THE PRINCIPLES AND PRACTICE
OF NAVIGATION

The Principles and Practice of Navigation

BY

A. FROST

Master Mariner, M.R.I.N.

GLASGOW
BROWN, SON & FERGUSON, LTD.
4-10 DARNLEY STREET

First Edition   1978
Revised   1983

ISBN 0 85174 310 2 (First Edition)
ISBN 0 85174 444 3
© 1983 BROWN, SON & FERGUSON, LIMITED, GLASGOW, G41 2SD
Printed and Made in Great Britain

LIST OF CONTENTS

v

THE PRINCIPLES AND PRACTICE OF NAVIGATION

For All Courses Leading to Department of Trade Certificates of Competence

1. The earth, the measurement of position, direction, and distance.
2. The Mercator Chart and its use in navigation.
3. The sailings.
4. Great circles—great circle sailing and the gnomonic chart.
5. The celestial sphere, the measurement of position on the sphere —the nautical almanac.
6. Correction of altitudes.
7. Time and its measurement.
8. The earth moon system.
9. Planetary motion.
10. Figure drawing.
11. The motions of the heavens.
12. The plotting of position lines.
13. The reduction of sights.
14. Meridian observations.
15. The pole star problem, pole star tables.
16. Amplitudes and azimuths.

CHAPTER 1

THE EARTH

The earth is a flattened sphere, which is rotating about one of its diameters, referred to as the axis of rotation. The two points where the axis meets the surface of the earth are called the poles of the earth. The circle drawn around the earth midway between the poles so that every point on it is equidistant from each pole is called the Equator.

The flattening is around the poles, and is caused by the tendency of the mass of the earth to fly off the surface at a tangent to the circle which it describes about the axis. This causes an acceleration away from the centre of the circle around which any mass is moving.

Thus in Figure 1.1 a mass M tends to move along a direction M . M'. Any mass on the equator therefore is accelerated away from the centre of the earth, C.

A mass m at some point off the equator, tends to move along a direction m . m' and is therefore accelerated away from L, the centre of its rotation. This acceleration can be resolved into two directions one directed away from the centre of the earth, and the other at right angles to this direction along the surface of the earth towards the equator. Thus any mass not on the equator has tendencies to move away from the centre of the earth and towards the equator. This means that the earth's rotation is causing a

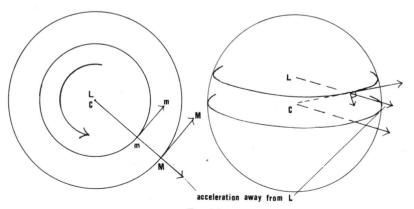

acceleration away from L

FIG. 1.1

1

shifting of mass towards the equator and a bulging outwards of the equatorial mass away from the earth's centre. The earth is therefore distorted into an oblate spheroid, which is the solid formed by rotating an ellipse about its minor axis. Any cross section of the earth taken through the poles therefore will be an ellipse.

If we imagine all the irregularities of the land surfaces planed off so that we have a sea level earth, it is this figure that would be the ellipsoid. This is given the name of the geoid. Describing the geoid as an ellipsoid is an oversimplification. In fact any cross section of the geoid departs from a perfect ellipse. The ellipse to which this cross section approximates to is called the reference ellipse. The amount by which the geoid departs from the reference ellipse is small but measurable by modern gravimetric readings. In recent years much has been learned about the true shape of the earth by the study of perturbations in artificial earth satellites.

The Figure of the Earth

This is the name given to the mathematical description of the reference ellipse, and it describes the amount by which it departs from a circle.

It is measured as the ratio of the difference between the maximum and minimum radii of the ellipse and the maximum radius. Thus the figure of the earth is:

$$\frac{\text{equatorial radius} - \text{polar radius}}{\text{equatorial radius}}$$

this equals $\dfrac{6378 \cdot 16 - 6356 \cdot 77}{6378 \cdot 16}$ expressed in kilometres

$$= \frac{1}{298 \cdot 25}$$

the only importance of this figure in navigation is in the definition of the unit of distance in navigation, the nautical mile.

The Measurement of Position on the Earth's Surface

Great Circle. This is a circle on the surface of a sphere, whose plane passes through the centre of the sphere. It is, therefore, the largest circle that can be drawn on a sphere of given radius. Between any two points on the surface of the sphere there is only one great circle that can be drawn, except if the two points are at opposite ends of a diameter. In this case there is an infinite number of great circles that can be drawn through them. The shortest distance between two points on the surface lies along the shorter arc of the great circle between them.

Poles of a great circle. These are the points on the sphere which are 90° removed from all points on the great circle. Each great circle will have two poles, the line joining which will be perpendicular to the plane of the great circle.

Small Circle. This is any circle on the surface of a sphere which is not a great circle. The plane does not pass through the centre of the sphere and the circle therefore does not divide the sphere into two equal halves.

Secondary great circles. Any great circle which passes through the poles of another great circle is said to be secondary to that circle, which is then referred to as its primary. Thus it could be said that the great circles that pass through the poles of the earth's rotation are secondaries to the earth's equator. It does not specifically refer to this special case however. It is a general term which may be used with reference to any great circle on a sphere and those great circles that cut it at right angles, hence passing through its poles.

To define a position on any plane surface we can assume two axes of reference at right angles to each other. The definition of any point is obtained by stating the distance of the point from each of the two axes of reference. In mathematics the axes are usually called the *x*-axis and the *y*-axis, and the distances of the point from these lines are called the co-ordinates of the point. So defined the position is unambiguous.

On a spherical surface such as the earth the two axes of reference are two great circles, and instead of linear distance we use angular distances.

The co-ordinates used to define a position are called LATITUDE and LONGITUDE.

LATITUDE. The axis from which this co-ordinate is measured is the equator, the plane of which is perpendicular to the earth's axis of rotation. Every point on this great circle will be at an angular distance of 90° from each of the earth's poles.

A parallel of latitude. This is a small circle on the surface of the earth whose plane is perpendicular to the earth's spin axis, and therefore parallel to the plane of the equator.

The latitude of any point can therefore be defined as the arc of a secondary to the equator which is contained between the equator and the parallel of latitude through the point being considered. It is measured 0° to 90° North or South of the equator in degrees minutes and seconds of arc.

Thus all positions on the same parallel of latitude have the same latitude. The latitude of the equator is 0° and that of each pole is 90° N. or S.

LONGITUDE. The axis from which this co-ordinate is measured is a semi-great circle which runs between the two poles of the earth and passes through an arbitrary point in Greenwich. This line is a secondary to the equator and is called the Prime Meridian.

There are an infinite number of semi-great circles that can be drawn between the poles. Each one of these is called a meridian. Given a position on the earth there is one meridian that passes through it. The meridian that passes through the antipodal point of the position is called the anti-meridian of that position. A meridian and its anti-meridian together form a great circle which is a secondary to the equator.

The longitude of any point can be defined as the lesser arc of the equator or the angle at the pole, between the meridian of Greenwich and the meridian through the point being considered. It is measured from 0° to 180° on either side of the prime meridian and named east or west.

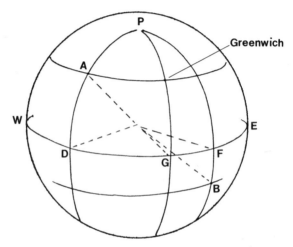

FIG. 1.2

Point A in north latitude (arc AD) and west longitude (arc DG).
Point B in south latitude (arc FB) and east longitude (arc GF).

To avoid any misunderstanding, the latitude is always stated first. The latitude and longitude of a position define that position on the earth's surface unambiguously.

Geographical Latitude

The fact that the earth is not a true sphere means that the definition of latitude given must be modified. The geographical latitude is the latitude of a position as observed. This assumes that the earth is a sphere with radius the same as the radius of curvature of the meridian at the position being measured. As the earth is an oblate spheroid the shape formed by a meridian and its anti-meridian is an ellipse. The radius of curvature of the ellipse will be greatest at the poles and least at the equator.

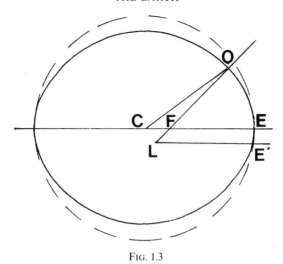

FIG. 1.3

In the figure let L be the centre of curvature of the meridian at O. LO is therefore the radius of curvature of the meridian at O. It will cut the earth's surface at O in a right angle and is therefore the vertical at O. The geographical latitude is angle OLE'. This will equal angle OFE.

The geographical latitude of an observer can be defined therefore as the angle between the vertical at the observer and the plane of the equator.

Geocentric Latitude

This is the angle at the centre of the earth between the line joining the earth's centre to the observer and the plane of the equator. In the diagram the geocentric latitude will be angle OCE.

The term latitude in navigation means geographical latitude or latitude as observed. The difference between the geographical and the geocentric latitudes is zero at the equator and the poles and maximum in 45° N. and S. The difference here will be about 11' of arc.

The geocentric latitude is given approximately by the formula:

$$\phi - 11 \cdot 6 \sin 2\phi$$

where ϕ = the geographical latitude.

Thus in geographical latitude 60° the geocentric latitude becomes:

$$60° - 11 \cdot 6 \times \sin 120°$$
$$= 60° - (11 \cdot 6 \times 0 \cdot 866)$$
$$= 60° - 10 \cdot 04'$$
$$= 59° \, 49 \cdot 96'$$

Change of Position on the Earth's Surface

When sailing between any two positions on the earth's surface, a knowledge of the necessary change in latitude and longitude is essential. This information is described by the 'Difference of Latitude', (d. lat.) and the 'Difference of Longitude' (d. long.), between the two positions.

The d. lat. between any two positions on the earth's surface is the arc of a meridian which is contained between the two parallels of latitude which pass through the two positions. This is illustrated in Figure 1.4. From the figure it can be seen that if the two positions have latitudes of the same name then the d. lat. will be the numerical difference between the two latitudes, i.e. the greater minus the smaller. If the latitudes are of different name then the d. lat. will be the sum of the two latitudes.

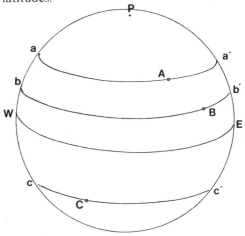

FIG. 1.4

WE = Equator
aa′ = parallel of latitude through A
bb′ = parallel of latitude through B
cc′ = parallel of latitude through C
d. lat. between A and B = Latitude A − Latitude B = arc ab
d. lat. between A and C = Latitude A + Latitude C = arc ac
d. lat. between B and C = Latitude B + Latitude C = arc bc

D. lat. is named according to the direction travelled, North or South.

The d. long. between any two positions on the earth's surface is the lesser arc of the equator contained between the two meridians which pass through the two positions. This is illustrated in Figure 1.5. From the figure it can be seen that if the two positions are on the same side of the Greenwich meridian then the d. long. will be the numerical difference between the longitudes, i.e. the greater minus the smaller. If they are on opposite sides of the Greenwich meridian, i.e. if the longitudes are of opposite name, then the d. long. will be found by the sum of the two longitudes. If however the d. long found by this means is more than 180°, as the d. long. is defined as the LESSER arc of the equator between two positions, then the d. long. is obtained by subtracting the result from 360°. The d. long. is named East or West according to the direction travelled.

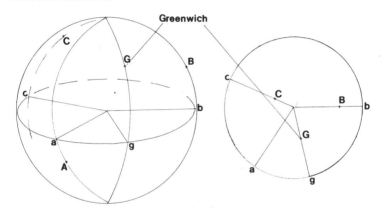

FIG. 1.5

Point A and point C are in westerly longitude.
Point B is in easterly longitude.
D. long. between A and C = Long. A ~ Long. C = arc ac
D. long. between A and B = Long. A + Long. B = arc ab
D. long. between C and B = 360 − (Long. C + Long. B) = arc cb

Examples

1. Find the d. lat. and d. long. between the positions 43° 15·5′ N. 43° 30·8′ W. and 31° 37·7′ N. 48° 18·0′ W.

Pos. A	43° 15·5′ N.	43° 30·8′ W.
Pos. B	31° 37·7′ N.	48° 18·0′ W.
d. lat.	11°37·8′ S. d. long.	4° 47·2′ W.
	= 697·8′ S.	= 287·2′ W.

Note

D. lats and d. longs are usually required in minutres of arc. The number of degrees is therefore multiplied by 60 and the odd minutes added on to express them in this manner. To get from A to B a vessel must sail to the south and to the west. D. lat. is therefore named S., and d. long. W. For both d. lat. and d. long. the rule in this case is 'same name take the difference'.

2. Find the d. lat. and d. long. between the two positions 20° 10·4′ N. 13° 04·5′ W. and 5° 18·0′ S. 8° 40·8′ E.

Pos. A	20° 10·4′ N.	13° 04·5′ W.
Pos. B	5° 18·0′ S.	8° 40·8′ E.
d. lat.	25° 28·4′ S. d. long.	21° 45·3′ E.
	= 1528·4′ S.	= 1305·3′ E.

Note

Latitudes and longitudes are of the opposite name and the d. lat. and the d. long. therefore are obtained by the sums. The direction travelled in is south and east. D. lat. is therefore named S., and d. long. E.

3. Find the d. lat. and d. long. between the two positions 10° 00·0′ S. 30° 15·0′ E. and 67° 40·0′ N. 70° 30·0′ W.

Pos. A	10° 00·0′ S.	30° 15·0′ E.
Pos. B	67° 40·0′ N.	70° 30·0′ W.
d. lat.	77° 40·0′ N. d. long.	100° 45·0′ W.
	= 4660·0′ N.	= 6045·0′ W.

4. Find the d. lat. and d. long. between the two positions 5° 15·6′ S. 168° 15·0′ E. and 17° 56·0′ N. 128° 16·5′ W.

Pos. A	5° 15·6′ S.	168° 15·0′ E.
Pos. B	17° 56·0′ N.	128° 16·5′ W.
d. lat.	23° 11·6′ N.	296° 31·5′
	= 1391·6′ N.	= 63° 28·5′ E.
		= 3808·5′ E.

Note

The d. long. found by adding the longitudes of opposite name is more than 180°. It is therefore subtracted from 360°. Note that the direction of travel is east across the 180th meridian.

5. A vessel steaming north and east makes good a d. lat. of 925·8′ and a d. long. of 1392·6′. If the initial positions was 25° 20·7′ N. 46° 45·2′ W. find the position at which the vessel arrived.

initial position	25° 20·7′ N.	46° 45·2′ W.
d. lat.	15° 25·8′ N.	23° 12·6′ E.
final position	40° 46·5′ N.	23° 32·6′ W.

EXERCISE 1A

Find the d. lat. and d. long. between the following positions:

	Initial position		Final position	
1.	40° 10·6′ N.	9° 25·2′ W.	47° 15·7′ N.	21° 14·3′ W.
2.	35° 15·6′ N.	22° 12·4′ W.	50° 25·9′ N.	11° 37·7′ W.
3.	10° 12·6′ N.	5° 03·8′ E.	5° 18·7′ S.	7° 18·8′ W.
4.	20° 40·0′ S.	170° 09·1′ E.	13° 06·5′ N.	178° 51·1′ E.
5.	30° 03·3′ N.	152° 43·3′ W.	42° 24·0′ N.	174° 01·8′ W.
6.	11° 31·7′ N.	178° 00·0′ E.	5° 14·9′ S.	177° 00·8′ W.
7.	8° 42·6′ S.	162° 41·7′ W.	7° 53·8′ N.	135° 27·9′ E.
8.	15° 20·0′ S.	130° 35·4′ E.	33° 10·5′ N.	155° 40·0′ W.
9.	52° 10·7′ S.	171° 08·0′ E.	27° 02·3′ S.	34° 02·3′ E.
10.	60° 40·5′ S.	151° 23·5′ W.	10° 57·7′ S.	92° 47·6′ W.

EXERCISE 1B

1. Given initial position 20° 50·5′ S. 178° 49·7′ E., d. lat. 33° 14·0′ N. d. long. 15° 37·7′ E. Find the final position.

2. Given initial position 39° 40·6′ N. 9° 21·8′ W., d. lat. 3° 57′ N., d. long. 27° 07·0′ E. Find the final position.

3. If a vessel's arrival position is 30° 10·6′ S. 4° 40·3′ E., and the d. lat. and d. long. made good was 72° 18·8′ S. and 38° 54·7′ E. respectively, what was the initial position?

4. A ship steered a course between north and east making good a d. lat. of 38° 55·5′ and a d. long. of 20° 41·8′. If the position reached was 21° 10·4′ N. 168° 18·7′ W., what was the initial position?

The Measurement of Distance

The unit of distance used in navigation is the nautical mile. Subunits are the cable which is 0·1 of a nautical mile, and the fathom which is 0·001 of a nautical mile.

In navigation calculation of position is made in units of arc, degrees and minutes. It is convenient therefore to use as a unit of distance, the length of a minute of arc of a great circle upon the surface of the earth. Thus the nautical mile is taken as the length of a meridian which subtends an angle of one minute at the centre of the earth.

This definition however assumes a perfectly spherical earth which is not the case. It can be modified such that one minute of geographical latitude is equal to one nautical mile in any given latitude.

Thus redefined with reference to a spheroidal earth the nautical mile is:

The length of a meridian between two parallels of latitude whose geographical latitudes differ by one minute.

Consider the diagram.

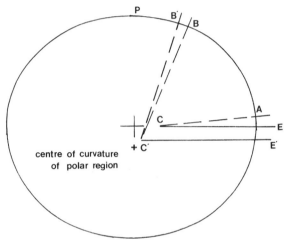

FIG. 1.6

The geographical latitude of A will be angle ACE. If this angle is 0° 1' then the geographical latitude of A will be 0° 1' N. and AE will be the length of a nautical mile at the equator. C is the centre of curvature of the meridian at the equator.

The geographical latitude of B is angle BC'E', and that of B' is angle B'C'E'. If the difference, i.e. angle B'C'B is one minute then the length of BB' is the nautical mile in that latitude.

The centre of curvature of the meridian at B is C', and the radius of curvature BC', is greater than the radius of curvature at the equator AC. Therefore the length of arc BB' is greater than the length of the arc AE. The length of the nautical mile as defined varies as the latitude. At the equator the length is 1842·9 metres. At the poles it is 1861·7 metres. In practice a value of 1853 metres (6080 ft) is used and this is considered a standard nautical mile.

The true length of the nautical mile in any latitude is given by the formula:

$$1852·3 - 9·4 \cos (2 \times \text{Latitude})$$

The variation in the length of the nautical mile has no significance in practical navigation. Any units of d. lat. are taken as units of distance, and the distance between two places on the same meridian but in different latitudes is equal to the d. lat. between the two places. The unit of speed at sea is the knot. This is a speed of one nautical mile per hour.

The Geographical Mile

This is the length of one minute of arc of the equator, or the length of the equator which subtends an angle of one minute at the centre of the earth.

The equator is the only true great circle on the reference ellipsoid, and the centre of the equator is the centre of the earth. The geographical mile therefore is a constant length of 1855·3 metres. It will be equal to the length of one minute of longitude at the equator by definition.

The Measurement of Direction

The three figure notation
The observer is considered to be at the centre of his compass, the plane of which represents the plane of the horizon. The direction of the meridian through the observer towards the north geographical pole is taken as the reference direction and called 000°. The circumference of the compass card representing the horizon is divided into 360 degrees and any direction from the observer is expressed as the angle measured clockwise from the reference direction of 000°.

Thus the direction of east in 3-figure notation is 090° (never 90°)
Thus the direction of south in 3-figure notation is 180°
Thus the direction of west in 3-figure notation is 270°
Thus the direction of north in 3-figure notation is 360° or 000°
The 3-figure notation is used to express:

1. Course. The direction of movement of the observer.
2. Bearing. The direction of an object from the observer.

Any instrument which is designed to measure these quantities is called a compass and to measure direction correctly the reference or zero mark on the compass card must be aligned with the direction of 000° on the horizon. If this is not the case then it is necessary to find the true direction in which the compass zero points in order that a correction may be applied to find the true direction of north.

The gyro compass
Gyroscopic compasses are liable to small errors which should not exceed one or two degrees.

If the north point of the compass card points to the left (to the west), of the true direction of the meridian, then all indications of direction taken from the compass will be greater than the true value.

Example

True bearing	050°
Compass bearing	051°
Gyro reading	1° high

In this case the gyro is said to be reading high, and any error of the compass will be negative to the compass reading to give the true reading.

If the north point of the compass card points to the right (to the east), of the true direction of the meridian, then all indications of direction taken from the compass card will be less than the true value. In this case the gyro is said to be reading low and any error of the compass will be positive to the compass reading to give the true reading.

Example

True bearing	050°
Compass bearing	049°
Gyro reading	1° low

The magnetic compass

Although nowadays the magnetic compass is very much a standby, taking second place to the gyro compass, it remains the most reliable compass available to the navigator. Its errors should always be known ready for immediate use.

The magnetic compass is disturbed from the true direction of north by:

Variation

The magnetic compasses directive power is derived from the property of a magnetised rod freely suspended to align itself with the lines of force of the earth's magnetic field. The magnetic poles of the earth are not coincident with the geographical poles (the poles of the earth's rotation). The zero mark on the compass will not therefore point towards the true direction of north as defined by the geographical poles.

The direction in which the lines of force of the earth's magnetic field run at any point on the earth's surface can be thought of as the direction of the magnetic meridian. The angle between the true meridian and the magnetic meridian is called the variation. This angle varies with position on the earth's surface. It is named west if the direction of the magnetic meridian lies to the left of the true meridian and east if it lies to the right of the true meridian, as determined by an observer facing north. The direction of the magnetic meridian is called Magnetic North.

The value of the variation is given in the compass roses of all Admiralty charts and on the Admiralty charts of variation which cover the world.

Deviation

The compass zero will align itself with the magnetic meridian only if the compass needle is free from all influences other than that of the earth's magnetic field. This is rarely so, particularly on a ship that is constructed of steel. The magnetism induced in the steel by the earth's magnetism will cause the compass needle to deviate from the magnetic meridian, by an amount which is called the Deviation. This will vary for any particular vessel for a number of reasons such as, change of course, change of angle of heel, change of position on the earth's surface.

Deviation is named West if the compass needle points to the left of the magnetic meridian, and East if the compass needle points to the right of the magnetic meridian. The direction in which the compass needle points is called Compass North.

Note that in any position on the earth's surface the deviation will vary mainly because of a change in course. It is dependant upon the ship's head therefore and for any given ship's head the deviation will be the same for ALL BEARINGS, taken from the compass.

Finding the Value of the Deviation

A ship's magnetic compass should be compensated, by the use of magnets which should correct for the effect of the ship's magnetism. However although deviations can be reduced, they can rarely be eliminated. The residual deviations after compensation should be found for each heading of the vessel and plotted in the form of a graph that can be referred to by the navigator when he needs to know the deviation for any particular ship's head.

The value of the deviation on any given heading does however vary for many reasons. If the ship is not in the same condition of loading as when the curve of deviations was made out, then such a curve may give an incorrect deviation. The changing of position of any of the ship's fittings will possibly affect the deviations. The positioning of the ship's derricks or cranes can have a large effect in this respect. For these reasons a deviation taken from a curve of deviations should be treated with suspicion.

A log of deviations observed for each compass should be kept by the navigators. At least once in every watch if possible a compass error and hence a deviation should be observed and the results recorded in the ship's log. The condition of the ship in respect of loading and position of derricks should be noted and in this way a complete record of deviations for any compass can be built up. If in an emergency a magnetic compass is required to be used this record can be consulted if it is not possible at the time to observe deviations.

Methods of observing compass errors and deviations are given later under the headings 'the azimuth problem' and 'the amplitude problem'.

Compass error

The error of the compass is the angle between the direction of compass north and the direction of the true meridian. This will be the combination of the variation and the deviation. If they are of the same name then the compass error will be the sum of their two values and will be named the same as they are. If they are of different names the compass error will be the difference between the two and will be named the same as the greater of the two.

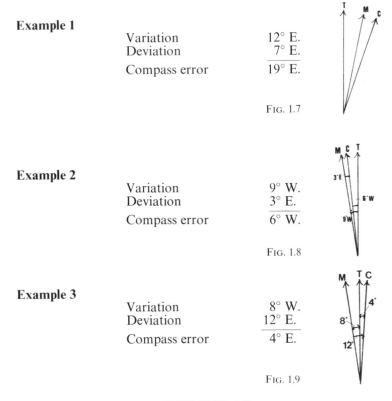

Example 1

Variation	12° E.
Deviation	7° E.
Compass error	19° E.

Fɪɢ. 1.7

Example 2

Variation	9° W.
Deviation	3° E.
Compass error	6° W.

Fɪɢ. 1.8

Example 3

Variation	8° W.
Deviation	12° E.
Compass error	4° E.

Fɪɢ. 1.9

EXERCISE 1C

Find the compass error given

1. Dev. 14° W. var. 8° E.
2. Dev. 9° E. var. 9° W.
3. Dev. 10° W. var. 6° E.
4. Dev. 21° W. var. 7° W.
5. Dev. 2° E. var. 8° W.

6. Dev. 0° W. var. 4° E.
7. Dev. 7° E. var. 11° E.
8. Dev. 4° E. var. 15° W.
9. Dev. 9° W. var. 4° W.
10. Dev. 3° E. var. 1° W.

Courses and Bearings

We have defined three directions which we can call north.
True north. The direction of the meridian through the observer towards the north geographical pole.
Magnetic north. The direction of the earth's magnetic field at the position of the observer towards the north magnetic pole.
Compass north. The direction indicated by the north point of the compass.

The difference between True North and Magnetic North measured as an angle at the observer, is the Variation.

The difference between Magnetic North and Compass North measured as an angle at the observer is the Deviation.

The difference between True North and Compass North measured as an angle at the observer is the Compass Error.

Any course or bearing can be denoted using any of these three directions of north.

True course or bearing. The angle at the observer between the direction of True North and the direction being measured, measured clockwise from the direction of True North.

Magnetic course or bearing. The angle at the observer between the direction of Magnetic North and the direction being measured, measured clockwise from the direction of Magnetic North.

Compass course or bearing. The angle at the observer between the direction of Compass North and the direction being measured, measured clockwise from the direction of Compass North.

The course or bearing indicated by the compass is the compass course or bearing and before being used for navigation it must be corrected to a true course or bearing. To do this the variation and the deviation should be combined to give the compass error which is then applied, either to the true to give compass or the compass to give true.

If the compass error is west the compass course or bearing will be greater than the true course or bearing.

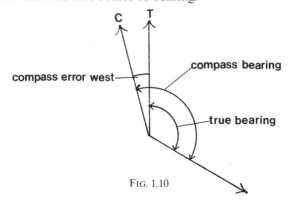

Fig. 1.10

If the compass error is east then the compass course or bearing will be less than the true course or bearing.

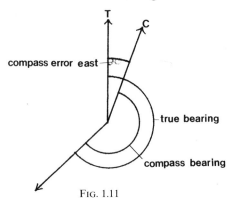

Fig. 1.11

From which may be deduced the mnemonic

Error West, compass Best,
Error East, compass Least.

Example 1

A vessel is steering 070° by compass. The deviation for the ship's head is 9° E. Variation is 16° W. Find the true course.

Variation	16° W.	or	Compass course	070°
Deviation	9° E.		Deviation	9° E.
Error	7° W.		Magnetic course	079°
			Variation	16° W.
Compass course	070°		True course	063°
Compass error	7° W.			
True course	063°			

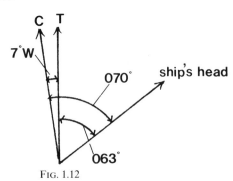

Fig. 1.12

Example 2
Find the compass course to steer to make good a true course of 340° if the variation is 5° E. and the deviation is 6° E.

Variation	5° E.	or	True course	340°
Deviation	6° E.		Variation	5° E.
Error	11° E.		Magnetic course	335°
			Deviation	6° E.
True course	340°		Compass course	329°
Compass error	11° E.			
Compass course	329°			

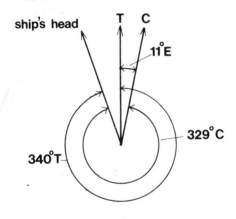

FIG. 1.13

EXERCISE 1D

Find the true course
1. Compass course 225° deviation 2° W. variation 16° W.
2. Compass course 006° deviation 8° W. variation 4° E.
3. Compass course 352° deviation 4° E. variation 8° E.
4. Compass course 257° deviation 9° E. variation 7° W.
5. Compass course 054° deviation 1° E. variation 15° E.
6. Compass course 338° deviation 2° W. variation 12° E.
7. Compass course 134° deviation 14° E. variation 3° W.
8. Compass course 206° deviation 7° W. variation 7° W.
9. Compass course 359° deviation 12° W. variation 2° E.
10. Compass course 001° deviation 4° W. variation 1° W.

EXERCISE 1E

Find the compass course
1. True course 265° deviation 5° W. variation 7° E.
2. True course 358° deviation 10° E. variation 3° E.
3. True course 180° deviation 3° W. variation 4° W.
4. True course 065° deviation 8° W. variation 9° E.
5. True course 003° deviation 15° E. variation 10° E.
6. True course 357° deviation 19° W. variation 11° E.
7. True course 350° deviation 3° E. variation 1° W.
8. True course 004° deviation 5° W. variation 3° E.
9. True course 090° deviation 3° E. variation 5° E.
10. True course 208° deviation 10° W. variation 9° E.

To find the deviation given the compass error and the variation.

Example 1.
The true bearing of the sun was calculated to be 225° T. At the time a bearing by compass was 221° C. If the variation at the position was 8° E., find the deviation of the compass for the ship's head.

The compass error can be found from the true and compass bearings given. The compass bearing is less than the true bearing and therefore the compass error will be east.

True bearing	225°
Compass bearing	221°
Compass error	4° E.
Variation	8° E.
Deviation	4° W.

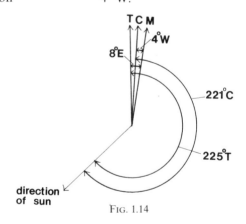

Fig. 1.14

Example 2
The true bearing of the sun at sunrise was calculated to be 095° T.
A compass bearing was observed to be 110° C. If the variation
was 5° E., find the deviation of the compass for the ship's head.

True bearing	095°
Compass bearing	110°
Compass error	15° W.
Variation	5° E.
Deviation	20° W.

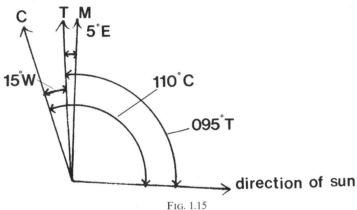

FIG. 1.15

EXERCISE 1F

Find the deviation
1. True bearing 050° T. compass bearing 061° C. variation 11° E.
2. True bearing 005° T. compass bearing 359° C. variation 5° W.
3. True bearing 075° T. compass bearing 070° C. variation 9° W.
4. True bearing 114° T. compass bearing 119° C. variation 16° E.
5. True bearing 207° T. compass bearing 201° C. variation 13° W.
6. True bearing 354° T. compass bearing 005° C. variation. 8° W.
7. True bearing 224° T. compass bearing 235° C. variation 10° E.
8. True bearing 290° T. compass bearing 309° C. variation 3° E.
9. True bearing 100° T. compass bearing 100° C. variation 3° W.
10. True bearing 002° T. compass bearing 359° C. variation 5° W.

CHAPTER 2

THE MERCATOR CHART

In portraying a portion of the spherical surface of the earth, upon a flat chart or map, some amount of distortion is inevitable. Just what form this distortion takes will depend upon the projection used. In selecting a projection for any particular purpose, the distortion inherent in that projection must have the minimum of effect upon the use to which the chart is going to be put.

The mercator projection is the projection chosen for the navigators chart. The main requirements of the navigator are that the rhumb line, the line of constant course on the earth's surface, is represented as a straight line, and that the value of the course angle can be measured directly from the chart. Except for long ocean passages a rhumb line course is invariably, for convenience, followed by a ship. For ease of laying off such a course and of measuring it these requirements are of paramount importance, and compromises are made in other respects in order to satisfy them.

The mercator projection is a cylindrical projection, the meridians being formed by rolling the plane surface of the chart around the globe, into the form of a cylinder, which is tangential to the globe around the equator, as in Figure 2.1.

When the chart is 'unrolled' then the meridians will appear as straight parallel lines running north south and cutting the equator in a right angle. The scale of longitude is now determined by the distance between the meridians, and as they are parallel this will be constant over the whole area of the chart. This property will ensure that any rhumb line will project as a straight line. This can be understood if the definition of a rhumb line is considered. A rhumb cuts all meridians at the same angle. Parallel meridians will result in straight rhumbs.

Although a rhumb line must, on such a chart appear as a straight line, the angle in which it cuts the meridians cannot be considered the course angle. This must depend upon the scale of latitude, as is shown in Figure 2.2 in which the same chart is shown using two differing latitude scales. A rhumb line drawn between the same two positions cuts the meridians at differing angles.

The Departure

As the meridians on the surface of the earth, converge towards the poles, then the distance between two given meridians measured

20

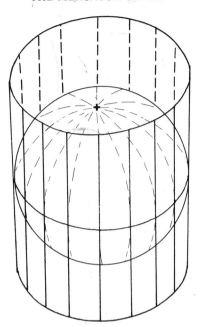

FIG. 2.1

Meridians are projected from the centre of the earth, through the sphere, and onto the cylindrical surface.

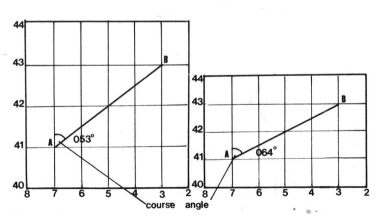

FIG. 2.2

along a parallel of latitude will decrease with increase of latitude. The distance between any two given meridians, measured along a parallel and expressed in nautical miles is called the departure. To maintain the property of course angles being accurately represented as the angle between the meridians and the rhumb line then the projection of the chart must be orthomorphic. A projection is orthomorphic if the scale of distance at any point on the chart is equal in all directions. The scale along a meridian in any latitude must be equal to the scale along the parallel which marks that particular latitude. As the meridians, which converge towards the poles are represented on the chart as parallel straight lines, the distance on the chart between two parallels will be constant. This constant distance represents a distance on the earth's surface which is a maximum at the equator and zero at the poles. It is evident therefore that the scale of distance on the chart varies with latitude. To retain orthomorphism then the scale of distance along the meridians must also increase towards the poles.

To find the scale of distance along a parallel

In Figure 2.3 let the distance AB be the departure between two positions on the same parallel of latitude $\theta°$. On a mercator chart this will be represented by ab. If the d. long. is EQ then this will be represented by eq on the chart where

eq = EQ × longitude scale.

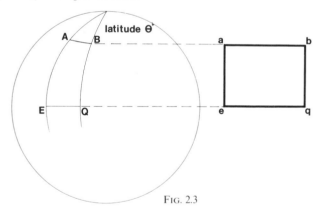

Fig. 2.3

Then AB = EQ × cos $\theta°$ (see parallel sailing in Chapter 3).
Thus the departure is represented on the chart by

$$\text{departure} = \text{eq} \times \cos \theta°$$
$$= \text{ab} \times \cos \theta°$$

Thus ab = departure × sec $\theta°$.

Thus the length of a parallel on a mercator chart, between any two meridians is given by the departure, in units of the longitude scale, multiplied by the secant of the latitude. Thus the scale of distance on a mercator chart increases with latitude. This is shown in Figure 2.4 in which the length on a chart which represents a nautical mile is illustrated in two latitudes.

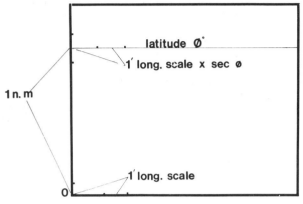

FIG. 2.4

This gives rise to distortion in the shape of land masses over large areas. The amount of distortion over small areas is not noticeable however and this particular distortion proves no disadvantage to the navigator. The only instance when the exact shape of the land portrayed is of importance to the navigator is for comparison with radar displays and over such small areas any distortion can be neglected. The main disadvantage which arises from the variation in the scale of latitude is the measurement of distance on a chart. The scale of distance on a mercator chart is the latitude scale, and accurate measurement of distance from a chart must take into account the variation of the scale. For practical purposes, on large scale charts the variation in the scale is not significant. On medium scale charts particularly in high latitudes then care must be taken to use that portion of the latitude scale which is in the same latitude as the distance being measured. Over long distances, on small scale charts, 'stepping off' a distance can only be an approximation. The most accurate results will be obtained if the length of the nautical mile on the chart in the mean latitude is used (or more accurately the middle latitude *see* Mid. lat. sailing).

To find the distance between parallels on a mercator chart

Meridional parts
The only constant scale inherent in the mercator projection is the scale of longitude. This scale is used therefore to position the parallels

with respect to each other. In order to do this the length of the meridians between any two parallels of latitude must be known, measured in units of the longitude scale.

The length of a meridian on a mercator chart between the equator and any parallel of latitude, expressed in units of the longitude scale is called the meridional parts for that latitude.

The length of a meridian on a mercator chart between any two parallels, expressed in units of the longitude scale is known as the difference of meridional parts between those latitudes.

The difference of meridional parts (dmp) between any two parallels will be the numerical difference between the meridional parts for the two parallels if they are in the same hemisphere, and the sum of the two meridional parts if they are in opposite hemispheres. This therefore is the same rule as for finding the difference of latitude between two parallels. The actual distance between any two parallels on a chart will depend upon the scale of the chart and will be found by multiplying the dmp by the length in centimetres of one minute of longitude on that chart.

The length of a small part of a meridian of difference of latitude 1', is given by

$$\text{length of } 1' \text{ d. long.} \times \text{secant latitude.}$$

If the length of the minute of longitude is taken as unity then this becomes

$$1 \times \text{secant latitude.}$$

As over any small length of a meridian the latitude varies then to find the total length of a meridian between any two parallels it is necessary to apply this formula to an infinitely large number of infinitely small segments of the meridian and summate.

This can be expressed in the integral calculus notation as

$$\int \sec 1\Delta1.$$

where $\Delta1$ is expressed in radians.

To find the meridional parts for any latitude, $\theta°$, this must be integrated between latitude $0°$ and latitude $\theta°$

$$\text{thus mer parts} = \int_0^\theta \sec l. \, dl.$$

or in minutes of arc

$$3438 \int_0^\theta \sec l. \, dl.$$

This integral is evaluated for values of latitude and tabulated in nautical tables as a table of meridional parts. The method given above however assumes a spherical earth, which means that the length of the nautical mile on the earth's surface is constant. For accuracy in navigation the meridional parts must be calculated for a spheroidal earth, and the resultant variation in the length of the nautical mile thus accounted for. The meridional parts given in nautical tables are calculated for the terrestrial spheroid.

The use of meridional parts in constructing a graticule on the mercator's projection.

To construct a graticule covering a stated range of latitude and longitude, a scale of longitude must first be chosen for the chart. This will enable the meridians to be constructed as vertical parallel lines, the distance between them being determined by the longitude scale. A parallel of latitude may then be inserted cutting the meridians in right angles from which to reference all other parallels. This may be chosen as the lowest parallel on the chart or more conveniently a parallel in the middle of the chart. This may then be referred to as the standard parallel.

The difference of meridional parts must now be calculated between the standard parallel and the other parallels to be inserted. The distance in centimetres between these and the standard parallel can then be found by

length on the chart of one minute of longitude × d.m.p.

The parallels may now be drawn at their appropriate distance north or south of the standard parallel.

Example

Construct a graticule on the mercator's projection to cover the parallels from 50° N to 54° N and the meridians from 8° W to 12° W, using a scale of longitude of 5 centimetres to one degree of longitude.

Total east-west dimension of chart = 5 cms × d. long.
= 5 × 4 = 20 cms.

Vertical meridians at 1° intervals may now be erected 5 cms apart.

Let the parallel of 52° N be chosen as the standard parallel.

then	m.p. 52°	3646·7		m.p. 52°	3646·7
	m.p. 50°	3456·5		m.p. 51°	3550·6
d.m.p.		190·2	d.m.p.		96·1
	m.p. 52°	3646·7		m.p. 52°	3646·7
	m.p. 53°	3745·1		m.p. 54°	3845·7
d.m.p.		98·4	d.m.p.		199·0

distance in centimetres between 50° and 52° = d.m.p. × length
$$1' \text{ long.}$$
$$= 190 \cdot 2 \times \frac{5}{60}$$
$$= 15 \cdot 85 \text{ cms.}$$

Similarly for 51° N., 53° N., and 54° N.

distances are $\dfrac{96 \cdot 1 \times 5}{60}$, $\dfrac{98 \cdot 4 \times 5}{60}$, and $\dfrac{199 \cdot 0 \times 5}{60}$

$= 8 \cdot 01$ cms, $8 \cdot 2$ cms, and $16 \cdot 58$ cms.

The parallels may now be inserted at the appropriate distance north or south of the standard parallel, that of 52°.

Example
Find the dimensions of the graticule of a mercator chart which covers the area from latitude 40° S. to latitude 46° S., and from the meridian of 178° W. to 170° E., if the scale of longitude is 10 cms to one degree of longitude.

$$\text{East west dimension} = \text{d. long.} \times 10 \text{ cms}$$
$$= 12 \times 10 \text{ cms}$$
$$= 120 \text{ cms.}$$

To find the north south dimension,

mer. parts 40°	2607·6
mer. parts 46°	3098·7
d.m.p.	491·1

$$\text{north south dimension} = \text{d.m.p.} \times \text{length } 1' \text{ long}$$
$$= 491 \cdot 1 \times \frac{10}{60}$$
$$= 81 \cdot 85 \text{ cms.}$$

Natural Scale

The natural scale of a chart or map is the ratio which is given by a length in any units on the chart, divided by the length on the earth's surface, in the same units, which that charted length represents. This is represented as a fraction with the numerator equal to unity. Thus a natural scale of $\dfrac{1}{50,000}$, means that a length of one centimetre on the chart represents a length of 50,000 cms on the earth's surface.

A natural scale is given on every Admiralty chart, under the title of the chart. As the scale of distance of a chart varies with the latitude however, the natural scale of the chart will also vary with latitude. The scale given therefore is for one parallel only, usually in the middle of the chart, and this will be stated.

To find the natural scale of a mercator chart, given the scale of longitude

The natural scale in any latitude $\theta°$ is given by:

$$\frac{\text{length of } 1' \text{ latitude in } \theta° \text{ on chart}}{\text{length of the nautical mile in latitude } \theta°}$$

$$= \frac{1' \text{ of longitude scale} \times \sec \theta}{1852\cdot3 - 9\cdot4 \cos 2\theta°}$$

Example

Find the natural scale of a mercator chart in latitude $58°$, given that the longitude scale is 10 cms to one degree of longitude.

Length of a nautical mile in $58°$:

$$1852\cdot3 - 9\cdot4 \cos (2 \times 58°)$$
$$= 1852\cdot3 - 9\cdot4 \cos 116°$$
$$= 1852\cdot3 + 9\cdot4 \cos 64°$$
$$= 1856\cdot4 \text{ metres}$$
$$= 185\,640 \text{ centimetres.}$$

$$1' \text{ latitude in } 58° \text{ on chart} = 1' \text{ longitude scale} \times \sec 58°$$
$$= \frac{10}{60} \times \sec 58°$$
$$= 0\cdot31452 \text{ cms.}$$

$$\text{natural scale} = \frac{0\cdot31452}{185640}$$

$$= \frac{1}{590240}$$

Limitations of the Mercator Projection

The scale along a meridian on a mercator chart is given by the longitude scale multiplied by the secant of the latitude. The secant of angles approaching $90°$ gets very large and approaches infinity. The length of one minute of latitude therefore approaches infinity towards the poles. It is not possible for this reason, to use the mercator projection for polar regions. This is of no great disadvantage to the marine navigator as very little navigation is done in these regions. Polar charts are usually constructed on the polar gnomonic projection.

The Transverse Mercator

The distortion of a mercator chart is very small near the equator. If an orthomorphic projection is required of equatorial regions, then this projection is most suitable. The variation in the scale of distance is also very small in these regions.

For maps of relatively large north south extent, the properties of the mercator projection are utilized by treating a meridian which passes through the area to be mapped, in the same way that the equator is used in the conventional mercator projection. The projection is therefore turned through 90°, and is called the transverse mercator projection. The projection of the meridian used is shown in Figure 2.5. Compare this with Figure 2.1, which shows how the equator and meridians are projected in the mercator projection.

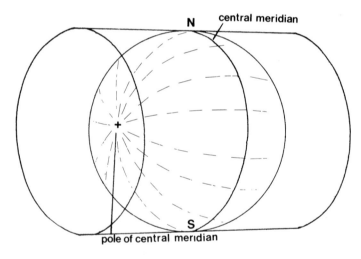

FIG. 2.5

The distortion away from the central meridian will be the same as that away from the equator on the mercator projection. This will be small as long as the east west extent of the map is small.

If neither the equator nor a meridian is used as the central great circle of the map then the projection is called a skew orthomorphic. This projection is used for mapping countries whose shape is long and narrow. A great circle which runs down the longer axis of the country is used as the central great circle.

EXERCISE 2

1. On a mercator chart one degree of longitude is represented by 5 centimetres. Find the spacing between the parallels of 12° and 14° N.

2. On a mercator chart the spacing between parallels of 40° N. and 45° N. is 5·8 cms. Find the scale of longitude and the spacing between the parallels of 30° and 33° N.

3. Given that the length of a nautical mile in any latitude is found by:

$$1852·3 - 9·4 \times \cos (2 \times lat).$$

Find the natural scale of a mercator chart in latitude 30° if the longitude scale is 1 cm to 1° longitude.

4. A chart is constructed to a natural scale of 1/50 000 in latitude 50° N. Two points on the chart in 50° N. are 90 mm apart. A is to the west of B and is in longitude 5° 30′ W. Find the distance between the two points and the longitude of B.

5. Find the dimensions of a mercator chart covering the area 45° N. to 56° N. and 7° W. to 19° E., if the scale of longitude is 5 centimetres to one degree of longitude. Find the natural scale in latitude 50° N.

6. A mercator chart covers the area between latitudes 50° N. and 56° N. and between longitudes 170° E. and 180° E. If the total length of the longitude scale is 100 centimetres, find the total length of the latitude scale, and the position in which the diagonals of the chart intersect.

7. A mercator chart covers the area from 50° N. to 45° N. and from 4° E. to 16° E. If the distance between two points on the parallel of 48° N. is measured against the longitude scale instead of the latitude scale, find the error incurred if the d. long. between the points is 6° 15′.

8. The scale of longitude of a mercator chart is 12 cms to 1° longitude. Find the error incurred in measuring the distance between two points 28 cms apart, against the longitude scale instead of the latitude scale, if one of the points is on the parallel of $51\frac{1}{2}$° N. and the other on the parallel of $52\frac{1}{2}$° N.

CHAPTER 3

THE SAILINGS

In this chapter the problem of finding the course and distance between two positions on the earth's surface is considered.

The Rhumb Line

If a constant course is steered between two positions then by definition the course line will cross each meridian at the same angle. Such a line on the surface of the earth is called a Rhumb Line. On the surface of the earth the meridians converge towards the poles, and this will mean that the rhumb line will take the form of a spiral towards the poles, approaching infinitely close to each pole. This form is also called a Loxodromic curve.

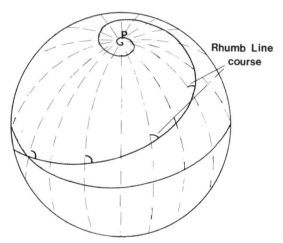

FIG. 3.1

The distance between two positions measured along a rhumb line will not represent the shortest distance along the earth's surface between those points. It is however the most convenient way of steaming between the points as any other track would involve a constant change of course. Only over long ocean passages does the extra distance steamed amount to anything of consequence.

30

Parallel Sailing

This may be used when steaming between two positions on the same parallel of latitude. The distance along a parallel between two specified meridians decreases as the meridians converge towards the poles. The distance decreases as the latitude increases. The distance along any specified parallel expressed in nautical miles is called the Departure.

The relationship between Departure, d. long. and latitude can be shown thus:

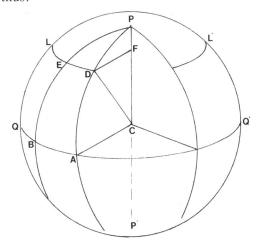

Fig. 3.2

In the figure let the circle represent the earth, C its centre, QQ′ the equator, LL′ a parallel of latitude, PP′ the earth's axis and F the centre of the small circle LL′.

D and E are two positions on the parallel LL′ with PAP′ and PBP′ the meridians through these positions. CA, CB and CD are radii of the earth.

By circular measure, the length of an arc, which subtends any given angle at its centre, is proportional to the radius.

Thus $\dfrac{DE}{DF} = \dfrac{BA}{AC}$ where DE is the departure and BA is the d. long.

Therefore $\dfrac{DE}{BA} = \dfrac{DF}{AC}$

and as DC and AC are both radii of the earth

$$\dfrac{DE}{BA} = \dfrac{DF}{DC}$$

Thus $\dfrac{DE}{BA}$ = cosine angle FDC

Thus $\dfrac{\text{departure}}{\text{d. long.}}$ = cosine latitude.

The finding of distance between any two positions on the same parallel requires the solution of this formula for departure (see definition of departure).

Example 1
Find the distance to steam between the following positions

$$
\begin{array}{llll}
A & 50°\ 25'\ N. & 48°\ 20'\ W. \\
B & 50°\ 25'\ N. & 38°\ 00'\ W. \\
\end{array}
$$

d. long. $\underline{10°\ 20'\ E.}$
= 620' E.

		no.	log.
Departure = d. long. × cos lat.			
= 620 × cos 50° 25′		620	2·79239
= 395·06		cos 50° 25′	$\overline{1·80428}$
distance = 395·1 miles			2·59667

Example 2
In what latitude will there be a distance of 120 miles between the meridians of 40° 15′ W. and 43° 55′ W.

43° 55′ W.
40° 15′ W.

d. long. $\underline{3°\ 40'}$
= 220′

	no.	log.
120 = d. long. × cos lat.	120	2·07918
$\cos \text{lat.} = \dfrac{120}{220}$	220	2·34242
latitude = 56° 56·6′ N. or S.		$\overline{\overline{1·73676}}$

Example 3
A ship leaves a position in latitude 49° 00′ N. longitude 160° 00′ W. and steams 000° T. for 90 miles, 090° T. for 90 miles, 180° T. for 90 miles and 270° T. for 90 miles. What is her final position?

This problem can best be done by considering the difference between the d. long. made good in the higher latitude and that made good in the lower latitude. As the 000° T. and the 180° T. will cancel out and return the ship to the same parallel of latitude, then the difference between the initial and the final positions will be the difference between the two d. longs.

Arrival latitude after 000° T. × 90 miles
       49° 00′ N.
d. lat.   1° 30′ N.
       ─────────
       50° 30′ N.

d. long. made good = 90 × sec 50° 30′   no.   log.
                   = 141·5′ E.   sec 50° 30′   0·19649
                                              90   1·95424
                                                        ─────────
                                                        2·15073

In latitude 49° d. long. = 90 × sec 49°   sec 49°   0·18306
                        = 137·2′ W.   90   1·95424
                                                          ─────────
                                                          2·13730

Thus initial longitude   160° 00′ W.
           d. long.   2° 21·5′ E.
                          ─────────────
                          157° 38·5′ W.
           d. long.   2° 17·2′ W.
                          ─────────────
       final longitude   159° 55·7′ W.

This may be illustrated as in Figure 3.3.

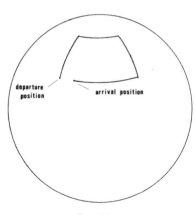

FIG. 3.3

Example 4
In what latitude will an aeroplane steering 270° T. experience perpetual noon if its speed is 400 knots.

Note
To experience perpetual noon (sun always bearing north or south) the plane must be flying at the same speed as the linear speed of the earth's rotation in that latitude.

Thus change of d. long in one hour $\dfrac{360}{24} = 15 \times 60'$ per hour

$$= 900' \text{ per hour.}$$

Speed of the earth's rotation in lat $\theta° = 900 \cos \theta°$
thus $400 = 900 \cos$ lat.

$$\cos \text{lat.} = \frac{400}{900} = 0\cdot444$$
$$\text{lat.} = 63° \ 36\cdot8' \text{ N. or S.}$$

EXERCISE 3A

1. In what latitude will a departure of 275 miles correspond to a d. long. of 6° 15'?

2. In latitude 49° 10' the departure between two meridians is 350 miles. Find the d. long.

3. A vessel steams a course of 090° T. from a position 22° 30' S. 58° 30' E. to a position 22° 30' S. 120° 30' E. How far did the vessel steam?

4. From a position, a vessel steams 000° T. for 50 miles and then 270° T. for 50 miles. If the d. long. made good was 230' find the latitude of the original position.

5. A ship leaves latitude 40° 12' N. for a port on the same meridian. The latitude of the port is 51° 12' N. If she steams 293 miles due east and then 660 miles due north, what is the distance of the ship from the destination?

6. In what latitude is the speed of rotation of the earth's surface about its axis, 120 knots slower than in latitude 28° 12'?

7. An aeroplane steering 270° at 204 knots experiences perpetual noon. In what latitude is the plane flying?

8. Two ships on the same parallel of 25° N. are steaming 000° T. at 15 knots. Find their distance apart after 24 hours if their original d. long. was 3° 35'.

9. Two vessels 200 miles apart on the same parallel steam 180° T. to the parallel of 20° N., where their d. long. was found to be 5° 20'. How far did each steam?

10. An arctic explorer leaves the north pole and walks 50 nautical miles south. He then walks 10 miles due west. How far is he away from his original position?

Plane Sailing (Mean Lat. Sailing)

This may be used when sailing between two positions which are not on the same parallel. Due to inherent inaccuracies however it should be limited to small distances.

If the quantities d. lat. and distance are imagined to be the two adjacent sides of a right angled triangle, the distance being the hypotenuse, then the angle between them can be made to represent the course angle. The third side, opposite the course may be thought of as the departure between the two positions. This triangle is called the plane sailing triangle. It should not however be thought of as a triangle on the surface of the earth. It is merely a trigonometrical representation of the quantities involved. See Figure 3.4.

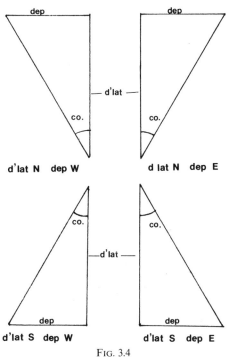

Fig. 3.4

In order to solve for course and distance then the departure must be known. It can be found by use of the parallel sailing formula:

$$\text{dep.} = \text{d. long.} \times \text{cosine latitude.}$$

The problem arises however—which is the correct latitude to use in the formula? The simple answer is, that latitude which will give a departure which, when used in the plane sailing triangle will give the correct values of course and distance. As yet we have no means of knowing this latitude, as an approximation we may use the mean latitude.

The procedure for the plane sailing problem is therefore:

1. Calculate the d. lat. and the d. long.
2. Use the parallel sailing formula to find departure using the numerical mean latitude.
3. Use the formulae $\dfrac{\text{dep.}}{\text{d. lat.}} = \tan$ course, and dist. = d. lat. × sec co., derived from the plane sailing triangle in order to solve for course and distance.

Example 1

Find the course and distance between the following positions.

A	37° 31′ N.	14° 00′ W.		35° 11′ N.	
B	35° 11′ N.	9° 05′ W.	½ d. lat.	1° 10′ N.	
d. lat.	2° 20′ S.	4° 55′ E. = d. long.		36° 21′ N. = mean lat.

dep. = d. long. × cos lat.

	no.	log
= 295 × cos 36° 21′	295	2·46982
= 237·6 miles	cos 36° 21′	$\overline{1}$·90602
		2·37584

$$\frac{\text{dep.}}{\text{d. lat.}} = \tan \text{ co.}$$

$$\tan \text{ co.} = \frac{237\cdot6}{140}$$

course = S. 59° 29·5′ E.

	no.	log
	237·6	2·37584
	140	2·14613
		0·22971

distance = d. lat. × sec course

	no.	log
= 140 × sec 59° 29·5′	140	2·14613
= 275·8 miles	sec 59° 29½′	0·29442
		2·44055

Example 2

From a position 50° 28′ N. 179° 40′ W. a vessel steams 204° T. for 155 miles. Find the arrival position.

d. lat. = dist. × cosine course

	no.	log.
= 155 × cos 24	155	2·19033
= 141·6′	cos 24°	$\overline{1}$·96073
		2·15106

initial lat.	50° 28′ N.
d. lat.	2° 21·6′ S.
arr. lat.	48° 06·4′ N.
½ d. lat.	1° 10·8′
mean lat.	49° 17·2′ N.

dep. = d. lat. × tan course   141·6   2·15106
    = 141·6 × tan 24   tan 24 $\overline{1·64858}$
    = 63·04   1·79964

and d. long. = dep. × sec mean lat.   141·6   1·79964
       = 63·04 × sec 49° 17·2′   sec 49° 17·2   0·18557
       = 96·7′ $\overline{1·98521}$

initial longitude   179° 40′ W.
     d. long.   1° 36·7′ W.
final longitude   181° 16·7′
       = 178° 43·3′ E.
final position = 48° 06·4′ N.   178° 43·3′ E.

EXERCISE 3B

1. Find the course and distance between the following positions.

   A. 35° 12′ N.   178° 12′ W.
   B. 37° 06′ N.   177° 00′ E.

2. A vessel leaves position 45° 12′ N. 161° 12′ W. and steams 213° T. for 406 miles. Find the arrival position.

3. Find the course and distance between the following positions.

   P. 5° 21′ N.   168° 17′ E.
   Q. 16° 38′ S.   153° 48′ W.

4. From a position in latitude 40° 30′ S. a vessel steams 050° T. In what latitude will the vessel cross the 180th meridian if the longitude of the initial position was 175° 45′ E. How far must the vessel steam on this course before crossing the 180th meridian.

5. Two vessels A and B are in different latitudes on the same course. A is in lat. 17° N. and is travelling twice as fat as B. The rate of change of longitude of A is $1\frac{1}{2}$ times that of B. Find the latitude of B.

6. Find the course and distance between the following positions.

   X. 7° 45′ N.   80° 30′ W.
   Y. 41° 00′ S.   178° 15′ E.

Mercator Sailing

It has been shown that on a mercator chart all meridians are represented by straight parallel lines. A rhumb line therefore appears as a straight line and the course angle may be measured as the angle between such a line and any meridians.

A right angled triangle may be formed on a mercator chart by:
1. The meridian through a departure position.
2. The parallel through the arrival position.
3. The rhumb line through the two positions.

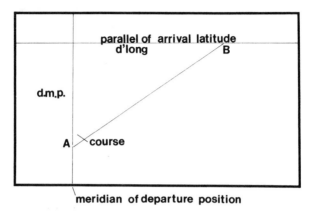

FIG. 3.5

The course angle in such a triangle may be found by plane trigonometry if a suitable scale is chosen by which to measure the opposite and adjacent sides. The scale of distance cannot be used as, on a mercator chart, this varies with latitude. There is however in the mercator projection principle a constant scale of longitude. The side opposite the course angle, will, against this scale be equal to the d. long. between the two positions. The length of the adjacent side, the length of a meridian between the parallels through the two positions, measured in these units, is the difference of meridional parts (see Chapter 2).

Hence by using the formula $\dfrac{\text{d. long.}}{\text{d.m.p.}} = \tan \text{course}$, the value of the course angle can be found accurately, without the use of the departure, and the inaccuracy involved in its use. Having found the course, then we may revert back to the plane sailing triangle and find the distance by the formula

$$\text{distance} = \text{d. lat.} \times \sec \text{course}.$$

Note that there is no point in finding the length of the hypotenuse in the units of d. long.

This method is almost invariably used at sea, because as well as being more accurate than the plane sailing method, there is less work involved in the computation.

Procedure
1. Find the d. lat. and the d. long. and also the difference of meridional parts for the two latitudes. The rule for d.m.p. will always be the same as that for finding d. lat., i.e. same names take the difference; different names take the sum of the mer. parts.
2. Find the course using the formula $\dfrac{\text{d. long.}}{\text{d.m.p.}} = \tan \text{course}$.
3. Find the distance using the formula distance = d. lat. × sec course.

Example 1
Find the course and distance between position 2° 21′ N. 5° 14′ W. and position 1° 47′ S. 0° 52′ E.

2° 21′ N.	5° 14′ W.	mer. parts 140·1
1° 47′ S.	0° 52′ E.	mer. parts 106·3
d. lat. 4° 08′ S.	d. long. 6° 06′ E.	d.m.p. 246·4

$$\tan \text{course} = \frac{\text{d. long.}}{\text{d.m.p.}}$$

	no.	log.
$= \dfrac{366}{246\cdot4}$	366	2·56348
	246·4	2·39164
course = S. 56° 03′ E.		0·17184

distance = d. lat. sec course	248	2·39445
= 248 × sec 56° 03′	sec 56° 3′	0·25301
= 444·1 miles		2·64746

Example 2
From a position 50° 28′ N. 179° 40′ W. a vessel steams 204° for 155 miles. Find the arrival position. (This example is also worked in 'plane sailing'.)

d. lat. = distance × cosine course	no.	log.
= 155 × cos 24°	155	2·19033
= 141·6′	cos 24°	1·96073
		2·15106

initial latitude = 50° 28′ N.	m.p.	3500·2
d. lat. 2° 21·6′ S.		
final latitude 48° 06·4′ N.	m.p.	3283·7
	d.m.p.	216·5

d. long. = d.m.p. × tan course	216·5	2·33546
= 216·5 × tan 24	tan 24°	1·64858
d. long. = 96·4′		1·98404

initial longitude $= 179° 40'$ W.
    d. long. $1° 36·4'$ W.
final longitude $181° 16·4'$ W.
        $= 178° 43·6'$ E.

The discrepancy between the mercator method and the plane sailing method is small over such a short distance.

EXERCISE 3C

By mercator sailing find the course and distance between the following positions.
1. A. $20° 35'$ N. $32° 15'$ W.
   B. $16° 24'$ S. $39° 55'$ W.
2. P. $20° 18'$ S. $178° 38'$ E.
   Q. $7° 00'$ N. $84° 45'$ W.
3. Z. $5° 00'$ N. $80° 05'$ E.
   Y. $24° 15'$ S. $111° 34'$ E.
4. R. $48° 24'$ N. $124° 44'$ W.
   S. $34° 50'$ N. $139° 50'$ E.
5. A vessel steams $065°$ T. for 1858 miles from position $21° 00'$ N. $178° 59'$ E. find the arrival position.
6. A vessel leaves position $40° 00'$ N. $47° 28'$ W. and steams $130°$ T. for 400 miles. Find by mercator sailing her final position.

MID. LAT. SAILING

The Middle Latitude

It has been shown that the course and distance between two positions on the earth's surface can be found if the departure between the two meridians is known. The Plane Sailing problem suffered the disadvantage of not knowing the exact value of the departure, but only an approximation found by using the numerical mean latitude in the formula:

departure = d. long. × cosine mean latitude.

The correct value of latitude to use in this formula is a latitude known as the middle latitude. If this is used in the plane sailing method, instead of the mean latitude, then the results will be accurate. The same results will be obtained as in the mercator sailing method. The problem is then called the Mid. Lat. Sailing problem.

The correct departure is found by using, in the parallel sailing formula a latitude whose secant is the mean of the secants of the individual parallels between the two positions being considered.

This can be found by integrating the secants over the required range.

Thus if L = middle latitude and l_n and l_s the parallels between which a vessel is sailing, then:

$$\sec L = \frac{1}{d.\,lat.} \int_{l_s}^{l_n} \sec l.\,dl.$$

To evaluate this formula the d. lat. must be expressed in radians. The values of mid. lat. are tabulated in nautical tables as a correction to apply to the mean latitude in order to get the middle latitude. The arguments for the tables are d. lat. and mean latitude. Middle latitude sailing involves using this correction to convert the mean latitude into the middle latitude. Otherwise the procedure is exactly the same as for the plane sailing problem.

It was shown in Chapter 2 that the d.m.p. between two parallels is given by:

$$d.m.p. = \int_{l_t}^{l_n} \sec l.\,dl.$$

therefore

$$\sec mid.\,lat. = \frac{d.m.p.}{d.\,lat.}$$

or

$$\cos mid.\,lat. = \frac{d.\,lat.}{d.m.p.}$$

as cos mid. lat. is also equal to

$$\frac{departure}{d.\,long.},$$

then

$$\frac{dep.}{d.\,long.} = \frac{d.\,lat.}{d.m.p.}$$

transposing

$$\frac{d.\,long.}{d.m.p.} = \frac{dep.}{d.\,lat.}$$

both these terms are equal to the tangent of the course, one derived from the mercator sailing triangle, and the other from mid. lat. sailing. The two methods therefore will give exactly the same result.

The exercise on mercator sailing may be reworked to show that this is so, using the mid. lat. sailing method.

CHAPTER 4

GREAT CIRCLES

If a circle is drawn on the surface of a sphere with the greatest possible radius (or the greatest possible circumference), then the circle will divide the sphere into two equal hemispheres. The plane of the circle will pass through the centre of the sphere and the centre of the circle will be coincident with the centre of the sphere. Such a circle is called a Great Circle.

Given any two positions on the surface of a sphere there is only one great circle which can be drawn passing through the two positions. The shorter arc of that great circle represents the shortest distance along the surface of the sphere between the two points. The exception to this is if the two points are at opposite ends of the same diameter. In this case there is an infinite number of great circles that can be drawn through the positions. To illustrate this we have the example of the two poles of the earth, which have an infinite number of meridians which can be drawn through them.

The Vertex of a Great Circle

The point on a great circle on the surface of the earth, which is closest to a geographical pole is called a vertex of the great circle. There will be two vertices on each great circle, a southerly one and a northerly one. Their latitudes will be numerically equal but opposite in name of course. At the vertex the direction in which the great circle is running must be 090°/270° thus forming a right angle with the meridian through the vertex.

Defining a great circle on the earth's surface

Any particular great circle drawn on the earth's surface may be unambigously defined by stating the longitude in which it crosses the equator and its inclination to the equator.

There will be two positions in which the great circle crosses the equator, and these must be 180° removed in longitude from each other. Each vertex must be 90° removed in longitude from the positions where it cuts the equator, and therefore 180° removed from each other. The latitude of the vertices will be given by the inclination of the great circle to the equator, where the direction of the great circle is given by the complement of this angle. A

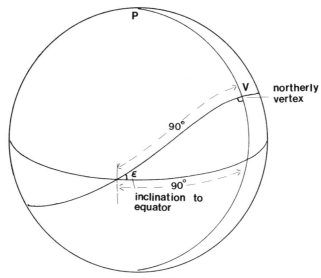

FIG. 4.1

thorough understanding of the facts outlined in this paragraph will be found invaluable in working the problems given later in this chapter.

Great Circles on the Mercator Chart

Any great circle other than the equator or a meridian, will appear on a mercator chart as a curve, the curvature of which will be more pronounced in high latitudes than in low ltitudes. The curvature will always be concave to the equator. Figure 4.2 shows the appearance of a complete great circle on a world wide mercator map. Although symmetrical about the equator, the curve is not sinusoidal. The equation of such a curve is given by:

$$\tan \phi = \tan \varepsilon \sin (x - \lambda)$$

this refers the curve to the equator as the x axis and the prime meridian as the y axis and the constants in the equation are:

ε = the inclination to the equator
λ = the longitude of the ascending node. (The point where the great circle cuts the equator moving eastwards from south to north of the equator.)
ϕ = latitude
x = longitude

It can be seen that the direction of the great circle with reference to the meridian is constantly changing and that a vessel steaming along a great circle must constantly change course.

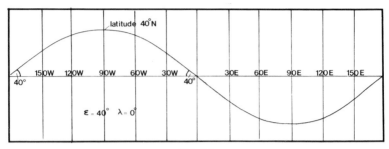

FIG. 4.2

Convergency of the Meridians

All meridians converge towards the poles. The convergency between two points on the earth's surface is defined as the change of direction of a great circle between the two points.

The true direction of a point on the earth's surface from an observer lies along the great circle between the two. The direction measured on a compass will be the direction of that great circle at the observer's position, as a line of sight or a radio wave follows a great circle path. If this direction is laid off on a mercator chart it will be in error as illustrated in Figure 4.3.

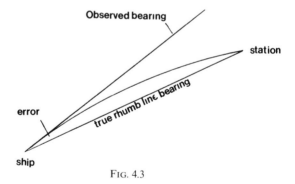

FIG. 4.3

Before laying off a bearing on a mercator chart it should be converted to a mercator bearing which is the direction of the rhumb line passing through the observer and the point whose bearing has been measured.

In the small distances, over which visual bearings are taken, the difference between the curve of a great circle and a rhumb line bearing on a mercator chart would not be discernable. The great circle bearing is laid off without any error. However a radio wave will also follow a great circle over the earth's surface and the distances involved in D/F bearings are sufficient to make a correction necessary.

In Figure 4.4 the observed bearing of B from A would be the direction in which the great circles is lying at A. In other words angle NAX. If this direction is laid off on a mercator chart it is in error by angle XAB. The mercatorial bearing of B is angle NAB. This will always lie on the equatorial side of the great circle bearing.

To find the value of the correction to apply to the great circle bearing to obtain the mercator bearing

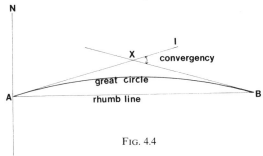

FIG. 4.4

In the diagram the direction AI is the initial direction of the great circle between A and B. The direction XB is the final direction. The angle IXB is therefore the change of direction of the great circle between the two positions, i.e. the convergency.

And angle IXB = angle XAB + angle XBA. (The exterior angle of a triangle is equal to the sum of the two interior and opposite angles.)

As over the short distances involved the two angles XAB and XBA can be considered small, then they are also considered equal to each other without material error.

Thus the correction to apply to the great circle bearing is half of angle IXB or half of the convergency.

Formula for convergency

In the diagram the convergency of the great circle between A and B is angle PBV − angle PAB.

$$\text{Thus convergency} = \angle\,PBV - \angle\,PAB$$
$$c = 180° - \angle\,PBA - \angle\,PAB$$
$$\text{In triangle PAB } \frac{c}{2} = 90 - \frac{\angle\,B + \angle\,A}{2}$$

In triangle PAB by Napier's analogies
$$\tan\frac{A + B}{2} = \frac{\cos\frac{1}{2}(PA - PB)}{\cos\frac{1}{2}(PA + PB)} \cdot \cot\frac{P}{2}$$

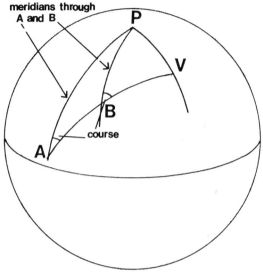

FIG. 4.5

Thus

$$\cot \frac{c}{2} = \frac{\cos \frac{1}{2} \text{ d. lat.}}{\cos \text{ mean co-lat.}} \cdot \cot \frac{1}{2} \text{ d. long.}$$

$$\tan \frac{1}{2} \text{ conv.} = \frac{\cos \text{ mean co-lat.}}{\cos \frac{1}{2} \text{ d. lat.}} \cdot \tan \frac{1}{2} \text{ d. long.}$$

$$\tan \frac{1}{2} \text{ conv.} = \frac{\sin \text{ mean lat.}}{\cos \frac{1}{2} \text{ d. lat.}} \cdot \tan \frac{1}{2} \text{ d. long.}$$

This is an accurate formula which can be used for any values of d. lat. and d. long. However over small distances this can be simplified by considering the convergency, the d. lat., and the d. long. to be small.

Then

$$\tan \tfrac{1}{2} \text{ convergency} = \tfrac{1}{2} \text{ convergency,}$$

$$\tan \tfrac{1}{2} \text{ d. long.} = \tfrac{1}{2} \text{ d. long.}$$

and

$$\cos \tfrac{1}{2} \text{ d. lat.} = 1.$$

The formula becomes

$$\tfrac{1}{2} \text{ convergency} = \tfrac{1}{2} \text{ d. long.} \times \text{ sine mean lat.}$$

or

$$\text{convergency} = \text{ d. long.} \times \text{ sine mean lat.}$$

The assumption that the two angles XBA and XAB are equal to each other is only correct if the two positions are in the same latitude. Errors caused by this assumption are not great enough to be meaningful in navigation.

To ascertain the direction of the correction
As a great circle on a mercator chart is always concave to the equator, the mercator bearing will always lie on the equatorial side of the great circle bearing. This is illustrated in the four cases of:

(a) westerly bearing in north latitude,
(b) easterly bearing in north latitude,
(c) westerly bearing in south latitude,
(d) easterly bearing in south latitude.

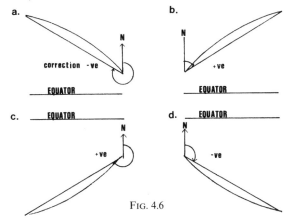

FIG. 4.6

Example
From a ship in D.R. position 44° 10′ S. 144° 50′ E., a D/F station bore 055°. If the position of the D/F station was 42° 53′ S. 147° 14′ E., find the rhumb line bearing.

44° 10′ S.	144° 50′ E.	mean lat. = 43° 31′ S.
42° 53′ S.	147° 14′ E.	

$$\begin{array}{cc} 1° 17′ \text{ N.} & 2° 24′ \text{ E.} \\ = \quad 77′ & 144′ \end{array}$$

convergency = d. long. × sine mean lat.
= 144′ × sine 43° 31′

= 99·156′

½ convergency = 49·58′

$$\begin{array}{r} 2·15836 \\ \overline{1}·83795 \\ \hline \overline{1}·99631 \end{array}$$

g.c. bearing   055°
½ conv.   49·6′
rhumb line brg.   054° 10·4′   or 054¼°

The Curve of Constant Bearing

A position line which is obtained from an observed bearing of an object from a ship, must be definition join points, from which the same great circle bearing would have been observed. This position line is neither the great circle joining the object and the observer, nor the rhumb line through them. From different points on the rhumb line there would be observed different great circle bearings. It is therefore theoretically wrong to draw the rhumb line on a mercator chart and assume that the observer is somewhere on that line.

The correct position line is the curve of constant bearing. The relationship between the great circle, the rhumb line, and the curve of constant bearing through the observer is shown in Figure 4.7.

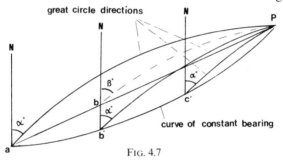

Fig. 4.7

In Figure 4.7 if a is the position of the observer, the observed great circle bearing of P will be angle $\alpha°$. The great circle bearing observed from point b, on the rhumb line joining a and P, will be $\beta°$ and this will not be equal to $\alpha°$. The great circle bearing $\alpha°$ would be observed from a point b′ and also from c′. The curve joining a, b′ c′, etc., is the curve of constant bearing.

The distances over which visual bearings are taken are small enough to ignore both the correction to the great circle bearing to obtain the rhumb line bearing, and the correction to the rhumb line to obtain the curve of constant bearing. Over greater d. longs however, as in the case of D/F bearings then it is practice to apply the half convergency correction to obtain the rhumb line bearing but to ignore the correction to find the curve of constant bearing. Laying off the curve of constant bearing is not so conveniently done as the simple process of putting a mercator bearing onto a chart. The resultant errors are small enough to be negligible compared with the errors inherent in the D/F system from other causes.

The angle between the great circle bearing and the curve of constant bearing is given by the formula:

d. long. × sine latitude of observer.

This can be seen to be almost equal to the convergency. The sign of the correction will always be the same as the sign of the half convergency correction to obtain the mercator bearing. It is evident therefore that the difference between the mercator bearing and the direction of the curve of constant bearing will also be the half convergency.

To find a position through which the curve of constant bearing passes
The curve of constant bearing may be taken as a straight line on a mercator chart only in the small area around the D.R. position. It will not pass through the D.R. position and therefore a position through which it passes must be calculated as well as the direction. This may be done employing the mercator sailing principle as follows.

Example
A vessel in D.R. position 44° 10′ S. 144° 50′ E. observes a bearing by D/F of a station in position 42° 53′ S. 147° 14′ E. Find the direction of the position line and a position through which it passes.
From the previous example the convergency is given by:

$$144' \times \sin 43° 31'$$
$$= 99·156'$$
$$= 1·7°$$

direction of rhumb line between vessel and station:

$$= 055° - 0·85°$$
$$= 054·15°$$

direction of curve of constant bearing:

$$= 055° - 1·7°$$
$$= 053·3°$$

To find the latitude in which the curve of constant bearing cuts the D.R. lontitude

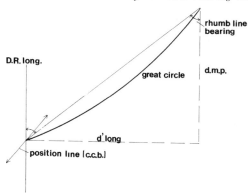

Fig. 4.8

$$\frac{\text{d. long.}}{\text{d.m.p.}} = \tan \text{ rhumb line bearing}$$

$$\frac{144}{\text{d.m.p.}} = \tan 054 \cdot 15°$$

d.m.p. = 144 × cot 54·15°	2·15836
= 104·05	1·85887
	2·01723

mer. parts for station (42° 53′)	2837·6
d.m.p.	104·05
mer. parts for required latitude	2941·65
required latitude = 44° 08·7′ S.	

Hence the position line runs in the direction 053·3° through position 44° 08·5′ S. 144° 50′ E.

The position line may now be laid off through this position as a straight line. It will not therefore pass through the position of the station as the assumption of a straight line only is valid for the small region around the D.R. position. The inaccuracy inherent in laying off bearings on a chart over long distances is avoided if this procedure is followed.

Great Circle Sailing

As the shortest distance between any two positions on the earth's surface lies along the arc of a great circle, then the methods of calculating such a track must be known. In order to plot a great circle track on a mercator chart we must know the latitude and longitude of a series of positions along the track. We have seen that a great circle on a mercator chart appears as a curve, but if positions along the curve are plotted at sufficiently short intervals, then the straight lines between these positions will approximate to the great circle curve.

Initially then the problem is to find the co-ordinates of these positions and the direction of the great circle (the course) at the positions, the initial course from the departure position, and the distance in nautical miles along the great circle track.

To solve for these quantities a spherical triangle is formed by the intersection of the three great circles,

    (i) the great circle track,
    (ii) the meridian through the departure position,
    (iii) the meridian through the arrival position.

thus the three points of the triangle are the two positions involved and one of the poles of the earth, usually the nearest one. Such a triangle is illustrated in Figure 4.9.

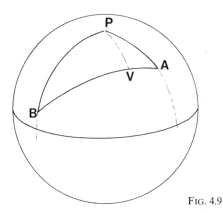

F<small>IG</small>. 4.9

In the figure

PA = colat. of A = 90° − lat. A
PB = colat. of B = 90° − lat. B
∠ P = d. long. between A and B
∠ A = the initial course along the great circle from position A
AB = the angular distance along the track between A and B.

If we express the angular distance AB in minutes of arc, then assuming a spherical earth this will be the distance in nautical miles, by definition of the nautical mile.

Thus in triangle APB, knowing PA, PB, and angle P we can by the haversine formula solve for AB and angle A.

Thus

$$\text{hav. } AB = (\text{hav. } P \sin PA \sin PB) + \text{hav. } (PA \sim PB)$$

or

$$\text{hav. dist.} = (\text{hav. d. long. } \cos \text{lat. A } \cos \text{lat. B}) + \text{hav. d. lat.}$$

The initial course is then found by:

$$\text{hav. } A = \left\{ \text{hav. } PB - \text{hav. } (AB \sim PA) \right\} \times \text{cosec } AB \text{ cosec } AP$$

The final course can be found by similarly calculating angle B, but in practice this is not required.

In order to complete the problem we first find the position of the nearest vertex. As the direction of the great circle at the vertex is 090°/270° a right angle is formed with the meridian through the vertex. This enables Napier's rules to be used to solve the rest of the problem.

To find the position of the vertex
In Figure 4.9 let V be the vertex of the great circle through A and B. (The vertex may or may not be between the two positions.)
Thus ∠ PVA = ∠ PVB = 90°.

Solving the right angled triangle PAV for side PV will give the colat. of the vertex, and hence the latitude. Solving for angle P will give the d. long. between A and the vertex, and hence the longitude of the vertex.

Thus given

$$\angle A = \text{initial course}$$
$$PA = \text{colat. of A.}$$

Then

$$\sin PV = \sin PA \sin \angle A$$

and

$$\cot \angle P = \cos PA \tan \angle A \quad \text{(by Napier's rules).}$$

To find latitude and longitude of positions along the track
If a position X is assumed anywhere along the track then a right angled spherical triangle is formed by P, V, and X. Knowing the position of V gives us PV.

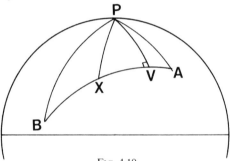

Fig. 4.10

In choosing a position X on the track we must assume either a longitude or a latitude. If a longitude is assumed then this will give angle P, the d. long. between our assumed position and the vertex. We can then find the latitude where our assumed longitude cuts the track. In this way a number of longitudes at regular intervals of d. long. can be taken and a series of positions along the track found. Solving the side PX in the triangle PVX will give the colat. of the position X, and solving for angle X will give the course along the great circle at X.

Thus given in PVX

$$PV = \text{colat. of vertex}$$
$$P = \text{d. long. between X and the vertex}$$

then

$$\cot PX = \sin \angle P \cot PV$$

and

$$\cos \angle X = \cos PV \sin \angle P \quad \text{(by Napier's rules).}$$

The work involved in this procedure is repetative and can be reduced by a system of tabulation as in the following examples.

Note
In the Figure 4.10 the vertex lies between the two positions. This need not be so, in which case the figure might appear as in Figure 4.11. In this case one of the angles of the triangle at the initial or final position will be greater than 90°. The courses between the two positions will then lie all in the same quadrant. If the vertex lies between the positions the course will change quadrants at the vertex. After solving the angles of the triangle to find the initial or the final course then these courses must be found by inspection, as to which quadrant they lie in. The procedure for the solution of the triangle will be the same in both cases.

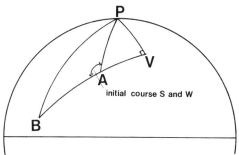

Fig. 4.11

Example 1
Find the great circle distance and the initial course from a position off Cape Palliser of 41° 40′ S. 175° 25′ E. to a position 7° 00′ N. 80° 50′ W. off Panama. Also find the positions where the track crosses the meridians of 180°, 160°, 140°, 120°, and 100° W. and the courses at these positions.

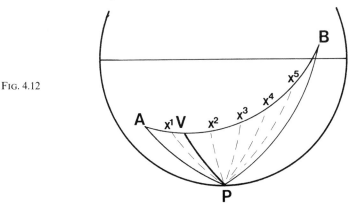

Fig. 4.12

A	41° 40·0′ S.	175° 25·0′ E.
B	7° 00·0′ N.	80° 50·0′ W.
d. lat.	48° 40·0′ N.	256° 15·0′
		360°
		103° 45·0′ E. = d. long.

hav. dist. = (hav. 103° 45·0′ cos 41° 40′ cos 7° 00′) + hav. 48° 40′

		no.	log.
	hav. 103° 45′		1̄·79158
	cos. 41° 40′		1̄·87334
dist. = 104° 54·4′	cos. 7° 00′		1̄·99675
= 6294·4′			1̄·66167
= 6294·4 miles.			0·45885
	nat. hav. 48° 40′		0·16978
			0·62863

To find the initial course
hav. ∠ A = {hav. PB − hav. (AB ∼ PA)} cosec AB cosec PA
hav. ∠ A = (hav. 97° − hav. 56° 34·4′) cosec 104° 54·4′
cosec 48° 20′

	no.	log.
nat. hav. 97°	0·56093	
nat. hav. 56° 34·4′	0·22457	
	0·33636	
		1̄·52680
log. cosec 104° 54·4′		0·01487
log. cosec 48° 20·0′		0·12666
		1̄·66833

∠ A = 86° 05·7′
initial course = S. 86° 05·7′ E.

To find the position of the vertex
In triangle APV by Napier's rules:

sin PV = sin A sin PA

	no.	log.
= sin 86° 05·7′ sin 48° 20′	sin 86° 05·7′	1̄·99899
PV = 48° 11·1′	sin 48° 20·0′	1̄·87334
Latitude of vertex = 41° 48·9′ S.		1̄·87233

and

$$\cot \angle P = \cos PA \tan \angle A$$
$$= \cos 48° \ 20·0' \tan 86° \ 05·7'$$
$$\angle P = 5° \ 52·0'$$

	no.	log.
	$\cos 48° \ 20·0'$	$\overline{1}·82269$
	$\tan 86° \ 05·7'$	$1·1657$
		$0·98839$

Longitude A	175° 25·0'
∠ P	5° 52·0'
Longitude V	181° 17·0' E.
	= 178° 43·0' W.

Position of vertex = 41° 48·9' S.   178° 43·0' W.

To find the latitudes where the track cuts the given longitudes and the course at these points

In triangle PVX by Napier's rules:

$$\cot PX = \cos \angle P \cot PV$$

and

$$\cos \angle X = \sin \angle P \cos PV$$

Longitude	180° W.	160° W.	140° W.	120° W.	100° W.
angle VPX ($\angle$ P)	01° 17'	18° 43'	38° 43'	58° 43'	78° 43'
cos ∠ P	$\overline{1}·99989$	$\overline{1}·97640$	$\overline{1}·89223$	$\overline{1}·71539$	$\overline{1}·29150$
cot PV	$\overline{1}·95161$	$\overline{1}·95161$	$\overline{1}·95161$	$\overline{1}·95161$	$\overline{1}·95161$
cot PX	$\overline{1}·95150$	$\overline{1}·92801$	$\overline{1}·84384$	$\overline{1}·66700$	$\overline{1}·24311$
PX	48° 11·5'	49° 43·6'	55° 05·2'	65° 05·1'	80° 04·3'
Latitude	41° 48·5' S.	40° 16·4' S.	34° 54·8' S.	24° 54·9' S.	09° 55·7' S.
sin ∠ P	$\overline{2}·35020$	$\overline{1}·50635$	$\overline{1}·79621$	$\overline{1}·93177$	$\overline{1}·99152$
cos PV	$\overline{1}·82395$	$\overline{1}·82395$	$\overline{1}·82395$	$\overline{1}·82395$	$\overline{1}·82395$
cos X	$\overline{2}·17415$	$\overline{1}·33030$	$\overline{1}·62016$	$\overline{1}·75572$	$\overline{1}·81547$
∠ X	89° 08·7'	77° 38·8'	65° 21·2'	55° 15·8'	49° 09·9'
course	S. 89° E.	N. 77½° E.	N. 65½° E.	N. 55° E.	N. 49° E.

Solution

	Position	
Latitude	Longitude	Course
41° 48·5' S.	180° 00·0'	S. 89° E.
41° 48·9' S.	178° 43·0' W.	East
40° 16·4' S.	160° 00·0' W.	N. 77½° E.
34° 54·8' S.	140° 00·0' W.	N. 65½° E.
24° 54·9' S.	120° 00·0' W.	N. 55° E.
09° 55·7' S.	100° 00·0' W.	N. 49° E.

Example 2
Find the great circle distance and the initial course on a voyage from Vancouver to Hawaii between the positions 48° 20′ N. 125° 00′ W., and 21° 15′ N. 157° 25′ W. Find also the position of the vertex.

In this case the vertex of the great circle will lie outside the track between the two positions.

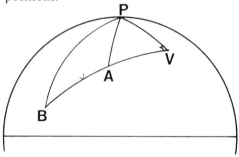

FIG. 4.13

Hav. AB = (hav. d. long. cos lat. A cos lat. B) + hav. d. lat.
Hav. AB = (hav. 32° 25′ cos 48° 20′ cos 21° 15′) + hav. 27° 05′

	no.	log.
log. hav. 32° 25′		$\overline{2}$·89162
log. cos 48° 20′		$\overline{1}$·82269
log. cos 21° 15′		$\overline{1}$·96942
		$\overline{2}$·68373
		0·04828
nat. hav. 27° 05′		0·05483
nat. hav. AB		0·10311

AB = 37° 27·6′
= 2247·6′
dist. = 2247·6 miles

To find initial course

Hav. ∠ A = {hav. PB − hav. (AB ∼ PA)} cosec AB cosec PA
Hav. ∠ A = (hav. 68° 45′ − hav. 4° 12·4′) cosec 37° 27·6′
cosec 41° 40·0′

	no.	log
nat. hav. 68° 45′	0·31878	
nat. hav. 4° 12·4′	0·00135	
	0·31743	
	$\overline{1}$·50164	
log. cosec 37° 27·6′		0·21595
log. cosec 41° 40·0′		0·17731
		$\overline{1}$·89490

A = 124° 45·5′

By inspection of the triangle:

initial course = S. 55° 14·5′ W.

or   235° 14·5′

The only indication that the vertex lies outside the two positions is the fact that angle A was calculated to be more than 90°. The initial course is therefore N. 124° 45·5′ W. or S. 55° 14·5′ W. expressed in the correct quadrantal notation.

To find the position of the vertex
In triangle APV by Napier's rules:

	no.	log.
Sin PV = sin ∠ A sin PA		
= sin 124° 45·5′ sin 41° 40′	sin 124° 45·5′	1·91465
	sin 41° 40·0′	1·82269
PV = 33° 06·4′		1·73734

Latitude of vertex = 56° 53·6′ N.

and

	no.	log.
Cot ∠ P = cos PA tan ∠ A		
= cos 41° 40′ tan 55° 14·5′	cos 41° 40·0′	1·87334
	tan 55° 14·5′	0·15867
∠ P = 42° 53·4′		0·03201

Longitude of A   125° 00·0′ W.
∠ P   42° 53·4′

Long. of vertex   82° 06·6′ W.
Position of vertex = 56° 53·6′ N.   82° 06·6′ W.

EXERCISE

1. Find the shortest distance, and the initial course of the great circle between the following positions.

A   41° 00′ S.   175° 00′ E.
B   33° 00′ S.   71° 30′ W.

Find also the latitudes where the track cuts the longitudes of 90° W., 110° W., 130° W., 150° W., and 170° W., and the course at these points.

2. Find the distance and the initial course along the great circle between the following positions.

A   48° 30′ N.   5° 10′ W.
B   22° 00′ S.   40° 40′ W.

Find also the position of the vertex.

3. Find the initial course, the final course and the great circle distance between the following positions.

A 55° 25' N.   7° 12' W.
B 51° 12' N.   56° 10' W.

4. Find the great circle distance, the initial course, and the position of the vertex of the great circle from:

A 34° 55' S.   56° 10' W.
to B 33° 55' S.   18° 25' E.

5. Find the saving in distance by steaming a great circle track, as opposed to the mercator track from:

A 43° 36' S.   146° 02' E.
to B 26° 12' S.   34° 00' E.

6. Find the distance and the initial course along the great circle between the following positions.

A 48° 24' N.   124° 44' W.
B 34° 50' N.   139° 50' E.

Find also the positions where the meridians of 140° W., 160° W., 180°, and 160° E., cut the great circle track, and the courses at these positions.

Composite Great Circle Sailing

If the vertex of a great circle lies between the two positions involved, then the great circle track will take the vessel into higher latitudes than either of the two positions. The further the positions are separated in longitude, the higher will be the latitude of the vertex. In the limit, if the two positions are 180° apart in longitude, then the great circle will pass over one of the poles. This kind of track is obviously undesirable.

In the composite great circle problem a limit is placed on the latitude to which the navigator wishes his vessel to go. An example of the circumstances in which a composite great circle may be used is the voyage from Cape of Good Hope to Australia or New Zealand. A great circle course would reach latitudes as high as 70° S. A composite great circle can be steamed, with a maximum latitude of about 50°, whilst still retaining a considerable saving in distance.

The track now becomes a great circle track down to the limiting latitude, a parallel sailing along the parallel of the limiting latitude, and then another great circle track from the limiting latitude up to the destination position.

The great circle to be taken from the departure position is that great circle which has its vertex in the limiting latitude. It will therefore form a right angle with the meridian through the vertex which enables the problem to be solved with Napier's rules. The track from the limiting latitude to the arrival position will be along that great circle through the arrival position which has its vertex in the limiting latitude.

Figure 4.14 represents such a track in the southern hemisphere. The broken line shows the true great circle track between the two positions. Note that this does not coincide with the great circles of the composite great circle.

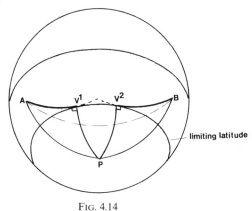

FIG. 4.14

Description of figure

> A = departure position
> B = arrival position
> AP = colat of A
> BP = colat of B
> V_1 = vertex of great circle AV_1
> V_2 = vertex of great circle BV_2
> V_1V_2 = parallel of limiting latitude
> $PV_1 = PV_2$ = colat of limiting latitude

To find the total distance and the initial course
The two right angled triangles can be solved for any part using Napier's rules.

The sides PA and PB are known.

The sides PV_1 and PV_2 are known.

The value of angle PAV_1 will give the initial course expressed in quadrantal notation.

To find angle PAV_1 by Napier's rules:
In triangle PAV_1

$$\sin A = \sin PV_1 \operatorname{cosec} PA$$

The value of sides AV_1 and V_2B expressed in minutes of arc will be the distances between these points. The sum of these plus the distance V_1V_2 will give the total distance.

To find AV_1 by Napier's rules:
In triangle PAV_1

$$\cos AV_1 = \cos PA \sec PV_1$$

In triangle BPV_2

$$\cos BV_2 = \cos PB \sec PV_2$$

The distance along the parallel of the limiting latitude can be found by the parallel sailing formula:

$$\frac{\text{departure}}{\text{d. long.}} = \cos \text{latitude}$$

The d. long. is found by subtracting the values of the angles P in the two triangles APV_1 and BPV_2 from the total d. long. between the two positions.

The problem of finding a series of positions along the two great circle tracks is solved in the same way as for great circle sailing.

Note
If one of the positions given is in north latitude and the other is in south latitude, then one of the sides PA or PB must be greater than 90°. The working of the problem is exactly the same but the introduction of negative signs for the values of the functions of angles in the second quadrant must be carefully watched. Remember that the cosine, the secant, the tangent and the cotangent are negative for angles between 90° and 180°. .

Example 1
Find the total distance, and the initial course along a composite great circle track between the positions given. Find also the positions

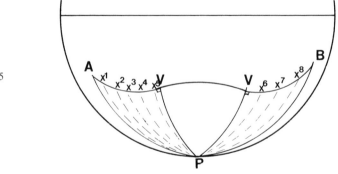

Fig. 4.15

where the track cuts the meridians of 30° E., 40° E., 50° E., 60° E., 70° E., 120° E., 130° E., and 140° E. The vessel must not go to the south of the parallel of 50° S.

Position off Cape of Good Hope	34° 35′ S.	18° 30′ E.
Position off Tasmania	43° 40′ S.	146° 50′ E.

$$34° \ 35·0' \ \text{S.} \qquad 18° \ 30·0' \ \text{E.}$$
$$43° \ 40·0' \ \text{S.} \qquad 146° \ 50·0' \ \text{E.}$$

In triangle AV_1P and BV_2P by Napier's rules:

$\cos AV_1 = \cos AP \sec VP$
$= \cos 55° \ 25' \sec 40°$

	no.	log.
	$\cos 55° \ 25'$	$\bar{1}·75405$
	$\sec 40°$	$0·11575$
		$\bar{1}·86980$

$AV_1 = 42° \ 11·2'$
dist. $AV_1 = 2531·2$ miles

$\cos BV_2 \cos BP \sec VP$
$= \cos 46° \ 20' \sec 40°$

	no.	log.
	$\cos 46° \ 20'$	$\bar{1}·83914$
	$\sec 40°$	$0·11575$
		$\bar{1}·95489$

$BV_2 = 25° \ 40·0'$
dist. $BV_2 = 1540·0$ miles

$\sin \angle A = \sin VP \ \text{cosec} \ AP$
$= \sin 40° \ \text{cosec} \ 55° \ 25'$

	no.	log.
	$\sin 40°$	$\bar{1}·80807$
	$\text{cosec} \ 55° \ 25'$	$0·08444$
		$\bar{1}·89251$

$\angle A = 51° \ 19·7'$
initial course = S. 51° 19·7′ E.

In APV_1

$\cos \angle P = \tan PV \cot PA$
$= \tan 40° \cot 55° \ 25'$

	no.	log.
	$\tan 40°$	$\bar{1}·92381$
	$\cot 55° \ 25'$	$\bar{1}·83849$
		$\bar{1}·76230$

$\angle P = 54° \ 39·3'$

In BPV$_2$

$$\cos \angle P = \tan PV \cot PB$$
$$= \tan 40° \cot 46° 20'$$
$$\angle P = 36° 46.9'$$

	no.	log.
tan 40°		$\bar{1}$·92381
cot 46° 20'		$\bar{1}$·97978
		$\bar{1}$·90359

To find distance V$_1$V$_2$
In triangle PV$_1$V$_2$

angle V$_1$PV$_2$ = d. long. $-54° 39.3' - 36° 46.9'$
$= 128° 20' - 91° 26.2'$
$= 36° 53.8'$
$= 2213.8'$
thus distance V$_1$V$_2$ = 2213.8' cos 50°
$= 1423.0$

	no.	log.
2213·8		3·34514
cos 50°		$\bar{1}$·80807
		3·15321

thus total distance = $1423.0 + 2531.2' + 1540.0'$
$= 5494.2$ miles
initial course = $\underline{S.\ 51° 19.7'\ E.}$

To find the latitudes in which the track cuts the longitudes of 30° E., 40° E., 50° E., 60° E., 70° E., 120° E., 130° E., and 140° E.
In triangles PVX:

$$\cos \angle P = \tan PV \cot PX$$

thus

$$\cot PX = \cos \angle P \cot PV$$

and

$$\cos \angle X = \cos PV \sin \angle P$$

Long.	30° E.	40° E.	50° E.	60° E.	70° E.	120° E.	130° E.	140° E.
∠ P	43° 09·3′	33° 09·3′	23° 09·3′	13° 09·3′	3° 09·3′	9° 56·9′	19° 56·9′	29° 56·9′
cos ∠ P	$\bar{1}$·86302	$\bar{1}$·92283	$\bar{1}$·96352	$\bar{1}$·98845	$\bar{1}$·99934	$\bar{1}$·99342	$\bar{1}$·97312	$\bar{1}$·93776
cot PV	0·07619	0·07619	0·07619	0·07619	0·07619	0·07619	0·07619	0·07619
cot PX	$\bar{1}$·93921	$\bar{1}$·99902	0·03971	0·06464	0·07553	0·06961	0·04931	0·01395
PX	48° 59·8′	45° 03·9′	42° 23·0′	40° 45·1′	40° 02·6′	40° 25·7′	41° 45·3′	44° 04·8′
Lat. (S.)	41° 00·2′	44° 56·1′	47° 37·0′	49° 14·9′	49° 57·4′	49° 34·3′	48° 14·7′	45° 55·2′
sin P	$\bar{1}$·83504	$\bar{1}$·73791	$\bar{1}$·59464	$\bar{1}$·35714	$\bar{2}$·74070	$\bar{1}$·23745	$\bar{1}$·53298	$\bar{1}$·69829
cos PV	$\bar{1}$·88425	$\bar{1}$·88425	$\bar{1}$·88425	$\bar{1}$·88425	$\bar{1}$·88425	$\bar{1}$·88425	$\bar{1}$·88425	$\bar{1}$·88425
cos X	$\bar{1}$·71929	$\bar{1}$·62216	$\bar{1}$·47889	$\bar{1}$·24139	$\bar{2}$·62495	$\bar{1}$·12170	$\bar{1}$·41723	$\bar{1}$·58254
X	58° 24·1′	65° 13·9′	72° 28·1′	79° 57·6′	87° 35·0′	82° 23·7′	74° 51·0′	67° 31·0′
course	S. 58¼° E.	S. 65¼° E.	S. 72½° E.	S. 80° E.	S. 87½° E.	N. 82¼° E.	N. 75° E.	N. 67½° E.

Solution

Position		Course
Latitude	Longitude	
41° 00·2′ S.	30° 00·0′ E.	S. $58\frac{1}{2}°$ E.
44° 56·1′ S.	40° 00·0′ E.	S. $65\frac{1}{4}°$ E.
47° 37·0′ S.	50° 00·0′ E.	S. $72\frac{1}{2}°$ E.
49° 14·9′ S.	60° 00·0′ E.	S. 80° E.
49° 57·4′ S.	70° 00·0′ E.	S. $87\frac{1}{2}°$ E.
50° 00·0′ S.	73° 09·3′ E.	East
50° 00·0′ S.	110° 03·1′ E.	East
49° 34·3′ S.	120° 00·0′ E.	N. $82\frac{1}{2}°$ E.
48° 14·7′ S.	130° 00·0′ E.	N. 75° E.
45° 55·2′ S.	140° 00·0′ E.	N. $67\frac{1}{2}°$ E.

Example 2

Find the initial course to steer and the shortest distance between the following positions, if the vessel is not to go to the south of the parallel of 45° S.

A. 10° 18·0′ S. 20° 10·0′ E.
B. 45° 00·0′ S. 160° 10·0′ E.
140° 00·0′ E. = d. long.

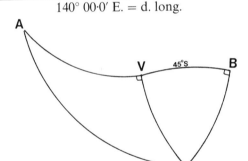

FIG. 4.16

In triangle AVP:

$$PA = 79° 42·0′$$
$$PV = 45°$$

To find angle A by Napier's rules:

$$\sin PV = \sin PA \sin A$$
$$\sin A = \sin 45° \operatorname{cosec} 79° 42·0′$$
$$A = 45° 56·8′$$
initial course = S. 45° 56·8′ E.

	no.	log.
	sin 45	1·84947
	cosec 79° 42′	0·00706
		1·85655

To find AV:

$$\cos PA = \cos AV \cos VP$$
$$\cos AV = \cos 79° \; 42·00' \; \sec 45°$$
$$AV = 75° \; 21·2'$$
distance AV = 4521·2 miles

	no.	log.
cos 79° 42'		1·25237
sec 45°		0·15051
		1·40288

To find angle P:

$$\cos P = \tan PV \cot PA$$
$$= \tan 45° \cot 79° \; 42·0'$$
$$= 79° \; 31·7'$$

	no.	log.
tan 45°		0·00000
cot 79° 42'		1·25943
		1·25943

Longitude of A	20° 10·0' E.
angle P	79° 31·7'
Longitude of V	99° 41·7' E.
Longitude of B	160° 10·0' E.
d. long. V − B	60° 28·3'

Distance V − B = 3628·3 × cos 45°
            = 2565·6 miles
distance AV   = 4521·2
total distance = 7086·8 miles

EXERCISE 4B

1. Find the initial course and the total distance along a composite great circle from:

A   35° 00' S.   20° 00' E.
to B   43° 40' S.   146° 50' E.

The maximum latitude is to be 48° S. Find also the longitudes of the vertices of the great circles.

2. A composite great circle track between Montivideo (34° 55' S. 56° 10' W.) and Cape Town (33° 55' S. 18° 25' E.), is required with limiting latitude 38° S. Find the initial course and the total distance to steam.

3. Find the total distance, the initial course, and the longitudes in which the track reaches and leaves the limiting latitude, on a composite great circle from:

A   26° 12' S.   34° 00' E.
to B   43° 36' S.   146° 02' E.

Limiting latitude 45° S.

4. Find the total distance and the initial course on the composite great circle from:

A   45° 30′ S.   71° 37′ W.
to B   46° 40′ S.   168° 20′ E.

Limiting latitude is to be 49° S.

5. Calculate the shortest distance to steam from A in 4° 00′ N. 31° 00′ E., to B in 42° 00′ S. 145° 00′ E., given that the vessel is not to go south of latitude 42° S. State also the direction of the track where it crosses the equator.

The Gnomonic Chart

The point of projection of a gnomonic chart is the centre of the earth. As this point lies in the plane of every great circle then all great circles must project onto any plane as straight lines. The plane of projection is a plane placed tangentially to the earth's surface at some chosen point. This point is chosen near the centre of the area to be portrayed, and the choice will affect the appearance on the chart of the meridians and the parallels. Such a chart is used to produce a quick solution to the great circle sailing problem, as any great circle course may be laid off as a straight line between the two points involved.

The Polar Gnomonic Chart

As the mercator projection cannot be used for high latitudes this type of projection is often used in polar regions. The plane of projection is tangential to the earth at the pole.

As the meridians form great circles and they all pass through the point of projection, they will appear as straight lines radiating from the pole.

The parallels of latitude will all project onto the plane as circles, as every point on a parallel is at the same distance from the point of projection and from the plane of projection. The radius of the projected circles will be proportional to the cotangent of the latitude.

From the diagram

$$\frac{r}{R} = \tan \text{ colatitude}$$

$$\frac{r}{R} = \cot \text{ latitude}$$

where r is the radius of the projected parallel and R is the radius of the globe being projected.

The scale of the chart therefore increases as the latitude decreases. This results in high distortion away from the tangential point. In the limit it is impossible to project the equator.

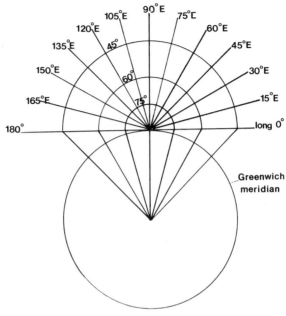

FIG. 4.17

The Equatorial Gnomonic Projection

This is a gnomonic chart with the tangential point of the plane of projection on the equator.

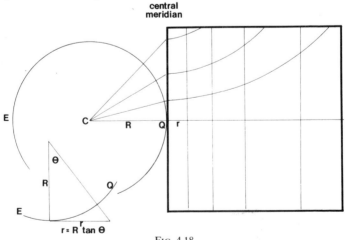

FIG. 4.18

Meridians will appear as straight lines, all at right angles to the straight line representing the equator. The spacing of the meridians will increase away from the tangential point until in the limit the meridian 90° removed from the meridian of the tangential point cannot be projected. The parallels of latitude will project onto the plane as hyperbolae, symmetrical about the central meridian, i.e. that of the tangential point.

The plane of projection may be tangential at any other position on the earth's surface, but the meridians will always appear as straight lines radiating from the projected position of the pole. All great circles will appear as straight lines. The gnomonic chart is particularly useful therefore for plotting great circle tracks.

If the two positions between which the vessel is sailing are plotted on the chart a straight line can be drawn between them to represent the track. Positions at intervals along the track can then be lifted off the gnomonic chart and transferred to a mercator chart. If these positions on the mercator chart are joined with straight lines the resulting construction will approximate to the great circle curve on the mercator chart. The mercator courses can then be measured from the chart.

The courses cannot be measured at any point on the gnomonic chart. This type of projection is not orthomorphic and angles are distorted at every point except the tangential point. Distance cannot be measured as the scale is increasing away from the tangential point.

A composite great circle track can be picked off a gnomonic chart by drawing from the initial position a tangent to the curve which represents the parallel of the limiting latitude. Similarly a tangent from the destination position to the same parallel will give the other great circle. The two straight lines can then be transferred to the mercator chart as before.

Methods of Effecting a Great Circle Sailing

Once the series of short mercator courses are plotted on the mercator chart, the navigator can measure the courses and endeavour to keep the vessel on these course lines. When the ship deviates from a mercator course, a new course can be set to the next alteration position on the great circle track.

However a better method of effecting a great circle sailing is to treat each observed position as the initial position of a new great circle problem. Thus once the vessel has deviated from the original great circle track there is no reason to try to get the ship back onto it. A new initial great circle course is set from the fix to the destination. This method is much simplified by the use of Azimuth tables (ABC) to solve the spherical triangle involved. The initial course of a great circle track may readily be found from the ABC tables by using the latitude of the initial position as the argument latitude in

Table A. The latitude of the destination is used as the declination in Table B. The d. long. between the positions is used as the argument hour angle. Initial course is then extracted as the azimuth from Table C. By this means the ship may quickly be put onto the new initial course as each observed position is obtained. The distance to go may then be worked by the haversine formula.

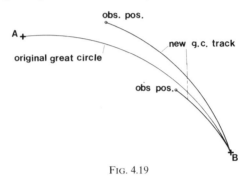

FIG. 4.19

Great circle courses should be adjusted to allow for set and leeway in order to prevent the ship from leaving the original great circle course line. If the ship does deviate however the shortest distance to steam to the destination is along a new great circle track, ignoring the original track from which the ship has deviated.

EXERCISE 4C

1. Define 'vertex of a great circle'. What is the course along a great circle at the vertices? State the relationship between the direction of a great circle at the equator and the latitude of the vertices.

2. Given that a great circle is inclined to the equator at 42°, and crosses the equator in longitude 50° W., the direction here being S.W./N.E., give the positions of the two vertices. What is the convergency between a vertex and a point where the great circle crosses the equator?

3. Define 'convergency of the meridians'. If a vessel steams directly towards a point which is in sight does she follow a mercator track or a great circle track. Explain why a D/F bearing must be corrected before laying off on a mercator chart. Why is this not done for a visual bearing?

4. Two places on the parallel of 50° N. have a d. long. between them of 100°. Find the difference in steaming distance between them over a great circle course and a mercator course.

5. Find by use of the half convergency formula the great circle bearing of A in position 50° N. 176° 14′ E. from B in position 50° N. 170° 21′ W.

6. Why is the gnomonic projection unsuitable for use for general navigation?

7. Explain the use of a gnomonic chart in navigation.

CHAPTER 5

THE CELESTIAL SPHERE. THE MEASUREMENT OF POSITION ON THE SPHERE. THE NAUTICAL ALMANAC

The Celestial Sphere

It is easy to imagine, when looking at the night sky, that the stars are on the inside of a huge dome, which could be part of a sphere surrounding the earth. It appears that the earth is at the centre of such a sphere. This concept is useful to the navigator, and it can be used because he is primarily concerned with angular measurement. Although each body in the heavens is at a different distance from the earth, this fact can be neglected. Distances will not affect the angle subtended at the centre of the earth by any two points or planes in the heavens.

Thus the concept of the celestial sphere is a sphere which is of infinite radius and is centred upon the earth. Upon the inside of this sphere are projected from the centre of the earth, the positions of all the celestial bodies. The earth and the celestial sphere are concentric.

We have therefore returned to the idea of the earth being the centre of the universe, and therefore, of the sun orbiting the earth. However whether we think of the sun orbiting the earth or vice versa makes no difference to the apparent position of the sun upon the celestial sphere. The distance between the sun and the earth is negligible compared with that between the solar system and the stars. Whether we think of the sun as being at the centre of the sphere or the earth being at the centre is irrelevant in this respect.

The apparent motion of the sun on the celestial sphere

The sun will appear to move against the background of the stars because of the motion of the earth in orbit around the sun. The path of the sun around the sphere is therefore a great circle which lies in the same plane as the earth's orbit around the sun (see Fig. 5.1).

This great circle is called the Ecliptic. The sun will move around the ecliptic once in the period that it takes the earth to go around its orbit, i.e. the year. It will move anticlockwise as viewed from the north, or eastwards as viewed from the earth.

The position of all bodies on the sphere will of course change over a period of time. In general the closer a body is to the earth, the

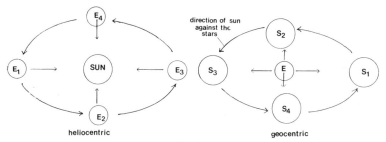

FIG. 5.1

greater will be that body's movement on the sphere, although this must depend also upon the magnitude of the body's own velocity. The closer celestial bodies such as the moon, the sun, and the planets all have much greater motions around the sphere than the more distant stars. These motions are discussed in greater detail in 'Motions of the Heavens'.

Before we can measure a body's movement on the celestial sphere, we must be able to express its position at any given instant. Position is measured on the celestial sphere exactly as position is measured on the surface of the earth, that is as an angular distance from a reference plane. An angular distance may be expressed as an arc of a great circle or as an angle at the centre of the sphere subtended by two points.

The first plane of reference that must be introduced is the equivalent on the celestial sphere to that of the equator on the earth. If the plane of the equator is extended outwards until it meets the sphere, it will do so in a great circle whose plane will be the same as that of the equator. This great circle is called the Equinoctial or the Celestial Equator. Similarly if the earth's axis of rotation is produced in both directions it will meet the sphere in points which may be called the poles of the equinoctial, or the poles of the celestial sphere. These points are important because as the earth rotates on its axis within the sphere it will appear as if the sphere were rotating about the earth in the opposite direction. Only the poles of the sphere will appear stationary, the heavens appearing to rotate around them.

The plane of the equinoctial is a constant plane in space, or very nearly so. The plane of the earth's orbit around the sun is also a constant plane in space. The angle between the two planes must therefore be a constant. The value of this angle is important because of its effects on conditions on the earth and on the way our heavens appear to move during the daily rotation of the earth. The plane of the ecliptic is inclined to the plane of the equinoctial at about 23° 27′ due to the fact that the axis of the earth's rotation is inclined to the perpendicular to the ecliptic by this angle. The two planes will cut the celestial sphere in great circles which are oblique to each other, by 23° 27'. This angle is called the Obliquity of the Ecliptic (see Fig. 5.3).

If the two celestial poles are joined by semi-great circles, a grid of celestial meridians is formed. These are sometimes referred to as Hour Circles.

The first co-ordinate by which position is measured on the celestial sphere, may now be defined. This co-ordinate expresses the angular distance of a point on the sphere north or south of the equinoctial, and is called declination.

Declination is defined as the arc of the celestial meridian which is contained between the equinoctial and the point being considered. A parallel of declination will join all points having the same declination and will form a small circle on the sphere whose plane is parallel to that of the equinoctial. Declination is measured from 0° to 90° north or south of the equinoctial. Figure 5.2 shows that the declination of a point on the celestial sphere is equal to the latitude of the position on the earth's surface directly beneath it. This position is called the Geographical Position of the point on the sphere and may be defined as the position where a line joining the point to the centre of the earth cuts the surface.

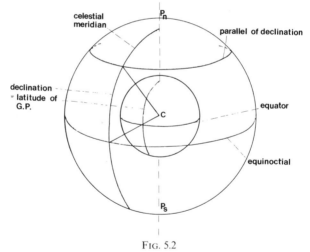

FIG. 5.2

The second plane of reference must be at right angles to the equinoctial, i.e. one of the celestial meridians. In defining a terrestrial position the Greenwich meridian was chosen from which to measure longitude. Similarly a celestial meridian must be chosen arbitrarily from which to measure the second celestial co-ordinate.

The celestial meridian chosen is that one which passes through the point where the ecliptic crosses the equinoctial. As this is the point of intersection of two constant planes in space then the direction of the point of intersection will lie in a constant direction in space. There must be two points of intersection. The one chosen is that one where the sun crosses the equinoctial when moving from south to north. This is called the First Point of Aries. The meridian through the first point of Aries is that from which the second co-ordinate is measured. The angular distance of any celestial meridian from this reference meridian may be expressed as an arc of the equinoctial. This arc is called the Sidereal Hour Angle (S.H.A.).

The S.H.A. of any body can be defined as the arc of the equinoctial measured westwards from the first point of Aries to the meridian passing through the body, and expressed in degrees minutes and seconds of arc.

Thus a position on the celestial sphere is defined by its declination and its sidereal hour angle. For any fixed point on the sphere these quantities will remain constant over short periods of time. Small long term changes will be explained in Chapter 7.

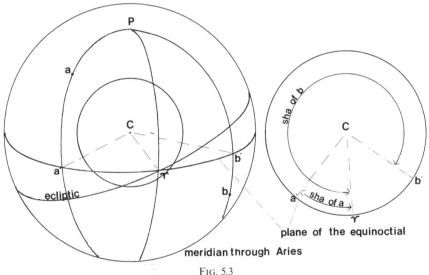

FIG. 5.3

Geographical position

If a line is projected from the centre of the earth to a body on the celestial sphere it will cut the earth's surface at a point which can be said to be the position on the earth directly under the body. This position is called the body's Geographical Position (G.P.).

It is a body's G.P. in which the navigator is primarily concerned when using a celestial body for navigation.

Latitude and longitude of the G.P. Greenwich hour angle

It has been shown that the declination of a body is equal to the latitude of its geographical position (see Fig. 5.2).

However it must be understood that the S.H.A. of a point on the sphere cannot be considered the longitude of the G.P. The reference planes from which these two co-ordinates are measured are not coincident. The plane from which longitude is measured, the Greenwich meridian, is rotating about the earth's axis, whereas the plane from which S.H.A. is measured can be considered fixed in space. Therefore a body with constant S.H.A. will change its terrestrial longitude by 360° each time the earth rotates about its axis within the celestial sphere. Hence the apparent daily motion of the heavens.

To find the longitude of the G.P. at any instant

In order to find the longitude of the G.P. of a body, whose S.H.A. is known, it is necessary to know the angular distance between the meridian of Greenwich and the meridian through the first point of Aries. This angle will be the difference between the S.H.A. and the longitude of the G.P., at any instant and is called the Greenwich Hour Angle of the first point of Aries (G.H.A.♈).

G.H.A. ♈ can be defined as the arc of the equinoctial contained between the meridian through Greenwich and that through the first point of Aries. It is measured westwards from the meridian of Greenwich from 0° to 360°.

If the S.H.A. of a body gives the angular distance of the body west of the first point of Aries, and the G.H.A. of Aries gives the angular distance of this point west of Greenwich, then the sum of these two will be the angular distance of the body west of the meridian of Greenwich. This angular distance is called the Greenwich Hour Angle of the body (see Fig. 5.4).

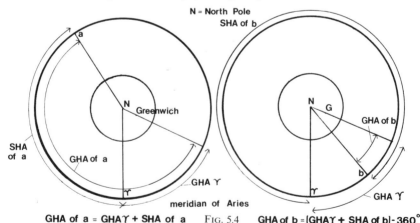

GHA of a = GHA♈ + SHA of a   Fig. 5.4   GHA of b =[GHA♈ + SHA of b]-360°

If the sum of the S.H.A. of the body and the G.H.A. of Aries is more than 360° then the G.H.A. of the body is obtained by subtracting this amount from the sum.

G.H.A. of any position on the celestial sphere can be defined as the arc of the equinoctial contained between the meridian of Greenwich and the meridian through the position being considered, measured westwards from the meridian of Greenwich from 0° to 360°.

Note

The Greenwich Hour Angle is synonymous with longitude of the G.P. except that G.H.A. is measured westwards from Greenwich from 0° to 360° and longitude is measured westwards or eastwards from 0° to 180°. If the G.H.A. found therefore is more than 180°, the longitude can readily be found by subtracting the G.H.A. from 360° and calling it east.

Example

Given that the G.H.A. ♈ = 126° 15′ and S.H.A. Rigel is 281° 41′, find the G.H.A. of Rigel and the longitude of its G.P.

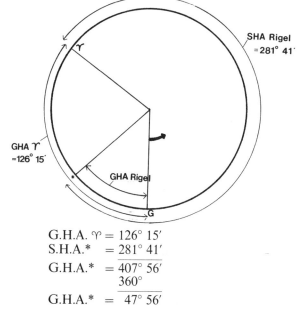

FIG. 5.5

$$\begin{aligned}
\text{G.H.A. } ♈ &= 126°\ 15' \\
\text{S.H.A.}^* &= 281°\ 41' \\
\hline
\text{G.H.A.}^* &= 407°\ 56' \\
&\quad\ 360° \\
\hline
\text{G.H.A.}^* &= \ \ 47°\ 56'
\end{aligned}$$

There must be at the disposal of the navigator, information about the geographical position of bodies, which are used for navigation, at any given time. This information is found in the *Nautical Almanac*. The greater part of the almanac consists of the 'daily pages', which together with the increment tables (the yellow pages in the H.M.S.O. publication), enable the navigator to extract the co-ordinates of the G.P.s of the sun, the moon, four navigational ·planets, and a list of selected navigational stars, for each second throughout the year. In the case of the sun, the moon, and the planets the information is given in the form of the G.H.A. and the declination. In the case of the stars, because their S.H.A.s remain fairly constant, it is less cumbersome to give these values and to tabulate the G.H.A. of the first point of Aries, to enable the navigator to derive the G.H.A. of any of the stars. The declinations of the stars, which also remain fairly constant, are given alongside the S.H.A.s.

The arrangement of the daily pages

G.H.A.
In columns headed 'Venus, Mars, Jupiter, Saturn, Sun, and Moon', the value of G.H.A. is given for each hour of G.M.T. throughout the year, each double page containing the figures for three days. The value for each second between the integral hours can be found by adding an increment to that value for the hour of the G.M.T. This increment is taken from the interpolation tables at the back of the almanac. These tables are entered with the number of minutes in the G.M.T. at the top of the page, and the number of seconds down the left hand side of the table. Note that different tables are provided for the sun and planets, for Aries, and for the moon.

The 'v' correction
The increment tables are merely interpolation tables which multiply an hourly change of hour angle by the fraction of an hour that is given by the number of minutes and seconds in the G.M.T. For each column (sun and planets, Aries, or moon), a fixed value for the hourly change of G.H.A. is specified. For the 'sun and planets' column a rate of change of hour angle of 15° per hour is used. In the case of the sun the actual rate of change is always close enough to this figure so that any errors are negligible. However the rate of change of hour angle of planets is variable to a much greater extent (see 'Planetary Motion'). In order that one increment table can be used a fixed rate of change of hour angle of 15° per hour is also used for planets and any departure from this value is allowed for by a correction referred to as the 'v' correction.

A value called 'v' is given once for each daily page at the foot of the column for each planet. This value is the difference between the actual hourly change of hour angle of the planet on that page and the hourly change of 15° assumed in the increment tables. Thus if the 'v' value given on one of the daily pages under Venus is +2·0 then the mean rate of change of G.H.A. on that page is 15° 02·0′ per hour. This can be verified by inspection of the hourly figures.

A value of 'v' of −2·0, would mean an hourly change of G.H.A. of 14° 58·0′ for those three days on that page.

However, as the increment tables multiply the hourly change of hour angle by a fraction, then the 'v' value must also be multiplied by the same fraction before being applied to the increment. This is done by the columns on the right hand side of each increment table headed 'v or d'. When extracting the increment for the minutes and seconds of the G.M.T., these columns should be entered with the 'v' value and the 'v' correction against it extracted. This correction should then be applied to the increment before the increment is added to the G.H.A. for the integral hour of G.M.T. The 'v' correction is always positive for Mars, Jupiter and Saturn, but is sometimes negative for Venus. The correct sign should be noted therefore when using Venus.

The change in G.H.A. of the moon varies between 14° 19′ and 14° 37′ per hour. The interpolation table for the moon is calculated on the minimum hourly change of 14° 19′. The 'v' value for the moon is the excess of the actual hourly change over this amount. This value is given for each hour of G.M.T. in the daily pages next to the hourly value of G.H.A. Interpolation of the 'v' value is done exactly as that for planets. Because the moon's interpolation table is based on the minimum hourly change of G.H.A., the moon's 'v' correction is always positive.

The increment tables for the first point of Aries are calculated with an hourly change of G.H.A. of 15° 02·46′. This value is constant and therefore there is no 'v' correction required for Aries.

Declination

The declination for each of the bodies mentioned is given for each hour of G.M.T. abreast of the G.H.A. The change in declination over one hour is given at the foot of the columns for planets and the sun, and against each hourly figure in the case of the moon, under the heading of 'd'. This is given for the purpose of interpolation and this can be done with the increment tables in exactly the same way that the 'v' value is interpolated, or in most cases it can be done mentally. When interpolating the declination note particularly whether the declination is increasing or decreasing, as this will determine the sign of the 'd' correction (see worked examples).

Example 1

Find the G.H.A. and declination of:

1. the sun at G.M.T. January 4th, 13h 14m 16s.

G.H.A. 13h	13° 46·1′	Dec. 22° 43·7′ S. (d = 0·3′)
incr. 14m 16s	3° 34·0′	d − 0·1′
G.H.A. sun	17° 20·1′	Dec. 22° 43·6′ S.

2. The moon at G.M.T. January 5th, 18h 50m 12s.

G.H.A. 18h   311° 08·2' (v = 3·5) Dec. 23° 19·1' N. (d = 3·3')
incr. 50m 12s   11° 58·7'   d   +2·8'
v   2·9'   ———————————
          ——————————   23° 21·9' N.
          323° 09·8'

3. Betelgeuse at G.M.T. January 6th, 00h 20m 20s.

G.H.A. 00h   105° 11·6'   Dec. 7° 24·2' N.
incr. 20m 20s   5° 05·8'
S.H.A. star   271° 32·9'
          ——————————
G.H.A. star   381° 50·3'
        =   21° 50·3'

4. Saturn at G.M.T. January 5th, 13h 59m 59s.

G.H.A. 13h   209° 32·8' (v = 2·7) Dec. 22° 24·7' N.
incr. 59m 59s 14° 59·8'
v   2·7'
          ——————————
G.H.A. Saturn 224° 35·3'

Local hour angle
This may be defined in the same way as the Greenwich hour
angle except that the observer's meridian is used as the reference
meridian instead of the Greenwich meridian. The L.H.A. is therefore the angular distance of a body west of the observer's meridian,
measured as an arc of the equinoctial, or the equator. A body on
the celestial sphere will have a different L.H.A. for observer's on
different meridians. Furthermore the L.H.A. of any fixed point on
the sphere will change as the earth rotates, the rate of change of
L.H.A. being exactly the same as the rate of change of G.H.A.
The L.H.A. of a fixed point will for a stationary observer, increase
by 360° each time the earth rotates about its axis.

Definition of L.H.A.
The arc of the equinoctial which is contained between the celestial
meridian of the observer, and the meridian passing through the
point being considered, measured westwards from the observer's
meridian from 0° to 360°.
    Clearly there must be a relationship between the L.H.A. of a
body to any given observer, and its G.H.A. at any instant. The
difference between the two must be the angle between the planes
of the observer's and the Greenwich meridian, i.e. the observer's
longitude.
    Figure 5.6 shows the earth, the celestial sphere and a body, X, on
the sphere with a G.H.A. of about 150°. Let A and B be the posi-

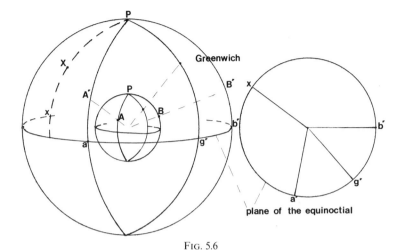

FIG. 5.6

tions of two observers, one in west longitude and the other in east longitude.

Then A′ is the position of the zenith of A, B′ is the position of the zenith of B, a and b are the positions where their meridians cut the equinoctial.
Then L.H.A. of X for observer A is given by:

G.H.A. of X − westerly longitude of A

thus for observer A

L.H.A. = gx − ag = ax

and L.H.A. for X for observer B is given by:

G.H.A. of X + easterly longitude of B

thus for observer B

L.H.A. = gx + gb = bx

The above rules hold good for any values of G.H.A. and longitude. If however G.H.A. + easterly longitude is greater than 360°, this figure should be subtracted from the result to give the L.H.A. If the longitude is west and the longitude is greater than the G.H.A. then a negative value would result. In this case 360° is added to give the L.H.A.
The above figure can be represented on the plane of the equinoctial as in Figure 5.7.

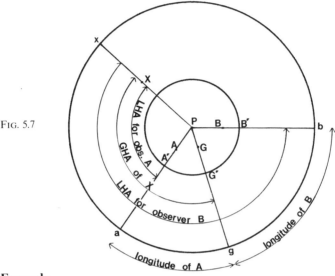

FIG. 5.7

Example

Find the L.H.A. of the moon at G.M.T. November 1st, 5h 35m 30s to an observer in longitude 94° 15′ W.

G.H.A. 5h	65° 26·2′ (v = 8·3)
incr. 35m 30s	8° 28·2′
v	4·9′
	73° 59·3′
long. W.	−94° 15·0′
	339° 44·3′

The horizon system

When observing a celestial body for navigational purposes, any observations made must be necessarily with reference to the position of the observer. We cannot observe any of the co-ordinates already defined, as the planes of the equinoctial and the Greenwich meridian are not conveniently marked in the sky. The only planes which we can readily identify from any position on the earth are those of the horizontal and the meridian. The horizontal plane is identified by the rim of the sea horizon. The meridian is identified by the compass. Using these planes of reference we can also fix a body's position on the celestial sphere.

The rational horizon

This is defined as the plane which passes through the centre of the celestial sphere, and is perpendicular to the observer's vertical. This plane will cut the celestial sphere in a great circle.

The zenith
This is the point on the celestial sphere which is directly above the observer. The declination and the G.H.A. of the zenith are therefore the same as the latitude and longitude of the observer.

The zenith will be the pole of the great circle which is the intersection of the rational horizon with the celestial sphere, and is therefore 90° removed from all points on the rational horizon.

The point on the sphere diametrically opposed to the zenith is called the Nadir.

If a number of semi-great circles joining the zenith and the nadir are drawn, a graticule on the sphere, which is analogous to that formed by the equator and the meridians, is produced. In this analogy the rational horizon corresponds to the equator, the zenith and the nadir to the two poles, and the semi-great circles joining the zenith and the nadir correspond to the celestial meridians. The great circles which pass through the zenith and the nadir are called vertical circles. They will cut the rational horizon in a right angle, and therefore to any observer his vertical circles appear as lines rising from the horizon vertically and passing directly overhead.

If this graticule now described is used to measure position on the celestial sphere, it is called the Horizon System. Figure 5.8 shows the graticule in this system for an observer in latitude 50° N. and longitude 90° W. The broken lines describe the equator and the celestial meridians.

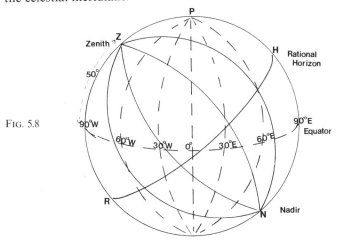

Fig. 5.8

The co-ordinates with which position is measured in the horizon system are:
True altitude: This is the angular distance of a body above the rational horizon. It can be defined precisely as the arc of the vertical

circle which passes through the body contained between the rational horizon and the body. (Arc XH in Figure 5.10.)

If all points on the sphere which have the same altitude are joined then a small circle is formed whose plane is parallel to that of the rational horizon. (Compare this to a parallel of latitude in the equinoctial system.) Such a small circle is called a circle of equal altitude.

Zenith distance: The true altitude may also be defined by stating the arc ZX in Figure 5.10. This is the arc of the vertical circle through the body which is contained between the zenith and the body, and it will be the complement of the true altitude.

Bearing: One of the vertical circles is chosen as a reference circle from which to measure the second co-ordinate. The circle chosen is that vertical circle which passes through the celestial poles. This vertical circle therefore must be, by definition, a meridian and its antimeridian. The point where it cuts the rational horizon will be the north point of the horizon as indicated by a compass.

The arc of the rational horizon contained between the north point of the horizon and the vertical circle through the body is called the bearing of the body if it is measured clockwise from the north point. This will be the bearing indicated by a compass in the three figure notation.

Azimuth

This is another method of expressing the bearing of a body. Azimuth is measured from 0° to 180° eastwards or westwards from the direction of the north point of the horizon if in north latitude, or from the south point of the horizon if in south latitude.

The conversion of Azimuth to bearing is done as follows.

If the azimuth is named north and east then the bearing will be the same as the azimuth. If the azimuth is named north and west then the bearing will be 360° − azimuth.

If the azimuth is named south and east then the bearing will be 180° − azimuth. If the azimuth is named south and west then the bearing will be 180° + azimuth.

Figure 5.9 illustrates each of these cases.

Conversion between the horizon system and the equinoctial system

To convert from one of these systems to the other, the angle between the equator and the horizon must be known or must be found. This angle will depend upon the observer's latitude. Figure 5.10 shows a position on the celestial sphere, X, and its declination and its L.H.A. Also shown is the rational horizon for an observer in latitude 50° N. and longitude 90° W. and hence the body's altitude and bearing. Conversion may be done by the solution of the spherical triangle formed by the intersection of the two meridians through the observer and the body and the vertical circle through the

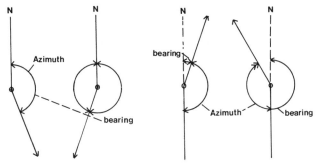

FIG. 5.9

position. In the figure this is triangle PZX. The elements of this triangle include the L.H.A. and the bearing, the complement of the latitude, the complement of the declination, and the complement of the altitude. If any three of these are known the triangle can be solved.

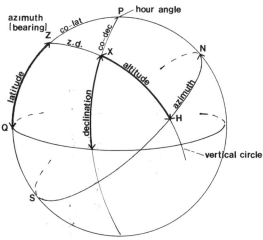

FIG. 5.10

Example
Given declination 48° N., G.H.A. 65°, find the altitude and bearing to an observer in position 50° N. 90° W.

$$\begin{array}{ll} \text{Longitude} & 90° \text{ W.} \\ \text{G.H.A.} & 65° \\ \hline \text{L.H.A.} & 335° \end{array}$$

The angle P = 360 − 335 = 25°
side PX = co-dec. = 42°
PZ = co-lat. = 40°

Thus in triangle PZX by the haversine formula:

hav. ZX = (hav. P sin PZ sin PX) + hav. (PZ ∼ PX)
 = (hav. 25° sin 40° sin 42°) + hav. 2°

	no.	log.
log. hav. 25°		$\overline{2}$·67067
log. sin 40°		$\overline{1}$·80807
log. sin 42°		$\overline{1}$·82551
log. hav.		$\overline{2}$·30425
nat. hav.		0·02015
nat. hav. 2°		0·00030
nat. hav. ZX		0·02045

ZX = 16° 26·5'   True altitude = 73° 33·5'

and

hav. Z = [hav. PX − hav. (PZ ∼ XZ)] cosec PZ cosec ZX
 = (hav. 42° − hav. 23° 33·5') cosec 40° cosec 16° 26·5'

	no.	log.
nat. hav. 42°		0·12843
nat. hav. 23° 33$\frac{1}{2}$'		0·04167
nat. hav.		0·08676
log. hav.		$\overline{2}$·93830
log. cosec 40°		0·19193
log. cosec 16° 26$\frac{1}{2}$'		0·54816
log. cosec Z		$\overline{1}$·67839

angle Z = 87° 20·8'   bearing = N. 87° 20·8' E.

EXERCISE 5A

Convert the following co-ordinates of the equinoctial system into altitude and bearing for the observer's positions given.

	S.H.A.	G.H.A. ♈	Dec.	Lat.	Long.
1.	208° 24'	243° 07·9'	12° 08·9' N.	34° 12' N.	40° 18' W.
2.	291° 33·2'	111° 37·0'	16° 26·1' N.	10° 14' S.	25° 36' W.
3.	54° 18·7'	317° 44·9'	56° 51·1' S.	36° 17' S.	9° 12' E.
4.	357° 09·6'	311° 31·0'	14° 59' N.	12° 17' S.	65° 58' E.

Use of the PZX triangle in navigation
The solution of the PZX triangle using known arguments derived from measurement of co-ordinates in the alt-azimuth or local

system, and from a knowledge of the bodies co-ordinates in the equinoctial system, will yield those parts of the triangle which define the relationship between the two sets of reference planes. This relationship will be defined by the side PZ from which is obtained the latitude, and by angle P from which the longitude is derived, using the G.H.A. of the body at the time of observation.

For a solution however three arguments are necessary. To have both PZ and angle P as respondents, the three arguments would have to be chosen from angle X, angle Z, side PX, and side ZX. Of these the two sides are suitable. PX is readily obtained, being the complement of the declination. ZX is obtained from a measurement of the true altitude. But, alas there is no third argument suitable. The angle X cannot be measured. The angle Z, the azimuth cannot be measured with sufficient accuracy to be used in the calculations.

We can therefore only obtain a solution by assuming a value for one of the parts PZ, P, or ZX, and hence calculating a value for those remaining. It is not possible therefore to calculate values for both PZ and P. One observation therefore cannot yield the ship's position.

The position line

If a value for latitude and hence PZ is assumed and used in the solution with PX and ZX, then a calculated value for P and hence longitude is obtained. The value arrived at for longitude depends upon the assumed value of latitude. Different assumed values of latitude will give correspondingly different values of calculated longitude. A line on the earth's surface joining all possible combinations of assumed latitude and calculated longitude will constitute a line of position, any point on which the ship might lie, consistent with the observed information used in the calculation.

The nature of a position line obtained from a celestial observation

The information observed at the ship consists of only an altitude, the instant of the observation being noted on a chronometer. There must be a circle centred upon the geographical position of the body, every point on the circumference of which, would give the same altitude and hence the same zenith distance. This constitutes a circle of position.

A point upon the position circle of any observation may be found by:

1. Assuming a value of latitude (PZ) and calculating the longitude in which the position line crosses that parallel.
2. Assuming a value of longitude (from which can be derived the angle P), and calculating the latitude in which the position line cuts that meridian.
3. Assuming both latitude and longitude (PZ and P), and calcu-

lating the value of zenith distance for that assumed position, for comparison with the observed zenith distance.

Each of these methods will be dealt with in detail in Chapter 13 under the headings of:

1. Longitude by chronometer.
2. Ex meridian problem.
3. Marq St. Hilaire problem.

Each of these methods is a calculation for finding a position on the position circle.

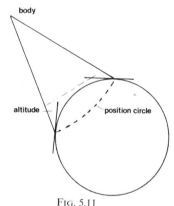

FIG. 5.11

The ecliptic system

The co-ordinates of a fixed point on the celestial sphere, in the equinoctial system, can, it has been stated, be considered constant over short periods of time. The equinoctial however is subject to small movements caused by the gravitational forces between bodies within the solar system (see Precession of the Equinoxes). This movement causes small changes in the values of the declination and the S.H.A. of a fixed point on the sphere. The plane of the ecliptic is fixed in space to a much greater extent, and therefore it is convenient for astronomers to use this plane instead of the equinoctial from which to measure a body's position.

The two co-ordinates used in this system are:

Celestial latitude. The angular distance of a body north or south of the ecliptic measured along a secondary to the ecliptic.

Celestial longitude. The arc of the ecliptic contained between the first point of Aries and the secondary to the ecliptic which passes through the position being considered. This arc is measured eastwards from the first point of Aries from 0° to 360°.

Figure 5.12 shows a point on the celestial sphere and its celestial latitude and longitude along with its declination and S.H.A.

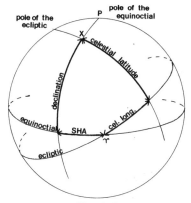

Fig. 5.12

Thus the only difference between the ecliptic system and the equinoctial system is that the ecliptic is used instead of the equinoctial from which to measure latitude and the secondaries to the ecliptic are used instead of the celestial meridians when measuring longitude. Knowing the value of the obliquity of the ecliptic it is a simple problem of spherical trigonometry to change the coordinates of a position in one system to those in the other. The ecliptic system is not used in practical navigation.

CHAPTER 6

CORRECTION OF ALTITUDES

Definitions

Rational horizon. This concept has already been discussed in Chapter 5, in which it was explained that this is the reference plane from which the altitude is measured. It can be defined as the plane through the centre of the celestial sphere, which is perpendicular to the observer's vertical. The plane will cut the celestial sphere in a great circle. All points on this great circle will be 90° removed from the observer's zenith, and will have a true altitude of zero. Great circles on the celestial sphere which pass through the zenith and cut the rational horizon in a right angle, are called vertical circles. The arc of a vertical circle contained between the rational horizon and a celestial body at any instant is the true altitude of that body. This will be the complement of the zenith distance, which may be defined as the arc of the vertical circle which passes through the body, contained between the body and the observer's zenith.

In order to find the zenith distance at any instant, it is necessary to observe the altitude above the visible horizon, and apply corrections to obtain the true altitude. To explain these corrections the following concepts are introduced.

Sensible horizon. This is a plane through the observer's eye and parallel to the rational horizon.

The visible horizon will always lie below the plane of the sensible horizon, the angle between them being called the angle of dip. An observed altitude must have the dip subtracted from it in order to obtain the apparent altitude, which may be defined as the angular height of a body above the sensible horizon.

The corrections to convert the observed altitude, which is the sextant reading corrected for any index error of the sextant, to a true altitude, are now dealt with in detail. They are introduced in the order in which they are applied, and this order should be strictly adhered to.

Dip

Dip is defined as the depression of the visible horizon below the plane of the sensible horizon.

If an altitude is observed relative to the visible horizon, then its value must be reduced by the amount of the dip to give the apparent

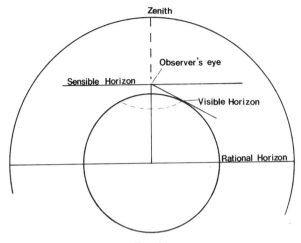

FIG. 6.1

altitude which is measured with respect to the sensible horizon. This is shown in Figure 6.2. The dip correction therefore is always negative to the observed altitude.

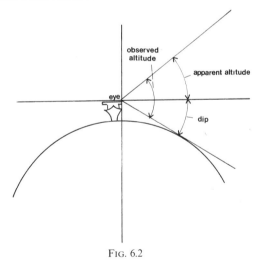

FIG. 6.2

Formula for dip

Assuming the horizon to be defined by the point where the straight line of sight from the observer touches the earth's surface tangentially then a simple formula for the dip can be found in terms of the height of eye of the observer, which is the only variable.

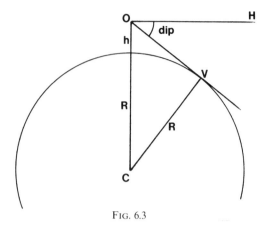

FIG. 6.3

In Figure 6.3, R is the radius of the earth, which is considered constant, h is the observer's height of eye in any suitable units, for example metres. V marks the limits of the earth's surface visible to the observer O. The angle of dip is shown below the plane of the sensible horizon OH.

$$\sin \text{ angle COV} = \frac{R}{R+h}$$

then

$$\cos \text{ dip} = \frac{R}{R+h}$$

To express the dip in minutes of arc in terms of the height of eye, h.

$$\cos \theta = 1 - 2 \sin^2 \frac{\theta}{2}$$

hence

$$1 - 2 \sin^2 \frac{\text{dip}}{2} = 1 - \frac{h}{R+h}$$

$$\sin \frac{\text{dip}}{2} = \sqrt{\frac{h}{2(R+h)}}$$

h is small compared with R, hence $R+h \simeq R$, and $\sin \text{dip} \simeq \text{dip}$ in rads. Thus approximately

$$\frac{\text{dip}}{2} = \sqrt{\frac{h}{2R}} \quad \text{where dip is in radians}$$

$$= \sqrt{\frac{h}{6,378,160 \times 2}} \quad \text{(R must also be in metres)}$$

$$\text{dip} = \frac{2 \times 57{\cdot}3 \times 60}{\sqrt{2 \times 6,378,160}} \sqrt{h} \quad \text{where dip is in minutes of arc}$$

$$= 1{\cdot}93\sqrt{h}$$

This formula does not allow for the fact that the visible horizon is lifted by the effects of refraction. The visible horizon will therefore be beyond the point V assumed in Figure 6.3. Figure 6.4 shows the visible horizon and the effect of refraction on the light reaching the observer from it.

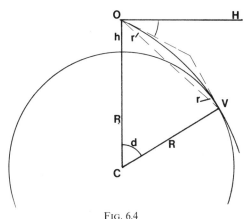

FIG. 6.4

The value of the dip will be less than that given by the formula $1{\cdot}93\sqrt{h}$.

The practical value of the dip may be determined by observation, and the amount of the refraction inferred. Uncertainty in the refraction at the time of any given observation, makes the dip correction the most inaccurate and unreliable of all the corrections to altitude. For practical prediction of the dip a refraction of 1/13 of the angle subtended at the centre of the earth by the observer and the visible horizon (angle d in Fig. 6.4) is assumed. Based upon this assumption the formula $1{\cdot}93\sqrt{h}$ may be shown to be amended to $1{\cdot}77\sqrt{h}$ thus.

In Figure 6.4 by the sine formula:

$$\frac{R}{\sin VOC} = \frac{R+h}{\sin OVC}$$

$$\frac{R}{R+h} = \frac{\sin VOC}{\sin OVC}$$

$$= \frac{\sin [180 - d - (90 - r)]}{\sin (90 - r)}$$

$$= \frac{\sin (90 - d + r)}{\sin (90 - r)}$$

$$= \frac{\cos (d - r)}{\cos r}$$

$$= \frac{\cos d \cos r + \sin d \sin r}{\cos r}$$

$$= \cos d + \tan r \sin d$$

as r is small sin r = r in radians

$$\frac{R}{R+h} = 1 - \sin^2 \frac{d}{2} + \tan r \sin d$$

$$= 1 - \frac{d^2}{2} + rd$$

substituting $\frac{d}{13}$ for r

$$\frac{d^2}{2} - \frac{d^2}{13} = 1 - \frac{R}{R+h}$$

$$d^2 = \left(1 - \frac{R}{R+h}\right)\frac{26}{11}$$

$$= \left(\frac{R+h}{R+h} - \frac{R}{R+h}\right)\frac{26}{11}$$

$$= \left(\frac{R+h-R}{R+h}\right)\frac{26}{11}$$

$$= \text{approx.} \ \frac{h}{R}\frac{26}{11}$$

$$d = 57 \cdot 3 \times 60 \times \sqrt{\frac{26}{11}} \times \sqrt{\frac{1}{6,378,160}} \times \sqrt{h}$$

where d is in minutes of arc, and h in metres

$$= 2 \cdot 09 \ \sqrt{h}$$

The angle d expressed in minutes of arc gives the arc of a great circle between the observer and the visible horizon. This will therefore give the distance of the horizon in nautical miles. The angle of dip can now be found by:

$$r = \frac{2 \cdot 09 \sqrt{h}}{13}$$

$$dip = 1 \cdot 93 \sqrt{h} - \frac{2 \cdot 09 \sqrt{h}}{13}$$

$$= 1 \cdot 77 \sqrt{h}$$

This is the formula upon which dip tables are based. The uncertainty in the refraction of the sea horizon should be born in mind however, when taking observations, as any inaccuracy will most likely be due to the incorrect value of dip being used, particularly in regions of abnormal refraction. This occurs mostly in high latitudes, and in regions of very high sea temperature such as the Red Sea, or the Persian Gulf.

Dip tables are given in all nautical tables and in the *Nautical Almanac*.

Refraction
All rays of light passing through the earth's atmosphere are affected by refraction when they pass between layers of air of different density. Light from astronomical bodies enters the atmosphere from the vacuum of space, and encounters air of gradually increasing density as it approaches the earth's surface. A refraction or bending towards the normal to the earth's surface, occurs, which is gradual rather than the abrupt change of direction which occurs when light passes through a well defined interface between two mediums of different density. The effect of refraction is to make objects appear at greater altitude than they really are.

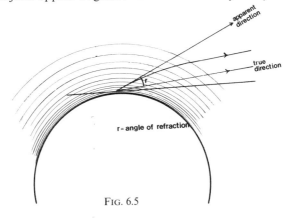

Fig. 6.5

As the altitude of the body increases the passage of the light through the atmosphere approaches the normal to the earth's surface at the observer. A body in the zenith will be seen along the normal and the light will therefore suffer no refraction. According to the laws of refraction, the amount of refraction will increase as the altitude decreases, producing a corresponding increase in the angle of incidence with the atmosphere. Light from bodies of low altitude is refracted a large and uncertain amount. A value of 34 minutes of arc is assumed in calculating the times of sunrise and sunset in the almanac, but uncertainty in this value, due to variable atmospheric conditions is sufficient reason to avoid observations at low altitudes. Because of the high value of the refraction any errors are also likely to be large.

The correct apparent altitude will be found by subtracting the value of the refraction from the altitude as observed (Fig. 6.5).

Formula for refraction
The thickness of the atmosphere is very small compared with the radius of the earth. If the zenith distance is not large then the light reaching the observer from a celestial body will have traversed a region of the atmosphere of small lateral extent. An approximate formula for refraction may be obtained by considering the earth a plane surface, and the atmosphere in layers of gradually decreasing density above the plane and parallel to it.

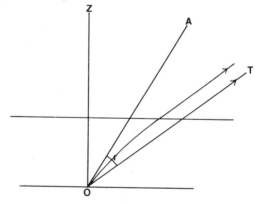

Fig. 6.6

In Figure 6.6:

    let angle ZOA = apparent zenith distance
        angle ZOT = (ZOA + r) = true zenith distance
where r is the angle of refraction.
    Then by the laws of refraction:

$$\frac{\sin \text{angle of incidence}}{\sin \text{angle of refraction}} = \text{refractive index}$$

Thus
$$\frac{\sin \text{ZOT}}{\sin \text{ZOA}} = \mu$$

and

$$\sin (\text{ZOA} + r) = \mu \sin \text{ZOA}$$
$$\sin \text{ZOA} \cos r + \cos \text{ZOA} \sin r = \mu \sin \text{ZOA}$$

Considering r is small then $\cos r \simeq 1$ and $\sin r = r$ in radians thus

$$\sin \text{ZOA} + r \cos \text{ZOA} = \mu \sin \text{ZOA}$$

$$r = \frac{\mu \sin \text{ZOA} - \sin \text{ZOA}}{\cos \text{ZOA}}$$

$$= \mu \tan \text{ZOA} - \tan \text{ZOA}$$
$$r = (\mu - 1) \tan \text{ZOA}$$

or

$$\text{refraction} = \text{constant} \times \tan \text{zenith distance}$$

This result shows that the refraction is approximately proportional to the tangent of the zenith distance. The constant of proportionality depends upon the refractive index of the medium through which the light is passing. The value of the constant $(\mu - 1)$ is best determined by practical observations, this constant being adjusted to give r in any desired units. To give r in minutes of arc the constant is found by observation to be $58\cdot3/60$, and this is called the coefficient of refraction.

Thus the refraction is given by:

$$r = \frac{58\cdot3 \ \tan \ \text{zenith dist.}}{60}$$

This formula will give reliable results for zenith distances of up to 70°. The constant is based upon observations in a standard atmospheric condition of temperature 10°C and pressure 1016 mb. The effect of variation from these standard conditions can be predicted and tables of corrections to the refraction for non-standard conditions are given in nautical tables. These are rarely used however, standard conditions being assumed. Any errors may be kept small by avoiding large zenith distances.

For zenith distances above 70° the formula given does not hold. The spherical nature of the shell of the atmsophere must then be considered. Cassini's formula gives the refraction as:

$$r = 58\cdot3 \ \tan \ \text{zenith dist.} - 0\cdot067 \ \tan^3 \ \text{zenith dist.}$$

r is given in seconds of arc and the constants are again determined by practical observation. Although the formula is mathematically proven, the uncertainty in the refraction at low altitudes, particularly under non-standard conditions, makes the results unreliable and such observations are avoided.

Observing the refraction
There are several methods of finding the refraction by observation. The simplest method is to observe the zenith distance of a body which passes through the zenith. At this point there is no refraction, and the theoretical rate of change of the zenith distance may be calculated, and the true zenith distance found at any time before or after meridian passage. Any departure from this theoretical zenith distance must be due to the refraction.

Terrestrial refraction
Refraction will also affect the apparent direction of the visible horizon, raising it above the true level. This effect is corrected for by adjusting the dip correction which gives the angle between the visible horizon and the horizontal through the observer's eye (see dip).

Semi-diameter
The apparent discs of the sun and moon are approximately one-half degree in diameter. It is the altitude of the centre of the disc that is required, and as it is inaccurate to judge the position of the centre when taking an altitude, it is practice to take the altitude of the lower edge or limb and apply a correction to obtain the altitude of the centre. If the lower limb is not visible because of clouds or in the case of the moon, because of the effect of phase, then the upper limb may be taken.

The value of the correction will be the angular radius of the body subtended at the observer. This is referred to as the semi-diameter. Evidently the correction will be positive to a lower limb observation and negative to an upper limb observation.

The angular semi-diameter will depend upon the size of the body concerned and its distance from the observer. Because of their vast distances, stars appear as points of light. The correction is not applicable to stellar observations therefore. The small apparent size of planets also makes the correction negligible in their case.

The size of the sun and moon is of course, constant, so that the only variable is the distance from the observer. Values of the semi-diameter of the sun, calculated taking into account the variation in the earth sun distance, and given once for each three day page, can be found at the foot of the sun column in the *Nautical Almanac*. The variation in the distance used is due to the ellipticity of the earth's orbit around the sun. A value for the moon's semi-diameter, which takes into account the ellipticity of the moon's orbit around the earth is given once for each day at the foot of the moon's column in the almanac.

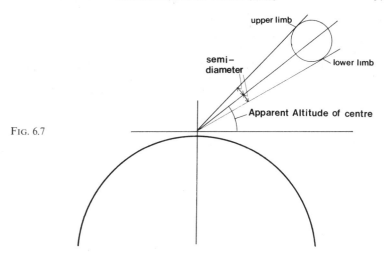

upper limb

semi–
diameter

lower limb

Apparent Altitude of centre

FIG. 6.7

Example
Given that the radius of the moon is $1·738 \times 10^6$ metres and its distance from the earth $3·844 \times 10^8$ metres find the semi-diameter.
Semi-diameter in circular measure approximately is given by:

$$\frac{1·738 \times 10^6}{3·844 \times 10^8}$$

$$= \frac{1·738 \times 10^6 \times 180 \times 60}{3·844 \times 10^8 \times \pi} \quad \text{minutes of arc}$$

$$= \frac{1·738 \times 18 \times 6}{3·844 \times \pi}$$

$$= 15·543'$$

The value of semi-diameter varies between $14·7'$ and $16·7'$ as the moon moves between perigee and apogee.

The augmentation
The point on the earth's surface closest to a celestial body is the geographical position of the body. An observer situated in this position would have the body in his zenith. The further the observer moves from the G.P. the greater will be his distance to the body until when the body is on his horizon, his distance from the body will be the same almost as the distance of the body from the centre of the earth.

In Figure 6.8 the observer at $0'$ is closer to the moon than the observer at $0''$ by an amount approximately equal to the earth's radius. $0'$ has the moon in his zenith and $0''$ has the moon on his horizon. The semi-diameter will vary accordingly being maximum for an altitude of 90° and minimum for an altitude of 0°.

Values of semi-diameter given in the almanac are calculated using the distance of the body from the earth's centre, which gives the semi-diameter for observers with the moon on the rational horizon. In the case of the sun the earth's radius is negligible compared with the earth sun distance, and no correction is necessary for altitude. In the case of the moon the variation in semi-diameter with altitude is significant and an additional correction which increases the semi-diameter must be applied. This correction is called the augmentation to the semi-diameter.

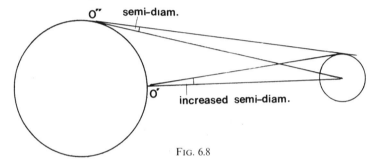

FIG. 6.8

Example
Find the maximum augmentation to apply to the moon's semi-diameter for the following conditions.

Moon's radius 1.738×10^6 metres.
Earth moon distance (between centres) 3.844×10^8 metres.
Earth radius 6.378×10^6 metres.

From the previous example the geocentric semi-diameter
$$= 15.543'$$

$$\text{increased semi-diameter} = \frac{1.738 \times 10^6 \times 180 \times 60}{(3.844 \times 10^8) - (6.378 \times 10^6) \times \pi}$$

$$= 15.803'$$

$$\text{Augmentation} = 15.803 - 15.543$$
$$= 0.26'$$

The value of the augmentation to the moon's semi-diameter is tabulated in nautical tables, and should be added to the values of semi-diameter given in the almanac.

Parallax
The co-ordinates used to measure a body's position on the celestial sphere are geocentric—they are measured from the centre of the

earth. Altitudes used in navigation must also be measured geocentrically. Of necessity altitudes must be observed from the earth's surface. The displacement of the point of observation from the centre of the earth to the earth's surface causes an apparent shift in the position of the body, which is called the body's geocentric parallax. It must be expressed in angular measure and applied to an altitude to correct to that altitude which would have been observed from the earth's centre.

It can be shown that the parallax is equal to the angle at the centre of the body, which is subtended by the radius of the earth through the observer. This ignores the height of eye which is negligible compared with the radius of the earth.

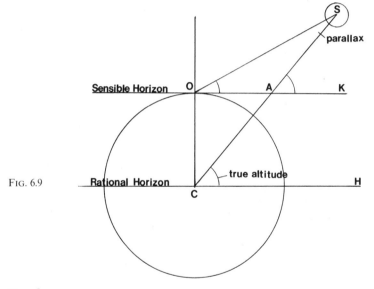

Fig. 6.9

Proof

In Figure 6.9 let angle AOS be the apparent altitude of the body S, i.e. the angular height above the sensible horizon. The true altitude is given by angle HCE, the angular height above the rational horizon. This is also equal to angle KAS.

If $\qquad \angle$ KAS = true altitude
and $\qquad \angle$ KAS = $\angle$ KOS + $\angle$ OSA
(External angle of a triangle is equal to the sum of the interior and opposite angles.)
$\qquad$ True alt. = apparent alt. + angle of parallax.

Thus the correction to altitude for parallax is always positive to the apparent altitude to give the true altitude.

It should be clear that the angle of parallax will be maximum when the body is on the horizon and will be zero when the body is in the zenith.

The maximum value of parallax, occurring when the body is on the sensible horizon or the rational horizon, is called the horizontal parallax. The value of the horizontal parallax will depend upon the radius of the earth and the distance of the body from the earth's centre. In the case of the sun the horizontal parallax will be given by:

$$\sin \text{H.P.} = \frac{\text{radius of earth}}{\text{earth–sun distance}}$$

$$= \frac{3963 \cdot 4}{93,000,000} \quad \text{expressed in statute miles}$$

$$= 1 \cdot 46'$$

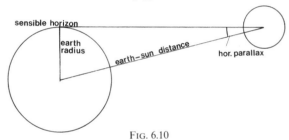

FIG. 6.10

The variation in the value of the sun's horizontal parallax can be considered negligible, and a constant figure used to calculate the parallax for any altitude. This is tabulated in nautical tables as the sun's parallax in altitude.

In the case of the moon the value will be given by:

$$\sin \text{H.P.} = \frac{\text{earth radius}}{\text{earth–moon distance}}$$

$$= \frac{3963 \cdot 4}{240,000}$$

$$\text{H.P.} = 56 \cdot 7'$$

This value is variable however, due to the variation in the earth–moon distance.

In this case a mean value for the earth moon distance is used. The variation in this distance means that the horizontal parallax varies between 61′ and 54′ of arc. A figure which takes this variation into account, is given for the moon's horizontal parallax, in the *Nautical Almanac* for each hour of G.M.T.

The horizontal parallax will also vary with the value for the earth's radius, which considering the ellipticity of the figure of the earth, will decrease with increasing latitude. The value of horizontal parallax given in the *Nautical Almanac* is based upon the equatorial radius of the earth, and can therefore be called the equatorial horizontal parallax of the moon. The horizontal parallax for any other latitude will be reduced by an amount, which can be found in nautical tables, tabulated under 'reduction to the moon's equatorial horizontal parallax for latitude'.

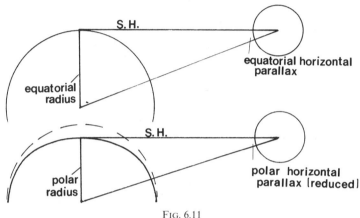

FIG. 6.11

Parallax of planets
The distance of any planet from the earth varies over a considerable range. The parallax is therefore also variable, and may sometimes be negligible and at other times quite considerable. It may at times be very much larger than that of the sun. The greatest parallax will occur at the time of the planets opposition, in the case of a superior planet, and at the time of inferior conjunction in the case of an inferior planet. The least value will occur at the time of conjunction—the superior conjunction in the case of the inferior planet. No parallax tables are therefore included in nautical tables, and the correction is conveniently ignored when correcting by individual corrections. Parallax is allowed for however in the total correction tables given in the *Nautical Almanac* in the form of an additional correction for planets included in the star correction tables. These will be discussed in more detail later.

Parallax of stars
The distance of any star is so great as to render the geocentric parallax minute and the correction can be ignored. Do not confuse this geocentric parallax of stars with the annual parallax which is the change of the stars apparent position as the earth moves to

extremities of its orbit around the sun. This movement of approximately 186 million miles produce a parallax of a few seconds of arc in some nearer stars. A change of position of 3963 miles from the earth's surface to its centre will not produce any detectable change of apparent position of a star.

To find the parallax in altitude given the horizontal parallax
In Figure 6.12 angle OHC is the horizontal parallax, angle OAC the parallax in altitude. The plane of OH is the plane of the sensible horizon.

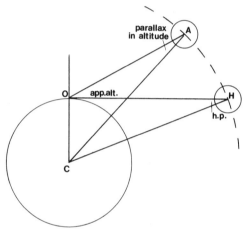

Fig. 6.12

In triangle OAC by the sine formula:

$$\frac{OC}{\sin A} = \frac{CA}{\sin COA}$$

$$\sin A = \frac{OC \sin COA}{CA}$$

$$\sin A = \frac{OC \sin (90 + \text{app. alt.})}{CH}$$

$$= \frac{OC}{CH} \cos \text{app. alt.}$$

Sine parallax in altitude = sine horizontal pa'x cos app. alt. Hence for small angles

parallax in alt. = horizontal pa'x cosine app. altitude.

This calculation must be done when correcting the moon's altitude. In the case of the sun however a constant value of horizontal parallax is used to calculate the parallax in altitude and the results tabulated in nautical tables.

Summary
A table giving the corrections which are applicable to the observations of the various bodies used in navigation is now given.

Sun	Moon	Planet	Stars
Dip	Dip	Dip	Dip
Refraction	Refraction	Refraction	Refraction
Semi-diam.	Semi-diam.		
Parallax	(after augmentation)		
	Parallax		
	(e.h.p. to be		
	reduced for		
	latitude)		

The index error of the sextant must, of course, be applied to all observations. This is done first to obtain the observed altitude. The corrections are then applied in the order given above.

Example 1
The sextant altitude of the sun's lower limb was observed to be 42° 05·7′. Index error 3·0′ on the arc. Height of eye 12·0 metres. Find the true altitude, if the observation was made on April 21st.

Sextant altitude	42° 05·7′
Index error	− 3·0′
Observed altitude	42° 02·7′
Dip	− 6·1′
Apparent altitude	41° 56·6′
Refraction	− 1·1′
	41° 55·5′
Semi-diameter	+ 16·0′
	42° 11·5′
Parallax	+ 0·1′
True altitude	42° 11·6′

Example 2
The sextant altitude of the star Aldebaran was observed to be 57° 18·5′. Index error 2·5′ off the arc. Height of eye 10·3 metres.

Find the true altitude.

Sextant altitude	57° 18·5′
Index error	+2·5′
Observed altitude	57° 21·0′
Dip	−5·6′
Apparent altitude	57° 15·4′
Refraction	−0·7′
True altitude	57° 14·7′

Example 3

The sextant altitude of the planet Mars was observed to be 31° 05·3′. Index error 2·0′ off the arc. Height of eye 9·5 metres. If the observation was taken on Sept. 14th, find the true altitude.

Sextant altitude	31° 05·3′
Index error	+2·0′
Observed altitude	31° 07·3′
Dip	−5·4′
Apparent altitude	31° 01·9′
Refraction	−1·7′
True altitude	31° 00·2′

Example 4

The sextant altitude of the moon's upper limb, at 0800 G.M.T. on June 24th, in D.R. latitude 48° N., was observed to be 47° 16·8′. Index error 1·6′ on the arc. Height of eye 11·5 metres. Find the true altitude.

Sextant altitude	47° 16·8′		
Index error	−1·6′		
Observed altitude	47° 15·2′		
Dip	−6·0′		
		Semi-diam. (from almanac)	16·3′
Apparent altitude	47° 09·2′		
Refraction	−0·9′	Augmentation	0·2′
	47° 08·3′	S.D. in altitude	16·5′
Semi-diameter (U.L.)	−16·5′	E.H.P. (from almanac)	59·9′
	46° 51·8′		
Parallax-in-alt.	+40·9′	Reduction for lat.	0·1′
True altitude	47° 32·7′	H.P. for 48° N.	59·8′

Par-in-alt. = 59·8′ × cos 46° 51·8′

59·8	1·77670
cos 46° 51·8′	1·83489
40·9	1·61159

EXERCISE 6.1A

Correct the following sextant altitudes to true altitudes.

1. Sun's L.L. 59° 15·8′. Index error 2·3′ off the arc. Height of eye 10 metres. Date Oct. 31st.

2. Sun's U.L. 38° 14·8′. Index error 3·0′ on the arc. Height of eye 9·4 metres. Date June 26th.

3. Sun's L.L. 74° 56·5′. Index error 1·3′ off the arc. Height of eye 12 metres. Date November 2nd.

4. Star Vega 56° 40·0′. Index error 0·5′ off the arc. Height of eye 10 metres.

5. Star Canopus 28° 15·0′. Index error 1·0′ on the arc. Height of eye 13·6 metres.

6. Star Rigel Kent 60° 00·0′. Index error nil. Height of eye 9·5 metres.

7. Planet Mars 59° 14·7′. Index error 1·5′ off the arc. Height of eye 10·5 metres. Date Jan. 6th.

8. Planet Venus 24° 50·8′. Index error 1·6′ on the arc. Height of eye 14·6 metres. Date November 1st.

9. Planet Saturn 74° 05·5′. Index error nil. Height of eye 10 metres.

10. Moon's L.L. 54° 03·3′. Index error 3·5′ off the arc. Height of eye 6·5 metres. G.M.T. 1700 hrs on January 5th. D.R. latitude 50° N.

11. Moon's U.L. 31° 16·0′. Index error 2·0′ on the arc. Height of eye 8·0 metres. G.M.T. 1200 November 2nd. D.R. latitude 30° S.

12. Moon's L.L. 40° 56·5′. Index error 1·5′ on the arc. Height of eye 12·0 metres. G.M.T. 1400 June 26th. D.R. latitude 55° N.

Total correction tables

In practical problems, time can be saved by using tables which combine the corrections. Answers obtained from these tables may differ slightly from those obtained using the individual corrections, as seasonal variations in semi-diameter cannot fully be allowed for. The accuracy of the total corrections, however, is well within the limits of accuracy required for practical navigation. Use of the tables is allowed in all examinations leading to Department of Trade certificates of competency, for practical problems. The tables most favoured are those given in the *Nautical Almanac*, and these are described here. Other total correction tables may be found in nautical tables, all giving similar answers.

The argument used in the tables in the almanac is the apparent altitude, so that the dip correction must be applied to the observed altitude before the main correction. A dip table is provided with the total correction tables. The sun's total correction table has one argument, the apparent altitude. Two tables are given, however, one for the summer months, and one for the winter months. This allows two values of semi-diameter to be used, a mean value for the summer table, and the mean value over the winter months for the winter table. Care must be taken to ensure that the correct table is used. Two values are given in each table, the one in bold type to be used for lower limb observations and the lighter figures for the upper limb observations. The corrections allow for refraction, the semi-diameter, and the parallax.

The star correction table is merely a table of refraction, as after the dip correction this is the only remaining correction. With the star correction table, however, are given additional corrections for planets to allow for their parallax and the effect of any phase shown by the planet. There will only be significant figures for certain dates and for certain altitudes. These are the arguments used therefore for these small corrections.

The moon's correction table is in two parts, the main correction being given against apparent altitude, correcting for semi-diameter, refraction and parallax, using mean values for semi-diameter and for horizontal parallax. Variation from these mean values are allowed for in the second correction, which is taken from the same vertical column as the main correction, and against the horizontal parallax given in the daily pages. Separate corrections for lower and upper limb observations are given. There is added to the upper limb figures, for ease of tabulation, 30 minutes of arc and this must be subtracted from the final result of an upper limb correction.

Full instructions are given with the tables for their use. It should be noted however that the dip table, and the sun and star total correction tables give values of the correction which apply between two critical values of the argument. If the table is entered with one of the critical values then the upper correction should be taken. Note that this does not mean the numerically greater value, but the upper value in the table. For example the dip correction for a height of eye of 11·0 metres should be noted to be 5·8′ and not 5·9′. Similarly the total correction for the sun's lower limb for a winter observation should be noted to be for an altitude of 26° 36′, + 14·3′ and not + 14·4′.

The examples used for the method of individual corrections are now used to illustrate the use of these total correction tables.

Example 1	Sextant altitude	42° 05·7′
	Index error	− 3·0′
	Observed altitude	42° 02·7′
	Dip	− 6·1′
	Apparent altitude	41° 56·6′
	Total correction	+ 14·9′
	True altitude	42° 11·5′

Example 2

Sextant altitude	57° 18·5′
Index error	+ 2·5′
Observed altitude	57° 21·0′
Dip	− 5·6′
Apparent altitude	57° 15.4′
Total correction	− 0·6′
True altitude	57° 14·8′

Example 3

Sextant altitude	31° 05·3′
Index error	+ 2·0′
Observed altitude	31° 07·3′
Dip	− 5·4′
Apparent altitude	31° 01·9′
Total correction	− 1·6′
Additional corr.	+ 0·3′
True altitude	31° 00·6′

Example 4

Sextant altitude	47° 16·8′
Index error	− 1·6′
Observed altitude	47° 15·2′
Dip	− 6·0′
Apparent altitude	47° 09·2′
Main correction	+ 49·0′
Second corr.	+ 3·6′
	48° 01·8′
	− 30·0′
True altitude	47° 31·8′

EXERCISE 6.1B

Exercise 6.1A may now be reworked using total corrections and the answers compared with those obtained using individual corrections.

CHAPTER 7

TIME

The basis of our measurement of time must be the succession of day and night caused by the rotation of the earth, about its axis. There is however a need to define units of time with high precision. The degree of precision required has become so high that no longer can the movement of any astronomical body provide a satisfactory definition of our unit of time, the second. We cannot escape the fact however that the sun governs our lives and that any system of time measurement must be regulated to the daily motion of the sun.

The solar day
This is defined as the interval of time between two successive transits of the sun across the same meridian.

This motion of course is due to the rotation of the earth about its axis, and during this time the sun changes its L.H.A. by 360°. It is convenient to assume the day to begin when the sun crosses the antimeridian of any observer. At this time the L.H.A. of the sun is 180°, and this time is called midnight. The day ends at the next such transit and the period of time in the interval is divided into 24 hours, midnight being 0000 hrs and the next midnight 2400 hrs, or 0000 hrs of the following day. Thus midday is 1200 hrs and occurs when the sun is on the observer's meridian, when the L.H.A. is zero.

We can say therefore that the measurement of time is merely an expression of the position of the sun relative to the observer. Measurement of time and measurement of L.H.A. are therefore synonymous, and only one value of time corresponds to any one value of L.H.A. of the sun.

Thus:

when L.H.A. sun is 0° time is 1200 hrs
when L.H.A. sun is 90° time is 1800 hrs
when L.H.A. sun is 180° time is 24 hours or 0000 hrs
when L.H.A. sun is 270° time is 0600 hrs
when L.H.A. sun is 360° (0°) time is 1200 hrs.

Because we are using the sun to measure this time it is called solar time, and because we are measuring time with respect to the observer it is called LOCAL time.

The solar day is longer than the rotation period of the earth by approximately 4 minutes, due to the fact that the sun is moving against the background of the stars. If we define the day with reference to a fixed point on the sphere the interval would be the time taken for the earth to rotate through 360°. A fixed point on the sphere could be taken to be the first point of Aries, and the day so defined is called a sidereal day. Astronomically it is easier to measure sidereal time and convert it into solar time.

During the solar day the earth will rotate through 360° plus the daily change of S.H.A. of the sun.

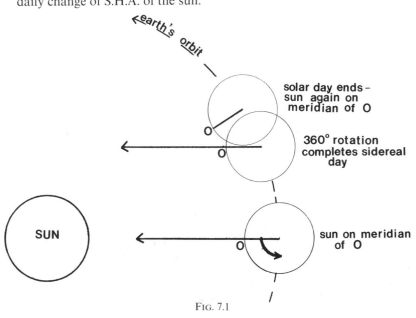

Fig. 7.1

The daily change of S.H.A. amounts to approximately 1°. Thus during a solar day the earth will rotate through approximately 361°, but note that the change of L.H.A. of the sun will be by definition 360° per day.

The use of the true sun (apparent sun), i.e. the sun we see in the sky, presents problems in accurate timekeeping, because of irregularities in its motion.

During a solar day the sun changes its L.H.A. by 360°, and because the earth is rotating from west to east, the L.H.A. is always increasing. The rate of change of L.H.A. is affected by two considerations.

1. The main cause of change of L.H.A. is the rotation of the earth, and this causes any body to change its L.H.A. by 15° 02·46′ per

hour (obtained from 361°/24). We can at this stage consider this to be constant.

2. The change caused by the earth's rotation is modified slightly by the change in the body's S.H.A. The sun changes its S.H.A. by 360° in a year which is 02·46′ per hour. As the sun is moving east-wards around the sphere this will decrease the hourly change of L.H.A. to exactly 15° per hour, as shown in Figure 7.2.

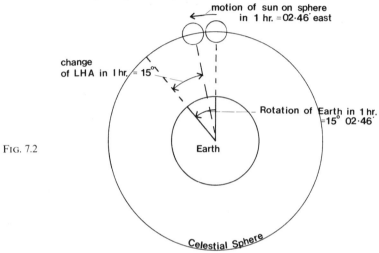

FIG. 7.2

The reason why the true sun is not an accurate timekeeper is due to the fact that this change of S.H.A. is not constant. Although the mean rate of decrease is 02·46′ per hour, the actual hourly change oscillates around this mean.

There are two causes of this irregularity.

1. The ellipticity of the earth's orbit. Kepler's second law of planetary motion states that the line joining the earth and the sun sweeps out equal areas in equal times (see planetary motion).

Let the time taken for the earth to go from E_1 to E_2, be the same as the time taken to go from E_3 to E_4, in Figure 7.3. If this is so then by Kepler's second law the two shaded areas are equal. The angle at the sun swept out by the line must be greater at perihelion than at aphelion. This angle at the sun swept out is the change of S.H.A. of the sun. Thus the ellipticity causes the sun's rate of change of S.H.A. to be maximum at perihelion, and minimum at aphelion. The solar day will be lengthened at perihelion and shortened at aphelion by this effect.

2. The obliquity. The sun is moving around the sphere in the ecliptic whereas we measure S.H.A. as an arc of the equinoctial. Consider the sun at the first point of Aries moving along the ecliptic at a constant rate (see Fig. 7.4).

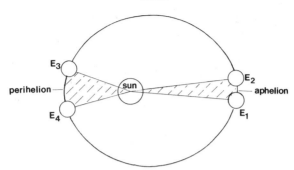

FIG. 7.3

If the sun moves from ♈ to S. in unit time the change of S.H.A. in that time would be ♈ E.

Consider the sun to be at the solstice where the ecliptic runs parallel to the equinoctial. If the sun moves from S′ to S″ in unit time where S′S″ is equal to ♈ E. then the change of S.H.A. will be QR. Because, at the equinoxes the ecliptic is running at an angle of $23\frac{1}{2}°$ to the equinoctial, and at the solstices it is parallel to it, then evidently QR will be greater than ♈ E.

Because of the obliquity the hourly change of S.H.A. will be greatest at the solstices and least at the equinoxes. Thus from this cause the solar day will be lengthened at the solstices and shortened at the equinoxes.

If we require the length of a solar day to be constant then the concept of the Mean Sun must be introduced.

The irregularity caused by the ellipticity can be smoothed out by introducing an imaginary body which moves around the

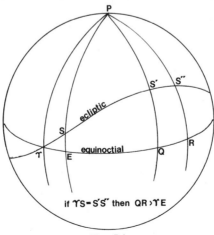

FIG. 7.4

ecliptic at a constant rate, which is the mean speed of the true sun for the year. This body is given the name of the Dynamical Mean Sun (D.M.S.). It is considered to be coincident with the true sun in the ecliptic at perihelion, which at the present time occurs on January 4th. As the true sun changes its S.H.A. at its maximum rate at this time it will move ahead of the D.M.S. in the plane of the ecliptic. Between perihelion and aphelion it will be ahead but as the true sun slows down, until at aphelion it is changing its S.H.A. at its slowest rate, the D.M.S. will again be coincident with it at aphelion. From here the D.M.S. will move ahead of the true sun, which now starts to speed up and they will again be coincident at the next perihelion.

If we draw a graph of the difference in S.H.A. between the D.M.S. and the true sun throughout the year it will appear as in Figure 7.5. The maximum difference amounts to about $1\frac{3}{4}°$ of S.H.A. Let the difference at any time throughout the year be called E_1.

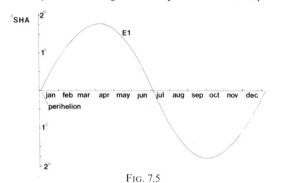

FIG. 7.5

As the D.M.S. moves in the ecliptic there will still be irregularities in its rate of change of S.H.A. due to the obliquity. To smooth these out we now imagine a further body to move in the equinoctial at the same constant angular rate as the Dynamical Mean Sun in the ecliptic. This body is called the Astronomical Mean Sun. The A.M.S. is therefore an imaginary body which moves around the equinoctial at a constant angular velocity and therefore changes its S.H.A. at a constant rate. Hence this body will as the earth rotates change its L.H.A. at a constant rate and the measurement of this L.H.A. will give us a means of measuring a uniform time. The rate of change of S.H.A. of the A.M.S. is 02·46′ per hour, which will therefore give an hourly rate of change of L.H.A. of exactly 15° per hour.

The A.M.S. is considered to coincide with the D.M.S. at the first point of Aries. If they then both move through 90° along the equinoctial and ecliptic respectively they will again occupy the same celestial meridian at the summer solstice. After both moving through a further 90° they will both occupy the first point of Libra, and again occupy the same celestial meridian at the winter solstice. At all times between these they will not occupy the same celestial meridian and the maximum difference between their S.H.A.s will occur half way between a solstice and an equinox. This amounts to about $2\frac{1}{2}°$ of S.H.A. If a graph is produced showing this difference throughout the year it will appear as a double sine curve having zero values at the equinoxes and the solstices. Let this value at any time be called E_2.

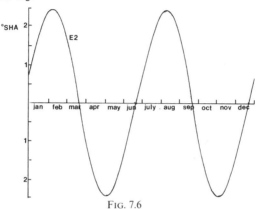

FIG. 7.6

It is the Astronomical Mean Sun which is used to measure solar time. Time measured with this body is called mean time as opposed to apparent time measured with the true sun. The difference between mean time and apparent time at any instant will be the arc of the equinoctial between the meridians through the mean sun and the true sun expressed in units of time. (If the term mean sun is used without any qualification then it is the Astronomical Mean Sun which is referred to and not the Dynamical Mean Sun.) This quantity, the difference between mean time and apparent time, is called the Equation of Time, and its value can be found by adding algebraically the values E_1 and E_2.

If we show graphically the addition of E_1 and E_2 then a graph of the Equation of Time throughout the year will be produced. Such a graph will have two positive maximums and two negative maximums, while the zero values occur on April 16th, June 4th, September 1st, and December 25th. Values for the Equation of Time are given in the *Nautical Almanac* for 0000 hrs and 1200 hrs G.M.T. for each day throughout the year.

By convention positive and negative signs are given to the Equation as shown in the graph. The sign given is that which should be applied to apparent time to give mean time. However in practice it is not necessary to consider the sign. All that is required is to determine whether the mean time is ahead of the apparent time or vice versa. This is readily done as follows. At the foot of the right hand page of each pair of daily pages of the almanac is given a time labelled 'mer pass' of the sun. This is the L.M.T. of the meridian passage of the true sun. The L.A.T. of the same occurrence by definition is 1200. Thus if the figure given is before 1200 then apparent time must be ahead of mean time. If the figure given is after 1200 then the mean time must be ahead of apparent time. From this it should be evident how the Equation should be applied. The difference between the L.M.T. given and 1200 hrs will be of course the Equation of Time to the nearest minute.

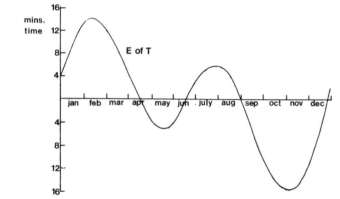

FIG. 7.7

Time defined as an angle
It has been said that the measurement of time and hour angle are synonymous. We can therefore define time, exactly as we define hour angle, as an angle between the meridians of the observer and that of the sun. However the reference meridian, from which time is measured, is 180° for 12 hours removed from that which we use to measure hour angle.

Thus we may define:

Local apparent time. The angle at the celestial pole contained between the antimeridian of the observer and the meridian of the true sun, measured westwards from the antimeridian of the observer and expressed in units of time.

Local mean time. The angle at the celestial pole contained between the antimeridian of the observer and the meridian of the mean sun, measured westwards from the antimeridian of the observer and expressed in units of time.

Relationship between hour angle and time
If expressed in similar units:

Local Mean Time = L.H.A. of mean sun ± 12 hours.
Local Apparent Time = L.H.A. of true sun ± 12 hours.

Greenwich time

At any instant different meridians will have different times. A standard meridian is required for world wide use and for this purpose the Greenwich meridian is used. Greenwich time is the local time of an observer on the Greenwich meridian.

Thus we may define:

Greenwich apparent time. The angle at the celestial pole measured westwards from the antimeridian of Greenwich to the meridian of the true sun, expressed in units of time.

Greenwich mean time. The angle at the celestial pole measured westwards from the antimeridian of Greenwich to the meridian of the mean sun, expressed in units of time.

Also

Greenwich Apparent Time = G.H.A. of true sun $\pm$ 12 hours.
Greenwich Mean Time = G.H.A. of mean sun $\pm$ 12 hours.

Relationship between Greenwich and local time

The difference between Greenwich time and local time at any instant will be the angle between the two meridians expressed in units of time, i.e. the longitude in time.

As the rotation of the earth is from west to east, the Greenwich meridian will pass under the sun before any meridian in west longitude and after any meridian in east longitude. Thus any longitude west will have a local time which is earlier than the Greenwich time, and any longitude east will have a local time which is later than the Greenwich time.

Thus

$$L.M.T. = G.M.T. + E. \text{ long.}$$
$$L.A.T. = G.A.T. + E. \text{ long.}$$

$$L.M.T. = G.M.T. - W. \text{ long.}$$
$$L.A.T. = G.A.T. - W. \text{ long.}$$

Universal time (U.T.)

This is the mean solar time on the Greenwich meridian. In other words the Greenwich Mean Time. However Universal Time is designated U.T.0, U.T.1, or U.T.2.

U.T0

This is universal time as observed. However because of the demand for higher and higher accuracy in the definition of our time system, two other causes of irregularities in the measurement of time must be considered.

1. *Polar variation*

This is an observed wandering of the poles of the earth relative to the earth's surface. The pole seems to be tracing out roughly circular motions of approximate diameter 20 metres. As the position of the pole changes the equator must also, and this will give rise to slight variations in the observed latitude of any point on the earth's surface. It was by such observations that the phenomenon was first discovered.

Latitude variations at any point will give rise to variations in observed time at points 90° removed in longitude. (A change of latitude in one position must be accompanied by a change of longitude 90° away.) The effect is not constant, but U.T.0 can be corrected by an estimated amount which can be as much as 30 milliseconds. When U.T.0 is corrected for polar variation it is designated U.T.1.

It is U.T.1 that is required from time signals by the navigator in theory. However the corrections now being discussed are hardly likely to affect navigation.

2. *Seasonal variation*

This is a variation in the rate of the earth's rotation. Previously we have considered the earth to rotate at a constant rate. Seasonal variations in the rate, probably due to annual variations in the distribution of the mass of the atmosphere is thought to amount to about plus or minus 30 milliseconds. If this effect is removed from U.T.1 it is designated U.T.2.

Co-ordinated universal time (U.T.C.)

This is a time system used internationally and is based upon atomic time. The measurement of time by atomic frequency standards is the most precise and uniform method available. It depends upon using the frequency of radiation associated with a transition between two different energy levels of an isotope of the Caesium atom, and summating the cycles of radiation. A system such as this is not linked to any astronomical phenomenon, but merely provides a running total of seconds from some arbitrary zero when the clock was started. This zero therefore must be defined in the astronomical time scale and it must be co-ordinated into solar time before being used for time signals.

Atomic time is now used for international time signals but it is never allowed to diverge from U.T.1 by more than 0·7s and coded information about the difference between the two at any time is broadcast. Atomic time is kept in step with U.T.1 by making step adjustments when necessary, either jumping a second forwards, or jumping a second backwards as required to keep within 0·7s of U.T.1. Such jumps are called leap-seconds. This time as disseminated by time transmissions is called Co-ordinated Universal Time (U.T.C.).

Sidereal time

It has already been said that sidereal time is defined with reference to the first point of Aries. The sidereal day is the interval of time between two successive transits of the first point of Aries across the same meridian. Its length is 23h 56m 4·09s of mean solar time. The sidereal day for any observer is assumed to begin when the first point of Aries crosses the observer's meridian, i.e. when the L.H.A. of Aries is zero. Thus as L.H.A. increases so sidereal time increases and the two are synonymous except that L.H.A. Aries is measured in arc and sidereal time is measured in units of time. Note that any unit of sidereal time will be slightly less than the corresponding unit of solar time.

Thus to find the sidereal time at any instant the L.H.A. of the first point of Aries can be converted into time.

Sidereal time and mean solar time
From Figure 7.8 the L.H.A. of the first point of Aries is equal to the L.H.A. of the mean sun plus the right ascension of the mean sun.

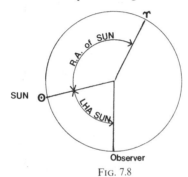

FIG. 7.8

Thus

Sidereal Time = L.H.A. mean sun + R.A. mean sun

or

S.T. = (L.M.T. ± 12 hours) + (360° − S.H.A.).

The measurement of time
The regulation of instruments with which we measure time is done by comparison with the time standard that is set by the rotation of the earth. The rotational period is marked by successive transits of a star across a stationary observer's meridian, and it is by observation of these occurrences that time is measured. Stellar observations are made in preference to solar observations, as a star appears as a point of light and may be chosen so that it passes through the zenith of an observatory in any latitude. Such an observation is more accurate than a meridional observation at low altitude when the rate of change of azimuth is small. Also more than one observation may be made in the course of one rotation of the earth.

Practical observation of time is done therefore by an instrument called a Photographic Zenith Tube, which records photographically an accurate time of meridian passage of any chosen star which passes within about 30 minutes of arc of the zenith. Observations are made of several stars whose celestial co-ordinates are accurately known. When such a star is on the observer's meridian then the local sidereal time is equal to the right ascension of the star. The observing instrument in Great Britain is in the Royal Observatory in Herstmonceux Castle in Sussex, situated on the Prime Meridian. Its local sidereal time is therefore the Greenwich sidereal time.

The sidereal time observed may now be converted to mean solar time by applying the right ascension of the mean sun. The result will be Universal Time designated $U.T._0$, that is uncorrected for polar variation and seasonal variation. Time signals disseminated by the primary time signal transmissions are derived from an atomic time standard. This is U.T.C. An atomic clock is the most consistent means available for the recording of time, but the earth's rotation is not so consistent. The atomic time standard will therefore diverge from $U.T._1$ which measures the earth's rotation, by an unpredictable amount. At present this amount is approximately $+$ or $-$ 1 second per year but this may change depending upon the way in which the earth behaves in its axial rotation. U.T.C., the atomic time standard, is kept in step with $U.T._1$ therefore by introducing leap seconds on January 1st and if necessary on July 1st. This ensures that the divergence of U.T.C. from $U.T._1$ is never more than the tolerated limit 0·7s. For marine navigation the uncorrected atomic time is taken as $U.T._1$ (G.M.T.), and this gives accuracy well within the limits obtainable at sea. Corrections to U.T.C. to obtain a more accurate $U.T._1$ are made available to users who require greater accuracy.

Calculations on solar time

The following is a summary of the relationships between L.M.T., L.A.T., G.M.T., G.A.T., Equation of Time, and Longitude.

L.M.T. $\pm$ Equ. of Time = L.A.T.
G.M.T. $\pm$ Equ. of Time = G.A.T.

L.M.T. = G.M.T. + E. Long.
L.A.T. = G.A.T. + E. Long.

L.M.T. = G.M.T. − W. Long.
L.A.T. = G.A.T. − W. Long.

By considering these relationships the following problems should be straightforward. A diagram on the plane of the equinoctial is drawn in each case showing the angles which represent each quantity. The definitions of the various quantities as angles should be remembered.

Example 1
Given L.A.T. 18h 06m 14s on January 4th, longitude 94° 15' W., find G.M.T.

Solution

L.A.T.	4th	18h 06m 14s
Long.		06h 17m
	4th	24h 23m 14s
G.A.T	5th	00h 23m 14s
E. of T.		05m 07s
G.M.T.	5th	00h 28m 21s

Notes
Longitude is west and is therefore additive to local time to give Greenwich time.

The Equation of Time is given in the almanac for 0000h and 1200h of G.M.T. for each day. The value is interpolated between these times to the nearest second. G.A.T. is sufficiently close to G.M.T. to use for this purpose but note that local time must not be used.

To determine whether to add or subtract the equation of time inspect the mean time of meridian passage of the true sun to find whether mean time is ahead of apparent time or vice versa. In this case the L.M.T. mer pass is after 1200. Thus mean time is later than apparent time and we must add the equation to G.A.T. to give G.M.T.

Example 2
Given G.A.T. 07h 14m 30s on November 1st, longitude 178° 14' E., find the L.M.T.

G.A.T.	1st	07h 14m 30s
E. of T.		16m 22s
G.M.T.	1st	06h 58m 08s
Long.		11h 52m 56s
L.M.T.	1st	18h 51m 04s

EXERCISE

1. Find the L.A.T. in the following.
   (a) June 24th, G.M.T. 17h 30m 00s, longitude 37° 30' W.
   (b) March 25th, G.M.T. 20h 00m 00s, longitude 150° E.
2. Find the G.M.T. in the following.
   (a) January 5th, L.A.T. 07h 20m 15s, longitude 56° 45' W.
   (b) October 21st, L.A.T. 17h 30m 15s, longitude 165° 48' E.

3. Find the L.M.T. in the following.
   (a) October 19th, G.A.T. 12h 00m 00s, longitude 7° 30′ W.
   (b) July 31st, G.A.T. 10h 50m 17s, longitude 157° 30′ W.
4. Find the longitude in the following.
   (a) G.M.T., March 24th, 17h 20m 23s, L.M.T., March 24th, 22h 50m 00s.
   (b) L.A.T., 02h 10m 30s, July 30th, G.M.T., 10h 40m 20s, July 30th.
   (c) G.M.T., October 31st, 21h 00m 30s, L.A.T., November 1st, 07h 30m 00s.

Precession of the Equinox—Nutation

The precession of the equinox is the westwards motion of the first point of Aries along the ecliptic. The mean rate of this motion is about 50″ of arc per year. Because of this the first point of Aries no longer lies in the section of the zodiac called Aries but has moved westwards into Pisces.

To understand the cause of the precession we must look briefly at the properties of the gyroscope.

A free gyroscope is a rotor or wheel, spinning about a spin axis passing through its centre of mass, which has the freedom to turn its spin axis to any direction in space. It has freedom to turn in azimuth, i.e. to turn about a vertical axis, and freedom to tilt, i.e. to turn about a horizontal axis. It is said therefore that a free gyroscope has three degrees of freedom:

1. to spin,
2. to turn in azimuth,
3. to tilt.

To have such freedom on the earth's surface a rotor must be supported in gymbals. The earth however is itself a free gyroscope, the mass of the bulge of the equator corresponding to the rotor of the gyro.

Such a free gyroscope has two basic properties.

1. Rigidity in space (gyroscopic inertia)
This means that if the rotor is set spinning as long as no forces act upon the rotor to disturb it the spin axis will maintain a constant direction in space. A star may be regarded as in a constant direction in space, thus any gyro set with its spin axis pointing to a star will remain so no matter what the movement of the earth. Thus the gyro axis will describe a circle as it follows the diurnal motion of the star. The circle described will of course be centred upon the celestial pole and have a period of one sidereal day. Thus considering the earth as a gyroscope we have the reason why the earth's axis points to the constant direction near Polaris.

2. *Gyroscopic precession*

If a force is applied to the rotor of a spinning gyroscope perpendicularly to the plane of the rotor, then the resultant effect will be
as if the force is moved around the rotor 90° in the direction of the
spin before acting.

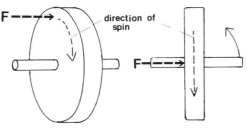

Fig. 7.9

Thus in Figure 7.9 the rotor would if acted upon by force F,
perpendicular to the rotor, turn its spin axis in an anticlockwise
direction as viewed from above. The axis is said to precess under
the influence of the force.

The cause of the precession of the equinox is the force of the
sun's and the moon's gravitational attraction acting on the rotor
formed by the equatorial bulge of the earth, spinning about the
spin axis of the earth.

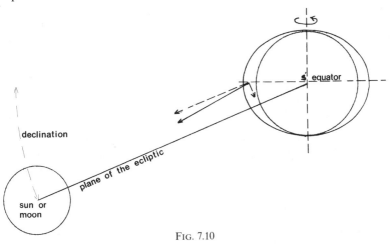

Fig. 7.10

From Figure 7.10 the attraction of the sun on the nearest part of
the equatorial bulge has a component which tends to pull the
equatorial bulge down into the plane of the ecliptic. This is a force

which is perpendicular to the plane of the rotor and it is effective after moving around the equator through 90° to S' to the eastwards. Acting here it would evidently have the effect of tilting the equator at S' downwards which would cause the north end of the earth's axis to move to the right as viewed from the sun. The south end would move to the left as viewed from the sun. If viewed from the pole of the ecliptic as in Figure 7.11 the north pole of the equinoctial would also move to the right thus continually making a circle westwards around the pole of the ecliptic.

In Figure 7.11 the pole of the equinoctial Q is moving in a circle westwards around the pole of the ecliptic.

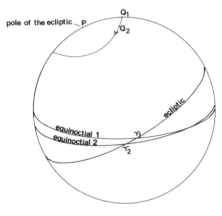

FIG. 7.11

The position of the equinoctial when the pole of the equinoctial is at Q1, is shown as Equinoctial 1. If the point Q now moves to Q2, then the equinoctial will move to Equinoctial 2. The first point of Aries has moved from ♈ 1 to ♈ 2, which is a shift westwards along the ecliptic.

The component of the gravitational force which causes the precession is greatest when the declination of the sun is maximum, that is when the sun is furthest from the plane of the equinoctial. When the sun is in the plane of the equinoctial, at the two equinoxes then the component goes to zero. At these times the solar precession disappears. It should be noted however that at both solstices the direction of the sun's attractive force is to pull the plane of the equator into the plane of the ecliptic and never out of it. The precession is always a westerly one therefore, whether the sun is at the summer solstice or the winter solstice. The movement will be periodic however with a period of six months reaching its maximum at the solstices.

The foregoing explanation could equally well describe the precession caused by the moon. In this case the plane of the ecliptic would be replaced by the plane of the moon's orbit. As these two planes are almost coincident then the resultant effect is for the two precessing forces to reinforce each other. The precession is the motion resulting from the two precessing forces. The effect of the moon however is more variable than that of the sun. Whereas because the obliquity of the ecliptic is almost constant, the inclination of the moon's orbit to the equinoctial is not, being sometimes as much as $28\frac{3}{4}°$ and sometimes as little as $18\frac{1}{4}°$. The moon's precessing force therefore, although it reaches a maximum, each time the declination of the moon does so, the amplitude of the maximum changes with a period of 18·6 years. The relatively high eccentricity of the moon's orbit also causes fluctuations in the precessing force (see Motion of the Moon).

The moon's precessing force will like the sun's be periodic, with a period of half the sidereal period, about 14 days. Although it tends to reinforce the precession caused by the sun, really it is causing a precession, which is making the pole of the equinoctial move westwards around the pole of the moon's orbit. The inclination of the moon's orbit to the plane of the ecliptic is about $5\frac{3}{4}°$, and therefore the pole of the moon's orbit is about this angular distance from the pole of the ecliptic. The pole of the moon's orbit itself goes around the pole of the ecliptic in a small circle of radius $5\frac{1}{4}°$ in a period of about 18·6 years (see Regression of the Moon's Nodes). The resultant of the two precessing forces will lie towards a direction somewhere between the two and this point will itself go around the pole of the ecliptic. (Shown by point R in Figure 7.12.)

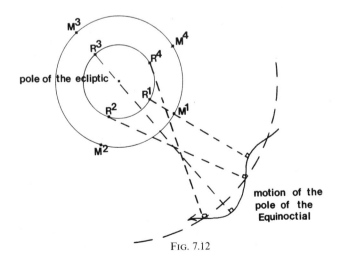

FIG. 7.12

In Figure 7.12 the pole of the moon's orbit is shown as M1, M2, M3, M4 as it circles the pole of the ecliptic. The motion of the pole of the equinoctial will always be at right angles to the direction of point R. As R circles the pole of the ecliptic the pole of the equinoctial will weave in and out of the small circle around the pole of the ecliptic.

The effect of the change of direction of the pole of the equinoctial and the variation in the rate of the precession means that the actual position of the pole of the equinoctial makes a small ellipse around the mean position, given by the mean precession around the small circle around the pole of the ecliptic. This effect is called the nutation, as it makes the pole of the equinoctial nod towards and away from the pole of the ecliptic.

The effects of precession and nutation

The pole of the equinoctial will complete one revolution around the pole of the ecliptic in a period of about 25,800 years, the mean rate of the precession being 50″ of arc per year.

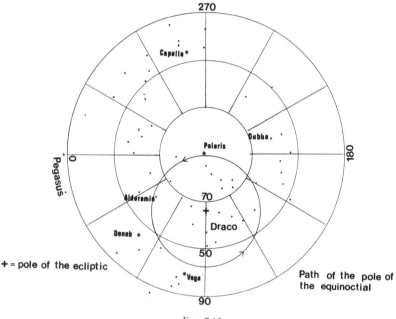

FIG. 7.13

In its journey around the pole of the ecliptic, the celestial pole now happens to be near a star which we call Polaris. It will move towards this star until about the year 2000 and then will move away. Eventually other stars will become pole stars as the celestial pole approaches them, as shown in Figure 7.13.

The precession of the equinoxes has the effect of making the recurrence of the seasons slightly less than the sidereal period of the earth in orbit (see Tropical Year). It also has the effect of making the sidereal day shorter than the earth's rotational period by about 0·008s, as the first point of Aries moves westwards to meet the easterly rotation of the earth (see Sidereal Time).

The precession also has the gradual effect of changing the values of declination and S.H.A. (or Right Ascension) for any fixed point on the sphere, as illustrated in Figure 7.14.

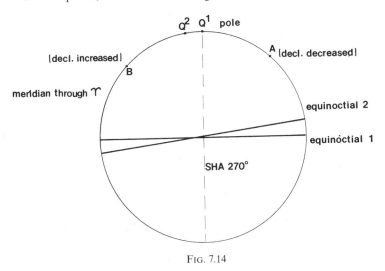

FIG. 7.14

All points on the sphere north of the equinoctial between the meridians of S.H.A. = 270° and S.H.A. = 90° will have their declination increased by the movement of the equinoctial from position 1 to position 2. All points north of the equinoctial but on the other side of the sphere, i.e. with S.H.A. from 90° to 270° will have their declination decreased. The opposite will occur in the southern hemisphere. If the first point of Aries is moving westwards then all S.H.A.s will decrease and all right ascensions will increase.

Nutation has the effect of changing slightly the value of the obliquity of the ecliptic. This will produce periodic variations in declination with the same period as the nutation.

The sidereal year
The period of the earth in orbit provides another natural unit of

time. The time taken for any planet to go around its orbit through 360° is called its sidereal period or year.

The sidereal year therefore in the case of the earth can be defined as the time taken for the sun to go 360° around the ecliptic. At the beginning and end of a sidereal year the sun will be in the same position relative to the fixed stars. In terms of mean solar time this period is 365d 06h 09m 09s.

The tropical year

This is the time taken for the sun to complete one revolution in the ecliptic, relative to the first point of Aries. Because of a motion of the first point of Aries westwards along the ecliptic this period is slightly shorter than the sidereal year (see Precession of the Equinoxes). In mean solar units this period is 365d 05h 48m 46s. It is this period which determines the recurrence of the seasons. Spring starts as the sun passes the first point of Aries. This is the period therefore that the civil calendar must keep in step with if the seasons are to recur at the same time within each year.

The anomalistic year

This is the time taken for the earth to go from perihelion to the next perihelion. This is longer than the sidereal year being of length 365d 6h 13m 53s.

The civil calendar

It is desirable that the seasons recur at the same time during each calendar year, therefore the civil calendar must keep in step with the tropical year.

The calendar must also contain a whole number of days, therefore 365 days are included in the civil year. Once in four years an extra day is inserted to account for the excess of 5h 48m 46s per year of the tropical year over the civil year. This means that 24 hours are inserted in the calendar when only 23h 15m 03s are required to keep in step with the tropical year. This inaccuracy was inherent in the calendar from the time of its inception by Julius Caesar (hence the name Julian Calendar), until 1582, when modification was introduced by Pope Gregory XIII.

In 400 years the error amounts to 3d 2h 55m 18s. Thus in every 400 years 3 days are missed out of the Julian calendar, or rather 3 leap years are not included. This modified calendar is called the Gregorian calendar.

The rules are if the year number is divisible by 4 then the extra day is included unless the year number is a whole number of centuries not divisible by 400, when the leap year is missed out. Thus 1700, 1800, and 1900 were not leap years but 2000 will be. 2100 will not be a leap year.

The residual error only amounts to a day in 4000 years.

EXERCISE 7

1. Define:
   (a) 'solar day',
   (b) 'sideral day'.
Explain why there is a difference in the lengths of these two units.

2. Explain why the motion of the true sun cannot be used as an accurate and constant timekeeper.

3. Define:
   (a) dynamical mean sun,
   (b) astronomical mean sun,
   (c) equation of time.
Explain the irregular shape of the graph representing the value of the equation of time throughout the year.

4. Define:
   (a) local apparent time,
   (b) Greenwich mean time.

5. Given, G.M.T. = 6h 50m 14s, longitude = 40° E., L.H.A. of apparent sun 322° 14·8′, find the value of the equation of time.

6. Discuss the relationship between the G.H.A. of the sun and the G.M.T.

7. Define Local Mean Time. If the L.M.T. of the meridian passage of the true sun is given in the almanac as 1152 is the apparent time greater or less than the mean time for any meridian?

8. Explain why the tropical year is shorter than the sidereal period of the earth in orbit. On which period is our calendar year based? Why?

9. What time would a sundial indicate in longitude 8° W. at 1200 hrs G.M.T. on January 4th?

10. Discuss the relationship between the sidereal time and the mean solar time at any instant.

CHAPTER 8

THE EARTH–MOON SYSTEM

The moon is the only natural satellite of the planet earth. Its motion around the earth may be described by Kepler's laws (see Planetary Motion). However a more correct description is that the centres of both earth and moon orbit a point which is the common centre of gravity of the system. This point is called the Barycentre and lies some way inside the surface of the earth. It is the barycentre which orbits the sun in a period of one year, as described by Kepler's laws, in an ellipse, the rotation of the earth and moon around the barycentre causing them to weave slightly inside and outside this ellipse.

All the superior planets, with the exception of Pluto, the small outermost planet, have more than one moon, the number varying from two for Mars, to thirteen for the massive Jupiter.

The eccentricity of the moon's orbit is relatively high the figure being about 1/18. The point on the moon's orbit where it is closest to the earth is called its perigee and the point furthest from the earth, apogee. The mean distance is 239,000 miles. This variation in distance has the effect of varying the moon's semi-diameter from 16·4 minutes of arc at perigee to 14·7 minutes at apogee. The line joining perigee to apogee is called the line of apsides.

The terms conjunction, quadrature, and opposition are used with reference to the moon in exactly the same sense as with the planets (see Planetary Motion for Definitions). The moon is therefore in conjunction when it has the same celestial longitude as the sun, and is in opposition when its celestial longitude is 180° removed from that of the sun.

The motion of the moon on the celestial sphere

The moon describes a great circle around the celestial sphere in the same period that it takes to orbit the earth. It therefore moves around this great circle through 360° in about $27\frac{1}{3}$ days. This period is known as the moon's sidereal period, or a sidereal month. The motion is direct and therefore the S.H.A. is always decreasing at a mean rate which is found by dividing the sidereal period into 360°. This represents a fairly rapid motion against the stars.

During the moon's sidereal period the sun will decrease its S.H.A. by about 29·9° due to the earth's motion around its orbit about the sun. If the moon is considered to be in conjunction at M^1 in

Figure 8.1, at the end of one sidereal period the moon will have arrived at M^2, the earth having moved around its orbit to E^2. The moon must continue to M^3 in order to return to a position of conjunction. The period of time required for the moon to complete a revolution around the sphere relative to the sun, i.e. the period from one conjunction to the next is called the moon's synodic period or a synodic month. As this is the period of the moon's phases it is also called a lunation.

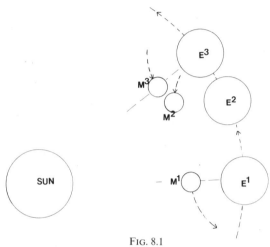

FIG. 8.1

The great circle which represents the moon's path around the celestial sphere is inclined to the ecliptic at an angle of about $5\frac{1}{4}°$. The moon will never be further from the ecliptic than this amount. During one orbit around this great circle the moon must cross the ecliptic twice, and the points on the orbit where this occurs are called the nodes of the moon's orbit. When the moon is crossing from south to north of the ecliptic, the node is specified as the ascending node and when crossing from north to south, as the descending node. Gravitational forces, acting on the moon cause the nodes to regress westwards around the ecliptic once in about 18·6 years. That is about 19° per year. A result of this motion is to change the limits, between which the declination of the moon oscillates as the moon moves around its orbit.

Consider the ascending node to be at the first point of Aries. This must occur once in 18·6 years. Figure 8.2 illustrates this.

The limits of the moon's declination at this time will be $23\frac{1}{2}° + 5\frac{1}{4}°$ north and south. The declination of the moon will therefore change from $28\frac{3}{4}°$ north to $28\frac{3}{4}°$ south in half the sidereal period; about 14 days. This is a very rapid motion in declination compared with any other body on the celestial sphere.

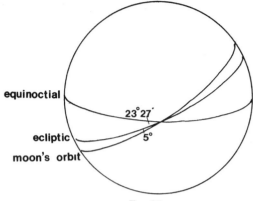

Fig. 8.2

After 9·3 years the ascending node will have moved to the first point of Libra, which is the point on the sphere diametrically opposed to the first point of Aries. The ecliptic and the moon's orbit will now be as shown in Figure 8.3.

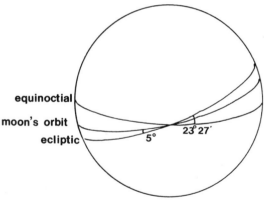

Fig. 8.3

The inclination of the moon's orbit to the equinoctial is now $23\frac{1}{2}° - 5\frac{1}{4}°$ and the declination of the moon will change between the limits of $18\frac{1}{4}°$ north and $18\frac{1}{4}°$ south, again in half the sidereal period which is about 14 days. During the following 9·3 years the limits will again increase to the maximum limits of $28\frac{3}{4}°$ north and south as the ascending node regresses around to the first point of Aries.

The position of the moon, relative to the earth and the sun determines the amount of the sunlit side of the moon which is visible from the earth. The period of the moon's phases will therefore be the moon's synodic period of 29d 12h 44m. The synodic period is considered to begin with the moon in conjunction. At this time the moon lies in the same direction as the sun and the sunlit half of the moon is not visible from the earth. The cycle of phases then proceeds as follows.

Phases during a lunation

Only half of the moon's surface can be illuminated at any time. Only part of the illuminated half will be visible from the earth at any given time during the lunation as shown in Figure 8.4. This shows the position of the moon at eight points in its synodic cycle with the sun's rays striking from the right hand side of the diagram. The moon as seen from the earth is shown at the correspondingly lettered positions above and below.

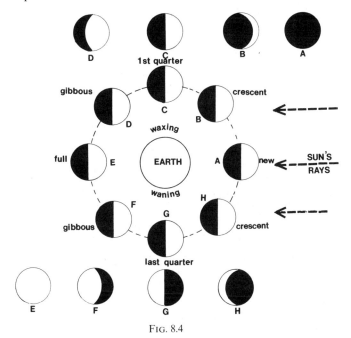

FIG. 8.4

At position A the whole of the illuminated half of the moon is turned away from the earth. This is the position of the moon's conjunction when the moon has the same celestial longitude as the sun. None of the moon's illuminated half is visible from the earth. In fact this can only occur if the earth, moon and sun all lie in the plane of the ecliptic, and with this configuration the moon would hide the sun from the earth. This does not occur at every conjunction because the moon does not orbit in the plane of the ecliptic. Therefore there will be a thin crescent of moon visible from the earth, on the side of the moon nearest the sun. In this position the moon is said to be new, and the age of the moon is said to be 0 days.

At B the moon's elongation (the difference between the longitudes of the sun and the moon), has increased and part of the moon's illuminated disc is visible from the earth. It will appear as a crescent with the cusps or horns turned away from the sun, as at B'. At C half of the illuminated disc is visible and the moon is said to be dichotomised. The moon here is in quadrature, and the age of the moon is about $7\frac{1}{4}$ days. When more than half of the illuminated moon is visible as at D the moon is said to be gibbous, and it will appear as in D' from the earth. At E the whole of the illuminated half of the moon is facing the earth and the moon appears full as in E'. The moon is now in opposition and the age of the moon is about $14\frac{1}{2}$ days.

During the time when the size of the visible moon is increasing it is said to be waxing. After full moon when the visible moon will start to decrease in size it is said to be waning. The phases will then repeat themselves at F, when the moon will appear as at F', at G and H when it will appear as at G' and H' respectively, except that the sunlit areas now appear on the other side of the moon (the eastern side). Finally the moon wanes until the new moon appears at the following conjunction when the age of the moon will be $29\frac{1}{3}$ days or 0 days of the next lunation.

The age of the moon therefore is the number of days ellapsed since the last new moon.

The part of the moon that is facing the earth but is not illuminated by the sun is often visible as a dim glow. This is due to light reflected from the earth, and is called earthshine. This corresponds to the moonshine on the earth which can illuminate partially the earth at night.

It is also worth noting that from the moon the earth would exhibit phases which would be opposite to the moon's phase as seen from earth. For example when the moon is new the earth would appear full from the moon.

Retardation in the meridian passage of the moon

It has been said that the moon moves around its orbit with a sidereal period of 27·3 days. The motion is direct, i.e. from west to east as viewed from the earth.

In the diagram let O' be the meridian of an observer at the time of meridian passage of the moon M'. Let the earth rotate through 360° so that O' returns to its original position. This will take 23h 56m. The moon because of its orbital motion will have moved to M", such that M'M" is 360°/27·3. Thus to produce the next meridian passage of the moon O must rotate through a further angle before 'catching up' with the moon. The meridian passage therefore gets later each day by an average of $50\frac{1}{2}$ minutes. Because of the varying speed of the moon in its orbit and hence the varying rate of change of S.H.A. this retardation may be between 40 minutes and 60 minutes.

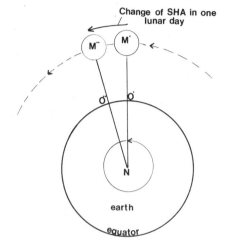

Fig. 8.5

Retardation of moonrise and moonset

There will be a corresponding retardation in both moonrise and moonset for the same reason as for the retardation of transit. However this retardation may be modified by the effects of a change of declination of the moon from one day to another. It has been shown that the moon can have a very rapid motion in declination, and it has also been shown that to an observer in north latitude the further north the declination then the longer will a body remain above the observer's horizon. Thus if a body is above the horizon in north latitude and is increasing its declination north it is tending to oppose the effect of the earth's rotation of making it sink towards the western horizon. If this is the case the retardation of moonset will be prolonged by the motion in declination. On the other hand if the declination is going south then the effect will be to hasten the moonset and the retardation will be shortened.

The same consideration will affect moonrise.

If the declination is the same name as latitude then an increase in the declination will shorten the retardation in moonrise. A decrease in declination will prolong the retardation.

The effect of change of declination is greatest in high latitudes. It can under extreme conditions amount to more than the retardation due to the moon's motion in orbit. If this is so it is possible for the moon to rise twice to a stationary observer within a period of 24 hours.

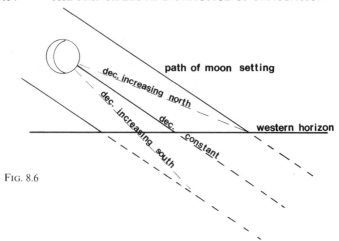

path of moon setting

dec. increasing north

dec. increasing south   dec. constant

western horizon

FIG. 8.6

When the sun is at the first point of Libra on September 23rd the full moon must be at the first point of Aries. When this is the case the moon is changing its declination to the northwards most rapidly. (This is most pronounced when the ascending node is at the first point of Aries. See Motion of the Moon on the Celestial Sphere.) Thus in the northern hemisphere the retardation in moon-rise is reduced to a great extent. Furthermore the full moon must rise at the approximate time that the sun is setting at the times of the equinoxes as the declinations are both near to zero and the difference in the S.H.A.s is 180°. Thus the full moon rises early to illuminate the evening at the time of the year when harvesting is done. For this reason this particular full moon was given the name of the harvest moon. At the next full moon the same conditions occur but to a less marked extent. This particular full moon is sometimes referred to as the hunter's moon.

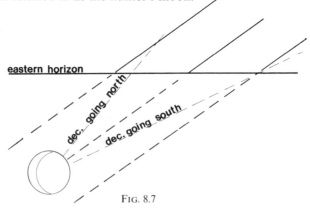

eastern horizon

dec. going north   dec. going south

FIG. 8.7

The moon's rotation

The moon rotates once around an axis which is almost perpendicular to the plane of its orbit around the earth. (Compare this with the earth's axis which is inclined to the plane of the earth's orbit at $66\frac{1}{2}°$.)

The rotation of the moon is captured or synchronous. This means that the same half of the moon is always facing the earth, due to the rotation period being the same as the sidereal period in orbit.

This is no mere coincidence, and the same phenomenon is suspected in other planets satellites in the solar system. It is caused by friction of tidal waves moving round the body (or more correctly the body rotating under the tidal wave), slowing down the rotation of the body. The ultimate effect is to slow the rotation down so that there is no rotation of the body relative to the tidal wave. As the tidal wave is constantly under the body that is causing the wave then the rotation will be synchronous with the orbital period. Tidal friction on the moon has already captured the moon's rotation. It should be realized that tidal effects occur in the solid matter of the body as well as the liquid that may be over the solid surface. The same effect is gradually slowing down the rotation of the earth, thus lengthening the day to the extent of 0·002 seconds per century.

Librations of the moon

Because of the moon's synchronous rotation the same lunar face is turned towards the earth at any time. Thus until the advent of space probes the other side of the moon was unknown to man. At any one time an observer on the earth can see approximately 49% of the moon's surface. However more than this is visible from the earth at some time or other though not all at the same time.

Libration in latitude

The moon's axis of rotation is not quite perpendicular to the plane of the moon's orbit, being about $6\frac{1}{2}°$ out of the perpendicular. Thus as the moon's axis is pointing to a constant direction in space, sometimes the moon's north pole and sometimes the south pole is tilted towards the earth, allowing earthlings to see alternately 'over the top' and 'underneath' the moon for short distances. Note that this is exactly the same phenomenon as that which causes the earth's seasons in the case of the earth–sun system. If an observer on the sun were to look towards the earth at summer solstice he would see 'over the top' of the earth's north pole, and at winter solstice he would see 'underneath' the south pole. This could be described as the earth's libration in latitude, as viewed from the sun.

Libration in longitude

As the moon's orbit is elliptical the moon's orbital angular velocity alternately increases and decreases. Thus the constant rotation of the moon, although of the same period as the orbital revolution, gets slightly out of step with it, sometimes lagging and sometimes leading, allowing us to see alternately round the 'leading edge' and then round the 'trailing edge' of the moon as shown in Figure 8.8.

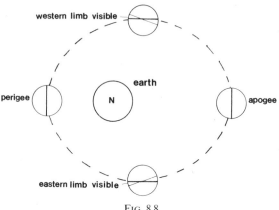

FIG. 8.8

Diurnal libration

This is merely an effect of parallax; arising from change of position on the earth's surface, relative to the moon. An observer to the west of the moon will see further round the western edge than someone under the moon. An observer to the east of the moon will see further round the eastern edge. As the rotation of the earth has the effect of carrying an observer from a position to the west of the moon to a position to the east of the moon during any day an observer will see slightly more than half the moon's surface.

In total about 59% of the moon's surface is visible from the earth at some time or other. The other 41% can only be seen from photographs taken by space probes.

Eclipses

When the sun, moon and earth lie in a straight line or very nearly so, then either the moon will cut off the light from the sun if it is at conjunction, or it will lie in the shadow of the earth, if it is at opposition. If the moon's orbit happened to be in the same plane as the ecliptic this would occur at each full moon and at each new moon. However as the moon's orbit is inclined to the ecliptic at about $5\frac{1}{4}°$ the moon is usually out of the plane of the ecliptic and thus the conditions of eclipse cannot occur. The only time that the moon is in or near the plane of the ecliptic is when it is passing one of the nodes of its orbit. If the sun also happens to be at one of these nodes in its journey around the ecliptic then an eclipse will occur.

If the sun is at the opposite node then an eclipse of the moon will occur when the moon passes through the earth's shadow.

If the sun is at the same node as the moon then an eclipse of the sun will occur when the moon passes between the sun and earth and cuts off the light of the sun from the observer.

Hence at an eclipse of the moon the moon must be full. At an eclipse of the sun the moon must be new.

The solar eclipse

When a solar eclipse occurs the shadow of the moon falls across the earth as the moon passes in front of the sun. To an observer in the shadow the sun's light will be cut off either partially or wholly. The length of the moon's shadow can readily be calculated given the diameters of the two bodies and the distance between them. This length is very near to the mean distance between the earth and the moon, so that the shadow only reaches the earth when the moon is near perigee, and it is only at these times therefore that the moon's disc is large enough to cover the whole disc of the sun. When this does occur it is called a total eclipse of the sun. It will only be total to an observer within the relatively small area of complete shadow or umbra. To an observer within the part shadow or penumbra the moon will only cover part of the sun and he will experience a partial eclipse of the sun. To any observer outside the region of penumbra no eclipse will occur.

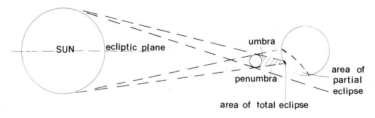

Fig. 8.9

If when the eclipse occurs the moon is near apogee then the shadow of the moon will not reach the earth. There will be no total eclipse therefore. An observer however who lies on the line through the centres of the sun and moon will see centres of the two bodies in line. The moon will be smaller than the sun and a ring of sun therefore will be seen around the moon. Such an eclipse is called an annular eclipse. Whether an eclipse is annular or total depends also on whether the earth is at aphelion or perihelion but to a lesser extent. To an observer outside the region where an annular eclipse is seen, a partial eclipse will be seen exactly as in the case of the total eclipse.

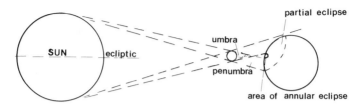

FIG. 8.10

The lunar eclipse

When at opposition, the moon is at or near a node, then it will pass through the shadow of the earth, which extends considerably further than the moon's orbit. The centre of the shadow area must lie in the plane of the ecliptic. Thus whether the moon passes completely, or partially through the shadow will depend upon the angular distance of the moon from the ecliptic (i.e. its celestial latitude), at the moment of opposition. If the latitude is small enough and the whole disc of the moon enters the umbra then a total eclipse of the moon is said to occur. If only part of the moon's disc passes through the shadow then a partial eclipse is said to occur. If no part of the moon touches the umbra but the moon passes through the penumbra of the earth then a penumbral eclipse is said to have occurred. This however only results in a slight diminishing of the moon's light. In Figure 8.11 M_1 shows the total lunar eclipse, M_2 the partial eclipse and M_3 the penumbral eclipse. In each case the moon is passing into the plane of the page.

Ecliptic limits

The celestial latitude of the moon is critical for the occurrence of an eclipse. In the case of the solar eclipse if the celestial latitude is zero (the moon is exactly in the ecliptic) then an eclipse will occur

FIG. 8.11

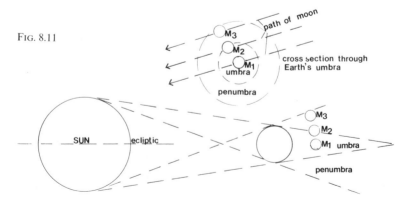

centrally on the earth in the equatorial regions. If the moon is slightly out of the ecliptic an eclipse will occur in higher latitudes. In the case of a lunar eclipse, if the moon is exactly in the ecliptic then it will pass through the centre of the earth's shadow. If slightly out of the ecliptic then it may pass through the shadow but not centrally. It may still completely enter the shadow however. A slightly greater celestial latitude will mean that the moon will not pass completely into the shadow but the conditions of partial eclipse may occur. In each case there will be a limit to the celestial latitude which the moon may have at the time of its conjunction for an eclipse to occur. If the obliquity of the moon's orbit to the ecliptic is now considered from Figure 8.12 then for any given celestial latitude of the moon at conjunction or opposition then the angular distance of the bodies from the node can be calculated. This angular distance which is consistent with an eclipse just occurring is called the ecliptic limit for the eclipse. The limits will be smaller for the lunar eclipse as in this case Figure 8.12 would have to show the cross section of the earth's shadow instead of the sun which will have a smaller angular diameter than the sun itself.

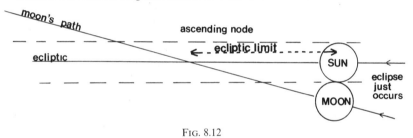

Fig. 8.12

Recurrence of eclipses

When the moon passes one of its nodes, the sun must be at or near the same node if a solar eclipse is to occur, or the opposite node for a lunar eclipse. Thus there will be two periods during the sun's passage around the ecliptic when eclipses can occur, that is when the sun is passing a node. Because of the regression of the nodes around the ecliptic the sun will return to a particular node in a period of less than one year. In fact the period is about $346\frac{1}{2}$ days. This is called the synodic period of revolution of the nodes. In this period there will be two occasions when the sun is within the ecliptic limits. When the moon goes through conjunction or opposition during these occasions then eclipses will occur.

Let Figure 8.13 represent the ecliptic and the moon's orbit and N and N' the nodes. Let S and S' be the extent of the solar ecliptic limits at each node and L and L' the extent of the lunar ecliptic limits at each node. Thus SS' is twice the solar limit and LL' twice the lunar limit. If the solar limit is a maximum then it can take as

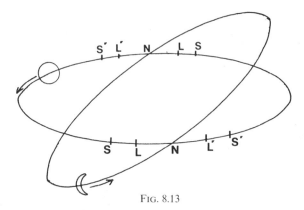

FIG. 8.13

much as 34 days for the sun to traverse this part of the ecliptic, and during this time the moon will go more than once around its orbit. Thus a solar eclipse must occur during this period and two may occur.

The angular distance LL′ is 23° when the lunar limits are maximum and in the time it takes the sun to go through this arc, the moon does not go completely around its orbit. Thus a lunar eclipse need not occur, but one may do so. (In fact a penumbral eclipse must occur but these are usually neglected as they are not particularly noticeable phenomena.)

Maximum number of eclipses
Under favourable conditions, i.e. if a solar eclipse occurs as soon as the sun enters a solar limit, then the sequence of events will produce a maximum number of eclipses within a period of twelve months. The maximum number is seven, either five solar and two lunar, or four solar and three lunar.

The least number of eclipses occurs when the moon is full just before the sun enters the lunar ecliptic limits, i.e. a lunar eclipse is just missed. This sequence of events will produce only two eclipses within a period of twelve months. Both of these must be solar.

Note that solar eclipses are more frequent than lunar eclipses but that at any one point on the earth more lunar eclipses are seen because these are visible over all the earth's surface where the moon is above the horizon, whereas a solar eclipse is only seen on that part of the earth where the moon's shadow falls.

EXERCISE

1. Explain the changing phases of the moon.

2. Define a lunation. Why is the moon's synodic period longer than its sidereal period?

3. Explain why the interval between two successive meridian passages of the moon over any given meridian is longer than the solar day.

4. Account for the moon's rapid motion in declination. Explain the limits between which the value fluctuates, and why these limits themselves change.

5. Define 'the ascending node'. How does the moon's ascending node move relative to the first point of Aries?

6. Explain exactly why only 59% of the moon's surface is ever visible from the earth.

7. Define the terms:
   (a) gibbous,
   (b) quadrature,
   (c) dichotomized.
Give the L.A.T. of the meridian passage of the moon over any meridian when the moon is:
   (a) new,
   (b) in quadrature,
   (c) full.

8. Explain why a lunar eclipse occurs. What are the conditions that are necessary for a lunar eclipse to occur?

9. Explain the phenomenon of a solar eclipse. Differentiate between a partial, a total, and an annular eclipse of the sun.

10. What are the ecliptic limits? Why do more solar eclipses occur than lunar eclipses?

11. Given that the ratio of the number of solar eclipses that occur to the number of lunar eclipses is about 3:2, why are more lunar eclipses observed from any position on the earth's surface?

12. Successive transits of the moon across any meridian occur about 24h 50m apart. How then is it possible for the moon to rise to a stationary observer twice in a period of 24 hours.

CHAPTER 9

PLANETARY AND SATELLITE ORBITS

Gravitation and orbiting bodies

Newton first expounded the law that every body attracts every other body with a force that varies as the product of their masses and inversely as the square of their distance apart. Thus

$$F = G \frac{mm'}{r^2}$$

where G is a constant called the constant of gravitation.

This force will cause the two bodies to accelerate together, but Newton's first law of motion states that every body moves in a straight line with a constant velocity, unless an external force acts upon it.

Consider an orbiting body P as in Figure 9.1. If no external force was acting upon it P would continue along the track PL. This involves an acceleration away from S. This is balanced by the acceleration due to the gravitational attraction between the two bodies which is shown in Figure 9.1 as an acceleration of P towards S. As these two accelerations balance the velocity of the body will cause it to move at right angles to them both. As the radius PS and therefore the tangent PL are constantly changing direction P will continue around a curved orbit.

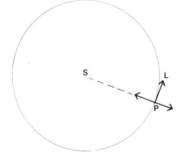

Fig. 9.1

The acceleration towards the parent body must be balanced by the tendency to accelerate away from the parent body. This

142

tendency depends upon the velocity of the body in orbit. Therefore, as the acceleration inwards, provided that the masses of the bodies are fixed, varies inversely as the square of the distance apart, for any given orbit radius there must be one value of velocity which will exactly balance the gravitational attraction. Thus the greater the radius of orbit, the less will be the velocity in orbit.

Planetary and satellite orbits

The three laws first discovered by Kepler, and first derived mathematically by Newton from his law of universal gravitation, describe the ideal planetary orbit.
These three laws state:

1. Each planet moves in an ellipse with the sun at one focus.
2. The line joining the orbiting body to the parent body sweeps out equal areas in equal times.
3. The square of the sidereal periods are proportional to the cubes of the mean distances apart of the orbiting and the parent body.

These three laws were formulated as the result of experimental observations over a long period of time and as far as the accuracy of the observations allowed they described exactly the path of the planet observed.

However now that more precise observations are possible it can be observed that these laws do not fully account for the observed motions of the planets, but only very nearly so. We may explain this by saying that Newton's mathematical proof of the laws hold good, but only if the two bodies are completely isolated from the influence of the attraction of any other body. This never occurs in the solar system. Each planet, although the controlling body is the sun by virtue of its great mass, is attracted by the gravitation of every body in the solar system. These forces, although small compared with that of the sun will perturb a planet from the perfect ellipse postulated in Kepler's laws. Only when the effect of these other attractions are taken into account can the motion of a planet or satellite be predicted and accounted for.

It should also be noted that even if two bodies were isolated we could not think of an orbiting body moving around a stationary parent body, at the focus of an ellipse.

The force which attracts the orbiting body to the parent body is their mutual gravitational attraction which is described by:

$$F = G \frac{Mm}{r^2}.$$

where M is the mass of the parent body and m is the mass of the satellite body.

Thus from $F = ma$ the acceleration of the satellite towards the parent body is given by:

$$a = G\frac{Mm}{r^2} \times \frac{1}{m}$$

$$= G\frac{M}{r^2}$$

But there will also be an acceleration of the parent body towards the satellite given by:

$$a = G\frac{m}{r^2}$$

Because of the usual small mass of the satellite, m, compared with the mass of the parent body, M, this acceleration will be small, but it should be realized that the two bodies will in fact both orbit around their common centre of mass. In the case of the sun and any planet the centre of mass lies very close to the centre of the sun. In the case of the earth and the moon then the mass of the moon is considerable compared with that of the earth and the centre of mass of this system lies some distance from the centre of the earth, although it is still well within the earth's radius. This centre of mass we call the Barycentre and it is this point which in fact describes an orbit around the sun according to Kepler's laws. The moon and the earth both weave in and out of this orbit as they in turn orbit around the Barycentre.

Newton's mathematical treatment also showed that Kepler's third law needed to be ammended slightly. Kepler's statement that the squares of the sidereal periods were proportional to the cubes of the distances from the sun was an oversimplification.

Stated mathematically, if T is the sidereal period and r the mean radius of orbit then:

$$\frac{T^2}{r^3} = \text{constant.}$$

But the acceleration of the planet towards the sun is given by:

$$a = G\frac{M}{r^2}$$

and that of the sun towards the planet,

$$a = G\frac{m}{r^2}$$

Thus the total acceleration is given by,

$$a = G\frac{M+m}{r^2}$$

The force acting on a planet towards the sun is given by $F = ma$. Thus

$$F = m \frac{v^2}{r} \qquad (1)$$

and as distance = velocity × time, if T is the sidereal period and $2\pi r$ the distance travelled in this time for a circular orbit then

$$v \times T = 2\pi r$$

and

$$v = \frac{2\pi r}{T}$$

Substituting in 1

$$F = \frac{m}{r} \frac{4\pi^2 r^2}{T^2} = \frac{m}{r^2} \frac{4\pi^2 r^3}{T^2}$$

Putting this into $F = ma$

$$\frac{m}{r^2} \frac{4\pi^2 r^3}{T^2} = m \frac{G(M+m)}{r^2}$$

and

$$\frac{4\pi^2 r^3}{T^2} = G(M+m)$$

thus

$$\frac{4\pi^2}{G} = \frac{T^2}{r^3}(M+m)$$

therefore

$$\frac{T^2}{r^3}(M+m) = \text{constant}$$

and not

$$\frac{T^2}{r^3} \text{ as Kepler's third law states.}$$

Because the mass of all planets is small compared with that of the sun then $(M+m)$ is almost a constant which is why Kepler's third law is a very close approximation to observable data.

Artificial satellites
Man made satellites, when put into space must of course be governed by the same laws as natural bodies. Earth satellites

however, because of their proximity to the earth have their orbits perturbed to a great extent by the irregularities in the gravitational attraction of the earth. Indeed these perturbations have proved to be a powerful method of studying the variations in the earth's gravitational field, and hence the shape, and distribution of mass of the earth. The equatorial bulge has the effect of making a satellite orbit drift to the westwards, and measurement of this drift has given a more accurate figure for the figure of the earth than was possible before. Latest measurements give a figure of 1/298·25 for the earth's flattening. Other irregularities alter the height of a satellite at various points in its orbit. Perhaps the most troublesome of the perturbations is the effect of air resistance. Although the atmosphere is extremely rarified at these heights, the closer satellites are slowed by air drag and eventually enter the denser atmosphere and burn up. The sun and moon also have their effects but these are small compared with the effects of the earth.

The methods of putting a satellite into orbit allow to a certain extent, the choice of type of orbit to be followed by the satellite. The method is to put the satellite at the required height above the earth by making it the final stage of a multi-stage rocket, and at the required height give it a velocity in the direction of the required orbit. This velocity is very critical in deciding the shape of the orbit. The direction is critical in deciding the inclination of the orbit to the equator.

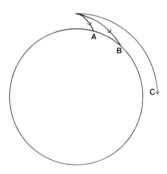

FIG. 9.2

In Figure 9.2 satellite A has been given a velocity which is insufficient to place the body in orbit. It falls to the earth's surface. Satellite B, which will start to fall towards the earth's centre at exactly the same rate and with exactly the same vertical acceleration as A, has been given a larger velocity, so that it falls to the earth at B. Satellite C has received a velocity which causes it to 'fall off' the earth, so that it continues to fall towards the earth's centre but at the same time its velocity keeps it in a closed orbit around the earth.

To produce a circular orbit the velocity imparted would have to be very accurately controlled. This type of orbit is very difficult to obtain, and any circular orbit would be quickly perturbed into an ellipse. If the velocity is slightly less than or slightly more than the circular velocity an elliptical orbit is produced as in Figure 9.3.

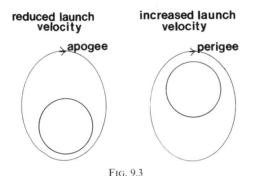

FIG. 9.3

In practice the rocket is fired into a precomputed curve which takes it smoothly into the required orbit but the foregoing describes the general principles involved.

Special orbits
Navigational satellites are placed in polar orbits. In other words their tracks pass over both of the earth's poles. (As viewed from the earth their tracks would describe in theory celestial meridians.) To understand the benefit of this type of orbit imagine the earth to be perfectly spherical and that the satellite has a circular polar orbit. In these circumstances the orbital plane would be fixed in space. The earth would be rotating inside the orbit, so that each time the satellite came round to a point on its orbit, a different meridian would be under the satellite. The period of revolution of the satellite would be in the order of one or two hours. Thus at every successive orbit the satellite would be displaced in longitude by about 15 or 30 degrees depending upon the period of revolution. Thus from one satellite coverage of all places on the earth would be obtained. In fact to provide adequate coverage in frequency of satellite passes five satellites in polar orbits are used in the Transit system.

Satellite orbits cannot be predicted far into the future, as the exact nature of the perturbations produced by the earth's irregular attraction is not known in sufficient detail. The information about a satellite's orbit must be continually observed and computed by ground tracking stations and injected into the satellite for storage each time the satellite passes over the station. This orbital information is then transmitted to ships that are using the system so that the ship receiver can compute its position given the position of the satellite.

Synchronous orbits

This type is often used for communications satellites. The satellite is put into an equatorial orbit the direction of which is in the same sense as that of the earth's rotation. The height is such that the orbital velocity just equals the rotational velocity of the earth. Thus as seen from the earth the satellite appears to remain in the same position relative to the horizon and the meridian. The necessary orbit for this is at a height of about 36,000 km. The orbital period will of course be a sidereal day.

The minimum height for a stable orbit is about 160 km. This would give an orbital period of about 88 minutes. Less than this air drag would destroy the satellite by heat of friction.

The solar system

There are nine known major planets in orbit around the sun, all in orbits of small eccentricity. Other minor members of the solar system include thousands of asteroids or minor planets, mostly between the orbits of Mars and Jupiter, and comets. These bodies often have orbits of great eccentricity. All these bodies however are subject to the same laws of planetary motion described.

The major planets all have orbits whose planes lie close to that of the earth's orbit, that is the plane of the ecliptic. It is convenient very often to think of them as all orbiting in the ecliptic. Those whose orbits lie inside that of the earth are termed inferior planets, of which there are two, Mercury and Venus. Of these only Venus is used for navigation. The six planets whose orbits lie outside that of the earth are called superior planets and of these, Mars, Jupiter, and Saturn are used for navigation. The others, Neptune, Uranus and Pluto are too faint to be seen with the naked eye.

Because of their proximity to the earth compared with the stars, the planets exhibit fairly rapid motions against the background of the stars. These motions are a result of the movement of the earth and the planets. All the major planets orbit the sun in an anti-clockwise direction as viewed from the north celestial pole. Because this includes the earth the motion of the other planets as seen from the earth is in general to move eastwards against the stars around the sphere fairly close to the ecliptic. Like the sun then the S.H.A. of all planets is changing from day to day.

The mean distance of the earth from the sun is often referred to as the astronomical unit. If this unit is accepted as unity it is a relatively easy problem to find the distance of the other planets from the sun, by measuring the time it takes for them to complete 360° of their orbits. This period is called a planet's sidereal period. Kepler's third law gives the relationship between the sidereal period of the earth, which is the year, the astronomical unit, the planet's sidereal period, and the planet's distance from the sun. The only unknown in this relationship is the planet's distance from the sun in terms of the astronomical unit.

To obtain the distance in miles, however, the astronomical unit must be determined in these units. This is a more difficult problem. Observing the parallax of a nearby planet at opposition from two stations on the earth as far apart as possible have provided solutions in the past, by giving the planet's distance from the earth. This will provide a solution when used in Kepler's third law. The closer the planet observed, the more accurate will be the results, and for this reason the minor planet Eros held a position of some importance in that it approached the earth much closer than any other planet at its opposition. The estimation of the astronomical unit is 93,005,000 miles. There are other methods of finding the astronomical unit, all giving similar results within the limits of observational errors.

The distances of the major planets with their sidereal periods are given in the table below.

Planet	Relative mean distance	Sidereal period	Dist. from sun (miles)
Mercury	0·387	87·97d	36,002,235
Venus	0·723	224·7d	67,270,516
Earth	1·000	365d 06h 06m	93,005,000
Mars	1·524	1·881 years	115,047,180
Jupiter	5·208	11·862 years	484,388,640
Saturn	9·539	29·457 years	887,156,090
Uranus	19·191	84·015 years	1,784,858,900
Neptune	30·071	164·788 years	2,796,725,400
Pluto	39·457	247·697 years	3,669,735,400

Bode's law

If the numbers 0, 3, 6, 12, 24, 48, 96, 192 are written (each one after 3 being double the previous one) and then 4 added to each, the resultant series gives very closely the relative distances of the planets frum the sun, taking the earth sun distance to be 10.

Thus

$$4, \quad 7, \quad 10, \quad 16, \quad 28, \quad 52, \quad 100, \quad 196.$$

There is a gap corresponding to the number 28, but this is filled by the minor planets or asteroids, most of which lie between the orbits of Mars and Jupiter. Neptune and Pluto do not conform but at the time of formulation of the law they had not been discovered. There seems to be no logical reason for this pattern. It is purely coincidental.

RELATIVE PLANETARY MOTION

There are certain positions in the orbit of a planet, relative to the sun and the earth that are given special names (see Fig. 9.4).

Inferior planets

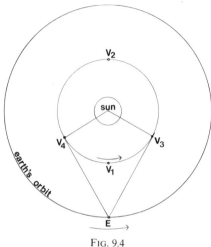

Fig. 9.4

Position v_1 = Inferior conjunction.
Position v_2 = Superior conjunction.
Position v_3 = Maximum elongation west.
Position v_4 = Maximum elongation east.

Definitions

Conjunction of a body is the position on its orbit when it has the same celestial longitude as the sun. If the planet is between the earth and the sun then it is termed an inferior conjunction. If the planet is on the opposite side of the sun to the earth then it is termed a superior conjunction.

Elongation of a body is the difference between the longitude of the sun and that of the body. Maximum elongation occurs when the angle at the body subtended by the earth and the sun is a right angle. At this time the line of sight from the earth to the body is a tangent to the body's orbit.

Sidereal period of an orbiting body is the time it takes to go 360° around its orbit.

Synodic period is the time taken for the planet to go from one conjunction to the next similar conjunction. Because of the movement of the earth in its own orbit this period for any inferior planet will be longer than that planet's sidereal period. For a superior planet the synodic period must be greater than the earth's sidereal period.

Because an inferior planet is orbiting the sun at a less distance from the sun than the earth then the planet as seen from the earth will always be in the same general direction as the sun. As the orbits of all the planets lie very nearly in the same plane as the earth's orbit, that of an inferior planet is viewed from the earth as end on and the planet appears to move almost in a straight line from side to side across the sun's disc. The positions in Figure 9.5 refer to the same positions as in the previous diagram.

FIG. 9.5

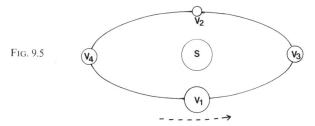

Because of the slight inclinations of the planetary orbits to the ecliptic the planet rarely transits across the face of the sun but passes above or below it.

Morning star and evening star

Because of the rotation of the earth both sun and planet will move from east to west across the sky. When the planet is at a westerly elongation it will preceed the sun and will therefore rise before the sun. When the planet has risen and can be seen in the eastern sky before sunrise it is referred to as a morning star. When the planet is at an easterly elongation it will set after the sun and as it is visible in the western sky after sunset it is termed an evening star. This happens for both Venus and Mercury.

Phases of an inferior planet

An inferior planet exhibits a full range of phase changes during its synodic period, the effect being most marked in the case of Venus, whose phases are clearly distinguishable with a small telescope or binoculars. The planet will appear full at superior conjunction, when the full sunlit half of the planet is facing the earth. The 'new' phase occurs at inferior conjunction, when a thin crescent is visible, as the planet is usually out of the plane of the ecliptic at inferior conjunction. If this occurs when the planet is in the plane of the ecliptic a transit of the planet across the face of the sun will be observed. This is a rare occurrence in the case of Venus. The planet will be dichotomized at maximum elongations. Phases are illustrated in Figure 9.6.

Brightness of Venus

At superior conjunction the distance of Venus from the earth averages 160 million miles (i.e. the sum of the earth sun distance and the Venus sun distance). From this position Venus emerges to the east of the sun and becomes an evening star, taking about 220 days to reach maximum elongation from superior conjunction. The position of maximum brightness occurs about 36 days after this maximum elongation. The journey from maximum elongation east to maximum elongation west takes about 144 days, through inferior conjunction, when it is only about 26 million miles from the earth. Maximum brightness again occurs about 36 days before maximum elongation west. Another 220 days brings the planet back to superior conjunction. The synodic period is therefore about 584 days.

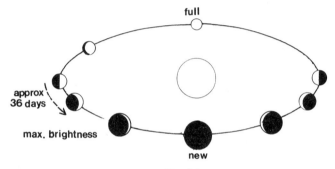

FIG. 9.6

Approximate brightnesses:

sup. conj.	-3.5
inf. conj.	-2.9
max.	-4.2

Retrograde motion of inferior planets

In Figure 9.7 let E_1V_1 and S represent the positions of the earth, Venus and the sun at an inferior conjunction of Venus and when the S.H.A. of the sun is 0°. (Hence this is occurring at the Vernal Equinox.) Let the circles represent the projections of the orbits onto the plane of the equinoctial.

Remembering that the inferior planet will have a greater angular velocity than the earth let positions V_2 and E_2 be the earth and Venus some time later. The line of sight from earth to Venus will have rotated to the west, such that angle $\alpha°$ is the increase in S.H.A. Thus at E_2V_2 the S.H.A. of Venus is $\alpha°$. If Venus is projected onto the background of the stars its projected position will have moved to the west.

As Venus curves around its orbit the rate of increase of S.H.A. will decrease until the S.H.A. reaches a maximum. This has occurred at V_3E_3 where the S.H.A. of Venus is $\beta°$. This position is called a stationary point. Venus has ceased to move westwards against the stars.

Thereafter the line of sight from the earth to Venus will rotate to the east and the S.H.A. will decrease. At V_4E_4 the S.H.A. has decreased to zero and the projected position of Venus has returned to its original position as at E_1V_1. It has moved eastwards. At V_5E_5 the S.H.A. of Venus has decreased to a value equal to $360° - \gamma°$.

When moving westwards against the stars the motion of the planet is termed retrograde.

When moving eastwards against the stars the motion of the planet is termed direct.

There will be another stationary point when Venus has moved through superior conjunction and is approaching inferior conjunction. Retrograde motion will therefore occur for a period before and after inferior conjunction.

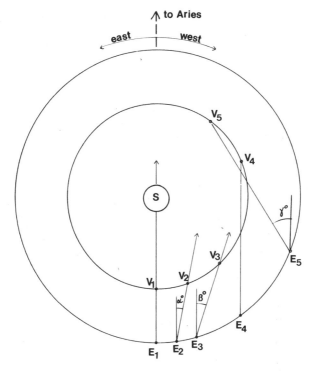

FIG. 9.7

Superior planets

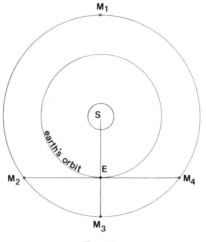

FIG. 9.8

Conjunction
The planet at M_1 is said to be at conjunction. This occurs when the celestial longitude of the planet is the same as that of the sun.

Quadrature
The planet at M_2 and at M_4 is said to be in quadrature. This occurs when the celestial longitude of the planet is 90° different from that of the sun.

Opposition
The planet at M_3 is said to be in opposition. This occurs when the celestial longitude of the planet is 180° away from that of the sun.

Note that these positions are relative to that of the earth, and the planet will pass through each of these positions once in its synodic period. Both planets are orbiting in an anticlockwise direction when viewed from the north pole of the sphere, the earth having the greater angular velocity. If the earth makes one orbit of 360°, the superior planet will have progressed around its own orbit something less than 360°. Thus the positions of the planet at each successive opposition will change, moving anticlockwise in the figure. Thus the synodic period of the planet is always greater than the sidereal period of the earth. The greater the distance of the superior planet from the sun, the closer will its synodic period approach the earth's sidereal period.

Synodic periods of superior planets

Planet	Mean dist. from sun	Synodic period
Mars	227,940,000 km	779·94 days
Jupiter	778,300,000 km	398·88 days
Saturn	1,427,000,000 km	378·09 days
Uranus	2,869,000,000 km	369·66 days
Neptune	4,498,000,000 km	367·49 days
Pluto	5,900,000,000 km	366·74 days

Retrograde motion of superior planets

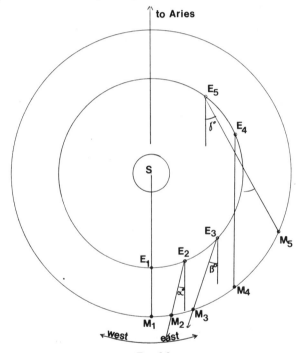

FIG. 9.9

Let Figure 9.9 represent the projection of the orbits of the earth and any superior planet onto the plane of the equinoctial. These will be very nearly circular. E_1, M_1 and S are the positions of the earth, the planet and the sun at an opposition of the planet. Let the S.H.A. of the sun be zero (Spring equinox). The sun therefore at this time lies in the same direction as the first point of Aries.

Remembering that the superior planet will have an angular velocity in orbit that is less than that of the earth let E_2 and M_2

represent the positions of the earth and the planet some time later. The line of sight from the earth to the planet has rotated to the west, that is clockwise as viewed from the north pole of the sphere, through an angle $\alpha°$. The angle $\alpha°$ is now the increase in S.H.A. of the planet so that the S.H.A. is now $180° + \alpha°$. If the planet is projected onto the background of the stars as viewed from the earth it will have appeared to have moved westwards against the stars.

As the earth curves around its orbit the rate of increase of the S.H.A. of the planet will decrease, until the S.H.A. reaches a maximum. This has occurred at E_3M_3 when the S.H.A. of the planet is $180° + \beta°$. This is the stationary point.

Thereafter the line of sight commences to rotate to the eastwards and the S.H.A. decreases. At E_4M_4 the S.H.A. has decreased back to $180°$ again and the projected position of the planet onto the background of the stars have moved to the east to its original position, as at E_1M_1. At E_5M_5 the S.H.A. has continued to decrease and is now equal to $180° - \gamma°$.

As with the inferior planet when the projected position of the planet on the background of the stars is moving westwards the planet is said to have retrograde motion. When it is moving eastwards it is said to have direct motion.

A stationary point will occur after quadrature west and the next stationary point will be before quadrature east. Between these two positions the planet will have retrograde motion. From then on until the planet reaches the next stationary point after quadrature west the motion will be direct.

Phases and brightness of superior planets

A superior planet can show a small change of phase, although the effect is only discernable in Mars being the nearest superior planet. At conjunction and at opposition an observer on the earth will be able to see the whole of the sunlit half of the planet. The planet is therefore full at these times. The least amount of the sunlit portion of the planet visible occurs at the positions of quadrature when the planet is gibbous.

The effect of change of phase is too small to have much effect on the planet's brightness. This is governed by the distance of the planet from the earth. Thus it will appear brightest at opposition and least bright at conjunction.

Loops of regression

If the path of a planet against the background of the stars is plotted, retrograde motion causes the planet to retrace its normal eastwards motion. At the same time however, slow changes in declination make the path traced out appear as an S-shape or a closed loop. These are referred to as loops of regression.

The relationship between the 'v' correction and the relative motion of planets

We have seen that the 'v' correction is necessary because when using the increment tables in the almanac to find the G.H.A. of planets we use the table that is computed for use with the sun. If the planet is changing its G.H.A. at the same rate as the sun then this will give correct results. If this is so we also say that the planet must also be changing its S.H.A. at the same rate as the sun. Remembering that the 'v' correction is the difference between the hourly change of hour angle of the planet and the change of 15° per hour assumed in the increment tables, then it follows that it may also be thought of as the difference between the hourly change of S.H.A. of the sun and that of the planet.

The hourly change of S.H.A. of the sun may be found by:

$$\frac{360°}{\text{length of tropical year in hours}}$$

This comes to 2·46′ of arc per hour, and the S.H.A. is always decreasing. In other words the sun has a direct motion relative to the fixed stars of 2·46′ per hour. From the foregoing when the planet has a similar direct motion the value of the 'v' correction will be zero.

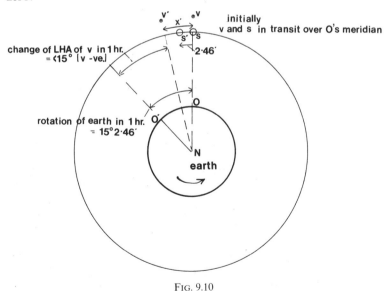

Fig. 9.10

Now from Figure 9.10, if the planet has a direct motion equal to x′ where x is greater than 2·46′ per hour, the change in hour angle in one hour will be decreased from that of the sun by an amount given by $x - 2.46'$. In this case the 'v' correction will be negative of value $x - 2.46'$. Similarly if the planet has a direct motion relative to the fixed stars equal to y, where y is less than $2.46'$ per hour, or if the planet has a retrograde motion of z' per hour, then the change of hour angle in one hour will be increased from that of the sun by an amount given by $2.46' - y$ if the motion is direct, or $2.46' + z$ if the motion is retrograde (see Fig. 9.11).

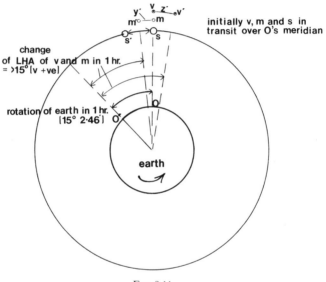

FIG. 9.11

In this case the 'v' correction will be positive and of value $(2.46' - y)$, or $(2.46' + z)$ as the case may be.

If the planet has no motion relative the fixed stars then the 'v' correction will be $2.46'$ positive. Consider the possibility of using the increment tables of the sun to find the G.H.A. of the first point of Aries. A constant 'v' correction of $+2.46'$ would have to be applied. Inspect the increment table for Aries to see that the hourly change of hour angle is in fact $15° 02.46'$.

The only navigational planet which ever has a direct motion greater than that of the sun is Venus. This is the only planet in the almanac therefore to have a negative 'v' correction at any time. All superior planets when their motion is direct have change of S.H.A. less than that of the sun therefore their 'v' corrections are always positive. Any inferior planet must of course at some time during its synodic period have direct motion greater than that of the sun.

Thus to sum up:
Superior planets always have positive 'v' corrections.
Venus has a negative 'v' correction when its motion is direct and
   greater than that of the sun.
Venus has a positive 'v' correction when it has direct motion less
   than that of the sun and when it has retrograde motion.

Or
When any superior planet is moving with direct or with retrograde
   motion its 'v' correction is positive.
When Venus is moving eastwards relative to the sun, i.e. when its
   S.H.A. is decreasing at a greater rate than the sun, then the 'v'
   correction is negative.
When Venus is moving westwards relative to the sun, i.e. when the
   S.H.A. is decreasing at a lesser rate than that of the sun, or the
   S.H.A. is increasing, then the 'v' correction will be positive.

The value and sign of 'v' at times during the synodic revolution
are shown in Figure 9.12.

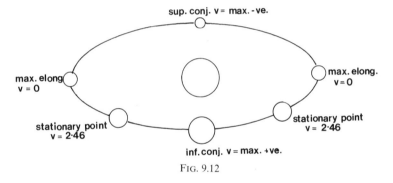

FIG. 9.12

EXERCISE

1. State Kepler's laws.

2. In what ways are Kepler's laws inaccurate in describing the
motion of the planets?

3. Explain why for any given radius of orbit of a satellite body
there is only one orbital velocity that the body may have.

4. Explain the circumstances in which a satellite can remain
permanently at an observer's zenith, if the observer is stationary.

5. Define:
   (a) conjunction,
   (b) elongation,
   (c) sidereal period of a planet,

(d) synodic period of a planet,

(e) quadrature of a planet.

6. Explain the variations in the brightness of Venus.

7. Explain why Venus exhibits phases. Explain the relationship between the phase of Venus and its brightness.

8. How is it possible for a superior planet to show a change of phase?

9. Explain the phenomenon of retrograde motion of planets.

10. What is the 'v' correction for? Explain why it is always positive for a superior planet and sometimes negative and sometimes positive for Venus. Relate your answer to the rate of change of the planet's S.H.A.

Given on a certain date, G.H.A. moon 13h = 135° 26·9′, G.H.A. moon 14h = 149° 56·7′, what is the value of the 'v' correction?

CHAPTER 10

THE PROJECTION OF THE CELESTIAL SPHERE

The conversion of co-ordinates in the equinoctial system to co-ordinates in the horizon system, can be done approximately by the use of scale drawing. Although scale figures have no significance in practical navigation, the ability to represent a navigational problem by an approximate figure is essential to the understanding of the computations involved. The two projections which are commonly used for this purpose are the stereographic and the equidistant projections. They are similar to each other and both are natural projections.

The stereographic and the equidistant projections
The plane of projection in both cases is a great circle on the celestial sphere. Such a great circle, i.e. one that forms the plane of projection, is called the primitive circle. Two primitives are commonly used, the observer's meridian and antimeridian, and the rational horizon. It is usual to produce a figure on the plane of the rational horizon.

The stereographic projection
The point of projection in this figure is one of the poles of the primitive. Thus if a figure on the plane of the rational horizon is required then the point of projection is the observer's nadir.

In Figure 10.1 let the plane NS be that of the rational horizon. Z is the observer's zenith and P the observer's nadir. The circle NZS is a vertical circle (i.e. one that is at right angles to the rational horizon), which can be taken to be the one that passes through the poles. It is therefore also the observer's meridian. N will be the north point of the horizon and S the south point. The points A, B, C, D, E, F, G, H, I, and J are equidistant points on the meridian. If lines of projection are drawn from P, the point of projection, these points will project onto the rational horizon at a, b, c, d, e, f, g, h, i, and j respectively. However the distances ab, bc, cd, etc., will not be uniform but will decrease towards the centre of the rational horizon. The zenith, Z, will project onto the centre of the primitive at z.

A most important property of the stereographic projection is that all circles great and small drawn on the sphere will project as circles or straight lines onto the plane of the primitive. The figure

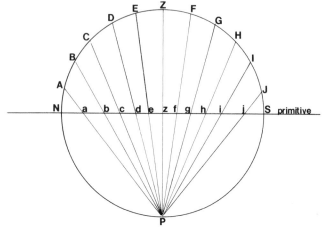

FIG. 10.1

is easily drawn therefore with compasses and ruler. The problem of drawing any particular circle becomes a problem of finding the point of projection of the centre of the circle and the projected radius.

Imagine how the following circles would project onto the rational horizon:

(a) *Vertical circles*
All vertical circles pass through the point of projection, and the zenith. If the point of projection lies in the plane of a great circle then that great circle must appear as a straight line from this point. Thus all vertical circles, including the observer's meridian must project as straight lines radiating from the zenith, because the planes of all vertical circles contain the point of projection.

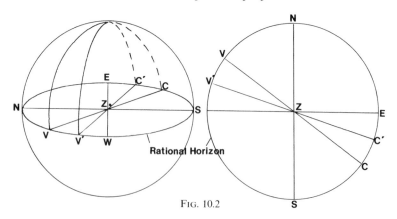

FIG. 10.2

The Prime Vertical will cut the observer's meridian in a right angle at Z.

(b) *Circles of equal Altitude*

The centres of all circles of equal altitude lie on the line joining the zenith and the nadir. Any point on such a line will project at the centre of the rational horizon at Z. All circles of equal altitude will appear therefore as concentric circles centred upon Z on the plane of the rational horizon.

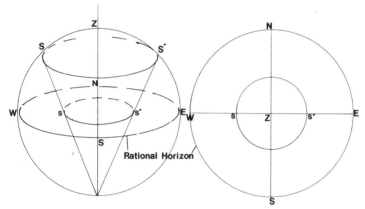

FIG. 10.3

(c) *Great circles*

(i) The equinoctial. This is a special case amongst great circles because the pole always lies on the meridian, and it must always cut the meridian in a right angle. It must therefore pass through the poles of the meridian which are the West and East points of the rational horizon. The pole of the equinoctial will be projected onto the straight line which is the projection of the vertical circle passing through the pole, i.e. the meridian.

In Figure 10.4 let QQ′ be the equinoctial. (The inclination of the equinoctial to the rational horizon will be the latitude.) Let N, S, W, and E be the north, south, east, and west points of the rational horizon. N′ is the nadir and Z the zenith.

The projections of P, Q, and Q′ will be at p, q, and q′. The projected circle will be therefore qWq′E. The less the inclination of the equinoctial to the rational horizon the closer will the projected equinoctial approach the rational horizon. Note that the centre of the projected circle is not the projected position of the pole.

(ii) The celestial meridians. The observer's meridian will be projected as a straight line through Z, because the point of projection lies in the plane of this great circle.

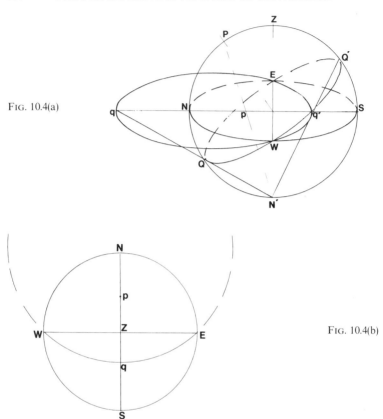

Fig. 10.4(a)

Fig. 10.4(b)

All other meridians will project as circles whose centres must be found in order to draw the projected meridians. If the two meridians which together form a great circle through P, W, and E (i.e. the two meridians whose L.H.A.s are 090° and 270°), are projected then the circle would appear as in Figure 10.5. (Note the similarity to Figure 10.4.) Point P is the projection of the north pole and point P' the projection of the south pole. All meridians pass through these two poles therefore the projections of all the meridians must pass through P and P'. The locus of all the centres of such circles is the line LL' at right angles to the observer's meridian at O, the centre of the projected meridian WPE.

(d) *Small circles* (*circles of declination*)
In Figure 10.6 let the small circle RR' be a parallel of declination which is circumpolar. Let LL' be a parallel of declination that is not circumpolar. QQ' represents the equinoctial.

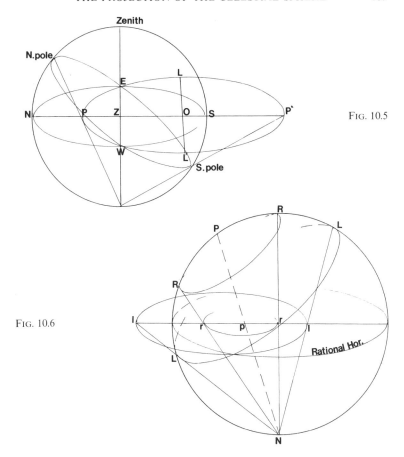

FIG. 10.5

FIG. 10.6

The circle RR' will project as a circle the whole of which lies inside the rational horizon. The non-circumpolar declination circle will project as a circle which lies partially outside the rational horizon. The projected positions at which the circle cuts the meridian and the horizon will define the circle. In the case of the circumpolar circle the centre of the projected circle will be at the projected position of the pole. This will not be so for the non-circumpolar circle, however, the centre of these receding from the projected position of the pole, as the declination decreases.

To construct a stereographic projection on the plane of the rational horizon

In Figure 10.7 let the circle N'NzS be the observer's meridian (and antimeridian). z is the observer's zenith and N' the observer's nadir, which is the point of projection. Let the latitude of the observer be 40° N. Then the point where the equinoctial cuts the meridian will be 40° to the southwards of z, at q. The north celestial pole, p, is 90° to the north of q.

It is required to represent on the figure,
(a) the circle of declination of 30° N.,
(b) the celestial meridian of a body whose L.H.A. is 050°.

It is required to find from the figure,
(a) the altitude,
(b) the azimuth.

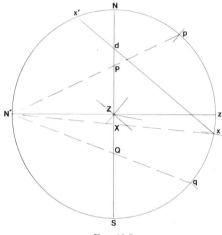

FIG. 10.7

The rational horizon in the figure is NS. The plane of the rational horizon lies perpendicularly to the page and therefore appears as a straight line. If lines of projection are drawn from N' to the points p, z, x and q then the positions where they cut the rational horizon at P, Z, X' and Q, are the projected positions of these points. The lines of projection are shown as broken lines in the figure.

If the small circle of declination of x is drawn it will appear as xx', where the arc qx is the declination 30°. The position where it cuts NS is shown as d.

The figure is now imagined to rotate through 90° to bring the plane of the rational horizon into the plane of the page. The figure will now appear as in Figure 10.8. In practice Figures 10.7 and 10.8 can be superimposed (see worked example).

The points P, X', and Q are projected points on the observer's meridian which now appears as a straight line NS. The two points d' and d" are the two points where the arc of declination cuts the rational horizon and are found by drawing a line through d parallel to WE, the prime vertical.

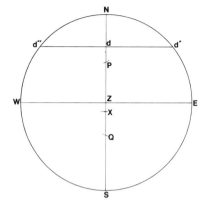

FIG. 10.8

The circle which is the projected equinoctial can now be drawn through W, Q and E by finding the centre, which is equidistant from the three points. The centre, by symmetry will lie on the meridian or the meridian produced. It can be located by bisecting the straight line WQ or QE. The point where the perpendicular bisector cuts the meridian is the centre of the circle.

Similarly draw the circle which represents the arc of declination. This circle will pass through d', X', and d'' and again the centre lies on the meridian or the meridian produced, and can be found by besecting the straight line d''X' or X'd'. The figure will now appear as in Figure 10.9 in which the construction lines are shown.

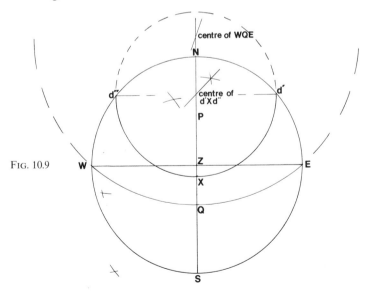

FIG. 10.9

Find the centre of the circle through W, P and E. This will lie on the meridian or the meridian produced. It can be located by bisecting the straight line WP or PE. Where the perpendicular bisector cuts the meridian will be the centre of the circle. Let this be point O. Through O draw a line at right angles to the meridian. This line is the locus line on which the centres of all the celestial meridians lie. To draw the required meridian, lay off from the meridian at P an angle equal to the hour angle (360° – the hour angle if the body is rising). Make sure that this angle is constructed on the correct side of the meridian, to the west if the body is setting (hour angle less than 180°), and to the east if the body is rising (hour angle greater than 180°). Draw a line at right angles to this line so drawn at P to cut the locus line. Let it cut the locus line at C. C is the centre of the required meridian, draw the circle through P to cut the arc of declination to give the position of the body X. The figure now appears as in Figure 10.10.

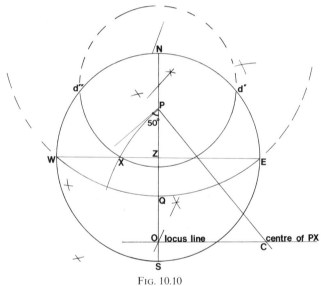

FIG. 10.10

The vertical circle which passes through the body can now be drawn in as a straight line radiating from Z. The final figure appears as in Figure 10.11.

To measure altitude or zenith distance
The length of the vertical circle ZX represents the zenith distance, but this must be measured against the scale along the meridian which is a variable scale. Draw in the arc of a circle of equal altitude through the body, X, to cut the meridian at Y in Figure 10.11. Using

the figure as if it were on the plane of the meridian (see Fig. 10.7), from the point of projection W (N′ in Fig. 10.7) project a line through Y onto the primitive at y′. The arc Ey′ is the zenith distance and the arc Sy′ is the altitude.

To measure the azimuth
Measure the angle PZX with a protractor.

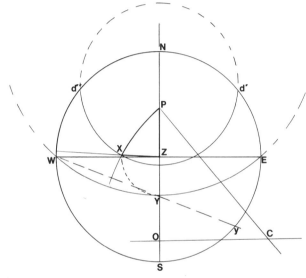

FIG. 10.11

Note
If the zenith distance is given in the problem, X may be located by drawing in the circle of equal altitude centred upon Z and radius, the zenith distance. The body is located where it cuts the arc of declination or the meridian of the body.

Example
Figure 10.12 represents on the plane of the rational horizon the following conditions.

      Latitude 35° S.   Declination 10° N.   L.H.A. 325°

Construction lines are left out for clarity and the original figure on the plane of the meridian (see Fig. 10.7), is incorporated in the figure. Where small letters are used in brackets they refer to the figure drawn on the plane of the meridian.

The equidistant projection
This projection is a natural projection which is very similar to the

stereographic. The only difference is that the point of projection instead of lying on the sphere at the pole of the primitive, lies outside the sphere at a distance of $1/\sqrt{2} \times$ radius of sphere from the pole of the primitive.

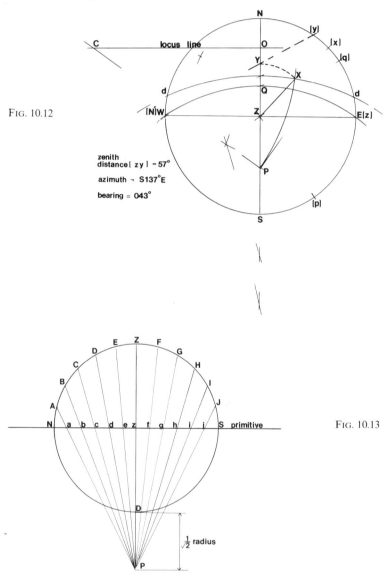

Fig. 10.12

zenith
distance| zy | = 57°

azimuth ⌐ S137°E

bearing = 043°

Fig. 10.13

In Figure 10.13 the points A, B, C, D, E, F, G, H, I, and J are equidistant points on the observer's meridian. Z is the zenith and D the nadir. These points are projected onto the plane of the rational horizon, NS, from the point of projection P at positions a, b, c, d, e, f, g, h, i, and j. The advantage of the equidistant projection is however that the distances ab, bc, cz, zd, etc., can without material error be considered constant. Therefore when the observer's meridian is projected onto the plane of the rational horizon as a straight line a constant scale is available along this line, and used as a scale of latitude or declination or altitude. The important property that all circles great and small are projected as circles or straight lines is retained, thus the projection has all the advantages of the stereographic projection with the added advantage of a constant scale along a vertical circle. The general appearance of the projection is the same as the stereographic and Figures 10.2 to 10.6 can be consulted for a guide to how the various circles will project.

To produce an equidistant projection of the celestial sphere on the plane of the rational horizon
The following conditions will be used,

Latitude 40° N. Declination 30° N. L.H.A. 050°

Figure 10.14 illustrates the given information on the plane of the observer's meridian. This diagram however is given for reference only and is not necessary to the problem.

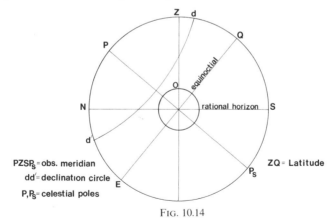

PZSP$_S$ = obs. meridian
dd' = declination circle
P,P$_S$ = celestial poles

ZQ = Latitude

FIG. 10.14

Procedure
1. Draw a circle to represent the rational horizon. It will be convenient to choose a radius of nine units, each unit representing an arc of 10°. Draw in the observer's meridian which conventionally

runs vertically on the page. The points where the meridian meets the rational horizon can be labelled N and S and the meridian divided into 18 equal parts between N and S. This will be the constant scale of latitude or declination. Note that any vertical circle can be so divided and the same scale therefore can be used for altitude or zenith distance. Draw in the prime vertical through the centre of the circle at right angles to the meridian. The points where the prime vertical meets the horizon are labelled W and E. The projection of the zenith is at the centre of the circle and is labelled Z. Figure 10.15 shows the figure drawn so far.

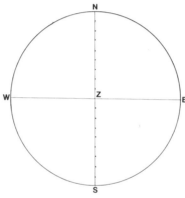

FIG. 10.15

2. To draw the equinoctial. Mark in a point Q where the equinoctial cuts the meridian. If the latitude is north then Q must be to the south of Z. If the latitude is south then Q must be to the north of Z. The arc of the meridian ZQ is equal to the latitude on the constant scale of the meridian, thus simply measure the amount of the latitude north or south of Z along the meridian. The position of the pole can then be marked 90° away from Q along the meridian. If the latitude is north then the north pole will be elevated, and if the latitude is south then it will be the south pole that is visible.

The equinoctial must also pass through W and E, thus with these three points through which the circle passes the circle is defined. The centre must be equidistant from the three points. Find this point and draw in the circle. (The centre must by symmetry lie on the meridian. It can be located by bisecting the straight line WQ or QE. Where the bisector cuts the meridian is the centre of the circle. Figure 10.16 shows the figure so far.

3. To draw in the arc of declination. Mark in a point d where the arc of declination cuts the meridian. The distance of d from Q will be the declination of the body as measured on the scale along the

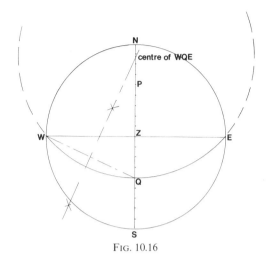

FIG. 10.16

meridian. The point will be either to the north of Q or to the south depending upon the name of the declination.

Two more points through which the circle passes can be found by ascertaining the bearing of the body when it crosses the horizon, i.e. when it sets (or rises). This may be extracted from amplitude tables which are entered with latitude and declination. Alternatively the amplitude can be calculated by the formula:

sine amplitude = sine declination × sec latitude.

(See 'The Amplitude Problem' for explanation of this formula.)

The bearing of the body expressed in quadrantal notation is the complement of the amplitude.

Construct an angle at Z to represent the bearing of the body when rising and when setting and draw in the two vertical circles. The points where they cut the rational horizon will be the positions of the body when rising and setting and will give two points through which to draw the declination circle. Draw a circle through these two points and through the point d. Find the centre by constructing the perpendicular bisector of the line d″d or dd′ to cut the observer's meridian. The figure now appears as in Figure 10.17.

4. To draw the celestial meridian through the body. Find the centre of the projected meridian through W, P and E. This must by symmetry lie on the meridian or the meridian produced, and can be located by bisecting WP or PE. Where the perpendicular bisector cuts the meridian will be the centre of the circle. Let this be called O. Draw a line at right angles to the meridian through O. This is the locus of the centres of all the meridians. Divide the equinoctial into equal parts to represent a scale of hour angle, and

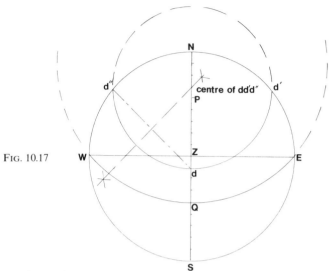

FIG. 10.17

mark a point where the required meridian crosses the equinoctial. Let this point be called s. Construct the perpendicular bisector of the line sP to cut the locus line at C. With centre C draw a circle through P and s to cut the arc of declination. The intersection of the meridian of the body and the arc of declination is the position of the body X. The figure now appears as in Figure 10.18.

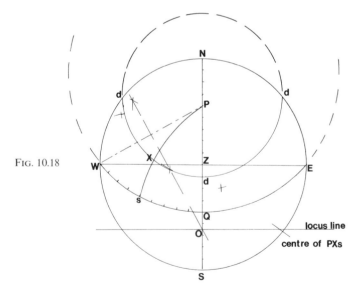

FIG. 10.18

To measure the altitude or zenith distance

Draw in the vertical circle which passes through the body. This is shown as ZA in Figure 10.19. The length of ZX measured against the constant scale of the meridian will give the zenith distance. The length XA will give the altitude.

To measure the bearing

Measure the angle PZX with a protractor. Figure 10.19 shows the completed figure in which all construction lines are deleted for clarity.

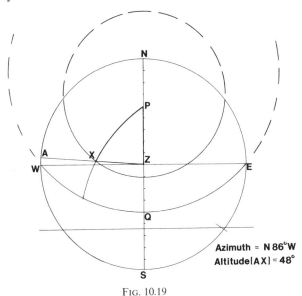

Azimuth = N 86°W
Altitude(AX) = 48°

FIG. 10.19

Example

Figure 10.20 gives a figure on the plane of the rational horizon drawn with an equidistant projection for the following conditions,

Latitude 20° S.   Declination 50° S.   L.H.A. 320°

Drawing sketch figures

Even when scale drawing is not required a student should have the ability to sketch a rough diagram to illustrate a calculation involving the PZX triangle. In doing this it should be sufficient to take note of the following considerations.

(i) Whether the latitude is north or south.

(ii) Whether the declination is of the same name or of opposite name to the latitude.

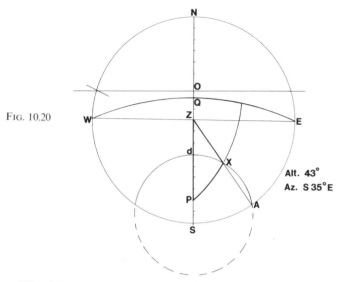

FIG. 10.20

(iii) If the declination is of the same name as the latitude whether it is greater than or less than the latitude.

(iv) Whether the body is circumpolar or not.

Study the following diagrams with reference to these conditions and note the differences between the figures given for each set of conditions.

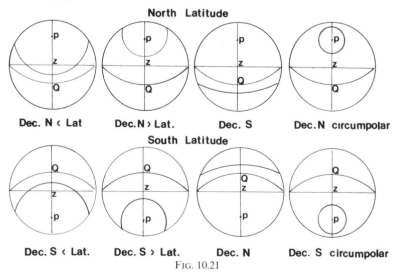

FIG. 10.21

The ability to illustrate a navigational problem with a figure approximately to scale, is essential to the solution of many theoretical problems on the principles of navigation. In general these can be solved by illustrating the appropriate PZX triangle and using the spherical trigonometrical formulae to solve from the parts given in the question. Napier's rules for the solution of right angled and quadrantal spherical triangles, figure largely in the range of problems encountered. In the PZX triangle a 90° angle or side will result from any of the following.

(a) An hour angle of 90° or 270°, giving an angle P of 90°.
(b) A body on the prime vertical (bearing 090° T. or 270° T.), giving an angle Z of 90°.
(c) A body at maximum azimuth, giving an angle X of 90°.
(d) A declination of 0°, giving a side PX of 90°.
(e) A latitude of 0°, giving a side PZ of 90°.
(f) A body setting or rising, giving a zenith distance (ZX), of 90°.

If any one or more of the above conditions are satisfied in a problem then Napier's rules may be used to solve the triangle.

Certain deductions may be made from the information given in a problem, as to the conditions of latitude and declination. Only if these deductions are made correctly can the appropriate figure be drawn. A familiarity with the figures given in Figure 10.21 will enable these deductions to be made. The following notes may be found helpful in this respect.

If a body crosses the prime vertical, i.e. bears due east or west, the latitude of the observer must have the same name as, and be of greater value than the declination.

If a body appears circumpolar to an observer, his latitude must be the same name as the declination, and the polar distance must be less than the latitude.

A body rising with a northerly amplitude must have a northerly declination. A body rising with a southerly amplitude must have a south declination.

A body which has a maximum azimuth must have a declination of the same name as the latitude and of greater value than the latitude. (It may be circumpolar or not.)

If declination is named the same as the latitude, then the hour angle on rising or setting must be greater than 90°. If the declination is opposite to latitude then the hour angle must be less than 90° on rising or setting.

If the declination is zero then the body will rise bearing due east and set bearing due west, the hour angle on rising and setting being 90°.

There is a very large variety of problems which may be asked to test theoretical knowledge of the PZX triangle. Some examples are now worked for illustration.

Example 1

The sun is on the equinoctial in September, and to an observer in position 40° N. 60° E. it bears 127°. Find the G.H.A. of the sun.

The declination of the sun is 0° as the sun is at the first point of Libra. From the PZX triangle the angle P can be found and hence the L.H.A. Application of the longitude will then give the G.H.A.

In triangle PZX, by Napier's rules,

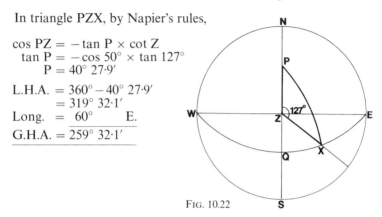

$$\cos PZ = -\tan P \times \cot Z$$
$$\tan P = -\cos 50° \times \tan 127°$$
$$P = 40° \ 27·9'$$

$$\begin{aligned} \text{L.H.A.} &= 360° - 40° \ 27·9' \\ &= 319° \ 32·1' \end{aligned}$$

$$\text{Long.} = \ \ 60° \qquad \text{E.}$$

$$\overline{\text{G.H.A.} = 259° \ 32·1'}$$

Fig. 10.22

Example 2

The sun crosses the observer's prime vertical to the west of the meridian with a true altitude of 14° 25'. If the declination is 10° 19·7' N., find the latitude of the observer and the L.H.A. of the sun.

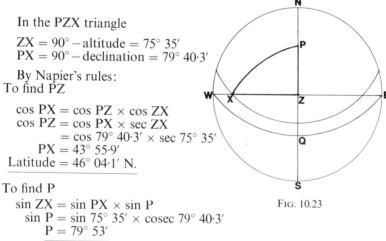

In the PZX triangle

$$ZX = 90° - \text{altitude} = 75° \ 35'$$
$$PX = 90° - \text{declination} = 79° \ 40·3'$$

By Napier's rules:
To find PZ

$$\cos PX = \cos PZ \times \cos ZX$$
$$\cos PZ = \cos PX \times \sec ZX$$
$$= \cos 79° \ 40·3' \times \sec 75° \ 35'$$
$$PX = 43° \ 55·9'$$
$$\text{Latitude} = 46° \ 04·1' \text{ N.}$$

To find P

$$\sin ZX = \sin PX \times \sin P$$
$$\sin P = \sin 75° \ 35' \times \operatorname{cosec} 79° \ 40·3'$$
$$P = 79° \ 53'$$

Fig. 10.23

As the body is to the west of the observer this equals L.H.A.

Example 3

Two stars are observed to rise simultaneously to an observer in latitude 27° N. The declination of star A is 16° N. The S.H.A. of star B is 60° greater than that of star A. Find the declination of star B.

Two PZX triangles must be shown here, and two formulae solved. The angle P in triangle PZB is 60° less than angle P in triangle PZA. Solution of triangle PZA for angle P will therefore enable angle P in triangle PZB to be found.

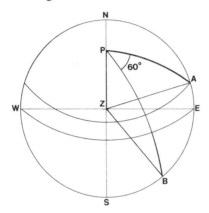

FIG. 10.24

Thus by Napier's rules in triangle PZA:

$$\cos P = -\cot PZ \times \cot PA$$
$$= -\cot 63° \times \cot 74°$$
$$= -81° \, 35\cdot9'$$
$$= 98° \, 24\cdot1' \text{ (angle in second quadrant)}$$

Angle P in triangle PZB $= 98° \, 24\cdot1 - 60°$
$$= 38° \, 24\cdot1'$$

In triangle PZB:

$$\cos P = -\cot PZ \times \cot PB$$
$$\cot PB = -\cos P \times \tan PZ$$
$$= -\cos 38° \, 24\cdot1' \times \tan 63°$$
$$PB = -33° \, 01\cdot8'$$
$$= 146° \, 58\cdot2'$$

Thus

declination $= 56° \, 58\cdot2'$ S.

Maximum azimuth

If the declination of the body is of the same name and of greater value than the latitude, then the azimuth as the body rises will increase. It will reach a maximum when the body reaches position X in Figure 10.25. It will thereafter decrease to zero when the body crosses the meridian and will reach another maximum with the body to the west of the meridian, finally decreasing as the body sets. At maximum azimuth the vertical circle through the body will be tangential to the declination circle. Angle X in the PZX triangle will therefore be a right angle.

Example 4

Find the maximum easterly azimuth of a star whose true altitude at lower transit is 10°, to an observer in latitude 35° N.

At lower transit:

$$\text{latitude} = \text{true altitude} + \text{polar distance}$$
$$\text{(see Meridian Altitudes)}$$
$$\text{polar distance} = 35° - 10° = 25°$$
$$\text{declination} = 65° \text{ N.}$$

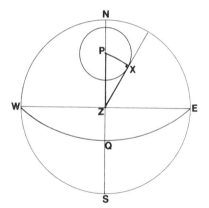

Fig. 10.25

In triangle PZX, by Napier's rules:

$$\sin PX = \sin PZ \times \sin Z$$
$$\sin Z = \sin PX \times \text{cosec } PZ$$
$$= \sin 25° \times \text{cosec } 55°$$
$$Z = 31° \ 03\cdot6'$$
$$\text{Maximum azimuth} = \text{N. } 31° \text{ E.}$$

EXERCISE 10

1. Find the L.A.T. when the sun will bear due east to an observer in latitude 35° N., if the declination of the sun is 23° 27′ N.

2. Find the maximum easterly azimuth of a star of declination 56° 15′ N. to an observer in latitude 45° 30′ N. Find the time

interval until the following meridian passage of the star over the observer's upper meridian.

3. At the September equinox the sun bore 236° T. to an observer in position 47° 18′ N. 149° 05′ E. Find the G.H.A. of the first point of Aries.

4. On June 25th an observer had the star Pollux in his zenith. Calculate the true altitude of the star Regulus at that time and its true bearing.

5. The sun crossed the observer's prime vertical to the west of the meridian at 4h 20m 16s G.M.T. on March 25th with a true altitude of 31° 15′. Calculate the observer's position.

6. Two stars are observed to rise simultaneously to an observer in latitude 36° N. The declination of star is 35° N. The S.H.A. of star B is 38° greater than that of star A. Find the decination of star B.

7. The change in azimuth of the sun between rising and crossing the prime vertical of a stationary observer is 38°. If the decination of the sun is 23° 27′ S., find the observer's latitude. Find also its change of hour angle during the period.

8. Given that the L.M.T. of a star's meridian passage to an observer in latitude 40° N. is 1200 hrs, find the L.M.T. of the star when it crosses the prime vertical to the east and to the west of the meridian. Declination of the star is 30° N.

9. If the declination of the sun is 20° N., find its hour angle and its altitude when it is on the prime vertical bearing 090° to an observer in 50° N.

CHAPTER 11

THE MOTION OF THE HEAVENS

All celestial bodies have an apparent motion, when viewed from the earth, which is a result of:

(a) the bodies' own motion,
(b) the earth's motion.

Of the two the earth's motion has the most apparent effect.

The earth's motion within the solar system
There are two motions to be considered.

1. The earth's rotation.
2. The earth's revolution in orbit.

The earth is rotating about one of its diameters, which is called the axis of rotation. The rotation is anticlockwise when viewed from the earth's north pole and this can be construed as a west to east rotation. The period of the rotation is the sidereal day of 23h 56m 04s (see Chapter 7 on 'Time').

Because of this rotation, to an observer on the earth's surface, every body in the heavens appears to rotate in the opposite direction, i.e. from east to west in the same period. To any observer on the earth most of the heavenly bodies will be visible for only part of this period, being hidden by the earth's mass when moving around the opposite side of the earth to the observer. This gives rise to the phenomenon of rising and setting as the bodies come into view and go out of view respectively, and to the phenomenon of the succession of day and night as the sun rises and sets.

The apparent path across the sky depends upon the latitude of the observer, and upon the decination of the body.

It is convenient to consider the celestial sphere as rotating from east to west, and the earth to have no rotation. If this was the case the celestial sphere would appear to rotate about an axis which is coincident with the earth's axis. The poles of the axis of the celestial sphere would be the points on the sphere where the earth's axis produced meets the sphere, and the whole sphere would appear to rotate about these points once in the period of rotation of the earth. Only the celestial poles would appear motionless relative to the horizon.

Imagine an observer on the earth's equator. The celestial poles would appear on the north and south points of the observer's rational horizon.

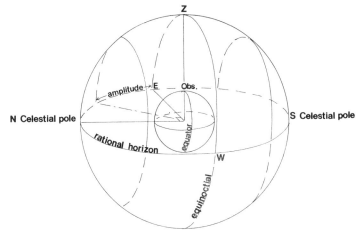

FIG. 11.1

In Figure 11.1 the celestial equator passes through the observer's zenith. All the parallels of declination, which can be thought of as representing the daily paths of celestial bodies around the sphere, are perpendicular to the rational horizon. Therefore every body as it rises or sets will be moving in a direction at right angles to the horizon. A body which lies on the equinoctial, i.e. with declination zero will rise in a direction due east from the observer and set bearing due west. Furthermore we can also say that all bodies having a northerly declination must rise to the north of east and set to the north of west. All bodies having a southerly declination must rise to the south of east and set to the south of west. It can also be seen that in this case the bearing of the body when it is rising or setting expressed in quadrantal notation will be the complement of the declination. The amplitude therefore will be equal to the declination.

The observer's horizon in the diagram cuts all circles of declination into two equal parts. Thus every body must be above the horizon for half of the rotation period and below it for the other half. This must of course apply to the sun also, thus any observer on the equator will experience equal day and night whatever the declination of the sun, i.e. at any time of the year.

Imagine now an observer at either of the earth's poles. The celestial pole in this case will lie at the observer's zenith, and the rational horizon will coincide with the equinoctial. All circles of declination will be parallel to the equinoctial. All bodies therefore, as the earth rotates will appear to describe a circle in the sky parallel to the horizon. Only a body with decination the same name as the latitude will ever be visible to such an observer. The altitude at which a body circles the sky will be equal to the bodies' declination. Of course no rising or setting phenomena will occur. This is illustrated in Figure 11.2.

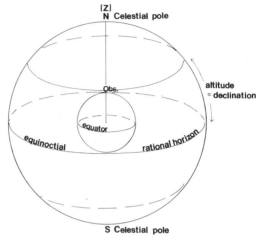

FIG. 11.2

At intermediate latitudes the motions will be more complex. Let Figure 11.3 represent an observer in north latitude and the sphere as it would appear to him.

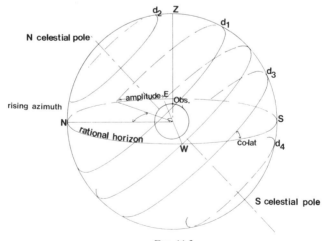

FIG. 11.3

The celestial pole will now appear in the sky bearing north, and between the horizon and the zenith. (Later it will be shown that the altitude of the pole above the horizon is equal to the latitude of the observer.) The circles of declination will run obliquely to the horizon. The angle between the horizon and the direction of the circles of declination will be equal to the complement of the latitude. When a body is rising or setting, its direction of motion against the sky will be at this angle to the horizon.

Even a casual look at the diagram shows that the circles of declination do not have equal arcs above and below the horizon. The only declination circle which is cut into two equal halves by the horizon is the equinoctial. Thus any body with declination 0° will, no matter what the latitude of the observer be above the horizon for exactly half of the period of rotation and below the horizon for the other half. Hence when the sun's declination is zero there is equal day and night for any observer.

A circle of northerly declination, i.e. of same name as the latitude, such as d₁, will have more than half of its arc above the horizon. A body with such a declination will therefore spend more than half the period of rotation visible to the observer. The greater north the declination the greater will be the proportion of its arc above the horizon, until at the point when the complement of the declination becomes less than the latitude, the whole of the declination circle lies above the horizon. The body is then said to be circumpolar.

Any circle of southerly declination, i.e. of declination opposite name to the latitude, will have the greater part of its arc below the horizon and will thus be hidden from the observer for most of its track. The greater south is the declination the less will be the period spent above the horizon until at the point when the complement of the declination becomes less than the latitude, the whole of the circle lies below the horizon. This gives rise to the phenomenon of total darkness for observers in high latitudes north during the northern winter and high latitudes south during the northern summer (see 'The Seasons').

From the diagram note that any body of declination 0° must rise bearing due east and set bearing due west. This will not be affected by the value of the observer's latitude. Furthermore all bodies with a northerly declination must rise to the north of east and set to the north of west. All bodies with southerly declination must rise to the south of east and set to the south of west.

Effect of change of latitude on the length of daylight
If in Figure 11.3 the earth's axis is imagined to tilt so that the pole approaches Z then the circles of declination which must remain perpendicular to the axis will approach parallelism with the horizon as the pole approaches Z. As this happens any circle of northerly declination will have less and less of its arc below the horizon and

as the observer moves north more and more bodies become circumpolar.

Consider the circle of declination of the sun at any instant when it is north of the equinoctial. Then as the observer moves north the sun's declination circle has an increasing amount of its arc above the horizon. Thus the length of daylight increases as latitude increases, if the declination is the same name as the latitude. By the same consideration the length of daylight will decrease with increasing latitude if the declination is of opposite name to the latitude.

The length of daylight to a stationary observer—the seasons
To any stationary observer the length of daylight will change throughout the year as the sun's declination changes. Change of declination of the sun is caused by the motion of the earth in orbit. The earth describes an approximately circular orbit around the sun in a period of one year. The direction in which the earth's axis of rotation points can be considered a constant direction in space over short periods of time (see 'Precession of the Equinox'). This direction is inclined to the plane of the earth's orbit around the sun at an angle of about $66\frac{1}{2}°$. Thus as the earth moves around its orbit each pole will be alternately tilted towards and away from the sun.

At position A in Figure 11.4 the earth's north pole is tilted away from the sun. An observer situated on the sun would see the earth as in A'. The direction of the sun from the earth's centre is about $23\frac{1}{2}°$ south of the equator or of the equinoctial, which means that the sun's declination is $23\frac{1}{2}°$ S., being the amount by which the earth's axis is tilted away from the perpendicular to the earth's orbital plane. The sun will therefore be overhead to any observer in a latitude of $23\frac{1}{2}°$ S., once in each rotation of the earth. This condition occurs around December 23rd each year, and any observer in north latitude will experience his least amount of daylight at this time. A southerly observer will have his longest period of daylight. This instant in the year is called the Winter solstice, and marks the beginning of the winter season in the nothern hemisphere.

At B the earth's axis is pointing in the same direction in space but as the earth has moved 90° around its orbit this direction will be at right angles to the direction of the sun. The earth will appear from the sun as in B'. The direction of the sun from the centre of the earth will be in the plane of the equator, which means that the declination of the sun is 0°, and any observer on the equator will have the sun overhead once in each rotation of the earth, about its axis. Because the declination is zero, every point on the earth will have equal lengths of day and night. For this reason this instant is called the Spring Equinox, occurring around March 21st each year. This marks the end of the northern winter and the beginning of spring.

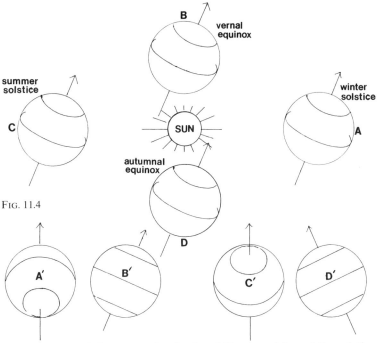

FIG. 11.4

At C the earth has moved a further 90° around its orbit and the north pole is now tilted towards the sun. The conditions in the northern and southern hemispheres on December 21st will now be reversed. The earth will appear to an observer on the sun as in C'. The direction of the sun from the centre of the earth will be $23\frac{1}{2}°$ north of the equator and thus the declination of the sun is $23\frac{1}{2}°$ N. Any latitude above $66\frac{1}{2}°$ N. will receive sunlight throughout the earth's period of rotation. To an observer in these latitudes therefore the sun will not set. This condition occurs on about June 22nd and is termed the summer solstice. This marks the end of the northern spring and the beginning of the northern summer.

At D(D') the conditions of the equinox occur again as the declination moves south and reaches 0°. This occurs around September 23rd and is called the Autumnal Equinox, marking the end of the northern summer and the beginning of autumn. During the autumn the sun's declination continues to increase southwards until the winter solstice recurs when the declination is maximum south.

The effect of the earth's orbital motion on the apparent motion of celestial bodies

The diameter of the earth's orbit is negligible compared with the vast distances of the stars from the solar system. If this were not so the movement of the earth from one side of the sun to the other would produce a movement of the closer stars against the background of the more distant stars. The absence of such motion was for centuries the stumbling block to the acceptance of the theory that the earth did in fact orbit the sun and not the sun the earth. Such change of relative position of the nearer stars can now be observed, but very precise observations are necessary. The measurable amount by which the nearer stars change their position is called the stars annual parallax and in the case of the nearest stars the amount is only in the order of 1 second of arc.

The distance of the sun from the earth is small compared with that of the stars. The earth's orbital motion around the sun means therefore that the sun will appear to change its position against the background of the stars. The sun will appear to move around the celestial sphere in the period of the earth's orbital motion, i.e. 360° around the sphere in 365 days. Thus the sun has a motion of about 1° per day against the stars. Stars which lie in the same general direction as the sun will not be visible from the earth because of the brightness of the sun's light. Stars which lie on the opposite side of the sphere to the sun will be visible at night. Thus during the year as the sun moves around the sphere different stars will be visible from the earth during the hours of darkness. The effect of this motion will be discussed in more detail under 'rates of change of hour angle' and in the chapter on 'time'.

The planet's and other minor bodies of the solar system have orbital motions of their own, which will have an effect on the bodies' position against the stars, as well as the earth's orbital motion. These effects are described under 'planetary motion'.

Change of sun's declination throughout the year

It has been shown that the sun's declination is zero at the times of the equinoxes and is changing most rapidly at these times. It is maximum at the solstices of value equal to the obliquity of the ecliptic. At times between these phenomena the declination will vary with the S.H.A. of the sun, being named South when the S.H.A. is between 0° and 180°, and North when the S.H.A. is between 180° and 360°.

Thus the declination is given by:

$$\tan \text{decl.} = \sin \text{S.H.A.} \times \tan \text{obliquity.}$$

The value throughout the year can be shown graphically as in Figure 11.5.

Rate of change of hour angle

In one year the sun appears to move completely around the celestial sphere, due to the earth's orbital motion. Stars may be regarded as fixed in position on the sphere, and the sun will therefore move

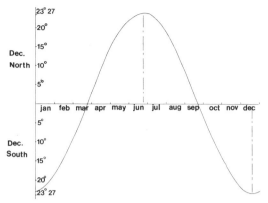

Fig. 11.5

against the background patterns of the stars. Their S.H.A.s will be constant but that of the sun must change by 360° in the period of one year. The sun is moving eastwards relative to the stars, and this motion, because S.H.A. is measured westwards from the first point of Aries, causes a decrease in the sun's S.H.A., never an increase. The daily change of S.H.A. may be found by dividing 360° by the number of days in the year. Thus the daily change of S.H.A. is about 1°. This gives a rate of change of 02·46′ per hour.

The change of local hour angle (or Greenwich hour angle), of any celestial body, in any given time is the result of:

1. The earth's rotation.
2. The body's change of S.H.A.

The main cause of change of hour angle is the rotation of the earth. The day as used for the measurement of time on earth, is defined by the earth's rotation with reference to the sun. Thus by definition, during the day the hour angle of the sun changes by exactly 360°, although during this time the earth actually rotates through almost 361°.

Let Figure 11.6 represent the earth at two positions in its orbit around the sun separated in time by one day.

If the meridian shown rotates through 360° it will not have returned to a position under the sun. Because of the earth motion around its orbit the sun will have appeared to have moved eastwards against the stars and the earth will have to rotate through the additional angle OCO′ to complete a revolution with respect to the sun. This additional angle is the sun's daily change of S.H.A. which is almost equal to 1°. The day so defined is called a solar day, during which, therefore, the earth will rotate through 361°.

It must be stressed though that in this period the change in the sun's hour angle to any observer is exactly 360°. Therefore the

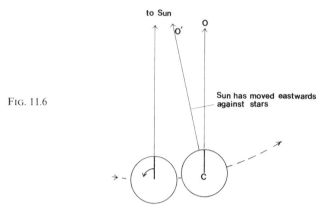

FIG. 11.6

hourly change of the sun's hour angle is 15° (or 15′ per minute of time).

The direction of rotation of the earth is such that the westerly hour angle increases.

From Figure 11.7 the change of hour angle of a fixed point on the sphere in one solar day will be 360° plus the change of S.H.A. of the sun in that period. Thus the first point of Aries changes its hour angle by 361° approximately in a solar day. This gives an hourly change of 15° 02·46′.

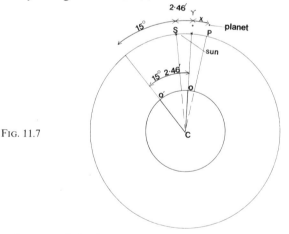

FIG. 11.7

In general the hourly change of hour angle of any body is given by:

$$15° \ 02·46 \pm x$$

where x is the body's hourly change of S.H.A. Its sign will be negative if the S.H.A. is decreasing and positive if the S.H.A. is increasing.

In Figure 11.7 consider the observer's meridian O. If at an initial point in time the sun, the first point of Aries, and a planet are over the observer's meridian, let one hour later the meridian be at O' due to the rotation of the earth. As the earth rotates through 361° in 24 hours, the angle OCO' will be 15° 02·46'.

Let also the sun to have decreased its S.H.A. by 02·46' and the planet to have increased its S.H.A. by x'.

The change of L.H.A. of the sun   = O'CS' = 15°
The change of L.H.A. of Aries   = O'CO = 15° 02·46'
The change of L.H.A. of the planet = O'CP = 15° 02·46' + x'

Effect of movement of the observer on the earth's surface

The rate of change of a body's hour angle will be modified by movement of the observer on the earth. The amount of the modification will be the rate of change of the observer's longitude. Thus if the observer is changing longitude by d' per hour, the rate of change of a body's hour angle will be given by

$$15° \ 02\cdot46' \pm x' \pm d' \text{ per hour.}$$

where x is the change of S.H.A. in one hour and d is the change in longitude in one hour.

The sign of d will be positive if the observer is moving eastwards, and negative if the observer is moving westwards.

Rate of change of altitude

Let Figure 11.8 represent the position of a body X on the sphere, and its position Y a small interval of time later. Then angle XPY is the change of hour angle in this interval.

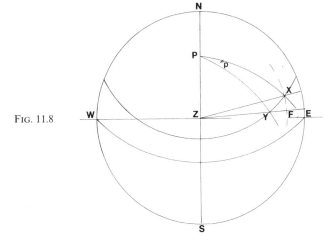

Fig. 11.8

Let the broken line represent the circle of equal altitude through X. Then YF is the change of altitude in this interval.

If the change in hour angle is very small then the triangle XYF can be treated as a plane triangle.

Then

$$YF = XY \sin \angle YXF \tag{1}$$

and

$$\angle YXF = \angle PXZ$$

(both complements of the same angle ZXY) and

$$XY = \angle p \times \cos \text{declination}$$

(expressed in minutes of arc of a great circle) substituting in 1

$$YF = \angle p \times \cos \text{dec} \times \sin PXZ \tag{2}$$

and in triangle PZX by the sine formula

$$\sin P\dot{X}Z = \frac{\sin PZ \times \sin PZX}{\sin PX}$$

substitute in 2

$$YF = p \times \cos \text{dec} \times \frac{\sin PZ \times \sin PZX}{\sin PX}$$

$$= p \times \cos \text{dec} \times \frac{\sin \text{colat} \times \sin Az}{\sin \text{codec}}$$

$$= p \times \cos \text{lat} \times \sin Az.$$

Thus if p is the change of hour angle in one minute then the change of altitude in one minute will be given by:

$$YF = 15' \times \cos \text{lat} \times \sin \text{azimuth.}$$

This gives the change in one minute for the mean sun. For any other body the rate of change of hour angle of the body can be substituted for 15′.

Twilight

Theoretical sunrise and sunset occur when the sun crosses the rational horizon. The period of daylight for any observer is the interval between these phenomena. When the sun sets below the rational horizon its light is not suddenly cut off from the observer. Although direct sunlight can no longer reach the observer, the upper atmosphere will still be sunlit. Reflection and scattering of the sun's light by the upper atmosphere allows some light to reach the observer by indirect means. The amount of this light reaching the observer will decrease as the sun's depression below the horizon increases.

The interval between the time when the sun sets, and the time when the sun is so far below the horizon that no light reaches the observer is called the period of evening twilight. The interval between when the sun approaches close enough to the eastern horizon to allow light to reach the observer, and the time of sunrise is called morning twilight.

It is impossible to define exactly the moment when all light to an observer ceases. Therefore arbitrarily twilight is considered to end when the centre of the sun sinks 18° below the rational horizon, and begin when the centre of the sun rises to within 18° of the eastern horizon.

Civil twilight
When the sun is more than 6° below the horizon it is considered that there is not enough natural light to perform the tasks of everyday life. The period of time between when the sun's centre is between 0° and 6° below the rational horizon is said to be the period of civil twilight.

Nautical twilight
The interval between when the sun's centre is between 6° and 12° below the rational horizon is said to be the period of nautical twilight. It is during this interval in normal weather conditions that star sights are possible at sea.

Astronomical twilight
This is the interval of time between when the sun's centre is more than 12° and less than 18° below the rational horizon. The limits of nautical twilight are given in the *Nautical Almanac* (see Chapter 5).

Variation in the length of twilight
The duration of twilight varies with the latitude of the observer. This can be understood by considering the rate of change of the sun's altitude which is caused by the earth's rotation. It has been shown that this decreases with latitude.

When the sun's diurnal path across the sky is perpendicular to the horizon then the rate of change of altitude will be maximum, and will be equal to the rate of the sun's motion along its diurnal arc. This is 15° per hour or 15′ of arc per minute of time. This is illustrated in Figure 11.9

This condition only occurs when the observer is on the equator, i.e. when the latitude is 0°.

At the other extreme if the sun's daily arc of motion is parallel to the horizon then the rate of change of the altitude must be zero. This occurs for an observer at the poles, i.e. when the latitude is 90°.

At any intermediate latitude the arc of the sun's daily motion makes an angle with the rational horizon equal to the complement

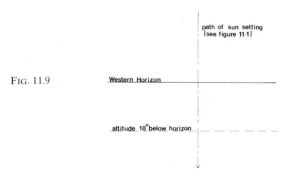

F̲ɪɢ. 11.9

of the latitude. From Figure 11.10 the smaller this angle is then the smaller will be any change of altitude for any given movement along the arc of declination.

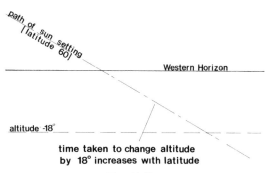

time taken to change altitude
by 18° increases with latitude

Fɪɢ. 11.10

Therefore the higher the latitude the smaller will be the rate of change of altitude and the longer it will take the sun to cover the required change of altitude during twilight, and the length of twilight will increase with an increase in latitude.

To find the times of sunrise or sunset for an observer

Given the observer's latitude and the declination of the sun, the times of sunrise and sunset can be found by solving the appropriate PZX triangle to find angle P. This will give the hour angle of the sun at this time from which can be derived the local apparent time of the phenomenon.

The value of angle P at sunrise will be the interval between the L.A.T. of sunrise and apparent noon, if expressed in units of time. The value of angle P at sunset will be the interval between apparent noon and the L.A.T. of sunset when expressed in units of time.

As the zenith distance at the time of sunrise or sunset is 90° then Napier's rules can be used to solve the triangle.

If necessary the chapter on 'Time' should be consulted for explanations of the terms 'local apparent time' and 'apparent noon'.

It should be noted here that the times of sunset and sunrise, and also the times of moonset and moonrise, which are given in the *Nautical Almanac* refer to the visible risings and settings. Due to the effects of refraction and height of eye, these will not coincide with the theoretical rising or setting, when the bodies' true altitude is 0°. Visible rising and setting is discussed in more detail in Chapter 16 under 'the Amplitude Problem'.

Example 1
Find the length of daylight to an observer in latitude 55° N. Declination 18° N. (assume that the declination remains constant over the period of daylight).

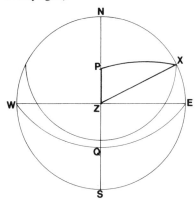

Fig. 11.11

$PX = 72°$
$PZ = 35°$
$ZX = 90°$

By Napier's rules

$$\text{sin comp. } P = -\tan \text{ comp. } PZ \tan \text{ comp. } PX$$
$$\cos P = -\cot PZ \cot PX \qquad \overline{\quad 0.15477 \quad}$$
$$\cos P = -\cot 35 \cot 72 \qquad \overline{\quad 1.51178 \quad}$$
$$P = 117° \ 39' \qquad \qquad \overline{\quad 1.66655 \quad}$$
$$= 7\text{h } 50.6\text{m}$$
$$2 \times 7\text{h } 50.6\text{m} = 15\text{h } 41.2\text{m}$$

Thus duration of daylight $= 15\text{h } 41.2\text{m}$
    time of sunrise $= 12\text{h } 00\text{m} - 7\text{h } 50.6\text{m} = 04\text{h } 09.4\text{m}$
    time of sunset $= 12\text{h } 00\text{m} + 7\text{h } 50.6\text{m} = 19\text{h } 50.6\text{m}$

To find the time of the beginning (or end) of twilight
Given the latitude of the observer and the declination of the sun the L.A.T. of the limit of twilight can be found in a similar manner

to the time of sunrise. The side ZX, the zenith distance, will in this case be 96°, 102°, or 108°, depending upon the twilight specified. There will be no right angle in the triangle and therefore the haversine formula should be used.

Example
Find the L.A.T. of the end of nautical twilight for an observer in latitude 55° N., when the declination of the sun is 18°.

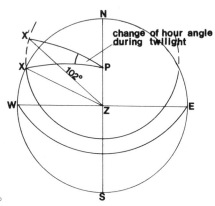

Fig. 11.12

$$PX' = 72°$$
$$PZ = 35°$$
$$PX' - PZ = 37°$$

In spherical triangle PZX' by haversine formula

$$\text{hav } P = \frac{\text{hav } ZX' - \text{hav } (PX' - PZ)}{\sin PZ \sin PX'}$$

hav P = (hav 102° − hav 37°) cosec 35° cosec 72°

0·60396
0·10068
0·50328
1·70181
0·24141
0·02179
1·96501

$$P = 147°\ 41\tfrac{1}{2}'$$
$$= 9\text{h } 51\text{m}$$

Twilight ends at 21h 51m.

To find the limits of latitude in which twilight will last all night
If twilight is to last all night then the sun must not go below 18° below the horizon. In the figure the arc of the sun's declination is

tangential to the circle of equal altitude which corresponds to a zenith distance of 108°.

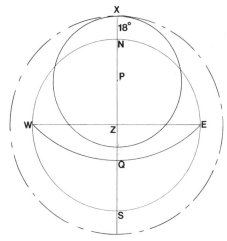

FIG. 11.13

On the observer's meridian arc PN = altitude of the pole, thus

$$PN = Latitude$$
$$PX = Polar\ Distance$$
$$NX = 18°$$

and

$$PN = PD - 18°$$
$$= 66\tfrac{1}{2}° - 18°$$
$$= 48\tfrac{1}{2}°\ N.$$

Thus any position north of this latitude will not experience total darkness at any time during the night, at the time of the summer solstice when the declination of the sun is maximum. This latitude will increase as the declination decreases.

EXERCISE 11

1. The sun sets bearing 292° T. to a stationary observer when the declination is 15° 07·5′ N. Find the latitude of the observer given that he is in:
   (a) north latitude,
   (b) south latitude.
2. Find the duration of nautical twilight to an observer in latitude 35° N. when the declination of the sun is 20° 30′ N.
3. (a) Why does the length of daylight (from sunrise to sunset) vary for any given latitude?

(b) To an observer in north latitude the ratio of the length of the longest day to the shortest day is 5:3. Calculate the latitude.

4. The sun is observed to rise bearing S. 80° E. to an observer in latitude 49° N. Find the L.H.A.

5. Calculate by spherical trigonometry the apparent time of theoretical sunrise for an observer in latitude 40° 22′ S. when the sun's declination is 21° 46′ S. Explain why to an observer on a stationary ship the times of theoretical and visible sunrise differ.

6. Find the length of daylight to an observer in latitude 48° N. when the sun's declination is 18° S.

7. Define the following:
astronomical twilight; circumpolar body; Prime vertical; theoretical sunrise.

Find the time of the end of civil twilight in latitude 20° N. if the declination of the sun is 20° N.

8. Under what conditions is a body circumpolar? Under what conditions will any latitude have total night? When will a body rise bearing due east and set bearing due west?

CHAPTER 12

POSITION CIRCLES AND POSITION LINES

Navigational computations are made in units of angular measure, degrees and minutes of arc. The arcs that are measured lie either on the earth's surface or upon the celestial sphere. As these two spheres are concentric however, angular distances upon one surface are directly transferable to the other. The angular distance between two observers on the earth's surface is exactly the same as the angular distance on the celestial sphere between the two observers' zeniths. Similarly the G.H.A. of a star is exactly the same as the longitude of the star's geographical position.

FIG. 12.1

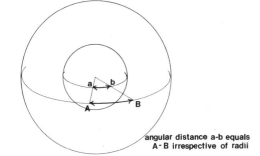

angular distance a-b equals
A-B irrespective of radii

It is convenient to consider the length of the earth's surface which corresponds to an arc of a great circle of one minute, as the nautical mile.

The observation of the altitude of a celestial body is a convenient way of measuring the distance of a body from the observer's zenith. Altitude and zenith distance are complementary. The distance of the body from the zenith in angular measure is the same as the distance of the geographical position of the body from the observer. If this angular distance on the earth's surface is expressed in minutes of arc this becomes by definition a distance in nautical miles.

Thus a sight of any one celestial body gives the distance of the observer from the geographical position of the body at the instant of taking the sight. From this information a circle can be drawn around the geographical position and the observer can be said to be somewhere on that circle. Such a circle is called a position circle. Note that a similar position circle is obtained by measuring a ship's distance off a point of land, perhaps by radar, but on a much smaller scale. In an astronomical sight the 'distance off' is the zenith distance, and the 'point of land' is the geographical position.

The intersection of two such position circles will give a 'fix' exactly as two position lines crossing will fix a ship's position. Why then is this not done in practice? If two geographical positions are plotted and circles drawn around them of radius the zenith distances a 'fix' should be obtained, the D.R. resolving the ambiguity caused by the two intersections.

Firstly circles cannot be easily drawn on a mercator chart. A circle on a globe does not appear as a circle on a chart, and a complete position circle would be extremely difficult to plot. Secondly the distances involved would mean a plotting chart covering a very large area, resulting in a very inaccurate plot. In order to make use of the simple basic concept of position circles, the method must be modified.

The approximate position of a ship is given by the D.R. or estimated position, and it can be assumed that each position circle runs reasonably close to the D.R. position. It is only that small part of the position circle that is of interest to the navigator, and generally the radius of curvature of a position circle is so large that such a small section of the circle can be considered a straight line without any significant error. This straight line will, strictly speaking, be a tangent to the position circle, and can be referred to as the position line. The direction in which the position line runs can be found by calculating the bearing of the body at the instant of taking the sight. If the position line is tangential to the position circle it must run at right angles to this bearing, which would form a radius of the circle.

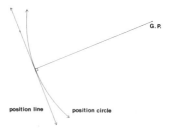

Fig. 12.2

Thus as long as one position through which the position line passes is known, such a position line can be drawn upon a large scale chart and it can be said that the ship's position is somewhere on that line. All methods of sight reduction now become problems of finding such a position, i.e. one that the position line passes through.

The Marcq St Hilaire method (intercept method)
Perhaps the most popular method of sight reduction used at sea because any sight can be worked in this way, no matter what the bearing and altitude. A D.R. position is assumed and the zenith distance or distance off the G.P. is calculated for that position. This calculated zenith distance is then compared with the true zenith distance obtained by direct observation.
In Figure 12.3 a D.R. position is shown with the G.P. The distance between the two will be the calculated zenith distance (CZX).

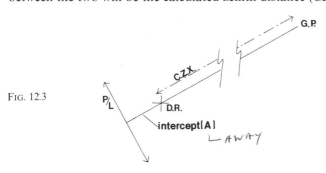

FIG. 12.3

If the true zenith distance is obtained and it is found to be greater than the calculated zenith distance then it should be apparent that the observer's position line must be shifted away from the G.P. instead of passing through the D.R. The difference between the CZX and the TZX is called the INTERCEPT. Thus if the CZX is increased by the amount of the intercept the position line can be drawn through the end of it at right angles to the bearing as shown in Figure 12.3. In this case the intercept is named AWAY because it is drawn away from the direction of the body.
If the TZX is found to be less than the CZX then the intercept must be drawn in the opposite direction, TOWARDS the body. Again the position line can be drawn through the end of the intercept at right angles to the bearing as in Figure 12.4.

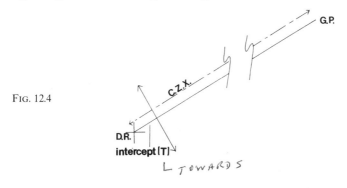

FIG. 12.4

The position line is always marked with an arrow at each end. Remember that this position line is in fact a small part of a circle of large radius centred upon the geographical position of the body observed.

If observations of two bodies are taken simultaneously and the same D.R. is used to calculate the two CZXs then two position lines can be plotted to scale on the same plot. The intersection of the two position lines gives an observed position, the latitude and longitude of which can be found by comparing it with the D.R. position on the plot, the latitude and longitude of which are known. In fact after having obtained the intercepts, the CZX is no longer of value and need not be included in the plot. For each observation it is only necessary to plot the D.R. position, the intercept in the appropriate direction and the position line.

The plot for one observation might appear as in Figure 12.5.

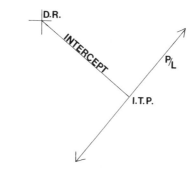

FIG. 12.5

Note
When plotting it is usual to use a scale of nautical miles. D. lats can therefore be plotted directly, but d. longs must be converted to departure before plotting. In order to obtain the latitude and longitude of the observed position, the d. lat. and the departure between it and the D.R. can be measured from the plot. The departure must be converted to a d. long. before being applied to the longitude of the D.R.

The plotting of position lines
To find the observed position from two simultaneous observations.

Procedure
1. Plot a convenient point to represent the D.R. position. It is convenient to use graph paper if a plotting chart with scales is not available.
2. From the D.R. position draw to a scale of nautical miles lines to represent the intercepts in magnitude and direction. Take particular care to plot an intercept labelled 'away' in the opposite

direction to the bearing and an intercept labelled 'towards' in the same direction as the bearing.

3. Through the intercept terminal points draw lines at right angles to the intercepts to represent the position lines. Mark the position lines with arrows and draw a small circle around their intersection to mark the observed position.

4. Measure the d. lat. and the departure between the observed position and the D.R. position, and convert the departure into d. long.

5. Apply d. lat and d. long. to the D.R. position to obtain the observed position.

Example 1
Two simultaneous observations, when worked assuming a D.R. position 52° 15′ N. 40° 30′ W., gave the following results.

(i) Bearing 175°, intercept 5·5′ away.
(ii) Bearing 250°, intercept 4·2′ towards.

Find the ship's position.

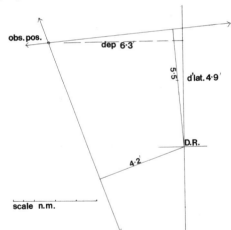

Fig. 12.6

By measurement

d. lat. = 4·9′ N.
dep. = 6·3′ W.

By traverse table

d. long. = 10·3′ W.

D.R. pos.	52° 15·0′ N.		40° 30·0′ W.
d. lat.	4·9′ N.	d. long.	10·3′ W.
Obs. pos.	52° 19·9′ N.		40° 40·3′ W.

To obtain a position from two observations with a run between them

If the two observations are not simultaneous, and the ship is steaming, then allowance must be made in the plot for the course and distance made good between the observations. It is necessary to transfer the position line obtained from the first observation up to the time of the second observation, by applying the d. lat. and d. long. made good, to the D.R. position. The second position line can then be crossed with the transferred position line to give an observed position at the time of the second observation.

In practice the position obtained after 'running up' the first D.R. position, would be used as a D.R. position with which to calculate the second position line. Both intercepts in this case can be plotted from the same position. If however the D.R. used in the second calculation is not the same position as the run up position then the intercepts must be laid off from different positions (see Example 3). Both these positions must be plotted in their correct positions on the plot relative to each other by finding the d. lat. and the departure between the two positions. This procedure may also be necessary if the second position line is obtained from a bearing of a terrestrial object such as a lighthouse. The position of the lighthouse must be plotted before its bearing can be laid off.

In the following examples note that the process of running up the first D.R. is carried out by means of the traverse table. It is not necessary to plot the run therefore and the actual plot will only be of the two intercepts and their position lines at the time of the second observation. A transferred position line is marked at each end with double arrows.

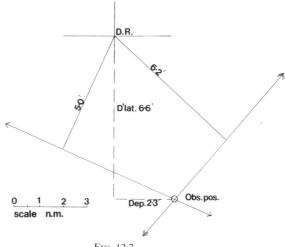

Fig. 12.7

Example 2

A vessel obtains an observation of a body bearing 132° T., which gives an intercept of 6·2′ towards using a D.R. position 25° 18′ S. 38° 20′ E. The ship then steams 245° T. for 45 miles, when a second observation gave an intercept of 5·0′ towards bearing 205° T. The position obtained by running up the first D.R. was used to calculate the second intercept. Find the ship's position at the time of the second observation.

By traverse table

Course 245° T.   D. lat. 19·0′ S.   Departure 40·8′ W.
        Mean lat. 25° 28′ S.   D. long. 45·2′ W.

1st D.R.	25° 18·0′ S.		38° 20·0′ E.
d. lat.	19·0′ S.	d. long.	45·2′ W.
2nd D.R.	25° 37·0′ S.		37° 34·8′ E.

By measurement

d. lat. = 6·6′ S.   dep. = 2·3′ E.   d. long. = 2·6′ E.

D.R. pos.	25° 37·0′ S.		37° 34·8′ E.
d. lat.	6·6′ S.	d. long.	2·6′ E.
Obs. pos.	25° 43·6′ S.		37° 37·4′ E.

Example 3

A vessel in D.R. position 32° 48′ S. 15° 35′ W. observed a body which was bearing 220° T., and obtained an intercept of 4·8′ away. The ship then steamed 335° T. for 68 miles. A second observation then gave a bearing of 290° T. and intercept of 2·0′ towards when

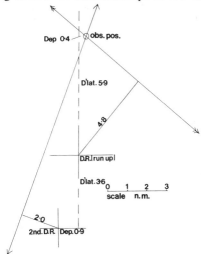

Fig. 12.8

calculated using a D.R. position of 31° 50′ S. 16° 10′ W. Find the ship's position at the time of the second observation.

D.R. pos.	32° 48·0′ S.		15° 35·0′ W.
d. lat.	1° 1·6′ N.	d. long.	33·9′ W.
run up pos.	31° 46·4′ S.		16° 08·9′ W.
2nd D.R.	31° 50·0′ S.		16° 10·0′ W.
d. lat.	3·6′ S.	d. long.	1·1′ W.

from traverse table dep. = 0·9′ W.

By measurement

d. lat. between run up pos. and observed pos. = 5·9′ N.
dep. = 0·4′ E.
from traverse table d. long. = 0·5′ E.

Run up position	31° 46·4′ S.	16° 08·9′ W.
	5·9′ N.	0·5′ E.
Observed pos.	31° 40·5′ S.	16° 08·4′ W.

Longitude by chronometer method
From any one observation there is only one position line that can be drawn. The positions through which the position line passes however are infinite. In the Marcq St Hilaire method the position which is nearest to the D.R. position is calculated. In the longitude by chronometer method the calculations use only the D.R. latitude and not the longitude. The longitude is then calculated in which the position line crosses the parallel of the D.R. latitude. The position through which to draw the position line is given by the D.R. latitude and the calculated longitude. Only if the ship is actually in the

Fig. 12.9

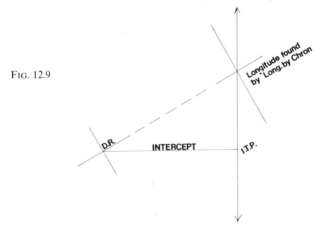

chosen D.R. latitude will the longitude calculated be the correct longitude. Thus the direction of the position line must be ascertained and the position line plotted through the position determined.

No intercepts are involved and in plotting it is only necessary to plot the position given by the D.R. latitude and the calculated longitude, and draw the position line through this position in the appropriate direction, i.e. at right angles to the bearing. If two simultaneous position lines are obtained then the two calculated longitudes have to be plotted on the D.R. latitude as in Example 4. Figure 12.9 shows a position line and the information obtained from the calculations and which would be used to plot the position line if the sight had been worked (a) by intercept method, and (b) by longitude by chronometer method.

Observed position from two simultaneous observations by longitude by chronometer

Procedure

1. Draw a line on the plot horizontally to represent the parallel of the D.R. latitude. Plot a suitable position on the line to represent one of the longitudes calculated.

2. Take the d. long. between the two longitudes and convert to departure. Plot the second longitude on the D.R. latitude at a distance from the first position to represent the departure to some suitable scale.

3. Draw in the position lines through their respective positions to obtain an observed position at their intersection.

4. Find the latitude and longitude of the observed position by measuring the d. lat. and departure between it and one of the known positions.

Example 4
Simultaneous observations of two bodies bearing 135° T. and 215° T., when worked by the longitude by chronometer method

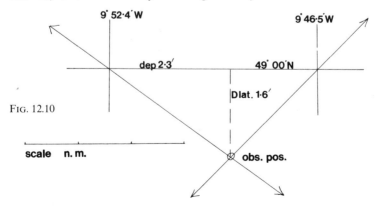

FIG. 12.10

using a D.R. latitude of 49° 00′ N. gave longitudes of 9° 46·5′ W.
and 9° 52·4′ W. respectively. Find the ship's position.

First longitude	9° 52·4′ W.
Second longitude	9° 46·5′ W.
d. long.	5·9′

from traverse table departure = 3·9′

By measurement
d. lat. between obs. pos. and pos. 49° 00′ N. 9° 52·4′ W. = 1·6′ S.
departure = 2·3′ E.
from traverse table d. long. = 3·5′ E.

Position	49° 00·0′ N.		9° 52·4′ W.
d. lat.	1·6′ S.	d. long.	3·5′ E.
Obs. pos.	48° 58·4′ N.		9° 48·9′ W.

Example 5
A vessel in D.R. latitude 26° 18′ S. obtains an observation of a
body bearing 300° T. which when worked by the longitude by
chronometer method gives a longitude of 164° 24′ W. The ship
then steams 280° T. for 40 miles when a second observation gives
a longitude of 165° 00′ W., bearing 020° T., when a D.R. latitude
of 26° 15′ S. was used. Find the ship's position at the time of the
second observation.

Position through which first p.l. is drawn	26° 18·0′ S.	164° 24·0′ W.
run (280° T. × 40 miles)	6·9′ N.	43·9′ W.
Position through which transferred p.l. is drawn	26° 11·1′ S.	165° 07·9′ W.
Position through which second p.l. is drawn	26° 15·0′ S.	165° 00·0′ W.
difference	3·9′	7·9′
		dep. 7·1′

By measurement
between obs. pos. and 26° 11·1′ S. 165° 07·9′ W. d. lat. = 1·1′ S.
dep. = 0·6′ W.
from traverse table d. long. = 0·7′ W.

	26° 11·1′ S.	165° 07·9′ W.
	1·1′ S.	0·7′ W.
obs. pos.	26° 12·2′ S.	165° 08·6′ W.

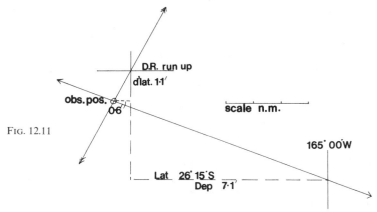

FIG. 12.11

Example 6

An observation of a body bearing 100° T., when using a D.R. latitude of 10° 07′ N., gives a longitude of 179° 45′ E. The ship then steams 095° T. for 38 miles, and a second observation of a body bearing 152° T. gives an intercept of 4·8′ towards. A D.R. was obtained by running up the D.R. latitude and the longitude by calculation from the first observation. Find the ship's position at the time of the second observation.

First D.R.	10° 07·0′ N.	179° 45·0′ E.
run 095° 38′	3·3′ S.	38·5′ E.
second D.R.	10° 03·7′ N.	180° 23·5′ E.
		= 179° 36·5′ W.

FIG. 12.12

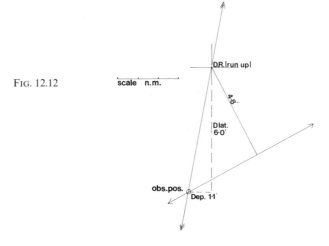

By measurement between pos. 10° 03·7′ N. 179° 36·5′ W. and observed position

$$
\begin{aligned}
\text{d. lat.} &= 6\!\cdot\!0'\ \text{S.}\\
\text{dep.} &= 1\!\cdot\!1'\ \text{W.}
\end{aligned}
$$

from traverse table d. long. = 1·1′ W.

D.R. pos.	10° 03·7′ N.	179° 36·5′ W.
	6·0′ S.	1·1′ W.
obs. pos.	9° 57·7′ N.	179° 37·6′ W.

Position lines from meridian altitudes

If a body is crossing the observer's meridian at the time of observation then the true bearing of the body is 000° T. or 180° T., i.e. north or south, depending upon which quantity has the most northerly value, the observer's latitude or the body's declination. In either case the position line obtained from the observation will run in the direction 090°/270° or east/west. It will therefore coincide with a parallel of latitude which must be that of the observer.

Such an observation is of particular value to the navigator for this reason, and as the calculations are much reduced in this special case it is an exercise which should be taken advantage of at every opportunity.

The usual way of obtaining a noon position at sea is to observe the sun during the forenoon and transfer the position line up to the time of noon, when the sun will be on the meridian. The transferred position line is then crossed with the position line from the meridian altitude observation. This problem can in fact be done without plotting but the principles involved in the problem as illustrated in Example 7 should be understood. The forenoon sight may be worked by the intercept method or by longitude by chronometer method.

Example 7

A ship in D.R. position 40° 15′ N. 36° 40′ W. obtained an observation of the sun during the forenoon which gave a bearing of 110° T. and an intercept of 5·5′ towards. The ship then steamed 250° T. for 20 miles when the latitude by meridian altitude of the sun was observed to be 40° 01·5′ N. Find the noon position.

Note

A plot of the complete problem would appear as in Figure 12.13. However the course and distance should be applied to the morning D.R. by traverse table. Only the part of Figure 12.13 inside the dotted lines should be plotted.

FIG. 12.13

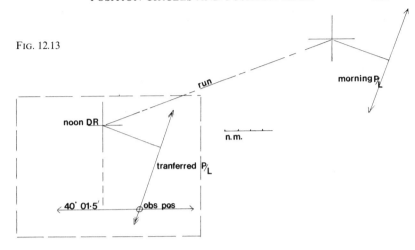

Procedure
1. Apply the course and distance, by traverse table, to the morning D.R. to obtain a noon D.R.
2. When the meridian altitude observation is obtained plot the noon D.R. position and lay off the transferred position line from the morning observation.
3. Taking the d. lat. between the noon D.R. and the observed noon latitude plot the noon position line which will run in the east–west direction.
4. The observed position is where the transferred position line cuts the noon latitude. Measure the departure between the observed

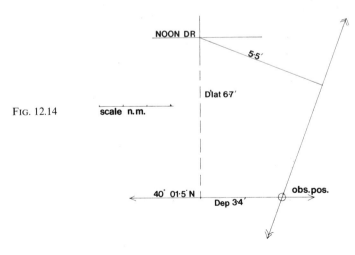

FIG. 12.14

position and the D.R. and convert it to d. long. Apply this to the D.R. to get the noon longitude.

morning D.R.   40° 15·0′ N.   36° 40·0′ W.
run 250°, 20′   6·8′ S.   24·6′ W.

noon D.R.   40° 08·2′ N.   37° 04·6′ W.

By measurement between observed position and noon D.R.
                          dep. = 3·4′ E.
        from traverse table d. long. = 4·4′ E.

        noon D.R. long.   37° 04·6′ W.
        d. long.   4·4′ E.

        obs. long.   37° 00·2′ W.

Observed position   40° 01·5′ N. 37° 00·2′ W.

Example 8

An observation in D.R. latitude 32° 30′ N. gave a longitude of 32° 08′ W., bearing of body 060° T. The ship then steamed 070° T. for 40 miles, when a meridian altitude gave a latitude of 32° 46′ N. Find the ship's position at the time of the meridian altitude.

D.R. at first sight   32° 30·0′ N.   32° 08·0′ W.
run 070°, 40 miles   13·7′ N.   44·6′ E.

D.R. at mer alt.   32° 43·7′ N.   31° 23·4′ W.

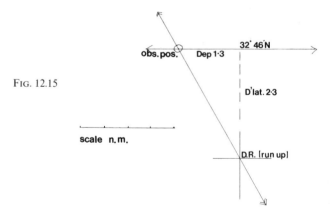

Fig. 12.15

By measurement between obs. pos. and D.R.
                          dep. = 1·3′ W.
        from traverse table d. long. = 1·6′ W.

D.R. long.	31° 23·4′ W.
d. long.	1·6′ W.
obs. long.	31° 25·0′ W.

Obs. position   32° 46′ N.   31° 25′ W.

Example 9

A point of land in 50° 20′ N. 7° 18′ W. bore 070° T. The ship then steamed 290° T. for 3 hours at 18 knots through a current that set 010° T. at 3 knots. A sight then gave a bearing and intercept of 245° T., 3·0′ towards, with a D.R. position of 50° 44′ N. 8° 34′ W. Find the ship's position at the time of the sight.

course steamed 290°, 54m.	d. lat. 18·5′ N.dep.	50·7′ W.	
current 010°, 9m.	d. lat. 8·9′ N.		dep. 1·6′ E.
total	27·4′ N.	49·1′ W.	
		d. long. 77·3′ W.	

Pt of land	50° 20·0′ N.	7° 18·0′ W.
	27·4′ N.	1° 17·3′ W.
transferred pos.	50° 47·4′ N.	8° 35·3′ W.
D.R. for sight	50° 44·0′ N.	8° 34·0′ W.
difference	3·4′	1·3′ = d. long.

departure = 0·8′

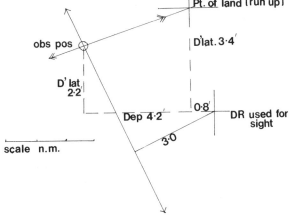

Fig. 12.16

By measurement between obs. pos. and D.R.

$$
\begin{array}{ll}
\text{d. lat.} & = 2 \cdot 2' \text{ N.}\\
\text{dep.} & = 4 \cdot 2' \text{ W.}\\
\text{d. long.} & = 6 \cdot 7' \text{ W.}
\end{array}
$$

D.R. position	50° 44·0′ N.	8° 34·0′ W.
	2·2′ N.	6·7′ W.
Obs. pos.	50° 46·2′ N.	8° 40·7′ W.

Example 10

A forenoon observation of the sun, when worked by longitude by chronometer method using a D.R. latitude of 30° 15′ S. gives a longitude of 50° 16′ E. If the same observation is worked using a D.R. latitude of 30° 21′ S. the calculated longitude is 50° 21·5′ E. What was the true bearing of the sun?

Note

The problem gives two positions through which the position line passes. It is sufficient to plot the two positions and join them with a straight line to find the direction of the position line. The ambiguity in the bearing is resolved by the fact that it is a forenoon sight and the sun must be bearing easterly.

d. long. between the two calculated longitudes = 5·5′
from traverse table departure = 4·8′
d. lat. = 6·0′

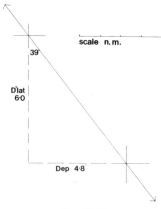

Fig. 12.17

By measurement the direction of the position line = 141°/321°
bearing of sun = 051°

EXERCISE 12

1. From the following position line information find the observed position.
1st obs. Intercept 6·0′ away, bearing 050° T.
2nd obs. Intercept 2·0′ towards, bearing 290° T.
D.R. position 47° 00′ N. 6° 40′ W.
2. In D.R. position 36° 05′ S. 122° 15′ E. simultaneous observations were made which gave intercepts of 9·5′ away and 4·3′ towards, bearings were 342° T. and 035° T. respectively. Find the ship's position.
3. In D.R. position 9° 30′ N. 177° 50′ E. simultaneous observations gave the following results
Intercept 2·5′ towards, bearing 175° T.
Intercept 2·5′ towards, bearing 270° T.
Find the ship's position.
4. Simultaneous observations were calculated using a D.R. position of 52° 20′ N. 164° 16′ W. The following results were obtained.
Intercept 1·0′ away, bearing 080° T.
Intercept 6·8′ towards, bearing 140° T.
Find the ship's position.
5. In D.R. latitude 34° 12′ N. simultaneous observations were taken which gave longitudes of 40° 27·4′ W. and 40° 31·9′ W. The calculated bearings were 255½° T. and 140° T. respectively. Find the ship's position.
6. Two simultaneous observations, when calculated using a D.R. latitude of 10° 14′ S., gave the following results.
Longitude 25° 46·3′ W., bearing 093° T.
Longitude 25° 44·7′ W., bearing 327° T.
Find the ship's position.
7. From the following information from longitude by chronometer calculations find the ship's position.
D.R. latitude 15° 20′ S.
Calculated longitude 159° 18′ W., bearing 095° T.
Calculated longitude 159° 12′ W., bearing 050° T.
8. From the following information from longitude by chronometer calculations, find the ship's position.
D. R. latitude 36° 40′ N.
Calculated longitude 146° 59′ E., bearing 310° T.
Calculated longitude 147° 10′ E., bearing 260° T.
9. In D.R. position 23° 40′ N. 52° 30′ W. a stellar observation gave an intercept of 4·0′ towards and bearing of 040° T. The vessel then steamed 090° T. for 24 miles through a current setting 000° T. Drift experienced was 5 miles. A second observation then gave an intercept of 5·0′ towards and a bearing of 120° T. when

using a D.R. position obtained by applying the run and the current to the first D.R. Find the ship's position at the time of the second observation.

10. In D.R. position 6° 18' S. 42° 19' W. an observation of the sun gave an intercept of 5·6' away, bearing 130° T. The ship then ran 145° T. for 53 miles when an observation of the moon, when using a D.R. obtained by running up the first D.R., gave an intercept of 1·6' towards, bearing 200° T. Find the ship's position at the time of the second observation.

11. In D.R. position 41° 10' S. 114° 00' E. an observation of Venus gave an intercept of 1·0' away, bearing 100° T. After steaming for 30 miles on a course of 100° T. the second observation of the sun gave intercept 4·0' away, bearing 314° T. Find the ship's position at the time of the second observation.

12. In D.R. position 19° 18' N. 160° 42' W. an observation of Jupiter gave intercept 4·0' towards, bearing 100° T. The ship then steamed 289° T. for 34 miles. An observation of the sun then gave intercept 7·0' away, bearing 200° T. Find the position at the time of the second observation.

13. In D.R. latitude 52° 50' N. an observation when worked by longitude by chronometer gave a longitude of 136° 10' W., bearing 285° T. The ship then steamed 150° T. for 15 miles when a second observation using a D.R. latitude of 52° 40' N. gave a longitude of 136° 05' W., bearing 205° T. Find the ship's position at the time of the second observation.

14. In D.R. latitude 52° 20' N. an observation gave a longitude of 164° 20' W., bearing 080° T. The ship then steamed 240° T. for 10 miles when a second observation, using the D.R. latitude obtained by running up the first D.R., gave a longitude of 164° 29' W., bearing 140° T. Find the position at the time of the second observation.

15. In D.R. position 50° 24' N. 22° 26' W. a forenoon observation of the sun gave an intercept of 3·1' away, bearing 102° T. The ship then steamed 265° T. for 48 miles when the latitude by meridian altitude of the sun was 50° 21·8' N. Find the noon position.

16. In D.R. 5° 57' N. 88° 16' E. a forenoon observation of the sun gave an intercept of 4·4' towards, bearing 121° T. The ship then steamed 088° T. for 33 miles when the latitude by meridian altitude of the sun was 5° 55·8' N. Find the position at noon.

17. In D.R. position 30° 45' N. 46° 40' W. an observation of the sun gave an intercept of 6·5' towards, bearing 110° T. The ship then steamed 115° T. for 20 miles, when the latitude by meridian altitude of the sun was 30° 30' N. Find the ship's position at the time of the meridian altitude observation.

18. An observation of a celestial body gave an intercept of 3·5′ away bearing 220° T., using a D.R. position of 32° 00′ S. 115° 00′ E. The ship then steamed 145° T. for 17 miles and then 063° T. for 12 miles. A point of land in position 32° 05′ S. 115° 31′ E. then bore 070° T. Find the ship's position at the time of the second position line.

19. An observation of a celestial body gave by longitude by chronometer a longitude of 152° 02′ E., bearing 220° T., when a D.R. latitude of 32° 00′ S. was used. Later a point of land in position 32° 00′ S. 152° 31′ E. bore 052° T. Between the observations the ship had steamed 148° for 18 miles, and then 065° for 10 miles. Find the ship's position at the time of the second observation.

CHAPTER 13

THE REDUCTION OF SIGHTS

In Chapter 10 the problem of representing the celestial sphere with a diagram was discussed, and the procedure for drawing the stereographic and the equidistant projection was outlined. By either of these projections it is possible to represent by projecting the observer's meridian, the meridian of a celestial body, and the vertical circle which passes through the body, a spherical triangle which may be imagined to lie on the celestial sphere. This is referred to as the PZX triangle, the triangle being formed between the three points the pole, the zenith, and X, the body. It is the solution of this triangle in one form or another which forms the basis of all navigational computations. The three sides and the three angles which form the triangle should therefore be discussed in more detail.

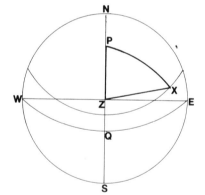

FIG. 13.1

The three sides of the triangle are:

PZ The arc of a great circle which joins the elevated pole, P, and the observer's zenith, Z, will form part of the observer's meridian. The angular distance from the observer to the pole (or from the observer's zenith to the celestial pole), is the complement of the observer's latitude. PZ is referred to as the co-lat therefore.

PX The arc of a great circle which joins the pole and the celestial body, X, is part of the celestial meridian which

218

passes through the body. The angular distance of the body from the pole is the complement of the declination, and therefore PX is referred to as the co-dec. It is more usual to refer to it as the body's polar distance however.

It is conventional to use in the PZX triangle the pole which lies in the hemisphere of the observer. If the name of the declination is opposite to that of the latitude, then the length of the side PX must be greater than 90°. In this case PX is found by 90° + declination.

ZX   The arc of a great circle which joins the zenith and the body is part of the vertical circle which passes through the body. As the altitude of the zenith is 90° then ZX (zenith distance) is found by taking the complement of the altitude of the body.

The three angles of the triangle are:

P   The angle at the pole contained between the observer's meridian and the meridian of the body. Note the similarity between this statement and the definition of the L.H.A. The angle P is always considered to be less than 180°. Therefore it will be the L.H.A. of the body when the body is to the west of the observer's meridian (body setting), and it will be 360° − L.H.A. if the body is to the east of the observer's meridian (body rising). Angle P is found from the G.H.A. of the body and the observer's longitude.

Z   The angle between the observer's meridian and the vertical circle which passes through the body. This is the azimuth, and is expressed from 0° to 180° east or west from the direction of the elevated pole. From the azimuth the bearing of the body is readily determined.

X   The parallactic angle. This angle is not normally used in the calculation of observer's position.

A knowledge or an assumption of any three of the six elements of the triangle will enable any of the remaining three to be calculated. The three elements which are used vary with the different methods of position line calculation. The methods which were introduced in Chapter 12 on position lines are discusssed here.

The Marcq St Hilaire (intercept) method

It was stated in Chapter 12 that to obtain a position line and position through which it passes, in this method a calculated zenith distance is compared with the observed zenith distance, to obtain an intercept, which is plotted from the D.R. position in the direction of the body's true bearing.

Thus from the solution of the PZX triangle is required a calculated zenith distance, and the true bearing of the body. These are obtained by solving for ZX and for angle Z.

The three elements which are used as arguments are:

PZ   This is obtained by assuming the observer's latitude (D.R. latitude), and taking the complement.

PX   Obtained from the declination of the body observed.

P   This is obtained by applying the D.R. longitude to the G.H.A., which is extracted from the *Nautical Almanac* for the G.M.T. of the observation.

With these three arguments the spherical haversine formula is used to find ZX thus:

$$\text{hav } ZX = (\text{hav P sin PZ sin PX}) + \text{hav} (PZ \sim PX)$$

This may be used more conveniently in the form:

$$\text{hav } ZX = (\text{hav P cos lat cos dec}) + \text{hav} (\text{lat} \underset{\sim}{+} \text{dec})$$

Note

If the name of the declination is opposite to that of the latitude the term (PZ $\sim$ PX) is given by (lat + dec).

Having calculated ZX it is compared with the observed zenith distance to obtain the intercept. The true bearing is found by use of the ABC tables as described in Chapter 16.

The effect of using different D.R. positions

If an observation is worked by Marcq St Hilaire several times each time using a different D.R. position. It should be understood that the same position line is arrived at each time. The value of the intercept and the direction of the intercept may vary. (Assume that the D.R.s are close enough together that the value of the true bearing is the same each time.) Figure 13.2 illustrates a position line, a selection of three random D.R. positions, and the intercepts that would result from using them. Note that the position lines drawn through each intercept terminal point are coincident so that only one position line is evident.

Procedure

1. From the chronometer reading, deduce the G.M.T., bearing in mind that the time indicated may be 12 hours ahead or retarded on G.M.T., i.e. 03h indicated may be either 03h or 15h. This is done by taking the approximate L.M.T. (clock time), and applying the longitude in time to obtain an approximate G.M.T.

From this approximate G.M.T. is deduced

(a) whether to add 12 hours to the chronometer time or not, and

(b) the date at Greenwich. (The date given in a problem will be, as in practice, the date at the ship. The date at Greenwich may be either the preceding date or the following date depending upon the longitude of the observer.

2. Extract the G.H.A. and the declination of the body for the G.M.T., from the *Nautical Almanac*.
3. Apply the D.R. longitude to the G.H.A. to obtain the L.H.A. of the body, and hence the angle P.
4. From the D.R. latitude and the declination obtain the term lat $\pm$ dec (PZ ~ PX). Latitude + declination if they are of opposite name and lat difference declination if they are of the same name.
5. Calculate ZX using the spherical haversine formula.
6. Convert the observed altitude to a true altitude and obtain the true zenith distance.
7. Compare the calculated and the true zenith distances to obtain the intercept.
8. Using ABC tables find the true bearing of the body.

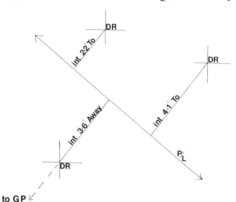

FIG. 13.2

Example 1. By observation of the sun

On October 31st in D.R. position 22° 10′ S. 31° 40′ W. the sextant altitude of the sun's lower limb was observed to be 35° 56·3′. Index error 3·1′ off the arc. Ht of eye 9·9 metres. The chronometer showed 5h 35m 21s and was correct on G.M.T. The approximate L.M.T. was 1526. Find the intercept and bearing of the sun.

Approx. L.M.T.   1526   31st
Longitude   0207
Approx. G.M.T.   1733   31st

G.M.T. 17h 35m 21s (12 hours to be added)

G.H.A. 17h	79° 05·2′	Dec.	14° 08·5′ S.	log hav P	1̄·34689
Increment	8° 50·3′	d	+0·5′	log cos L	1̄·96665
G.H.A.	87° 55·5′		14° 09·0′	log cos D	1̄·98662
Longitude	31° 40·0′ W.				1̄·30016
L.H.A.	56° 15·5′				

Latitude	22° 10·0′ S.		nat hav	0·19961
Dec.	14° 09·0′ S.			0·00489
L ~ D	8° 01·0′		L ~ D	0·20450
			CZX	53° 46·4′

Sext. alt.	35° 56·3′		A	0·273 +
I.E.	+ 3·1′		B	0·303 −
Obs. alt.	35° 59·4′		C	0·030 −
Dip	− 5·5′			
App. alt.	35° 53·9′		Bearing S. 88·4° W.	
Corr.	+ 14·9′			
True alt.	36° 08·8′			
TZX	53° 51·2′			
CZX	53° 46·4′		Answer: Intercept 4·8′ away	
Intercept	4·8′ away		Position line runs	
			358·4°/178·4°	

Example 2. By observation of a star

On June 24th in D.R. position 35° 18′ N. 175° 18′ W. during evening twilight the sextant altitude of the star Procyon was observed to be 17° 21·6′. Index error 1·5′ on the arc. Height of eye 13·0 metres. The chronometer, which was 1m 05s fast on G.M.T. showed 5h 59m 19s. Find the intercept and the direction of the position line.

Approx. L.M.T.	1800	(evening stars)
Longitude	1101	
Approx. G.M.T.	2901	
	= 0501	June 25th

G.M.T.	5h 59m 19s
error	− 1m 05s
G.M.T.	5h 58m 14s

G.H.A. 5h	347° 57·5′		Dec.	5° 17·4′ N.	log hav P	$\bar{1}$·54638
Incr.	14° 35·9′				log cos L	$\bar{1}$·91776
S.H.A.*	245° 30·6′				log cos D	$\bar{1}$·99815
G.H.A.*	608° 04·0′					$\bar{1}$·45629
	= 248° 04·0′					0·28596
Long.	175° 18·0′ W.				hav L ~ D	0·06703
L.H.A.	72° 46·0′					0·35299
Latitude	35° 18·0′ N.					
Dec.	5° 17·4′ N.				CZX	72° 54·1′
L ~ D	30° 00·6′					

Sext. alt.	17° 21·6′
I.E.	− 1·5′
Obs. alt.	17° 20·4′
Dip	− 6·3′
App. alt.	17° 14·1′
Corr.	− 3·1′
True alt.	17° 11·0′
TZX	72° 49·0′
CZX	72° 54·1′
Intercept	5·1′

A	0·219 +
B	0·097 −
C	0·122 +

Bearing S. 84·3° W.

Answer: Intercept 5·1′ towards
Position line runs
354·3°/178·3°

Example 3. By observation of the moon

On November 2nd in D.R. position 10° 45′ N. 141° 20′ E. at approximate L.M.T. 0545, a sextant altitude of the moon's lower limb was observed to be 23° 04·9′. Index error 4·0′ on the arc. Height of eye 16·9 metres. A chronometer which was correct on G.M.T. showed 8h 20m 10s. Find the intercept and the direction of the position line.

Approx. L.M.T.	0545	2nd
Longitude	0925	
Approx. G.M.T.	2020	1st

G.M.T. 20h 20m 10s (12 hours to be added)

G.H.A. 20h	282° 08·8′	(v = 7·3′)Dec.
Incr.	4° 48·7′	d
'v'	2·5′	

	21° 11·4′
	1·4′
	21° 12·8′ N.

G.H.A.	287° 00·0′
Long.	141° 20·0′
L.H.A.	428° 20·0′
	= 68° 20·0′
Latitude	10° 45·0′ N.
Dec.	21° 12·8′ N.
L ∼ D	10° 27·8′

log hav P	1̄·49886
log cos L	1̄·99231
log cos D	1̄·96953
	1̄·46070
	0·28887
hav L ∼ D	0·00832
	0·29719

CZX   66° 04·2′

Sext. alt.	23° 04·9′	A	0·076 +
I.E.	− 4·0′	B	0·418 −
Obs. alt.	23° 00·9′	C	0·342 −
Dip	− 7·2′		
App. alt.	22° 53·7′	Bearing N. 71·5° W.	
1st corr.	1° 01·5′		
2nd corr.	5·1′		
True alt.	24° 00·3′		
TZX	65° 59·7′	Answer: Intercept 4·5′ towards	
CZX	66° 04·2′	Position line runs	
Intercept	4·5′ towards	198·5°/018·5°	

Longitude by chronometer method

As detailed in Chapter 12 on position lines, from the longitude by chronometer method it is required to obtain a longitude, in which the position line cuts the D.R. latitude, and the true bearing. The three arguments which are used in the calculation are

PZ   The colat, or complement of the D.R. latitude.

PX   Obtained from the decination of the body.

ZX   The zenith distance obtained by observation of the body by sextant.

With these three arguments the haversine formula can be used to solve for angle P, in the form

$$\text{hav } P = [\text{hav } ZX - \text{hav}(PZ \sim PX)] \text{ cosine } PZ \text{ cosine } PX$$

It may be used more conveniently in the form

$$\text{hav } P = [\text{hav } ZX - \text{hav}(\text{lat} \stackrel{+}{\sim} \text{dec})] \text{ sec lat sec dec}$$

The L.H.A. can now be deduced from the value of the angle P. (L.H.A. = angle P if the body is setting. L.H.A. = 360° − angle P if the body is rising.) The L.H.A. is then applied to the G.H.A. to obtain the calculated longitude.

The longitude calculated is usually referred to as the observed longitude. It should be clearly understood that this is the ship's longitude only if the ship is in the D.R. latitude. The D.R. latitude and the calculated longitude together give a position through which the position line passes. The true bearing of the body must therefore be found by ABC tables in order to infer the direction in which the position line runs. The position line can then be plotted through the position described as shown in Chapter 12.

It should be stressed that any one observation, whether worked by longitude by chronometer method or by Marcq St Hilaire can only result in one position line. The position through which it passes however differs. Figure 12.9 should be consulted to illustrate this point.

Procedure
1. From the chronometer time obtain the G.M.T. as described under the procedure for Marcq St Hilaire.
2. Extract the G.H.A. and the declination of the body for the G.M.T., from the *Nautical Almanac.*
3. Correct the observed altitude to a true altitude and obtain the true zenith distance by taking the complement.
4. From the latitude and the declination, obtain the term lat $\pm$ declination (PZ $\sim$ PX).
5. Solve the PZX triangle for angle P and hence obtain the L.H.A.
6. Apply the L.H.A. and the G.H.A. to obtain the longitude.
7. Calculate the true bearing by use of the ABC tables.

Example 1. By observation of the sun
For illustration the same example is used as for the Marcq St Hilaire method. The results should be compared.
On October 31st in D.R. position 22° 10′ S. 31° 40′ W. the sextant altitude of the sun's lower limb was observed to be 35° 56·3′. Index error 3·1′ off the arc. Height of eye 9·9 metres. The chronometer which was correct on G.M.T. showed 5h 35m 21s. The approximate L.M.T. was 1526. Find the direction of the position line and the longitude in which it cuts the D.R. latitude.

Approx. L.M.T.	1526	31st
Longitude	0207	
Approx. G.M.T.	1733	31st

G.M.T. 17h 35m 21s

G.H.A. 17h	79° 05·2′	Dec.	14° 08·5′ S.	Sext. alt.	35° 56·3′
Incr.	8° 50·3′	d	0·5′	I.E.	+3·1′
G.H.A.	87° 55·5′		14° 09·0′ S.	Obs. alt.	35° 59·4′
				Dip	−5·5′
Latitude	22° 10·0′ S.			App. alt.	35° 53·9′
Dec.	14° 09·0′ S.			Corr.	+14·9′
L ∼ D	8° 01·0′			True alt.	36° 08·8′
				TZX	53° 51·2′

hav ZX	0·20507
hav L ∼ D	0·00489
	0·20018
	1̄·30142
log sec L	0·03335
log sec D	0·01338
	1̄·34815

angle P	56° 20·8′	(In the afternoon the sun is to the west of the observer.
L.H.A.	56° 20·8′	This must equal L.H.A. therefore.)
G.H.A.	87° 55·5′	
Long.	31° 34·7′ W.	

$$
\begin{array}{ll}
A & 0·273\ + \\
B & 0·303\ - \\
\hline
C & 0·030\ -
\end{array}
$$

Bearing = S. 88·4° W.
Position line runs 358·4°/178·4° through 22° 10′ S. 31° 34·7′ W.

Example 2. By observation of the moon

The same example is used as for the Marcq St Hilaire method.

On November 2nd in D.R. position 10° 45′ N. 141° 20′ E. at approximate L.M.T. 0545 a sextant altitude of the moon's lower limb was observed to be 23° 04·9′. Index error 4·0′ on the arc. Height of eye 16·9 metres. A chronometer which was correct on G.M.T. showed 8h 20m 10s. Find the direction of the position line and the longitude in which it cuts the D.R. latitude.

Approx. L.M.T.	0545	2nd
Longitude	0925	
Approx. G.M.T.	2020	1st

G.M.T. 20h 20m 10s (12 hours is added)

G.H.A. 20h	282° 08·8′ (V = 7·3)		Sext. alt.	23° 04·9′
Incr.	4° 48·7′		I.E.	− 4·0′
	v = 2·5		Obs. alt.	23° 00·9′
G.H.A.	287° 00·0′		Dip	− 7·2′
			App. alt.	22° 53·7′
Latitude	10° 45·0′ N.		1st corr.	1° 01·5′
Dec.	21° 12·8′ N.		2nd corr.	5·1′
L ∼ D	10° 27·8′		True alt.	24° 00·3′
			TZX	65° 59·7′

hav ZX	0·29659	
hav L ∼ D	0·00832	
	0·28827	
	1̄·45980	
log sec L	0·00769	
log sec D	0·03047	
	1̄·49796	

angle P   68° 15·2′

L.H.A.   68° 15·2′   (By considering the G.H.A. and the
G.H.A.   287° 00·0′   longitude, the moon is to the west
Long.   218° 44·8′ W.   of the observer.)
        =   141° 15·2′ E.

                    A   0·076 +
                    B   0·418 −
                    C   0·342 −

Bearing N. 71·5° W.
Position line runs 018·5°/198·5° through 10° 45′ N. 141° 15·2′ E.

Noon position by longitude by chronometer and meridian altitude

In Chapter 12 the problem of finding a noon position by a forenoon observation of the sun and a meridian altitude of the sun, was discussed. This exercise should be understood before proceeding with the following section.

It is possible to solve this problem without the use of scale plotting of position lines, as follows.

The position line resulting from the forenoon observation is to be transferred up to the time of noon by application of the course and distance made good. This can be done by use of the traverse table. It is advantageous to work the forenoon sight by the longitude by chronometer method, as the run can then be applied directly to the position which is given by the D.R. latitude and the calculated longitude. If the Marcq St Hilaire method is used to avoid the use of plotting, the intercept terminal point must be found, and this position run up to the time of noon.

However, having obtained a position for noon by application of the run to a morning position, the position obtained can be referred to as the noon D.R. position. But this position is only a position through which the transferred position line passes. The vessel may be anywhere on the transferred position line at noon. Figure 13.3 shows a forenoon D.R., the run to noon, and the transferred position line through the noon D.R. position.

The meridian altitude observation will now give the ship's true latitude. A second position line running east–west, along the parallel of the observed latitude could be drawn to cut the transferred position line. This may show that the ship is either to the north or to the south of the D.R. latitude. Now bearing in mind that the ship is somewhere on the transferred position line, it is possible to say whether the ship is to the east or to the west of the noon D.R. longitude.

In the example shown in Figure 13.3 because of the general S.W./N.E. trend of the position line we can say that if the ship is to the south of the D.R. latitude, she must also be to the west of the

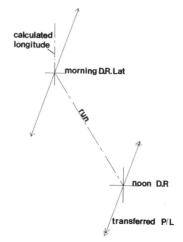

FIG. 13.3

D.R. longitude. Similarly if the ship is to the north of the D.R. latitude she must be to the east of the D.R. longitude. If the position line ran S.E./N.W. then this would be reversed. Each individual case may be assessed if necessary by a rough sketch of the position line.

By a knowledge of the d. lat. between the D.R. and the observed latitudes, and the direction of the position line, it should be possible by simple plane trigonometry to find the departure and hence the d. long. between the observed and the D.R. longitudes.

In Chapter 16 it is explained that the value of C in the ABC tabulations was in fact:

$$\text{cot azimuth} \times \text{sec latitude.}$$

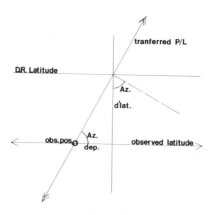

FIG. 13.4

From Figure 13.4 by plane trigonometry,

$$\text{departure} = \text{d. lat.} \times \cot \text{azimuth}$$

and

$$\text{d. long.} = \text{dep.} \times \sec \text{latitude}$$

thus

$$\text{d. long.} = \text{d. lat.} \times \cot \text{az.} \times \sec \text{lat.}$$
$$= \text{d. lat.} \times \text{'C'}$$

Thus it is found that by multiplying the value of the 'C' as found when calculating the true bearing of the forenoon observation, by the difference in latitude between the observed position and the noon D.R., the difference in longitude is given. This enables the problem to be easily solved without a plot, by comparing the latitude by meridian altitude with the D.R. latitude and multiplying the difference by 'C'. The result is then applied to the D.R. longitude of noon in the appropriate direction, to obtain the noon observed longitude.

Example 1

An observation of the sun taken during the forenoon gave the following results when using a D.R. latitude of 42° 46' N.

Longitude 31° 14' W. T. Bearing 128° ('C' value 1·06)

The ship then steamed 240° T. for 30 miles until noon when a meridian altitude observation gave a latitude of 42° 38·5' N.
Find the noon observed position.

D.R.	42° 46·0' N.	31° 14·0' W.
Run	15·0' S.	35·4' W.
Noon D.R.	42° 31·0' N.	31° 49·4' W.
Obs. lat.	42° 38·5' N.	
Difference	7·5' N.	
'C' corr.	× 1·06	
	7·95	7·9' E.
Obs. long.		31° 41·5' W.
Observed pos.	42° 38·5' N.	31° 41·5' W.

Example 2

The observation of the sun worked in Example 1 of the longitude by chronometer method gave a position line running $358\frac{1}{2}°/178\frac{1}{2}°$ through 22° 10' S. 31° 34·7' W. Time of sight 1526. The ship then steamed 100° T. for 35 miles when a meridian altitude of a star gave a latitude of 22° 02·6' S. Find the position at the star sight.

D.R. at 1526	22° 10·0′ S.	31° 34·7′ W.
100° T. × 35′	6·1′	37·2′ E.
	22° 16·1′ S.	30° 57·5′ W.
Obs. lat.	22° 02·6′ S.	
Difference	13·5′ N.	
'C' corr.	× 0.03	
	0·4′ W.	
D.R. long.		30° 57·5′ W.
		0·4′ W.
Obs. long.		30° 57·9′ W.
Observed pos.	22° 02·6′ S.	30° 57·9′ W.

The ex-meridian problem

In this problem the three arguments used to solve the PZX triangle are angle P, PX, and PZ. The triangle is solved for the term (PZ $\sim$ PX).

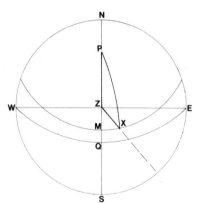

FIG. 13.5

In Figure 13.5 let X be the position of a celestial body and M its position when it crosses the observer's meridian. ZM will therefore be the zenith distance of the body when on that meridian. ZQ is the latitude and can be found by ZM $\pm$ QM, or

lat. = meridional zenith distance $\pm$ declination

(see 'Meridian Altitudes') and

$$ZM = PZ \sim PM \qquad (1)$$

If the declination of the body is assumed to be constant between the time of the observation and the time of the meridian passage then PM = PX = the body's polar distance.

Thus from (1)

$$ZM = PZ \pm PX.$$

The term (PZ $\sim$ PX) can be found from the haversine formula in the form,

hav (PZ $\sim$ PX) = hav ZX − hav P sin PZ sin PX.

This can be modified,

hav (PZ $\sim$ PX) = hav ZX − hav P cos lat. cos dec.

By solving the PZX triangle for the term PZ $\sim$ PX, the zenith distance which would be observed when the body is on the observer's meridian, assuming that the observer is in the D.R. longitude and is stationary.

A latitude can then be found by applying the declination to this meridional zenith distance exactly as described in the meridian altitude problem (see Chapter 14).

However note that the value of the latitude found is dependent upon the value of the D.R. longitude used to find the angle P. It is evident therefore that the latitude found, and the D.R. longitude together form a position through which the position line must pass. The true bearing of the body must be found also to give the direction in which the position line runs. Thus from the calculations there has been obtained a position line and a position through which it passes, at the time of the observation. It should be understood that the latitude found is in no way an observed latitude for the time of meridian passage. It can only apply to the time of the observation and will be calculated to have different values if different D.R. longitudes are used. The positions given by the calculated latitudes and the D.R. longitudes will all lie on the position line.

If the haversine formula with which the term (PZ $\sim$ PX) is calculated is inspected, it will be noted that a value for latitude is required to be assumed. We are in fact using a latitude with which to calculate a latitude. The calculated latitude can be said to be a closer approximation to the true latitude than the original assumed value. However the calculated latitude can only be accepted as a reasonable result if the value calculated is in fact close to the D.R. assumed. Also in order to keep the error which will result in an incorrect latitude being assumed, to as small a value as possible, the term 'hav P cos lat. cos dec.' must itself be kept small. This can only be achieved by limiting the value of angle P that is used in this method. The actual limits will be discussed later but the fact that angle P is limited, means that the method can only be used accurately when the body observed is close to the meridian of the observer. This will also ensure that the change in the body's declination in the interval between the observation and the meridian passage is negligible.

It should be noted that many navigators prefer to use the Marcq St Hilaire method instead of the ex-meridian. The same position line will result and the former method suffers none of the limitations of the ex-meridian method. The ex-meridian problem is of importance however because the same results can be obtained very quickly by the use of tabulated solutions of the ex-meridian problem. This makes the method considerably quicker than the intercept method.

Procedure for ex-meridian method
1. From the chronometer reading, deduce the G.M.T. as described in the procedure for the Marcq St Hilaire method.
2. Extract the G.H.A. and declination of the body from the *Nautical Almanac*.
3. Apply the longitude to the G.H.A. to obtain L.H.A. and hence the angle P. (This should be small.)
4. Correct the sextant altitude and obtain the zenith distance.
5. Solve the PZX triangle by the haversine formula to obtain the term (PZ ~ PX).
6. Using the term (PZ ~ PX) as the meridional zenith distance, apply the declination to obtain the latitude.
7. Combine the latitude so calculated with the D.R. longitude to give a position through which the position line passes.
8. Work the ABC tables to find the bearing and hence the direction of the position line.

Example
On January 6th in D.R. position 20° 30′ N. 113° 05′ E., the sextant altitude of the sun's lower limb was observed to be 46° 25·8′. Index error 3·0′ on the arc. Height of eye 12·0 metres. A chronometer at the time showed 03h 55m 35s and was 12m 35s slow on G.M.T. If the body was observed near the meridian find the direction of the position line and the latitude in which the position line cuts the D.R. longitude.

Approx. L.M.T.	1200	(mer. pass. sun)
Long.	0732	E.
Approx. G.M.T.	0428	6th

Chron.	3h 55m 35s
Error	+ 12m 35s
G.M.T.	4h 08m 10s

G.H.A. 4h	238° 35·2′	Dec. 22° 32·8′ S.	Sext. alt.	46° 25·8′
Incr.	2° 02·5′		I.E.	− 3·0′
G.H.A.	240° 37·7′		Obs. alt.	46° 22·8′
Long. E.	113° 05·0′		Dip	− 6·1′
L.H.A.	353° 42·7′		App. alt.	46° 16·7′

Angle P   6° 17·3'   Corr.   +15·3'

True alt.   46° 32·0'

TZX   43° 28·0'

log hav P	$\overline{3}$·47835
log cos L	$\overline{1}$·97159
log cos D	$\overline{1}$·96547
	$\overline{3}$·41541
	0·00260
hav TZX	0·13711
hav PZ ~ PX	0·13451

Meridional zenith dist. = 43° 01·9'
Declination   = 22° 32·8' S.

Latitude   20° 29·1' N.

A	3·39 +
B	3·79 +
C	7·18 +

Bearing = S. 8·5° E.
Position line runs 261½°/081½° through 20° 29·1' N. 113° 05' E.

Ex-meridian tables

Many navigators prefer to use the Marcq St Hilaire method as an alternative to the ex-meridian method. The same position line will result, and the former method does not suffer the limitations of the ex-meridian calculations. The ex-meridian method is of little importance in modern navigation therefore. The basic principles are retained however in the use of the ex-meridian tables, and these allow the method to be used with much less working than the intercept method.

Norie's and Burton's tables both include ex-meridian tables which allow a 'reduction' to be extracted, which corrects the observed zenith distance, to that which would be observed with the body on the meridian, assuming a constant declination and a stationary observer. In other words the correction will be the change in altitude of the body between the time of the observation and the time of the meridian passage. The reduction to the zenith distance is obtained in two stages. A factor 'F' (in Burton's) or 'A' (in Norie's) is obtained from Table 1 using the latitude and the declination. This factor is then used as an argument, with the hour angle, to extract the reduction, in minutes of arc, from Table II. A small additional correction is obtained from Table III. A full explanation of the tables is included in both Norie's and Burton's.

It must be realized however that the result obtained cannot be considered the observer's latitude. The reduction obtained depends upon the D.R. longitude used to calculate the hour angle. So therefore does the final result, the latitude. From such an observation as from any other, only a position line may be found. The latitude calculated and the D.R. longitude can only constitute a position through which the position line passes. The latitude can therefore be thought of as that in which the position line cuts the D.R. longitude. The position line, moreover, must still refer to the time of the observation, and not the time of meridian passage.

Burton's tables explain the reduction as a correction to apply to the meridional zenith distance, calculated from the D.R. latitude and the declination, in order to get a calculated ZX for the time of the ex-meridian observation. This can then be compared with the true zenith distance, as observed, to obtain an intercept. Both methods of approach will result in the same position line, and the ABC tables must be used to find the bearing of the body and hence the direction of the position line in either case. This method is usually less convenient however than the first.

The example worked by the haversine formula under ex-meridian problem is now shown worked by ex-meridian tables.

Example
On January 6th in D.R. position 20° 30′ N. 113° 05′ E., the sextant altitude of the sun's lower limb, near the meridian was observed to be 46° 25·8′. Index error 3·0′ on the arc. Height of eye 12·0 metres. A chronometer at the time showed 3h 55m 35s and was 12m 35s slow on G.M.T. Find, by ex-meridian tables, the direction of the position line and the latitude in which it cuts the D.R. longitude.

Approx. L.M.T.	1200	(mer. pass. sun)
Long.	0732	E.
Approx. G.M.T.	0428	6th

Chron.	3h 55m 35s	
Error	12m 35s	
G.M.T.	4h 08m 10s	6th

G.H.A. 4h	238° 35·2′	Dec. 22° 32·8′ S.
Incr.	2° 02·5′	
G.H.A.	240° 37·7′	
Long. E.	113° 05·0′	
L.H.A.	353° 42·7′	
Angle P	6° 17·3′	

From Table I   Factor = 2·49   (Burton's tables)

From Table II $2{\cdot}00 = 21{\cdot}1$
$\phantom{From Table II 2{\cdot}}0{\cdot}40 = 4{\cdot}2$
$\phantom{From Table II 2{\cdot}}0{\cdot}09 = 1{\cdot}0$
$\phantom{From Table II 2{\cdot}00 =}\overline{26{\cdot}3}$
2nd corr. $0{\cdot}1$
Reduction $= \overline{26{\cdot}2}$

Sext. alt.	46° 25·8′		
I.E.	− 3·0′		
Obs. alt.	46° 22·8′		
Dip	− 6·1′		
App. alt.	46° 16·7′		
Corr.	+ 15·3′		
True alt.	46° 32·0′		
TZX	43° 28·0′	A	3·40 +
Redct.	− 26·2′	B	3·79 +
Merid. ZX	43° 01·8′	C	7·19 +
Dec.	22° 32·8′ S.		
Latitude	20° 29·0′ N.	Bearing S. 8·5° E.	

Position line runs $261\frac{1}{2}°/081\frac{1}{2}°$ through 20° 29·0′ N. 113° 05′ E.

If, as is usually the case at sea, the ex-meridian method is being used as an alternative to a meridian altitude, with the sun as the observed body, then the longitude used will most likely have been obtained by running up a forenoon observation to the time of the ex-meridian sight. To obtain a position from these two observations then it is necessary to plot the two position lines and find their intersection as described in the chapter on position lines. The latitude obtained from the ex-meridian must not be run up to meridian passage and used as a meridian altitude latitude. This is shown in Figure 13.6. The intersection of the position lines can if desired be transferred to noon.

The limits of hour angle for the ex-meridian method

The limits for the hour angle in the method are given in Table IV of the ex-meridian tables. These can be expressed as a number of minutes of time either side of meridian passage during which the method is accurate.

In general it can be said that the further apart are the latitude and the declination then the greater will be the limits. In the extreme case of the latitude and declination being the same then the body will pass through the zenith and the method cannot be used.

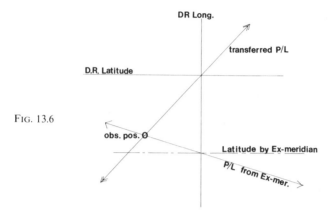

FIG. 13.6

EXERCISE 13

1. On October 31st in D.R. position 19° 50′ N. 66° 32′ E. an afternoon sight of the sun's lower limb gave a sextant altitude of 23° 29·5′. Index error 1·2′ off the arc. Height of eye 11·5 metres. A chronometer, which was fast on G.M.T. by 1m 40s, showed 11h 11m 00s. Find the direction of the position line and a position through which it passes.

2. On March 25th in D.R. position 40° 05′ S. 94° 05′ W. an observation during morning twilight, of the star Shaula gave a sextant altitude of 72° 10·5′. Index error nil. Height of eye 11·0 metres. A chronometer, which was 1m 06s slow on G.M.T., showed 1h 07m 12s. Find the direction of the position line and a position through which it passes.

3. On March 25th in D.R. position 40° 05′ S. 94° 05′ W. an observation of the star Fomalhaut, during morning twilight gave a sextant altitude of 42° 18′. Index error nil. Height of eye 11·0 metres. A chronometer which was 1m 06s slow on G.M.T., showed 1h 08m 12s. Find the direction of the position line and a position through which it passes.

4. On January 6th in D.R. position 20° 30′ N. 113° 05′ E. at L.M.T. 1150 the sextant altitude of the sun's lower limb when near the meridian, was 46° 25·8′. Index error 3·0′ on the arc. Height of eye 12·0 metres. A chronometer which was 12m 35s slow on G.M.T., showed 03h 55m 35s. Find the direction of the position line and the latitude in which it crosses the D.R. longitude.

5. On November 1st at approximate ship's time 2240, in D.R. position 7° 12′ S. 12° 18′ E., the sextant altitude of the moon's upper limb was 41° 47·9′. Index error 5·3′ off the arc. Height of eye 18·8 metres. A chronometer which was correct on G.M.T., showed

09h 50m 05s. Find the direction of the position line, and a position through which it passes.

6. On June 25th in D.R. position 30° 02′ S. 140° 20′ W., the sextant altitude of the sun's lower limb near the meridian was 36° 25·8′. Index error 1·4′ on the arc. Height of eye 12·0 metres. A chronometer at the time showed 9h 03m 55s and was 4m 11s slow on G.M.T. Find the direction of the position line and a position through which it passes.

7. On July 31st in D.R. position 16° 43′ S. 159° 40′ E. a morning altitude of the sun's lower limb was 34° 51′. Index error nil. Height of eye 12·5 metres. A chronometer which was correct on G.M.T. showed 10h 35m 29s. Find the direction of the position line and a position through which it passes.

8. On June 26th at approximate ship's time 0930, in D.R. position 29° 35′ S. 121° 25′ W., the sextant altitude of the sun's lower limb was 27° 25·2′. Index error 1·5′ off the arc. Height of eye 10·5 metres. A chronometer which was slow on G.M.T. by 0m 13s showed 5h 49m 56s. Find the direction of the position line and a position through which it passes.

9. On January 6th in D.R. position 20° 28′ N. 113° 06′ E., the sextant altitude of the sun's lower limb when near the meridian was 46° 25·4′. Index error 2·5′ off the arc. Height of eye 12·0 metres. A chronometer, which was 5m 40s slow on G.M.T., showed 04h 02m 30s. Find the direction of the position line and the latitude in which the position line cuts the D.R. longitude.

CHAPTER 14

MERIDIAN ALTITUDES

The coincidence of a celestial body with the observer's meridian as the earth rotates within the celestial sphere is of importance to the navigator as it produces position information quickly and simply. Such an occurrence is called the meridian passage or transit of the body.

The G.M.T. at which the meridian passage of a celestial body occurs will yield the observer's longitude, as at this time, by definition, the L.H.A. of the body is zero. The westerly longitude will therefore be equal to the G.H.A. of the body. Unfortunately it is not possible for the navigator at sea to observe the time of meridian passage with sufficient accuracy to obtain a meaningful longitude. It is necessary however to have the approximate time of any particular meridian passage and to obtain this the problem may be worked in reverse. From a knowledge of the D.R. longitude, the approximate time of meridian passage may be found. This is desirable because an observation of the altitude of a body at meridian passage will readily give the observer's latitude.

The observation of the latitude by meridian altitude is, because of its simplicity, widely used, and the noon observation of the sun is a daily occurrence on a ship at sea. At twilight very often it will happen that a star is crossing the meridian, and the moon may provide a good latitude during the daylight hours. In order to make such an observation, it will therefore be necessary to have the approximate time of the meridian passage. The time is not used in the calculations and therefore it is not important to have the time exactly. The procedure is to observe the altitude with a sextant, a few minutes before the meridian passage, and to watch the altitude increase as meridian passage approaches, adjusting the sextant continuously. The rate of increase of altitude will decrease until the body is no longer climbing. As soon as the image in the sextant is seen to dip into the horizon, the observer knows that meridian passage has occurred and the maximum altitude on the sextant is the meridian altitude.

Before the calculation of the latitude is explained, the methods used to find the approximate time of meridian passage will be discussed. There are two methods available to the navigator.

1. At meridian passage the L.H.A. is zero and

$$\text{L.H.A.} = \text{G.H.A.} - \text{W. long.}$$

thus at mer pass.

$$G.H.A. = W. long.$$

Hence express the longitude west from Greenwich (i.e. if the longitude is east subtract it from 360°), and this must equal the G.H.A. The almanac may now be inspected to find the G.M.T. at which this G.H.A. occurs for this particular body concerned. This sounds a simple task. It must be remembered however that the date at Greenwich may or may not be the same as the date at the ship. It must be ascertained for which day the appropriate G.M.T. should be extracted. The G.M.T. taken from the almanac should, after having the D.R. longitude in time applied to it, give an L.M.T. on the correct date at the ship. It is important to remember that the date given in any examination question will be the date at the ship, and this is the date which the navigator would have in practice. The Greenwich date may be the day before, the same, or the day after the local date, depending upon the longitude of the observer. The procedure is therefore:

1. Write down the G.H.A. (W. longitude).
2. Inspect the almanac on the appropriate day for the G.M.T. when the value of G.H.A. is next less than that given in (1). The difference between this value and that in (1) will be the increment, which will give the minutes and seconds of the G.M.T.
3. Inspect the increment tables after adjusting the increment in (2) for the 'v' correction if necessary.
4. The hour of G.M.T. in (2) and the minutes and seconds in (3) give the G.M.T. of meridian passage.
5. Check that the G.M.T. for the date used will after application of the longitude in time give a local time on the date required. If this is not so then the problem must be reworked using the preceding Greenwich date if in east longitude, or the following Greenwich date if in west longitude.

Example 1
Find the G.M.T. and L.M.T. of meridian passage of the sun over the meridian of an observer in longitude 52° 14' W. on January 5th.

G.H.A. = W. long. = 52° 14'
For G.M.T. 15h on 5th G.H.A. = 43° 38·8'

Difference 8° 35·2' = Increment
From sun increment table increment = 34m 21s
G.M.T. meridian passage = 15h 34m 21s on January 5th
Longitude in time 3h 28m 56s
.M.T. for long. 52° 14' W. 12h 05m 25s on January 5th

Example 2
Find the G.M.T. and L.M.T. of the meridian passsage of the moon

over the meridian of an observer in longitude 40° 38·0′ E. on November 2nd.

G.H.A. = W. long.   = 360 − 40° 38·0′
                        = 319° 22·0′
For G.M.T. 22h on 1st G.H.A. = 311° 01·5′   'v' = 7·2
Difference   8° 20·5′
'v'   − 4·1′
Increment   8° 16·4′
From moon increment table increment = 34m 40s
G.M.T. meridian passage   22h 34m 40s on November 1st
Longitude in time   2h 42m 32s
L.M.T. for longitude 40° 38′ E.   25h 17m 12s
                             = 01h 17m 12s on November 2nd

Notes
1. In order to obtain an L.M.T. on the date given in the problem it was necessary to use the Greenwich date of the previous day, the 1st. Sometimes if the longitude is west it is necessary to use the following day.
2. In practice the 'v' correction may be ignored as the exact time is never required. In some examination problems however it is required to give the time to the nearest second, and in a case like this it must be applied. As the problem is being worked in reverse the correction will carry the opposite sign to that used normally when extracting the G.H.A. of the body. In this case, the moon's 'v' correction being normally positive, the correction was subtracted to find the increment with which to enter the increment tables.

Example 3
Find the G.M.T. and L.M.T. of the meridian passage of the star Aldebaran over the meridian of an observer in longitude 150° 30′ W. on October 31st.

G.H.A. star   150° 30·0′
S.H.A. star   291° 22·3′
G.H.A. Aries   219° 07·7′
G.H.A. Aries 11h 31st   204° 22·0′
Difference   14° 45·7′ = increment
From Aries increment table increment = 58m 53s
G.M.T. meridian passage   11h 58m 53s on October 31st
Longitude in time   10h 02m 00s
L.M.T. for 150° 30′ W.   01h 56m 53s on October 31st

Note

In the case of a star the G.H.A. of Aries must be inspected. This may be found from:

$$G.H.A.* = G.H.A. \text{ Aries} + S.H.A.*$$

The advantage of this method is that the procedure is the same for all bodies, and the method may be used for sun, stars, planets and the moon. Care must be taken to use the correct increment table. The method will give the time to the nearest second for the particular longitude used in the problem. In practice this will be only the D.R. longitude, and the time obtained will therefore be approximate for an observer whose exact longitude is not known.

2. There is provided in the *Nautical Almanac*, the times to the nearest minute, of meridian passage for the sun, moon, planets, and the first point of Aries. It must be understood that these times are local mean times, and must be converted to Greenwich mean times before the declination can be inspected.

Sun

At the foot of the right hand of each of the daily pages, there is given a time under the heading 'Sun—mer. pass.'. This figure varies between 1144 and 1216, and may be taken as the L.M.T. of the meridian passage of the true sun across any meridian. The difference between this figure and 1200 will be, of course, the equation of time to the nearest minute.

This figure provides the easiest method of finding the time of the sun's meridian passage. All that it is necessary to do is to apply the longitude in time to obtain the G.M.T. This can then be used to find the declination of the sun.

Example

Find the G.M.T. of meridian passage of the sun over the meridian of 52° 14′ W. on January 5th.

From almanac for 5th L.M.T. mer. pass.	1205
Longitude in time	0329
G.M.T. mer. pass. sun over 52° 14′ W.	1534

This agrees to the nearest minute with the same example worked by method 1. This method however can be seen to be considerably quicker and easier than method 1. As the times given in the almanac are to the nearest minute, then it is of no benefit to introduce seconds into any subsequent figure such as the longitude in time.

Moon

The L.M.T. of meridian passage of the moon is given under the heading 'Moon—mer. pass.—upper', also at the foot of the right hand of each of the daily pages. However because of the retardation of the moon's meridian passage, this figure can only be taken as the L.M.T. for the Greenwich meridian, that for which it was calculated. A correction must be applied to obtain the L.M.T. for any observer's meridian. (This correction is not the longitude in time, and for this reason do not think of the figure given as a G.M.T.) To understand this correction consider the following.

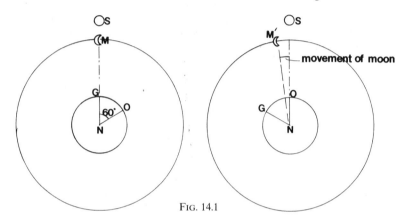

FIG. 14.1

Let G be the Greenwich meridian with the moon in transit. The figure is shown on the plane of the equinoctial, and therefore is seen as if looking down on the north pole. For simplicity let the sun also be in transit over the Greenwich meridian, i.e. the L.M.T. of mer. pass. of the moon given in the almanac would be 1200. Let O be an observer in longitude 60° W.

Now in the period of one rotation of the earth it has been shown that the moon moves eastwards around the celestial sphere by approximately 13°, the time it takes the earth to rotate through this amount being the daily retardation of the meridian passage. In the time it takes the observer O to reach a position with the sun in transit (L.M.T. for 60° W. will then be 1200), the moon will have moved to M', an amount given approximately by:

$$13° \times \frac{60}{360}.$$

The time it will take the earth to rotate this amount, in order to bring the moon in transit over the meridian of 60° W. will be given by:

$$\frac{\text{daily retardation} \times 60°}{360}$$

or in general:

$$\frac{\text{daily retardation} \times \text{longitude}}{360}$$

Hence the meridian passage of the moon over the meridian of 60° W. will be later than 1200 by this amount, which is referred to as the longitude correction. The daily retardation, which varies between 40 minutes and 60 minutes, must in this case be found by taking the difference in the times of meridian passage for the day in question, and for the following day.

Any meridian in easterly longitude will pass beneath the sun before the meridian of Greenwich. At such a time the moon would not yet have reached the sun in its easterly motion around the celestial sphere. The meridian passage of the moon over an easterly meridian would therefore have occurred before the meridian passage of the sun. The longitude correction will in this case, therefore be negative, again given by the above formula. The retardation must be found by taking the difference in the times of meridian passage for the day in question, and for the preceding day.

Solutions of the formula for the longitude correction are tabulated in the *Nautical Almanac*, against the variables longitude and daily retardation, under the name Table II. It can be found in the almanac (N.P.314) on the last of the increment (yellow) pages.

Hence the procedure is:

1. Write down the time of the moon's meridian passage for the day in question.

2. Under this write the time for the following meridian passage if the longitude is west, or the preceding meridian passage if the longitude is east. (Note that this will not necessarily occur on the following or preceding day as there is more than 24 hours between successive meridian passages.)

3. Take the difference and enter Table II with the longitude to extract the longitude correction, or solve the formula:

$$\text{long. correction} = \frac{\text{difference} \times \text{longitude}}{360}$$

4. Apply the correction to the L.M.T. of meridian passage for the day in question (from 1), positive for westerly longitude and negative for easterly longitude. (The result must lie between the two times in 1 and 2.)

5. The result is the L.M.T. for the meridian of the D.R. longitude, of the moon's meridian passage. The longitude in time must now be applied to obtain the G.M.T. This may then be used to extract the declination from the almanac.

Example 2
Find the G.M.T. of the meridian passage of the moon over the meridian of 40° 38′ E. on November 2nd.

L.M.T. mer. pass. for longitude 0° 2nd	0124
L.M.T. mer. pass. for longitude 0° 1st	0028
Difference = retardation =	56m

$$\text{Longitude correction} = \frac{56 \times 40° 38'}{360} = 7m$$

L.M.T. mer. pass. longitude 0° 2nd	0124
Longitude correction	7
L.M.T. mer. pass. longitude 40° 38′ E.	0117 November 2nd
Longitude in time	0243
G.M.T. mer. pass. longitude 40° 38′	2234 November 1st

Planets
The L.M.T. of meridian passage of the four navigational planets is given at the foot of each of the left hand daily pages. One figure is given for the three days on the page, this figure referring to the middle day on the page. Again this L.M.T. is for the Greenwich meridian and theoretically a longitude correction should be applied. However the amount of change over one day is never greater than a few minutes. Whether this is a significant change or not may be judged by inspecting the rate of change of the decination of the planets, for it is the declination which is to be extracted with the G.M.T. found. Inspection of the almanac will show that the change of declination over a few minutes is always negligble for any planet, and the longitude correction therefore may be ignored. The L.M.T. given on each daily page therefore may be taken as correct for any meridian on any of the three days on the page. It remains only to apply the longitude in time to obtain the G.M.T.

Example 3
Find the G.M.T. of meridian passage of the planet Mars over the meridian of 165° 15′ E. on March 24th.

L.M.T. mer. pass. Mars 24th	1644	24th
Longitude in time	1101	
G.M.T. mer. pass. Mars	0543	24th

Stars
The time of meridian passage of a star is not required in order to extract the declination from the almanac. As the declination of all stars remains constant over long periods, a value is given once for each three days for the brighter stars, and once per month for

others. A time will be required however to enable the navigator to commence his observations at the correct time, and for this extreme accuracy is not required.

The L.M.T. of meridian passage of the first point of Aries is given at the foot of the G.H.A. Aries column. This will always get approximately four minutes earlier each successive day. One figure is given for the three days on the page, the figure referring to the middle day of the page. It is therefore a simple matter to interpolate for each of the other two days on the page. The time for the first day on the page will be found by adding four minutes to the time given on that page, and the time for the last day on the page, by subtracting four minutes. This will give an L.M.T. for the Greenwich meridian for the day in question.

The longitude correction will never exceed two minutes and therefore may be ignored. Any star will cross a meridian earlier than the first point of Aries by an amount given approximately by the S.H.A. of the star in time.

More accurately the star will cross any meridian before the first point of Aries by the time it takes the earth to rotate through an angle equal to the S.H.A. The earth rotates through 15° 02·5′ per hour, hence this will be given by:

$$\frac{\text{S.H.A.}}{15° \ 02·5′}$$

In practice the error incurred by merely converting the S.H.A. to time cannot exceed four minutes. This gives a result which is accurate enough for practical purposes.

Example 4
Find the G.M.T. of meridian passage of the star Aldebaran over the meridian of 150° 30′ W. on October 31st.

L.M.T. mer. pass. Aries 31st	2121	(2117 + 4m)
S.H.A. in time	1925	
L.M.T. mer. pass. star	0156	31st
Longitude in time	1002	
G.M.T. mer. pass. star	1158	31st

To find whether any stars will cross the observer's meridian during the twilight period
If the S.H.A. of the celestial meridian, which coincides with the observer's celestial meridian, is found for the beginning of twilight, and also for the end of twilight, any star with an S.H.A. between the two values calculated will be suitable for a meridian altitude observation.

Example

Find any stars which will cross the meridian of 161° W. during the period 1712 L.M.T. to 1750 L.M.T. on October 31st.

L.M.T. beginning of twilight	1712
Longitude in time	1044

G.M.T. of beginning of twilight	2756	November 1st
G.H.A. Aries 03h	85° 01·4′	
Increment 56m	14° 02·3′	
G.H.A. Aries	99° 03·7′	
G.H.A. star = W. long.	161°	
S.H.A. star	61° 56·3′	will cross meridian at 1712 L.M.T. 31st

At 1750, i.e. 38 minutes later earth will have rotated through:

$$\frac{38 \times 15° 02·4′}{60} = 9·5° \text{ approximately}$$

Hence at 1750 the celestial meridian of 61° 56·3′ − 9° 30′ will be in transit over 161° W.

Any star with S.H.A. between 61° 56·3′ and 52° 26·3′ will cross 161° W. between 1712 and 1750.

By inspection of the almanac the star Peacock with S.H.A. 54° 04·8′ will be suitable, and the star Altair will be on the meridian a few minutes before (S.H.A. 62° 36·5′).

Finding the latitude

When the celestial body, and the observer's zenith occupy the same celestial meridian, then there is a simple relationship between the declination, the zenith distance and the latitude. All three are now arcs of the same great circle, and their values give the distance of each point from the equinoctial, and the distance of one from the other, the units of distance being the minute of arc of the great circle or nautical mile, if projected onto the earth's surface.

The relationships can be shown as in Figure 14.2.

Let Z be the observer's zenith, and X, X_1, and X_2 three bodies with declinations the same name and greater than the latitude, the same name and less than the latitude, and of opposite name to the latitude respectively. Let Q be the point where their meridian cuts the equinoctial.

Then

QZ = latitude
QX, QX_1, and QX_2 = the declinations of X, X_1, and X_2 respectively
ZX, ZX_1, and ZX_2 = the zenith distances of X, X_1, and X_2

In the case of X (declination same name as latitude and greater)

$$ZQ = QX - ZX$$
$$\text{latitude} = \text{declination} - \text{zenith distance.}$$

In the case of X_1 (declination same name and less than latitude)

$$ZQ = QX + ZX$$
$$\text{latitude} = \text{declination} + \text{zenith distance.}$$

In the case of X_2 (declination of opposite name to latitude)

$$ZQ = ZX - QX$$
$$\text{latitude} = \text{zenith distance} - \text{declination.}$$

These three simple relationships may be memorized, together with the conditions under which they apply, or each problem may be considered from first principles in the manner shown. The problem of finding the latitude by meridian altitude observation may now be summarized as follows.

1. Find the G.M.T. of meridian passage.
2. Extract the declination from the almanac.
3. Observe the altitude and correct to a true altitude.
4. Combine the zenith distance and the declination to find the latitude.
5. The same observation might have been taken from any meridian near the D.R. position, at slightly different times. The problem gives no information about longitude therefore. We may show this by stating that the position line runs 090° T./270° T. along the parallel of the latitude calculated.

Note

In order to find which formula is applicable, either the D.R. latitude must be known or the bearing of the body, north or south from the observer. In critical cases where the latitude and the

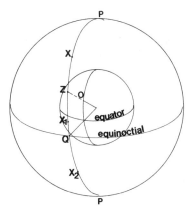

FIG. 14.2

declination are close to each other, then it is essential to resolve the ambiguity by considering whether the body passes to the north or to the south of the observer.

Example 1

On July 31st in D.R. position 15° 26′ N. 77° 18′ W. the sextant altitude of the sun's lower limb, when on the meridian to the north of the observer, was 87° 04·8′. Index error 2·0′ off the arc. Height of eye 12·0 metres. Find the latitude of the observer and state the direction of the position line.

L.M.T. mer. pass. 31st	1206	
Longitude W.	0509	
G.M.T.	1715	31st
Declination	18° 14·6′ N.	
'd'	−0·2′	
	18° 14·4′ N.	
Sextant altitude	87° 04·8′	
Index error	+2·0′	
Observed altitude	87° 06·8′	
Dip	−6·1′	
Apparent altitude	87° 00·7′	
T. correction	+15·9′	
True altitude	87° 16·6′	
Zenith distance	2° 43·4′	
Declination	18° 14·4′ N.	
Latitude	15° 31·0′ N.	

Position line runs 090° T./270° T.

Note

The body is about 18° north of the equator, while the observer is about 3° to the south of the body. The latitude is given therefore by declination minus zenith distance. The observer must also be to the north of the equator.

Example 2

On March 25th in D.R. position 30° 40′ S. 161° 20′ E., the sextant altitude of the planet Venus when on the meridian to the north of the observer, was 72° 37·6′. Index error nil. Height of eye 9·5 metres. Find the latitude and state the direction of the position line.

L.M.T. mer. pass. Venus 25th	0911	
Longitude in time	1045	
G.M.T.	2226	24th

Declination	13° 11·6′
'd'	− 0·2′
	13° 11·4′ S.
Sextant altitude	72° 37·6′
Index error	—
Observed altitude	72° 37·6′
Dip	− 5·4′
Apparent altitude	72° 32·2′
Correction	− 0·3′
True altitude	72° 31·9′
Zenith distance	17° 28·1′
Declination	13° 11·4′ S.
Latitude	30° 39·5′ S. P/L runs 090/270

In this case the body is to the south of the equator and the observer is to the south of the body. The latitude will therefore be found from the sum of the zenith distance and the declination. The observer must also be to the south of the equator.

Example 3

On October 20th in D.R. position 15° 30′ S. 32° 21′ W. the sextant altitude of the moon's lower limb when on the meridian to the south of the observer, was 83° 34·5′. Index error 2·0′ on the arc. Height of eye 10·0 metres. Find the latitude and state the direction of the position line.

L.M.T. mer. pass. for long. 0° 20th	1606	
L.M.T. mer. pass. for long. 0° 21st	1656	
Difference = retardation =	50m	
From Table II longitude correction = 4m		
L.M.T. mer. pass. for long. 0° 20th	1606	
Longitude correction	4	
L.M.T. mer. pass. for longitude 32° 21′ W.	1610	20th
Longitude in time	0209	
G.M.T. mer. pass.	1819	20th

Declination	21° 39·5′ S.
'd'	− 0·9′
	21° 38·6′ S.

	Sextant altitude	83° 34·5′
	Index error	− 2·0′
	Observed altitude	83° 32·5′

Dip	− 5·6'
Apparent altitude	83° 26·9'
Main correction	+ 17·2'
2nd correction	+ 4·1'
True altitude	83° 48·2'
Zenith distance	6° 11·8'
Declination	21° 38·6' S.
Latitude	15° 26·8' S.
P/L runs 090°/270°	

Example 4

On October 31st in D.R. position 50° N. 161° W. the sextant altitude of the star Altair when on the meridian to the south of the observer was 48° 58·1'. Index error 1·0' off the arc. Height of eye 11·5 metres. Find the latitude and state the direction of the position line. Also find the time when this meridian passage occurred.

Declination	8° 48·3' N.
Sextant altitude	48° 58·1'
Index error	+ 1·0'
Observed altitude	48° 59·1'
Dip	− 6·0'
Apparent altitude	48° 53·1'
Correction	− 0·8'
True altitude	48° 52·3'
Zenith distance	41° 07·7'
Declination	8° 48·3' N.
Latitude	49° 56·0' N.

To find the time of meridian passage.

G.H.A.* at mer. pass.	161° 00·0'
S.H.A.*	62° 36·5'
G.H.A. Aries	98° 23·5'
G.H.A. for 3h 1st	85° 01·4'
Difference	13° 22·1' = increment
Increment = 53m 20s	
G.M.T. = 3h 53m 20s	November 1st
Long. = 10h 44m 00s	
L.M.T. 17h 09m 20s	October 31st

Lower meridian passage
In Chapters 10 and 11, circumpolar bodies were discussed. During the daily rotation of the earth every body must not only cross the observer's meridian, but also the observer's lower meridian or antimeridian. A circumpolar body may be said to be one that is visible to an observer when this occurs. Whether a body is circumpolar or not depends upon the declination of the body and the latitude of the observer.
In general the conditions for circumpolarity are:

1. The declination must be the same name as the latitude.
2. The polar distance of the body must be less than the latitude.

Circumpolar bodies are discussed in more detail in Chapter 11.
Figure 14.3 shows the circle of declination of a circumpolar body to an observer in north latitude, on the plane of the observer's meridian.

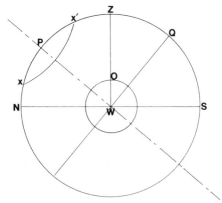

Fig. 14.3

Let Z be the observer's zenith.
Q the point where the observer's meridian cuts the equinoctial.
NWS the rational horizon.
xx' the circle of declination of a circumpolar body.
The arc NP = arc ZQ (both complements of PZ) and arc NP therefore is equal to the latitude.
When the body is at x then it is on the observer's lower meridian. Its true altitude is represented by the arc Nx, its angular height above the rational horizon. Px is the polar distance $(90° -$ declination).
Then at lower meridian passage:

$$NP = Px + Nx$$
$$latitude = polar\ distance + true\ altitude.$$

This formula holds good for all circumpolar bodies.

Finding the time of lower transit
Method 1. At lower transit the L.H.A. of the body is 180°. The G.H.A. therefore will be equal to the westerly longitude plus 180°. (subtracting if necessary 360°). Having found the G.H.A. thus the almanac may be inspected to find the G.M.T. at which this G.H.A. occurs for the body in question, in exactly the same way as described for the upper meridian passage.

Method 2. In the case of the moon, the L.M.T. of the lower transit is given for the Greenwich meridian under the heading 'Moon—mer. pass.—lower'. This figure is used in exactly the same manner as that described for finding the L.M.T. of the upper meridian passage.

In the case of the sun, planets and the first point of Aries, the lower meridian passage may be taken as 12 hours removed from the upper meridian passage, without any significant error resulting.

Example
On August 1st in D.R. position 55° 20′ N. 154° 30′ W. the sextant altitude of the star Alioth, when on the meridian below the pole was 21° 37·5′. Index error nil, height of eye 14·0 metres. Find the L.M.T. of this meridian passage and the observer's latitude.

$$\text{G.H.A.} = \text{W. long.} + 180° = 154° \ 30' + 180°$$

	$= 334° \ 30'$
S.H.A.*	$= 166° \ 46·3'$
G.H.A.* Aries	$= 167° \ 43·7'$
G.H.A. 14h 1st	$= 159° \ 47·8'$
Difference	$7° \ 55·9' =$ increment
Increment $= 31$m 38s	
G.M.T. $= 14$h 31m 38s	August 1st
Long. $= 10$h 18m 00s	
L.M.T. $= 04$h 13m 38s	

or

L.M.T. mer. pass. Aries 1st	0322
	+ 1200
L.M.T. lower transit (approx.)	1522
S.H.A.	1107
L.M.T. mer. pass. Alioth	0415 approx.
Declination	56° 06·0′ N.
Sextant altitude	21° 37·5′
Index error	—

Observed altitude	21° 37·5′
Dip	− 6·6′
Apparent altitude	21° 30·9′
Correction	− 2·4′
True altitude	21° 28·5′
Polar distance	33° 54·0′
Latitude	55° 22·5′ N.

P/L runs 090/270

Maximum and meridian altitudes

For a stationary observer the maximum altitude of a body of constant declination will occur when the body crosses the observer's meridian. If when the body is on the meridian, the declination or the observer's latitude are changing, then the meridian altitude will not be the maximum.

If the combined effect of a change of latitude and of declination is to bring the observer closer to the geographical position, then the meridian altitude will still be increasing. The observer's movement towards the G.P. will cause an increase of altitude. The maximum altitude will occur after the meridian passage. If the combined effect of the change of declination and of latitude is to open out the observer and the G.P. then the meridian altitude will be decreasing and maximum altitude will have already occurred before the meridian passage.

Maximum altitude will occur when the rate of change of altitude due to the rotation of the earth is equal and of opposite sign to the rate of change of latitude and declination combined.

When observing the meridian altitude, in fact the maximum altitude will be obtained. The difference between the two will in normal navigable latitudes be small and may be neglected. The time interval between meridian passage and maximum altitude will also increase with latitude and may be several minutes in high latitudes.

For example, assuming the following conditions:

Latitude 60° N.
Declination 5° S. changing south by 1·0′ per hour.
Ship steaming north at 19 knots.

Then maximum altitude will occur 9·3 minutes before the meridian passage and will exceed the meridian altitude by 1·5′. The same conditions except that the observer's latitude is 30° N. would give a maximum altitude occurring 3·4 minutes before the meridian passage and 0·5′ greater than the meridian altitude.

Although it is usual in practice to ignore this correction the effect should be borne in mind in high latitudes, particularly when observing a body with a rapid change in declination such as the moon. The effect will, of course be more pronounced in high speed vessels.

The time interval in minutes of time is given by the formula:

$$\frac{15\cdot3x\,(\tan \text{lat} \pm \tan \text{dec})}{60} \qquad \begin{array}{l} \text{sign} - \text{lat and dec same name} \\ \text{sign} + \text{lat and dec opposite} \end{array}$$

where x is the combined change of latitude and declination, in minutes of arc per hour.

Having found the interval the change of altitude between maximum and meridian altitude may be found approximately by extracting the reduction from the ex-meridian tables, using the interval as the hour angle.

EXERCISE 14

1. On January 5th in D.R. position 45° 05′ S. 75° 18′ E. the sextant altitude of the moon's upper limb when on the meridian to the north of the observer was 21° 15·4′. Index error 1·0′ off the arc. Height of eye 14·5 metres. Find the latitude and state the direction of the position line.

2. On June 25th in D.R. longitude 40° 20′ W. the sextant altitude of the sun's lower limb when on the meridian to the north of the observer was 41° 26·4′. Index error 2·4′ off the arc. Height of eye 7·3 metres. Find the latitude and state the direction of the position line.

3. On January 6th in D.R. longitude 96° 35′ W., the sextant altitude of the sun's upper limb when on the meridian to the north of the observer was 61° 25′. Index error 1·4′ on the arc. Height of eye 11·5 metres. Find the latitude and state the direction of the position line.

4. On January 5th in longitude 45° 20′ E. the observed altitude of the moon's lower limb when on the meridian to the north of the observer was 40° 18·5′. Height of eye 5·5 metres. Find the latitude.

5. On November 1st in D.R. position 45° 10′ N. 165° 18′ E. the sextant altitude of the moon's lower limb when on the meridian to the south of the observer was 62° 18·6′. Index error 2·0′ off the arc. Height of eye 10·5 metres. Find the latitude and state the direction of the position line.

6. Find the G.M.T. and the L.M.T. of the meridian passage of the star Sabik during morning twilight on March 25th in D.R. position 30° 09′ N. 133° 45′ E. Index error 1·5′ on the arc. Height of eye 10 metres. Find the latitude if the sextant altitude was 44° 18·8′.

7. On October 21st in D.R. longitude 150° 15′ E. the sextant altitude of the star Altair when on the meridian to the north of the

observer was 67° 15·6'. Index error nil. Height of eye 14·5 metres. Find the latitude and state the direction of the position line.

8. On June 24th in D.R. longitude 170° W. the sextant altitude of the star Fomalhaut when on the meridian to the south of the observer was 20° 37'. Index error 1·5' on the arc. Height of eye 15 metres. Find the latitude and state the direction of the position line.

9. On March 24th in D.R. longitude 165° 15' E. the sextant altitude of the planet Mars when on the meridian to the south of the observer was 62° 47·6'. Index error 1·0' off the arc. Height of eye 15·5 metres. Find the latitude and state the direction of the position line.

10. Compute the sextant altitude and find the L.M.T. when the star Aldebaran is on the meridian of an observer in longitude 142° 10' W. on August 1st. Index error 0·6' off the arc. Height of eye 13·3 metres. D.R. latitude 5° 25' S.

CHAPTER 15

THE POLE STAR PROBLEM

At the present time, the northern end of the axis of rotation of the earth, is pointing to a direction in space, which is less than one degree from a star which is known as Polaris. Due to the precession of the equinox the celestial pole is moving closer to Polaris and will be at its closest about the year 2000. From then on it will move away and eventually other stars will be approached and they will become pole stars. Any star whose celestial latitude is $66\frac{1}{2}°$ will be approached by the celestial pole as it moves around the pole of the ecliptic in the period of 25,800 years.

The proximity of Polaris to the pole means that by measuring the altitude of the star and applying corrections, which are pre-computed and published in the form of tables in the *Nautical Almanac*, the altitude of the northern pole can be ascertained.

It can be shown that the altitude of the pole is equal to the observer's latitude.

Figure 15.1, on the plane of the observer's meridian.

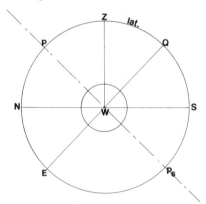

FIG. 15.1

Arcs   PN = altitude of the pole
          ZQ = observer's latitude
Plane NS = rational horizon
          EQ = equinoctial

From the diagram ZQ = PN (both are complements of the arc PZ). Thus the alt. of the pole = observer's latitude.

The problem is therefore to obtain the true altitude of the pole star and correct it to give the altitude of the pole.

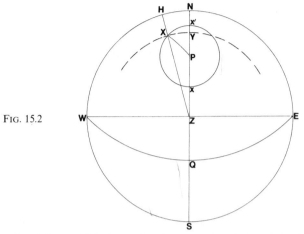

FIG. 15.2

Let Figure 15.2 show the circumpolar circle of declination of the pole star (polar distance is much exaggerated), and X the position of the star at any time.

Then the altitude of Polaris = HX and the altitude of the pole = NP.

Let XY be the circle of equal altitude passing through the star and cutting the observer's meridian at Y.

Then NY = HX = altitude of the pole star.

Clearly the difference between the altitude of the star and the altitude of the pole is the arc of the meridian PY and this is the correction which we must obtain.

There will be two occasions during the daily motion of the star around its circle of declination when the correction is zero, i.e. when the star is at x and x'. When the star is at its lower meridian passage at x' then the correction will be equal to the polar distance of the star and will be positive to the star's altitude to give the altitude of the pole. When the star is at its upper meridian passage then the correction will also be equal to the polar distance but will be negative. At any other time the correction will be equal to PY and will sometimes be positive and sometimes be negative.

At any time the correction can be found by considering the triangle PXY (note that this is not a spherical triangle as the arc XY is not part of a great circle). By considering this triangle to be small and treating it as a plane right angled triangle then the value of PY can be approximated as

$$PY = PX \cos P$$
$$= \text{polar dist.} \times \cos \text{local hour angle.}$$

However a more accurate solution is sought in the compilation of the pole star tables.

Let the correction $= y$; altitude of the pole $= a$; thus

$$\text{latitude} = a + y.$$

In the triangle PZX by the spherical cosine formula

$$\cos P = \frac{\cos ZX - \cos PX \cos PZ}{\sin PX \sin PZ}$$

$$\cos P = \frac{\sin a - \cos p \sin(a+y)}{\sin p \cos(a+y)}$$

$$\cos P \sin p \cos(a+y) = \sin a - \cos p \sin(a+y)$$

$$\cos P \sin p (\cos a \cos y - \sin a \sin y)$$
$$= \sin a - \cos p (\sin a \cos y + \cos a \sin y)$$

$$\cos P \sin p \cos a \cos y - \cos P \sin p \sin a \sin y$$
$$= \sin a - (\cos p \sin a \cos y + \cos p \cos a \sin y)$$

p and y are small angles therefore

$$\sin p = p^c \quad \sin y = y^c$$

$$\cos p = \left(1 - \frac{p^2}{2}\right) \quad \cos y = \left(1 - \frac{y^2}{2}\right)$$

$$\cos Pp \cos a \left(1 - \frac{y^2}{2}\right) - \cos Ppy \sin a$$

$$= \sin a - \sin a \left(1 - \frac{p^2}{2}\right)\left(1 - \frac{y^2}{2}\right) - \left(1 - \frac{p^2}{2}\right) y \cos a$$

multiplying out the brackets and neglecting third order terms.

$$\cos Pp \cos a - \cos Ppy \sin a = \sin a - \left(1 - \frac{p^2}{2} - \frac{y^2}{2}\right) \sin a - y \cos a$$

$$\cos P(p \cos a - py \sin a) = \sin a \left(\frac{p^2}{2} + \frac{y^2}{2}\right) - y \cos a$$

$$\frac{y \cos a}{\cos a} = \tan a \left(\frac{p^2}{2} + \frac{y^2}{2}\right) - \cos Pp + \cos Py \tan ap$$

$$y = -p \cos P + \tan a \left(\frac{p^2}{2} + \frac{y^2}{2} + \cos Ppy\right)$$

To the first approximation $y = -p\cos P$ so substituting this into the second order term

$$y = -p\cos P + \tan a \left(\frac{p^2}{2} + \frac{p^2 \cos^2 P}{2} - \cos^2 P p^2 \right)$$

$$= -p\cos P + \tan a \frac{p^2}{2}(1 + \cos^2 P - 2\cos^2 P)$$

$$= -p\cos P + \tan a \frac{p^2}{2}(\sin^2 P)$$

Using this formula the value of y, the correction to the altitude of the pole star to obtain the altitude of the pole, is calculated using mean values for declination and for a, the latitude of the observer (altitude of the pole). A mean value for S.H.A. of Polaris is used to tabulate the correction against L.H.A. of Aries instead of the L.H.A. of the star.

Thus a mean value of declination and S.H.A. are used for the year and a latitude of 50° is used. The value of y obtained is then a function of L.H.A. of Aries and is tabulated against this quantity and called a_0. A further correction is also computed which gives the change in a_0 caused by the use of a different latitude to the standard latitude of 50°. This quantity is called a_1. A correction which takes into account the changes in declination and S.H.A. throughout the year is then tabulated as a_2.

Thus:

a_0 is a function of the L.H.A. of the first point of Aries using mean values for S.H.A. and declination and a latitude of 50°. The computed values are adjusted by the addition of a constant so that the value is always positive.

a_1 is a function of L.H.A. of the first point of Aries and latitude and is the excess of the second order term over its mean value for latitude 50°. The values are increased by a constant such that they are always positive.

a_2 is a function of the L.H.A. of the first point of Aries and of date and is a correction to the first term for the variation of the S.H.A. and declination during the year. The values are increased by a constant so that they are always positive.

The sum of the three constants added is exactly one degree. This must be subtracted from the final answer, so that

latitude = true altitude Polaris $+ a_0 + a_1 + a_2 - 1°$

The azimuth of the pole star at any time is the arc HN.

$HN = XY \sec a$

$= PX \sin P \sec a$

$Az^c = $ polar dist^c sin hour angle sec lat.

This is tabulated in the pole star tables against the local hour angle of Aries using the mean value for S.H.A. for the year and the mean value of declination. These require no adjustment for variation in these quantities.

Procedure for the pole star problem
1. Find the G.M.T. of the observation and extract the L.H.A. of the first point of Aries from the almanac.
2. Correct the sextant altitude to obtain the true altitude.
3. With the L.H.A. of Aries enter the pole star tables and extract a_0, a_1, a_2, and the azimuth.
4. Find the latitude by adding the corrections to the true altitude and subtracting $1°$. Find the direction of the position line by inspection of the azimuth.

Worked example
On January 6th in D.R. longitude $52° 30'$ W. at L.M.T. 1845, an observation of the pole star gave a sextant altitude of $40° 15.5'$. Index error $1.5'$ off the arc. Height of eye 10 metres. Find the direction of the position line and the position through which it passes.

L.M.T.	1845	
Long. W.	0330	
G.M.T.	2215	6th

G.H.A. Aries 22h	$76° 05.8'$	
Increment 15m	$3° 45.6'$	
G.H.A.	$79° 51.4'$	
Longitude	$52° 30.0'$	W.
L.H.A. Aries	$27° 21.4'$	
Sextant altitude	$40° 15.5'$	
I.E.	$+1.5'$	
Observed altitude	$40° 17.0'$	
Dip	$-5.6'$	
Apparent altitude	$40° 11.4'$	
Correction	$-1.1'$	
True altitude	$40° 10.3'$	
a_0	$0° 08.0'$	
a_1	$0.6'$	
a_2	$0.7'$	
	$40° 19.6'$	
	$1°$	
	$39° 19.6'$	Bearing $= 000.1°$

Position line runs $270.1°/090.1°$ through $39° 19.6'$ N. $52° 30'$ W.

Note

Only if the bearing is exactly 000° can the latitude calculated be the ship's latitude. The position line in this case will run east-west. Usually in practice the bearing is close enough to 000° to assume that this is so. The bearing may, however, be up to 2° east or west of the meridian, which may introduce errors in the latitude if the D.R. longitude is very far from the actual longitude. Strictly, the latitude calculated and the D.R. longitude constitute a position through which the position line passes.

EXERCISE 15

1. In longitude 169° 14′ E. on October 20th at approximate ship's time 0630, the sextant altitude of the pole star was observed to be 40° 38·7′. Index error 1·5′ off the arc. Height of eye 11·0 metres. A chronometer at the time showed 7h 12m 14s and was 2m 05s slow on G.M.T. Find the direction of the position line and the position through which it passes.

2. In longitude 100° 01′ W. on November 1st at approximate ship's time 1815 the observed altitude of the pole star was 25° 14·6′. Height of eye 9·6 metres. A chronometer read 00h 58m 13s and was correct on G.M.T. Find the direction of the position line and the position, through which it passes.

3. Find the altitude to set on a sextant to observe the pole star at 0650 L.M.T. to an observer in longitude 52° 17′ W. The D.R. latitude is 46° 18′ N. and the date at ship June 24th. Index error 3·4′ on the arc. Height of eye 10·0 metres.

4. On June 24th in D.R. position 47° 15′ N. 125° 40′ W. at L.M.T. 0500 the sextant altitude of the pole star was observed to be 47° 52′. Index error 1·4′ off the arc. Height of eye 6·1 metres. A chronometer read 01h 20m 44s and was correct on G.M.T. Find the direction of the position line and a position through which it passes.

5. On January 4th at ship in D.R. position 22° 40′ N. 163° 20′ W. at 4h 58m 20s G.M.T., the sextant altitude of the pole star was observed to be 23° 40·4′. Index error 0·8′ off the arc. Height of eye 13·2 metres. Find the direction of the position line and a position through which it passes.

CHAPTER 16

AZIMUTHS AND AMPLITUDES

In order to ascertain the error of either a magnetic or a gyro compass, it is required to be able to find at any instant the true bearing of a celestial body from the observer. A comparison with a compass bearing taken at the chosen time will yield the error of the compass, and the deviation.

In Chapter 5 the term azimuth was explained. It may be defined as the angle at the zenith between the direction of the elevated pole and the vertical circle passing through the body, measured from 0° to 180° on either side of the meridian. The azimuth is named the same as the latitude and east if the body is rising or west if the body is setting. It should be clear therefore that the azimuth is the angle Z in the PZX triangle, and in order to find the azimuth a solution of the triangle is necessary.

The conversion of an azimuth into a true bearing is given in Chapter 5.

The arguments necessary for the solution of the PZX triangle for the azimuth are:

1. Local hour angle ($\angle$ P).
2. Declination (PX).
3. D.R. latitude (PZ).

Extreme accuracy is not required however for the purpose of finding the compass error, nor for the calculation of the direction of the position line in the reduction of sights. Answers to the nearest half degree are adequate. The problem is simplified therefore by the provision, in nautical tables, of tabulated solutions of the spherical triangle. These are named ABC tables and may be used for the solution of any spherical triangle. They are specifically designed however for the solution of the nautical triangle and the columns are headed accordingly. The true bearing is extracted from the tables and not the azimuth, although they are usually thought of as azimuth tables.

The ABC tables

The tabulations are based upon the application of the spherical four part formula to the PZX triangle. The formula states: if the four adjacent parts of a spherical triangle are considered, then

cot outer side × sin inner side = (cot outer angle × sin inner angle)
+(cos inner side × cos outer angle)

Applying this to the PZX triangle we have:

FIG. 16.1

P

P = inner angle

PX = outer side

PZ = inner side

X

Z = outer angle

Z

Considering the adjacent parts,

azimuth – PZ – ∠ P – PX

$$\text{cot PX sin PZ} = (\text{cot az. sin } \angle P) + (\cos PZ \cos \angle P)$$

or

$$\text{tan dec. cos lat.} = (\text{cot az. sin P}) + (\sin \text{lat. cos P})$$

Dividing by sin P cos lat.

$$\text{tan dec. cosec P} = (\text{cot az. sec lat.}) + (\text{tan lat. cot P})$$

The quantity cot az. × sec lat. is tabulated as 'C'. The quantity tan dec. × cosec P is tabulated as 'B'. The quantity tan lat. × cot P is tabulated as 'A'.

So that

$$C = B - A$$

or

$$-C = A - B \qquad (1)$$

if B is greater than A, C becomes negative, then

$$C = B - A \qquad (2)$$

If latitude and declination are of opposite names then the side PX is greater than 90° and its tangent and cotangent are negative. Thus a negative sign must be attached to B giving

$$-C = A + B \qquad (3)$$

Under the conditions of (1) and (3), which make C negative then the quadrant in which the bearing lies is named opposite to the latitude. When C is positive as in (2) then the bearing is named the same as the latitude. In fact the negative sign against C in (1) is ignored in the tabulation, which means that the above rules must be reversed. Thus if C is positive then the bearing is named opposite to the latitude. If C is negative then the bearing is named the same as the latitude.

If the hour angle is greater than 90° and less than 270° then the bearing must be the same name as the latitude. This can only occur if the latitude and declination are the same name. In such cases the sign of A is reversed.

The bearing will also be named east or west depending upon whether the body is rising or setting.

Full instructions for naming the bearing are given with the tables, and these should be followed carefully.

The procedure for the azimuth problem is therefore:

1. Observe the compass error and note the G.M.T.
2. Compute the L.H.A. of the body and extract the declination from the almanac.
3. With the D.R. latitude, solve the PZX triangle by ABC tables, to obtain the true bearing of the body.
4. Compare the true and compass bearings to obtain the compass error.
5. Apply the variation to find the deviation if necessary.

Example 1
On August 1st in D.R. position 52° 48′ N. 42° 18′ W. at L.M.T. 1609 the compass bearing of the sun was observed to be 262°. Find the error of the compass and the deviation for the ship's head if the variation was 4° W.

L.M.T.	1609	
Long.	0249	
G.M.T.	1858 1st	Declination = 17° 58·4′ N.
G.H.A.	88° 25·7′	
Incr.	14° 30·0′	
G.H.A.	102° 55·7′	
Long.	42° 18·0′ W.	
L.H.A.	60° 37·7′	
'A'	= 0·743 + (hour angle less than 90°)	
'B'	= 0·374 − (lat. and dec. same name)	
'C'	= 0·369 +	

Values of A and B must be found by interpolation, in this problem between values of hour angle of 60° and 61°, and values of latitude between 52° and 53°. Declination may be taken here as 18°.

Inspecting the C table for latitude 52·8° azimuth = 77·4°.

Following the instructions for naming C then the bearing is in the SW quadrant.

$$\text{True bearing} = \text{S. } 77.4° \text{ W.}$$

$$= 257.4°$$
$$\text{Compass brg} = 262.0°$$

Comp. error	=	4·6° W.
Variation	=	4·0° W.
Deviation	=	0·6° W.

Example 2

On March 24th in D.R. position 25° 40′ S. 175° 45′ W. at L.M.T. 0325 the compass bearing of the star Gacrux was observed to be $214\frac{1}{2}°$ by gyro compass. Find the error of the gyro.

L.M.T.	0325		
Long.	1143		
G.M.T.	1508	24th	Declination 56° 58·3′ S.

G.H.A. Aries 15h	46° 42·2′
Increment	2° 00·3′
G.H.A. Aries	48° 42·5′
S.H.A.*	172° 33·2′
G.H.A.*	221° 15·7′
Longitude	175° 45·0′ W.
L.H.A.*	45° 30·7′ (body is setting as L.H.A. is less than 180°)

'A' $= 0.472 + $ (interpolating between latitudes 25° and 26°)
'B' $= 2.160 -$
'C' $= \overline{1.688 -}$

Bearing $=$ S. 33·3° W.

$$= 213.3°$$
$$\text{Gyro brg} = 214.5°$$
$$\text{Error} = \overline{1.2° \text{ high}}$$

EXERCISE 16A

1. On March 24th in D.R. position 20° 00′ S. 160° 00′ W. at L.M.T. 0800 the compass bearing of the sun was observed to be 071°. Find the error of the compass and the deviation for the ship's head if the variation was 5° E.

2. On October 31st in D.R. position 35° N. 78° W. at L.M.T. 1420 the gyro bearing of the sun was observed to be 225° G. Find the error of the compass.

3. On November 1st in D.R. position 30° 30′ N. 158° 30′ E. at L.M.T. 1115, the compass bearing of the sun was observed to be 172°. Find the error of the compass and the deviation for the ship's head if the variation was 10° E.

4. On June 24th in D.R. position 18° S. 59° 30′ E. at L.M.T. 2330 the compass bearing of the star Arcturus was observed to be 300°. Find the error of the compass.

5. On January 4th in D.R. position 25° 14′ N. 138° 20′ W. at L.M.T. 0325 the compass bearing of the star Betelgeuse was observed to be 269°. Find the error of the compass.

6. On July 31st in D.R. position 38° 40′ S. 160° 20′ E. at L.M.T. 0030 the compass bearing of the star Achernar was observed to be 145°. Find the error of the compass.

7. On June 24th in D.R. position 38° 45′ N. 7° 15′ E. at G.M.T. 02h 12m the compass bearing of the star Rasalhague was observed to be 247°. If the variation was 8° W. find the error of the compass and the deviation for the ship's head.

8. On 26th June in D.R. position 5° 05′ N. 61° 30′ E. at approximate ship's time 2230 the gyro bearing of the moon was observed to be 262° G. A chronometer showed at the time 6h 25m 30s and was correct on G.M.T. Find the error of the gyro.

9. On January 5th in D.R. position 43° 46′ N. 34° 18′ E. at approximate ship's time 0115 the gyro bearing of the moon was observed to be 278° G. A chronometer correct on G.M.T. showed 11h 30m 10s. Find the error of the gyro.

Amplitudes
The special case for the solution of the azimuth is when the body is on the observer's rational horizon. The angle at the zenith between the prime vertical and the vertical circle passing through the body is called the amplitude of the body. It is named east or west depending upon whether the body is rising or setting, and north or south depending upon which quadrant of the compass the bearing lies in. Any body will rise to the north of east and set to the north of west, if the declination is north. If the declination is south then the body will rise to the south of east and set to the south of west. A body with zero declination will rise bearing due east and set bearing due west.

The value of the amplitude will always be the compliment of the bearing, expressed in quadrantal notation. It is then the difference between the rising bearing and 090°, or the difference between the setting bearing and 270°.

In Figure 16.2 the rising amplitude of body X will be the angle EZX, which is drawn equal to E. 20° N. The setting amplitude will be W. 20° N. The amplitude of body X′ will be angle EZX′, which is drawn equal to E. 30° S. The setting amplitude will be W. 30° S.

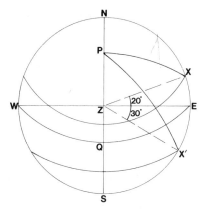

FIG. 16.2

The observation of the compass bearing of a body rising or setting, for comparison with the calculated true bearing, provides a quick and accurate check on the compass error. Only the sun and the moon are visible at rising and setting, as even in clear weather there is sufficient horizon haze to render stars and planets invisible. It must be remembered also that the visible rising and setting will not coincide with the theoretical rising and setting, when the body is on the rational horizon.

To find the observed altitude at theoretical rising or setting
At theoretical rising or setting the true altitude of the centre of the body will be 0°. Application of the altitude corrections in reverse order will give the observed altitude at that moment. Assuming a height of eye of 12·0 metres then:

True altitude	0° 00·0′
Parallax	− 00·15
	− 0° 00·15′
Semi-diam. (L.L.)	− 16·0
Apparent altitude	− 0° 16·15′
Refraction	+ 34·0
	+ 0° 17·85′
Dip	+ 6·1
Observed altitude	23·95′

At the moment of theoretical rising therefore the sun is above the visible horizon. As a guide it may be remembered that the lower limb is approximately a semi-diameter above the visible horizon for small heights of eye, and slightly higher than this for the heights of eye usually found in merchant ships. This is the time when the compass bearing should be observed.

To find the observed altitude at theoretical moonrise or moonset

True altitude	$0°\ 00\!\cdot\!0'$
Hor. parallax	$-58\!\cdot\!0'$
	$-0°\ 58\!\cdot\!0'$
Semi-diam. (L.L.)	$-15\!\cdot\!8'$
	$-1°\!\cdot\!13\!\cdot\!8'$
Refraction	$+34\!\cdot\!0$
Apparent altitude	$-0°\ 39\!\cdot\!8'$
Dip	$+6\!\cdot\!1'$
Observed altitude	$-0°\ 33\!\cdot\!7'$

Thus at theoretical rising and setting of the moon, the disc is not visible, being below the visible horizon by approximately a diameter. It is therefore more difficult to judge the exact moment of rising or setting of the moon than the sun.

Any errors incurred by not taking the compass bearing at the correct time of true rising or setting will be small in low latitudes. On the equator all bodies rise perpendicular to the horizon and no error will be incurred by taking the bearing at visible rising. As latitude increases the angle at which the path, taken by the body in its daily journey around the sky, cuts the horizon, decreases until at the poles all bodies will appear to circle the sky parallel to the horizon. This is discussed in detail in Chapter 11. In normal navigable latitudes, as long as the moment of theoretical rising or setting is judged according to the principles described above, the errors will be acceptably small. It should be born in mind however that in high latitudes significant errors may be introduced in doing this.

Times of rising and setting

The right hand of each of the daily pages in the *Nautical Almanac* contains times of rising and setting, given once for the three days for the sun and once for each day in the case of the moon. These times are for visible rising and setting and are calculated assuming a value of refraction of $34\!\cdot\!0'$ of arc. The times must be interpolated for latitude.

It must be remembered that the times given are Local Mean Times, calculated for the Greenwich meridian. They should be corrected for longitude in the manner explained in Chapter 14 for finding the times of meridian passages. The longitude correction for the sun however will be small enough to be neglected, and in order to find the G.M.T. with which to extract the declination, it will be sufficient to take the time given for the appropriate page and apply the longitude in time. The rate of change of declination of the sun is small enough such that extreme accuracy is not required.

When finding the times of moonrise or moonset however, it is most important that a longitude correction is applied, the procedure after interpolating the times given for the latitude is exactly the same as that described for finding the time of the moon's meridian passage. The following examples should make the problem clear.

Example 1
Find the G.M.T. of moonrise on March 25th for a position 57° N. 158° W.

L.M.T. moonrise 25th lat. 57° long. 0°	0543		(these figures
L.M.T. moonrise 26th lat. 57° long. 0°	0601		interpolated between lat. 56°
Difference	18m		and 58° N.)

$$\text{Longitude correction} = \frac{18 \times 158}{360} = 8\text{m}$$

L.M.T. moonrise 25th lat. 57° N. long. 0°	0543	
Longitude correction	8	
L.M.T. moonrise lat. 57° N. long 158° W.	0551	
Longitude in time	1032	
G.M.T. moonrise 57° N. 158° W.	1623	25th

Example 2
Find the G.M.T. of moonset on August 1st in position 64° N. 160° E.

L.M.T. moonset lat. 64° N. long. 0° 1st	0111	
L.M.T. moonset lat. 64° N. long. 0° 30th	2351	
Difference	0120	

$$\text{Longitude correction} = \frac{80 \times 160}{360} = 36\text{m}$$

L.M.T. moonset lat. 64° N. long. 0° 1st	0111	
Longitude correction	36	
L.M.T. moonset lat. 64° N. long. 160° E.	0035	1st
Longitude in time	1040	
G.M.T. moonset lat. 64° N. long. 160° E.	1355	31st

Note
The figure given for moonset on the 31st (2511) is the same moonset as the one on the 1st (0111). The retardation is found by taking the time of the previous moonset, which does not necessarily occur on the preceding day. In this case the previous moonset occurred on the 30th.

It is possible because of the effect of changing declination for successive moonrises or moonsets to get earlier and not later as normally happens. In this case the retardation has become an advance and the rules for the sign of the longitude correction must be reversed, i.e. for westerly longitudes the correction is negative, and for easterly longitudes the correction is positive.

The effect of the change of declination on the times of rising and setting is explained in Chapter 8.

The amplitude formula

The application of Napier's rules to the quadrantal triangle which is formed by the pole, the zenith and the body, when the body is on the rational horizon, gives a simple formula for the amplitude. At theoretical rising or setting the zenith distance of the body is 90°. Figure 16.3 show such a body on the plane of the rational horizon, for an observer in north latitude and a body of northerly declination.

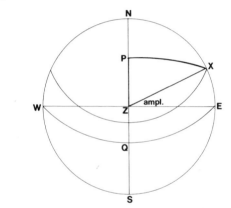

FIG. 16.3

In triangle PZX by Napier's rules

$$\text{sin comp. } PX = \text{cos comp. } pZ \times \cos Z$$
$$\text{sin dec.} = \cos \text{lat.} \times \sin \text{amplitude}$$
$$\text{sin amplitude} = \sin \text{dec.} \times \sec \text{latitude.}$$

The procedure for the amplitude problem may now be summarized.

1. Observe the compass bearing at the time of theoretical rising or setting. The G.M.T. of the occurrence may be worked before hand.
2. Extract the declination from the almanac.
3. With a D.R. latitude solve the amplitude formula.
4. Compare the true bearing with the compass bearing to find the compass error and if necessary the deviation.

Example

At sunrise on November 2nd the sun bore 101° by compass, to an observer in D.R. position 41° 29' N. 120° 30' E. Find the error of the compass.

L.M.T. sunrise November 2nd lat. 41½°	0631
Longitude in time	0802
G.M.T. sunrise Nov. 2nd 41° 29' N. 120° 30' E.	2229 1st Nov.

Declination   14° 32·2' S.

$\sin$ ampl. $= \sin 14° 32·3' \sec 41° 29'$
ampl. $= 19° 34·6'$

amplitude $=$ E. 19° 34·6' S.

	no.	log.
sin dec.		$\overline{1}$·39968
sec lat.		0·12543
sin amp.		$\overline{1}$·52511

Note
Named east because the body is rising and south, the same as the declination.

True brg.	109° 34·6'
Comp. brg.	101°
Compass error	8° 34·6' E.

Example 2
On June 24th in D.R. position 40° S. 172° W. the sun set bearing 302° by gyro. Find the error of the compass.

L.M.T. sunset 24th 40° S.	1642
Longitude	1128
G.M.T. sunset 40° S. 178° W.	0410 25th

Declination   23° 24·1' N.

$\sin$ ampl. $= \sin 23° 24·1' \sec 40°$

	no.	log.
$\sin 23° 24·1'$		$\overline{1}$·59898
$\sec 40°$		0·11575
sin amp.		$\overline{1}$·71473

amplitude $=$ W. 31° 13·9' N.

True brg. $=$	301¼°
Gyro brg. $=$	302
Error $=$	¾° high

Example 3
On July 30th in D.R. position 22° 15' S. 150° 30' W. the moon set bearing 253° by compass. Find the error of the compass.

L.M.T. moonset 30th $22\frac{1}{4}°$ S. long. 0°   0339
L.M.T. moonset 31st $22\frac{1}{4}°$ S. long. 0°   0426

Difference $\overline{47'}$

$$\text{Longitude correction} = \frac{47 \times 150\cdot5}{360} = 20\text{m}$$

L.M.T. moonset 30th $22\frac{1}{4}°$ S. long. 0°   0339
Longitude correction   20

L.M.T. moonset $22\frac{1}{4}°$ long. 150° 30′ W.   0359
Longitude in time   1002

G.M.T. moonset $22\frac{1}{4}°$ S. $150\frac{1}{2}°$ W.   1401   30th

Declination	22° 35·3′ S.
'd'	−0·1′
	22° 35·2′ S.

sin ampl. = sin 22° 35·2′ sec 22° 15′
amplitude = W. 24° 31·1′ S.
True bearing = $245\frac{1}{2}°$
Compass brg. = 253°

Compass error $7\frac{1}{2}°$ W.

	no.	log.
sin 22° 35·2′		$\overline{1}·58442$
sec 22° 15′		0·03360
		$\overline{1}·61802$

Amplitude tables
Amplitudes are tabulated in nautical tables against latitude and
declination. These are sufficiently accurate enough for practical
observations. The range of declinations covered extends to 28°,
which is the approximate maximum declination of the moon. If it
required to find the amplitude of a star, whose declination is greater
than 28° then the amplitude formula must be used. This is not likely
to be required in practice, but theoretical problems are encountered
particularly in figure drawing where this may have to be done.

Together with the amplitude is given a number of minutes of time,
which is referred to as the Time Amplitude. This is the number of
minutes that the time of rising or setting differs from 0600 hrs, or
1800 hrs. It will be the difference in the hour angle of the body when
rising or setting and 270° or 90°, expressed in time. The time
amplitude enables the L.A.T. of rising or setting to be found easily
if the observed body is the sun. It will not however give the L.M.T.
unless the equation of time is applied.

EXERCISE 16B

Find the error of the compass and the deviation in the following cases.

	Body	Date	D.R.		Compass brg.	Variation
1.	Sun rising	January 6th	6° 18′ S.	42° 19′ W.	100°	6° W.
2.	Moon setting	October 31st	19° 18′ N.	160° 42′ W.	268°	3° E.
3.	Sun setting	March 25th	5° 57′ N.	88° 16′ E.	269°	3° W.
4.	Sun rising	November 1st	32° 00′ S.	115° 00′ E.	095°	nil
5.	Moon setting	January 4th	23° 40′ N.	52° 30′ W.	285°	8° W.
6.	Sun rising	July 31st	40° 15′ N.	36° 40′ W.	074°	9° W.

APPENDIX 1

Practical Paper 1   **Time allowed 2 hours**

Answer all questions.

1. On June 25th at approximate L.M.T. 1530, in D.R. position 28° 18′ S. 175° 35′ W., the sextant altitude of the sun's lower limb was observed to be 18° 37·5′. Index error 1·5′ on the arc. Height of eye 11·5 metres. A chronometer showed 3h 08m 14s and was slow on G.M.T. by 0m 18s. Find the direction of the position line and a position through which it passes.

                                                      35 marks

2. A vessel left a position 28° 19·8′ S. 175° 32·6′ W. at 1530 L.M.T. on June 25th, for a position off Panama of 8° 30′ N. 79° 40′ W. Find the course and distance to steam by mercator sailing and the L.M.T. of arrival if the average speed of the vessel is 18·5 knots.

                                                      25 marks

3. From the following sights find the position of the ship at the time of the second observation.

    Time 1430. D.R. 43° 13′ N. 150° 46′ E. Intercept 1·6′ towards bearing 217° T.

    Run. Course 290° T. distance 60 miles and then 265° T. distance 35 miles.

    Time 1930. D.R. used from the first D.R. run up. Intercept 5·0′ away, bearing 100° T.

                                                      20 marks

4. On July 26th in position 10° N. 140° E. the moon set bearing 253° by gyro compass. Find the error of the gyro.

                                                      20 marks

Practical Paper 2   **Time allowed 2 hours**

1. On October 20th at approximate L.M.T. 0600 in D.R. position 12° 55′ N. 150° 15′ E. the sextant altitude of the star Denebola was 41° 46·2′. Index error 1·0′ on the arc. Height of eye 11·8 metres. A chronometer which was fast on G.M.T. by 1m 20s, showed 8h 36m 38s. Find the direction of the position line and a position through which it passes.

2. From the following information find the direction of the position line and the latitude in which it cuts the D.R. longitude.

    Approx. L.M.T. 1150 January 5th. D.R. 45° 18′ S. 53° 38′ W.

Sextant altitude sun's lower limb when near the meridian 67° 10'.
Index error 2·0' on the arc. Height of eye 13 metres.
Chronometer 3h 35m 01s. Error nil.

3. On March 24th in D.R. position 43° 20' N. 34° 20' W., during
morning twilight the sextant altitude of Polaris was 43° 00·5'. Index
error 1·5' off the arc. Height of eye 12 metres. A chronometer which
was 2m 20s fast on G.M.T. showed 7h 23m 05s at the time. Find
the direction of the position line and a position through which it
passes.

4. From the following sights find the position of the ship at the
time of the second observation.
  Time 1500. E.P. 25° 27' N. 112° 23' W. Intercept 2·5' away bearing
  043° T.
  Run. 279° T. distance 65 miles.
  Time 1900. From the first D.R. position run up. Intercept 5·4'
  towards bearing 135° T.

Practical Paper 3   **Time allowed 2 hours**

1. On July 31st during the forenoon in D.R. position 16° 45' S.
159° 42' E. the sextant altitude of the sun's lower limb was observed
to be 34° 25'. Index error 2·5' on the arc. Height of eye 12·3 metres.
A chronometer which was 0m 20s fast on G.M.T. showed 10h 34m
20s. Find the position line direction and a position through which
it passes.

2. Find the L.M.T. of the time of meridian passage of the star
Atria over the meridian of 35° 30' W. on March 24th. If the D.R.
latitude at this time is 20° 15' S., find the altitude to set on a sextant
to observe the meridian passage. Index error 1·6' off the arc.
Height of eye 9·4 metres.

3. A vessel leaves a position 54° 37' N. 45° 14' W. and steams
234° T. for 348 miles. Find the D.R. position at the end of the run
by mercator sailing.

4. From the following information, using the 'c' correction, find
the position at the time of the noon observation.
  Time 0800. D.R. 26° 28' N. 118° 14' W. Observed longitude
  118° 13' W. brg. 130° T.
  Run. 74 miles. Course 250° T.
  Time 1230. Meridian observation gives latitude 26° 06' N.

Practical Paper 4

1. On July 31st at evening twilight in D.R. position 15° 50' W.
105° 40' W. the sextant altitude of the moon's lower limb was
20° 18·9'. Index error 1·5' on the arc. Height of eye 8·6 metres.
A chronometer which was fast on G.M.T. by 1m 24s showed
1h 35m 39s. Find the direction of the position line and a position
through which to draw it.

2. From the following information find the compass error and the deviation for the ship's head.
Date June 26th. D.R. 38° 10′ N. 175° 16′ E.
Sun rose bearing 062° by compass. Variation 7° W.

3. On June 25th in D.R. longitude 150° W. the moon crossed the observer's meridian to the south of the observer with a sextant altitude (L.L.) 67° 07′. Height of eye 11·3 metres. The index error of the sextant was 0·5′ off the arc. Find the latitude and state the direction of the position line.

4. From the following information find the position of the ship at the time of the second observation.
D.R. 43° 13′ N. 150° 46′ E. Intercept 1·6′ towards azimuth 217° T.
Run. 299° T. distance 62 miles.
D.R. obtained from first D.R. run up. Intercept 5·3′ away azimuth 105° T.

Principles Paper 1

1. Define
(a) horizontal parallax,
(b) parallax in altitude.
Draw a sketch and show the relationship between the two.

2. If the obliquity of the ecliptic is 23° 27′, calculate the declination of the sun when its S.H.A. is 145° 35′.

3. Explain why the correction 'augmentation of the moon's semi-diameter' is applied to the semi-diameter of the moon tabulated in the *Nautical Almanac*. Why is the sun's semi-diameter not augmented by a similar correction?

4. During evening twilight on March 25th a stationary observer noted that the star Aldebaran was on the meridian bearing 180° T. with a true altitude of 52° 30′. After 1h 21m 15s a second star was on the meridian bearing 000° T. with a true altitude of 15° 25′. Find the S.H.A. and declination of the second star.

Principles Paper 2

1. Define with the aid of diagrams
(a) sidereal hour angle,
(b) local apparent time,
(c) vertical circle,
(d) rational horizon.

2. In what latitude will a star whose declination is 22° 30′ change its azimuth by 40° between crossing the prime vertical and setting?

3. On June 26th the sun's zenith distance was observed to be 0° 15′ at G.M.T. 1559. At G.M.T. 1601 the same zenith distance was observed, the sun having passed to the north of the observer. Find the position of the observer.

4. The d. long. between A and B both in north latitude, is 3° 40′, A being to the west and to the south of B. If the d. lat. between them is 2° 30′, and the departure 110′, find the latitudes of A and B.

Principles Paper 3

1. An observation of a celestial body bearing 050° when worked by Marcq St Hilaire, using a D.R. 30° 40′ S. 64° 18′ E. gave an intercept of 3·8′ away. Find by plotting, the intercept and bearing which would have been obtained if a D.R. of 30° 34′ S. 64° 24′ E. had been used. From your plot also give the longitude which would have been obtained if the sight had been worked by longitude by chronometer using a D.R. latitude 34° 40′ S.

2. Explain the conditions which give an eclipse of the moon. Why are more lunar eclipses than solar sclipses observed from any one position on the earth's surface?

3. A star of declination 21° 14′ N. takes two hours to change its bearing from 180° T. to 270° T. to a stationary observer. Find the latitude of the observer and the stars altitude when it crosses the prime vertical.

4. (a) Define
   (i) inferior conjunction,
   (ii) superior conjunction,
   (iii) maximum elongation.
   (b) Explain why the planet Venus is never visible at midnight in normal navigable latitudes.

Principles Paper 4

1. Calculate the initial course and great circle distance on a great circle track between the following positions. Find also the position of the vertex.
   A. 34° 22′ N.   140° 00′ E.
   B. 48° 28′ N.   126° 30′ W.

2. Draw a scale diagram on the plane of the rational horizon to illustrate the following conditions:
   Latitude 20° N., Declination 20° N., L.H.A. 60°.
   Measure the altitude and the azimuth on your figure.

3. Define
   (i) synodic period of the moon,
   (ii) sidereal period of the moon.
   Explain why they are not of the same length, using a diagram to illustrate your answer.

4. Define
   (i) sensible horizon,
   (ii) rational horizon,
   (iii) visible horizon.

On October 20th at 1200 G.M.T. in D.R. latitude 48° N. the sextant altitude of the moon's lower limb was 38° 14·5'. Index error 2·0' on the arc. Height of eye 14 metres. Using individual corrections find the true altitude.

Principles Paper 5

1. Find the composite great circle distance between the following positions, consistent with a limiting latitude of 33° S.

A. 18° 09' S.   178° 26' E.
B. 33° 00' S.   71° 37' W.

Give the longitude in which the track reaches the limiting latitude and the initial course.

2. Explain the two reasons why the sun does not have a constant rate of change of S.H.A.

Given that the G.M.T. is 6h 14m 16s on November 2nd find the L.A.T. of an observer in longitude 94° W.

Explain briefly the need for the 'leap second' as applied to the time signals promulgated to ship's.

3. Find the L.A.T. at which a position line obtained from a morning sight of the sun would run 000°/180° for an observer in latitude 35° N., if the declination of the sun is 23° 27' N. Also find the altitude to set on a sextant to observe the lower limb at the following meridian passage, assuming that the observer is stationary and that the declination remains constant. Index error 2·5' off the arc. Height of eye 10·5 metres.

4. Explain why the moon changes its declination so rapidly compared with the sun. Under what circumstances will the limits between which the moon changes declination, be maximum.

ANSWERS TO EXERCISES

Exercise 1A

1. 425·1' N.	709·1' W.		2. 910·3' N.	634·7' E.
3. 931·3' S.	742·6' W.		4. 2026·5' N.	522·0' E.
5. 740·7' N.	1278·5' W.		6. 1006·6' S.	299·2' E.
7. 996·4' N.	3710·4' W.		8. 2910·5' N.	4424·6' E.
9. 1508·4' N.	8225·7' W.		10. 2982·8' N.	3515·9' E.

Exercise 1B

1. 12° 23·5' N.	165° 32·6' W.	2. 43° 37·6' N.	17° 45·2' E.
3. 42° 08·2' N.	34° 14·4' W.	4. 17° 45·1' S.	170° 59·5' E.

Exercise 1C

1. 6° W.	2. Nil.	3. 4° W.	4. 28° W.	5. 6° W.
6. 4° E.	7. 18° E.	8. 11° W.	9. 13° W.	10. 2° E.

Exercise 1D

1. 207°	2. 002°	3. 004°	4. 259°	5. 070°
6. 348°	7. 145°	8. 192°	9. 349°	10. 356°

Exercise 1E

1. 263°	2. 345°	3. 187°	4. 064°	5. 338°
6. 005°	7. 348°	8. 006°	9. 082°	10. 209°

Exercise 1F

1. 22° W.	2. 11° E.	3. 14° E.	4. 21° W.	5. 19° E.
6. 3° W.	7. 21° W.	8. 22° W.	9. 3° E.	10. 8° E.

Exercise 2

1. 10·192 cms.
2. Longitude scale 0·8575 cm : 1° 3·003 cms.
3. $\dfrac{1}{9600415·6}$, 1847·6 metres.
4. Distance 4500 metres = 2·43 nm. Longitude 5° 26·22' W.
5. 130 cms × 86·76 cms, natural scale 1/14300617.
6. Lat. scale 99·66 cms. 53° 06·3' N. 175° E.
7. Dist. against longitude scale 375 miles. D.M.P. 375. D. lat. 4° 09·4'. Distance 249 miles, error 125·6 miles.
8. Dist. against longitude scale 140 miles. Correct distance 86·3 miles. Error 53·7 miles.

Exercise 3A

1. 42° 50' N. or S.	2. 8° 55·3'

279

3. 3436·8.
5. 240·4 miles.
7. 76° 54′ N. or S.
9. 1879·1 miles.

4. 76° 36·6′ N. or 78° 16·6′ S.
6. 41° 35′ N. or S.
8. 184·3 miles.
10. 50 miles.

Exercise 3B

1. Dep. 232·55. Course N. 63° 53·1′ W. Dist. 259 miles.
2. D. lat. 340·5′. Dep. 221·1. D. long. 229·3′. Position 39° 31·5′ N. 166° 11·3′ W.
3. Dep. 2263·98. Course S. 59° 46·5′ E. Dist. 2620·2 miles.
4. D. lat. 166′. Latitude 37° 44·0′ S. Dist. 258·2 miles.
5. 44° 10·4′ N.
6. Dep. 5821·1. Course S. 63° 19·3′ W. Dist. 6514·8 miles.

Exercise 3C

1. S. 11° 34·7′ W. 2265·1 miles.
2. N. 74° 04·3′ E. 5968·6 miles.
3. S. 46° 33·3′ E.
4. S. 79° 12·6′ W. 4347·9 miles.
5. D. lat. 13° 05·2′ N. D. long. 31° 35·3′ E. position 34° 05·2′ N. 149° 25·7′ W.
6. D. lat. 4° 17·1′ S. D. long. 6° 26·6′ E. position 35° 42·9′ N. 41° 01·4′ W.

Exercise 4A

1. Initial course S. 50° 39·5′ E. Dist. 5038·6 miles.

   positions   45° 10·7′ S.   90° W.   course   S. 55·9° E.
                51° 52·4′ S.   110° W.   S. 71·0° E.
                54° 14·1′ S.   130° W.   N. 87·0° E.
                53° 09·9′ S.   150° W.   N. 76·8° E.
                48° 15·6′ S.   170° W.   N. 61·2° E.

2. Distance 4638·8 miles. Initial course S. 33° 29·7′ W.
3. Initial course N. 77° 37·7′ W. Final course S. 62° 13·8′ W. Distance 1732·3 miles.
4. Initial course S. 67° 30·3′ E. Vertex 40° 44·8′ S. 20° 17′ W. Distance 3599 miles.
5. Great circle dist. 5190·4, mercator dist. 5594·1 miles, saving 403·7 miles.
6. Initial course N. 61° 50·5′ W. Vertex 54° 10·4′ N. 160° 19·7′ W. Distance 4076·6 miles.

   positions   52° 24·4′ N.   140° W.   course   N. 73° 38·4′ W.
                54° 10·3′ N.   160° W.   N. 89° 44·0′ W.
                52° 31·4′ N.   180°   S. 74° 09·7 W.
                46° 50·1′ N.   160° E.   S. 58° 49·7′ W.

Exercise 4B

1. Initial course S. 54° 46·3′ E. Distance 5484·6 miles (2368·9 + 1302·2 + 1813·5). Longitudes of vertices 70° 54·9′ E., 116° 05·2′ E.
2. Initial course S. 73° 56·6′ E. Distance 3613·4 miles (1296·6 + 816·8 + 1500).
3. Initial course S. 52°00·4′ E. Distance 5279·6 miles (3081·8 + 1431·5 + 766·3).
4. Initial course S. 69° 23·8′ W. Distance 4804·0 miles (1144·8 + 2731·1 + 928·1).
5. Distance 6630·6 (5759·0 + 871·6). Course at equator S. 48° E.

Exercise 4C

2. Vertices 52° N. 40° E., 42° S. 140° W., convergency 48°.
4. Mercator distance 3856·7 miles. Great circle dist. 3539·8 miles. Difference 316·9 miles.
5. Bearing of A from B 275° 08·3′.

Exercise 5A

1. Altitude 38° 39·1'	Bearing 257° 25·5'.
2. Altitude 58° 10·0'	Bearing 326° 42·0'.
3. Altitude 64° 59·6'	Bearing 207° 58·2'.
4. Altitude 59° 07·1'	Bearing 331° 35·4'.

Exercise 6A

1. True altitude 59° 28·1'.   2. True altitude 37° 49·5'.
3. True altitude 75° 07·5'.   4. True altitude 56° 34·3'.
5. True altitude 28° 05·7'.   6. True altitude 59° 54·0'.
7. True altitude 59° 09·9'.   8. True altitude 24° 40·4'.
9. True altitude 73° 59·6'.   10. True altitude 54° 53·3'.
11. True altitude 31° 41·3'.   12. True altitude 41° 47·8'.

Exercise 6B

1. True altitude 59° 28·1'.   2. True altitude 37° 49·4'.
3. True altitude 75° 07·6'.   4. True altitude 56° 34·3'.
5. True altitude 28° 05·7'.   6. True altitude 59° 54·0'.
7. True altitude 59° 10·0'.   8. True altitude 24° 40·5'.
9. True altitude 73° 59·6'.   10. True altitude 54° 53·5'.
11. True altitude 31° 41·2'.   12. True altitude 41° 47·7'.

Exercise 7A

1. (a) L.A.T.   24 Jun.   14h 57m 40s.
   (b) L.A.T.   26 Mar.   5h 54m 00s.
2. (a) G.M.T.   5 Jan.   11h 12m 35s.
   (b) G.M.T.   21 Oct.   6h 11m 48s.
3. (a) L.M.T.   19 Oct.   11h 15m 04s.
   (b) L.M.T.   31 Jul.   00h 26m 38s.
4. (a) Long. 82° 24·25' E.
   (b) Long. 125° 51·5' W.
   (c) Long. 153° 17·25' E.

Exercise 7B

5. E. of T. 1m 15s. Mean time greater than apparent.
9. E. of T. 4m 54s. G.A.T. 11h 23m 06s.

Exercise 10

1. L.A.T. 8h 33m 07s.
2. Maximum azimuth N. 52° 26' E. Interval 3h 08m.
3. L.H.A. 47° 27·2'. G.H.A. sun 259° 22·2'. G.H.A. ♈ 78° 22·2'.
4. Altitude 52° 57·2'. Bearing S. 71° 47·1' E.
5. G.H.A. sun 243° 30·9'. Declination 1° 38·8' N. L.H.A. 58° 47·3'. Position 3° 10·5' N. 175° 16·4' E.
6. 10° 04·7' S.
7. Lat. 49° 43·9' S. change H.A. 9° 14·5'.
8. 8h 54m 25s and 15h 05m 35s.
9. L.H.A. 287° 46·7'. Altitude 26° 31·8'.

Exercise 11

1. (a) 44° 09' N.   ⁻(b) 44° 09' S.

2. Time of sunset 1901. Time end twilight. 2009. Duration 0108.

3. (b) Lat. 41° 25·2′ N. or S.

4. Angle P 82° 25·2′. L.H.A. 277° 34·8′.

5. Angle P 109° 50·5′. L.A.T. sunrise 4h 40m 38s.

6. Angle P 68° 50·8′ = 4h 35m 23s. Duration daylight 9h 10m 46s.

7. Angle P 104° 31·7′ = 6h 58m 07s. Twilight ends 18h 58m 07s.

Exercise 12

1. 46° 55·3′ N. 6° 45·7′ W.

2. 36° 10·2′ S. 122° 33·3′ E.

3. 9° 24·6′ N. 177° 44·9′ E.

4. 52° 11·4′ N. 164° 15·4′ E.

5. 34° 14·6′ N. 40° 28·2′ W.

6. 10° 15·1′ S. 25° 46·4′ W.

7. 15° 13·6′ S. 159° 17·4′ W.

8. 36° 48·8′ N. 147° 08·1′ E.

9. 23° 45·2′ N. 52° 57·3′ W.

10. D.R. run up 7° 01·4′ S. 41° 48·4′ W. Obs. pos. 7° 00·6′ S. 41° 55·1′ W.

11. Run 5·2′ S. 39·2′ E. D.R. run up 41° 15·2′ S. 114° 39·2′ E. Obs. pos. 41° 23·3′ S. 114° 36·2′ E.

12. Run 11·1′ N. 34·1′ W. D.R. run up 19° 29·1′ N. 161° 16·1′ W. Obs. pos. 19° 34·7′ N. 161° 10·7′ W.

13. Run up position 52° 37·0′ N. 135° 57·6′ W. Obs. pos. 52° 37·8′ N. 135° 57·3′ W.

14. Run up position 52° 15·0′ N. 164° 34·2′ W. Obs. pos. 52° 12·6′ N. 164° 33·6′ W.

15. Run 4·2′ S. 1° 14·9′ W. Obs. pos. 50° 21·8′ N. 23° 45·3′ W.

16. Run 1·2′ N. 33·2′ E. Obs. pos. 5° 55·8′ N. 88° 53·3′ E.

17. Run up pos. 30° 36·5′ N. 46° 19·0′ W. Obs. pos. 30° 30′ N. 46° 13·7′ W.

18. Run 8·2′ S. 24·1′ E. Obs. pos. 32° 06·1′ S. 115° 27·3′ E.

19. Run 11·1′ S. 21·9′ E. Obs. pos. 32° 07·6′ S. 152° 18·9′ E.

Exercise 13

1. By M.S.H. L.H.A. 57° 57·0′. CZX 66° 18·7′. TZX 66° 21·2′. Int 2·5′ A. P/L runs 153·8°/333·8° through ITP 19° 51·1′ N. 66° 34·4′ E. By L.B.C. P 57° 59·9′. Longitude 66° 34·9′ E. T Brg. S. 63·8° W. P/L runs 153·8°/333·8° through 19° 50′ N. 66° 34·9′ E.

2. By M.S.H. L.H.A. 22° 37·9′. CZX 17° 53·5′. TZX 17° 55·6′. Int. 2·1′ A. P/L runs 002·3°/182·3° through ITP 40° 05·1′ S. 94° 02·4′ W. By L.B.C. P 22° 40·5′. Longitude 94° 02·4′ W. T. Brg. N. 87·8° W. P/L runs 002·2°/182·2° through 40° 05′ S. 94° 02·4′ W.

3. By M.S.H. L.H.A. 301° 47·9′. CZX 47° 57·9′. TZX 47° 48·9′. Int. 9·0′ T. P/L runs 006·5°/186·5° through ITP 40° 06·0′ S. 93° 53·3′ W. By L.B.C. P 58° 00·2′. Longitude 93° 53·1′ W. T. Brg. S. 83·5° E. P/L runs 006·5°/186·5° through 40° 05′ S. 93° 53·1′ W.

4. By M.S.H. L.H.A. 353° 42·7′. CZX 43° 28·9′. TZX 43° 28·0′. Int. 0·9′ T. P/L runs 261·6°/081·6° through ITP 20° 29·1′ N. 113° 05·1′ E. By ex-meridian. P 6° 17·3′. TZX 43° 28·0′. MZX 43° 01·9′. T. Brg. S. 8·4° E. P/L 261·6°/081·6° through 20° 29·1′ N. 113° 05′ E.

5. By M.S.H. L.H.A. 320° 56·3′. CZX 47° 46·2′. TZX 47° 48·2′. Int. 2·0′ A. P/L 322·4°/142·4° through ITP 7° 13·2′ S. 12° 16·4′ E. By L.B.C. P 39° 06·4′. Longitude 12° 15·3′ E. T. Brg. N. 52·5° W. P/L runs 332·5°/142·5° through 7° 12′ S. 12° 15·3′ E.

6. By M.S.H. L.H.A. 356° 02·7′. CZX 53° 33·3′. TZX 53° 27·0′. Int. 6·3′ T. P/L runs 274·5°/094·5° through ITP 29° 55·7′ S. 140° 19·4′ W. By ex-meridian. P 3° 57·3′. TZX 53° 27·0′. T. Brg. N. 4·5′ E. P/L runs 274·5°/094·5° through 29° 55·9′ S. 140° 20′ W.

7. By M.S.H. L.H.A. 316° 56·6′. CZX 55° 02·6′. TZX 55° 00·6′. Int. 2·0′ T. P/L runs 142°/322° through ITP 16° 41·8′ S. 159° 41·6′ E. By L.B.C. P 43° 00·8′. Longitude 159° 42·6′. T. Brg. N. 52·2° E. P/L runs 142°/322° through 16° 43′ S. 159° 42·6′.

8. By M.S.H. L.H.A. 325° 25·8′. CZX 62° 30·2′. TZX 62° 24·8′. Int. 5·4′ T. P/L runs 306°/126° through ITP 29° 30·6′ S. 121° 21·3′ W. By L.B.C. P 34° 23·5′. Longitude 121° 14·3′ W. T. Brg. N. 36° E. P/L runs 306°/126° through 29° 35′ S. 121° 14·3′ W.

9. By ex-meridian formula P 6° 16·3′. TZX 43° 22·9′. MZX 42° 56·8′. Latitude 20° 24·0′ N. T. Brg. S. 8·4° E. P/L runs 261·6°/081·6° through 20° 24·0′ N. 113° 06′ E. By ex-meridian tables. F = 2·49(A) Red. 26·1′ Latitude 20° 24·1′ N. P/L runs 261·6°/081·6° through 20° 24·1′ N. 113° 06′ E.

Exercise 14

1. G.M.T. 1610 5th Decl. 23° 12·7′ N. P/L 090°/270° Latitude 45° 00·5′ S.

2. G.M.T. 1444 25th Decl. 23° 23·5′ N. P/L 090°/270° Latitude 24° 57·6′ S.

3. G.M.T. 1832 6th Decl. 22° 28·5′ S. P/L 090°/270° Latitude 51° 27·5′ S.

4. G.M.T. 1815 5th Decl. 23° 20·0′ N. P/L 090°/270° Latitude 25° 24·4′ S.

5. G.M.T. 1303 31st Decl. 18° 11·2′ N. P/L 090°/270° Latitude 45° 14·7′ N.

6. G.M.T. 24th 20h 06m 16s. L.M.T. 25th 5h 01m 16s. Latitude 30° 07·6′ N.

7. Decl. 8° 48·3′ N. ZX 22° 51·5′. Latitude 14° 03·2′ S. P/L 090°/270°.

8. Decl. 29° 45·2′ S. ZX 69° 33·9′. Latitude 39° 48·7′ N. P/L 090°/270°.

9. G.M.T. 0543 24th P/L 090°/270°. Latitude 51° 22·7′ N.

10. ZX 21° 52·6′ to north. Sextant alt. 68° 13·6′. G.M.T. 17h 23m 23s 1st. L.M.T. 7h 54m 43s 1st.

Exercise 15

1. L.H.A. 125° 41·4′. T. alt. 40° 33·3′. P/L runs 268·9°/088·9° through 40° 36·7′ N. 169° 14′ E.

2. L.H.A. 315° 27·8′. T. alt. 25° 07·0′. P/L runs 270·9°/090·9° through 24° 55·5′ N. 100° 01′ W.

3. L.H.A. 14° 39·5′. T. alt. 47° 07·1′. Sextant alt. 47° 17·0′.

4. L.H.A. 346° 50·0′. T. alt. 47° 48·2′. P/L runs 270·9°/090·9°° through 47° 12·0′ N. 125° 40′ W.

5. L.H.A. 15° 39·7′. P/L runs 270·3°/090·3° through 22° 43·8′ N. 163° 20′ W.

Exercise 16A

1. G.M.T. 1840 24th L.H.A. 298° 25·0′. T. Brg. N. 77·9° E. Error 7° E. Dev. 2° E.

2. G.M.T. 1932 31st L.H.A. 39° 05·2′. T. Brg. S. 44·0° W. Gyro error 1° N.

3. G.M.T. 0041 1st L.H.A. 352° 50·4′. T. Brg. S. 9·8° E. Error 1·8° W. Dev. 11·8° W.

4. G.M.T. 1932 24th L.H.A. 51° 26·3′. T. Brg. N. 56·1° W. Error 3·9° E.

5. G.M.T. 1238 4th L.H.A. 66° 27·4′. T. Brg. S. 86·7° W. Error 2·3° W.

6. G.M.T. 1349 30th L.H.A. 291° 12·3′. T. Brg. S. 43·2° E. Error 8·2° W.

7. L.H.A. 48° 39·7′. T. Brg. S. 72·3° W. Error 5·3° E. Dev. 13·3° E.

8. G.M.T. 18h 25m 30s 26th L.H.A. 70° 28·5′. T. Brg. S. 81·4° W. Gyro 0·4° H.

9. G.M.T. 23h 30m 10s 4th L.H.A. 79° 14·8′. T. Brg. N. 80·7° W. Gyro 1·3° L.

Exercise 16B

1. G.M.T. 0840 6th Decl. 22° 31·5′ S. Ampl. E. 22° 40·2′ S. Error 12·7° E. Dev. 18·7° E.

2. G.M.T. 1723 31st Decl. 18° 42·6′ N. Ampl. W. 19° 52·2′ N. Error 21·9° E. Dev. 18·9° E.

3. G.M.T. 1218 25th Decl. 1° 46·7′ N. Ampl. W. 1° 47·3′ N. Error 2·8° E. Dev. 5·8° E.

4. G.M.T. 2236 31st Decl. 14° 13·1′ S. Ampl. E. 16° 50·1′ S. Error 11·8° E. Dev. 11·8° E.

5. G.M.T. 0556 4th Decl. 19° 42·6′ N. Ampl. 21° 36·4′ N. Error 6·6° E. Dev. 14·6° E.

6. G.M.T. 0724 31st Decl. 18° 20·5′ N. Ampl. E. 24° 21′ N. Error 8·4° W. Dev. 0·6° E.

Practical Paper 1

1. L.H.A. 50° 53·4′. CZX 71° 14·0′. TZX 71° 16·8′. Int. 2·8′ A. T. Brg. N. 48·8° W. P/L 221·2°/041·2° through ITP 28° 19·8′ S. 175° 32·6′ W.

2. Course 068° 27·5′. Distance 6018·3 miles. Steaming time 13d 13h 29m. L.M.T. arrival July 9th 11h 12m.

3. D.R. run up 43° 30·4′ N. 148° 40·3′ E. Obs. pos. 43° 32·0′ N. 148° 33·7′ E.

4. G.M.T. 1432 26th Decl. 17° 31·2′ S. Ampl. W. 17° 48′ S. Error ¾° High.

Practical Paper 2

1. L.H.A. 310° 03·8′. CZX 48° 25·7′. TZX 48° 21·9′. Int. 3·8′ T. P/L runs 351·6°/171·6° through ITP 12° 55·6′ N. 150° 18·9′ E.

2. G.M.T. 15h 35m 01s 5th P 1° 13·9′. MZX 22° 41·2′. P/L 272·9°/092·9° through 45° 17·6′ S. 53° 38·0′ W.

3. L.H.A. 257° 14·6′. T. Alt. 42° 54·9′. P/L runs 270·8°/090·8° through latitude 43° 30·7′ N. 34° 20′ W.

4. Obs. pos. 25° 31·7′ N. 113° 31·7′ W.

Practical Paper 3

1. G.M.T. 22h 34m 00s 30th L.H.A. 316° 36·3′. CZX 55° 19·2′. TZX 55° 29·1′. T. Brg. N. 52·4° E. P/L 322·4°/142·4° through ITP 16° 51·0′ S. 159° 33·8′ E.

2. G.M.T. 7h 02m 31s 24th L.M.T. 4h 40m 31s 24th. Sextant alt. 41° 21·1′ to the south of the observer.

3. D. lat. 204·5′. D.M.P. 338·5. D. long. 465·9′. Final position 51° 12·5′ N. 52° 59·9′ W.

4. Noon D.R. 26° 02·7′ N. 119° 30·5′ W. 'C' 0·937. Error in longitude 3·1′. Obs. pos. 26° 06·0′ N. 119° 27·4′ W.

Practical Paper 4

1. G.M.T. 1h 34m 15s Aug. 1st. L.H.A. 300° 33·7′. CZX 68° 36·2′. TZX 68° 45·0′. Int. 8·8′ A. Brg. S. 60·2° E. P/L runs 209·8°/029·8° through ITP 15° 54·4′ N. 105° 47·9′ W.

2. G.M.T. 1657 25th. Ampl. E. 30° 19·5′ N. Error 2° 19·5′ W. Dev. 4° 40·5′ E.

3. G.M.T. 0320 26th. Decl. 3° 03·9′ S. True alt. 67° 40·0′. Latitude 19° 16·1′ N.

4. Position 43° 44·9′ N. 149° 24·2′ E.

Principles Paper 1

2. 13° 46·5′ S.

4. Latitude 53° 57·5′ N. Declination 51° 27·5′ N. S.H.A. 91° 01·2′.

Principles Paper 2

2. 36° 32·25′ N. or S.

3. Position 23° 17·4′ N. 59° 21·85′ W.

4. Mid. lat. 60°. Mean lat. 60° 03′. Lat. A 58° 48′ N. Lat. B 61° 18′ N.

Principles Paper 3
1. Int. 11·6′ A. Bearing 050° T. Longitude by L.B.C. 64° 12·2′ E.
3. Altitude 62° 08·7′. Latitude 24° 10·9′ N.

Principles Paper 4
1. Initial course N. 46° 55·6′ E. Dist. 4025·9 miles. Vertex 53° 37·6′ N. 160° 14·7′ W. ?
2. Altitude 34°. Bearing N. 79° W.
4. 39° 03·5′.

Principles Paper 5
1. Initial course S. 61° 57·3′ E. Dist. 5836·2 miles. Longitude 21° 53·0′ W.
2. L.A.T. 00h 14m 40s 2nd.
3. L.A.T. 8h 33m 07s. Sextant altitude 78° 14·5′.

INDEX

INDEX

A2 ALTITUDE CORRECTION TABLES 10°–90°—SUN, STARS, PLANETS

SUN

OCT.–MAR. App. Alt.	Lower Limb	Upper Limb	APR.–SEPT. App. Alt.	Lower Limb	Upper Limb
9 34	+10·8	−21·5	9 39	+10·6	−21·2
9 45	+10·9	−21·4	9 51	+10·7	−21·1
9 56	+11·0	−21·3	10 03	+10·8	−21·0
10 08	+11·1	−21·2	10 15	+10·9	−20·9
10 21	+11·2	−21·1	10 27	+11·0	−20·8
10 34	+11·3	−21·0	10 40	+11·1	−20·7
10 47	+11·4	−20·9	10 54	+11·2	−20·6
11 01	+11·5	−20·8	11 08	+11·3	−20·5
11 15	+11·6	−20·7	11 23	+11·4	−20·4
11 30	+11·7	−20·6	11 38	+11·5	−20·3
11 46	+11·8	−20·5	11 54	+11·6	−20·2
12 02	+11·9	−20·4	12 10	+11·7	−20·1
12 19	+12·0	−20·3	12 28	+11·8	−20·0
12 37	+12·1	−20·2	12 46	+11·9	−19·9
12 55	+12·2	−20·1	13 05	+12·0	−19·8
13 14	+12·3	−20·0	13 24	+12·1	−19·7
13 35	+12·4	−19·9	13 45	+12·2	−19·6
13 56	+12·5	−19·8	14 07	+12·3	−19·5
14 18	+12·6	−19·7	14 30	+12·4	−19·4
14 42	+12·7	−19·6	14 54	+12·5	−19·3
15 06	+12·8	−19·5	15 19	+12·6	−19·2
15 32	+12·9	−19·4	15 46	+12·7	−19·1
15 59	+13·0	−19·3	16 14	+12·8	−19·0
16 28	+13·1	−19·2	16 44	+12·9	−18·9
16 59	+13·2	−19·1	17 15	+13·0	−18·8
17 32	+13·3	−19·0	17 48	+13·1	−18·7
18 06	+13·4	−18·9	18 24	+13·2	−18·6
18 42	+13·5	−18·8	19 01	+13·3	−18·5
19 21	+13·6	−18·7	19 42	+13·4	−18·4
20 03	+13·7	−18·6	20 25	+13·5	−18·3
20 48	+13·8	−18·5	21 11	+13·6	−18·2
21 35	+13·9	−18·4	22 00	+13·7	−18·1
22 26	+14·0	−18·3	22 54	+13·8	−18·0
23 22	+14·1	−18·2	23 51	+13·9	−17·9
24 21	+14·2	−18·1	24 53	+14·0	−17·8
25 26	+14·3	−18·0	26 00	+14·1	−17·7
26 36	+14·4	−17·9	27 13	+14·2	−17·6
27 52	+14·5	−17·8	28 33	+14·3	−17·5
29 15	+14·6	−17·7	30 00	+14·4	−17·4
30 46	+14·7	−17·6	31 35	+14·5	−17·3
32 26	+14·8	−17·5	33 20	+14·6	−17·2
34 17	+14·9	−17·4	35 17	+14·7	−17·1
36 20	+15·0	−17·3	37 26	+14·8	−17·0
38 36	+15·1	−17·2	39 50	+14·9	−16·9
41 08	+15·2	−17·1	42 31	+15·0	−16·8
43 59	+15·3	−17·0	45 36	+15·1	−16·7
47 10	+15·4	−16·9	48 55	+15·2	−16·6
50 46	+15·5	−16·8	52 44	+15·3	−16·5
54 49	+15·6	−16·7	57 02	+15·4	−16·4
59 23	+15·7	−16·6	61 51	+15·5	−16·3
64 30	+15·8	−16·5	67 17	+15·6	−16·2
70 12	+15·9	−16·4	73 16	+15·7	−16·1
76 26	+16·0	−16·3	79 43	+15·8	−16·0
83 05	+16·1	−16·2	86 32	+15·9	−15·9
90 00			90 00		

STARS AND PLANETS

App. Alt.	Corrn
9 56	−5·3
10 08	−5·2
10 20	−5·1
10 33	−5·0
10 46	−4·9
11 00	−4·8
11 14	−4·7
11 29	−4·6
11 45	−4·5
12 01	−4·4
12 18	−4·3
12 35	−4·2
12 54	−4·1
13 13	−4·0
13 33	−3·9
13 54	−3·8
14 16	−3·7
14 40	−3·6
15 04	−3·5
15 30	−3·4
15 57	−3·3
16 26	−3·2
16 56	−3·1
17 28	−3·0
18 02	−2·9
18 38	−2·8
19 17	−2·7
19 58	−2·6
20 42	−2·5
21 28	−2·4
22 19	−2·3
23 13	−2·2
24 11	−2·1
25 14	−2·0
26 22	−1·9
27 36	−1·8
28 56	−1·7
30 24	−1·6
32 00	−1·5
33 45	−1·4
35 40	−1·3
37 48	−1·2
40 08	−1·1
42 44	−1·0
45 36	−0·9
48 47	−0·8
52 18	−0·7
56 11	−0·6
60 28	−0·5
65 08	−0·4
70 11	−0·3
75 34	−0·2
81 13	−0·1
87 03	0·0
90 00	

Additional Corrn — 1974

VENUS

Jan. 1–Jan. 5
App. Alt.	Corrn
6	+0·5
20	+0·6
31	+0·7

Jan. 6–Feb. 9
4	+0·6
12	+0·7
22	+0·8

Feb. 10–Feb. 17
6	+0·5
20	+0·6
31	+0·7

Feb. 18–Mar. 4
11	+0·4
41	+0·5

Mar. 5–Mar. 31
46	+0·3

Apr. 1–May 15
47	+0·2

May 16–Dec. 31
42	+0·1

MARS

Jan. 1–Jan. 17
41	+0·2
75	+0·1

Jan. 18–Dec. 31
60	+0·1

DIP

Ht. of Eye (m)	Corrn	Ht. of Eye (ft)
2·4	−2·8	8·0
2·6	−2·9	8·6
2·8	−3·0	9·2
3·0	−3·1	9·8
3·2	−3·2	10·5
3·4	−3·3	11·2
3·6	−3·4	11·9
3·8	−3·5	12·6
4·0	−3·6	13·3
4·3	−3·7	14·1
4·5	−3·8	14·9
4·7	−3·9	15·7
5·0	−4·0	16·5
5·2	−4·1	17·4
5·5	−4·2	18·3
5·8	−4·3	19·1
6·1	−4·4	20·1
6·3	−4·5	21·0
6·6	−4·6	22·0
6·9	−4·7	22·9
7·2	−4·8	23·9
7·5	−4·9	24·9
7·9	−5·0	26·0
8·2	−5·1	27·1
8·5	−5·2	28·1
8·8	−5·3	29·2
9·2	−5·4	30·4
9·5	−5·5	31·5
9·9	−5·6	32·7
10·3	−5·7	33·9
10·6	−5·8	35·1
11·0	−5·9	36·3
11·4	−6·0	37·6
11·8	−6·1	38·9
12·2	−6·2	40·1
12·6	−6·3	41·5
13·0	−6·4	42·8
13·4	−6·5	44·2
13·8	−6·6	45·5
14·2	−6·7	46·9
14·7	−6·8	48·4
15·1	−6·9	49·8
15·5	−7·0	51·3
16·0	−7·1	52·8
16·5	−7·2	54·3
16·9	−7·3	55·8
17·4	−7·4	57·4
17·9	−7·5	58·9
18·4	−7·6	60·5
18·8	−7·7	62·1
19·3	−7·8	63·9
19·8	−7·9	65·4
20·4	−8·0	67·1
20·9	−8·1	68·8
21·4		70·5

Ht. of Eye	Corrn
m	
1·0	− 1·8
1·5	− 2·2
2·0	− 2·5
2·5	− 2·8
3·0	− 3·0
See table	
←	
m	
20	− 7·9
22	− 8·3
24	− 8·6
26	− 9·0
28	− 9·3
30	− 9·6
32	−10·0
34	−10·3
36	−10·6
38	−10·8
40	−11·1
42	−11·4
44	−11·7
46	−11·9
48	−12·2
ft.	
2	− 1·4
4	− 1·9
6	− 2·4
8	− 2·7
10	− 3·1
See table	
←	
ft.	
70	− 8·1
75	− 8·4
80	− 8·7
85	− 8·9
90	− 9·2
95	− 9·5
100	− 9·7
105	− 9·9
110	−10·2
115	−10·4
120	−10·6
125	−10·8
130	−11·1
135	−11·3
140	−11·5
145	−11·7
150	−11·9
155	−12·1

App. Alt. = Apparent altitude = Sextant altitude corrected for index error and dip.
For daylight observations of Venus, see page 260.

App. Alt.	0°–4° Corrⁿ	5°–9° Corrⁿ	10°–14° Corrⁿ	15°–19° Corrⁿ	20°–24° Corrⁿ	25°–29° Corrⁿ	30°–34° Corrⁿ	App. Alt.
′	° ′	° ′	° ′	° ′	° ′	° ′	° ′	′
00	0 · 33·8	5 · 58·2	10 · 62·1	15 · 62·8	20 · 62·2	25 · 60·8	30 · 58·9	00
10	35·9	58·5	62·2	62·8	62·1	60·8	58·8	10
20	37·8	58·7	62·2	62·8	62·1	60·7	58·8	20
30	39·6	58·9	62·3	62·8	62·1	60·7	58·7	30
40	41·2	59·1	62·3	62·8	62·0	60·6	58·6	40
50	42·6	59·3	62·4	62·7	62·0	60·6	58·5	50
00	1 · 44·0	6 · 59·5	11 · 62·4	16 · 62·7	21 · 62·0	26 · 60·5	31 · 58·5	00
10	45·2	59·7	62·4	62·7	61·9	60·4	58·4	10
20	46·3	59·9	62·5	62·7	61·9	60·4	58·3	20
30	47·3	60·0	62·5	62·7	61·9	60·3	58·2	30
40	48·3	60·2	62·5	62·7	61·8	60·3	58·2	40
50	49·2	60·3	62·6	62·7	61·8	60·2	58·1	50
00	2 · 50·0	7 · 60·5	12 · 62·6	17 · 62·7	22 · 61·7	27 · 60·1	32 · 58·0	00
10	50·8	60·6	62·6	62·6	61·7	60·1	57·9	10
20	51·4	60·7	62·6	62·6	61·6	60·0	57·8	20
30	52·1	60·9	62·7	62·6	61·6	59·9	57·8	30
40	52·7	61·0	62·7	62·6	61·5	59·9	57·7	40
50	53·3	61·1	62·7	62·6	61·5	59·8	57·6	50
00	3 · 53·8	8 · 61·2	13 · 62·7	18 · 62·5	23 · 61·5	28 · 59·7	33 · 57·5	00
10	54·3	61·3	62·7	62·5	61·4	59·7	57·4	10
20	54·8	61·4	62·7	62·5	61·4	59·6	57·4	20
30	55·2	61·5	62·8	62·5	61·3	59·6	57·3	30
40	55·6	61·6	62·8	62·4	61·3	59·5	57·2	40
50	56·0	61·6	62·8	62·4	61·2	59·4	57·1	50
00	4 · 56·4	9 · 61·7	14 · 62·8	19 · 62·4	24 · 61·2	29 · 59·3	34 · 57·0	00
10	56·7	61·8	62·8	62·3	61·1	59·3	56·9	10
20	57·1	61·9	62·8	62·3	61·1	59·2	56·9	20
30	57·4	61·9	62·8	62·3	61·0	59·1	56·8	30
40	57·7	62·0	62·8	62·2	60·9	59·1	56·7	40
50	57·9	62·1	62·8	62·2	60·9	59·0	56·6	50

H.P.	L U	L U	L U	L U	L U	L U	L U	H.P.
′	′ ′	′ ′	′ ′	′ ′	′ ′	′ ′	′ ′	′
54·0	0·3 0·9	0·3 0·9	0·4 1·0	0·5 1·1	0·6 1·2	0·7 1·3	0·9 1·5	54·0
54·3	1·1 1·4	0·7 1·2	0·7 1·2	0·8 1·3	0·9 1·4	1·1 1·5	1·2 1·7	54·3
54·6	1·1 1·4	1·1 1·4	1·1 1·4	1·2 1·5	1·3 1·6	1·4 1·7	1·5 1·8	54·6
54·9	1·4 1·6	1·5 1·6	1·5 1·6	1·6 1·7	1·6 1·8	1·8 1·9	1·9 2·0	54·9
55·2	1·8 1·8	1·8 1·8	1·9 1·9	1·9 1·9	2·0 2·0	2·1 2·1	2·2 2·2	55·2
55·5	2·2 2·0	2·2 2·0	2·3 2·1	2·3 2·1	2·4 2·2	2·4 2·3	2·5 2·4	55·5
55·8	2·6 2·2	2·6 2·2	2·6 2·3	2·7 2·3	2·7 2·4	2·8 2·4	2·9 2·5	55·8
56·1	3·0 2·4	3·0 2·5	3·0 2·5	3·0 2·5	3·1 2·6	3·1 2·6	3·2 2·7	56·1
56·4	3·4 2·7	3·4 2·7	3·4 2·7	3·4 2·7	3·4 2·8	3·5 2·8	3·5 2·9	56·4
56·7	3·7 2·9	3·7 2·9	3·8 2·9	3·8 2·9	3·8 3·0	3·8 3·0	3·9 3·0	56·7
57·0	4·1 3·1	4·1 3·1	4·1 3·1	4·1 3·1	4·2 3·1	4·2 3·2	4·2 3·2	57·0
57·3	4·5 3·3	4·5 3·3	4·5 3·3	4·5 3·3	4·5 3·3	4·5 3·4	4·6 3·4	57·3
57·6	4·9 3·5	4·9 3·5	4·9 3·5	4·9 3·5	4·9 3·5	4·9 3·5	4·9 3·6	57·6
57·9	5·3 3·8	5·3 3·8	5·2 3·8	5·2 3·7	5·2 3·7	5·2 3·7	5·2 3·7	57·9
58·2	5·6 4·0	5·6 4·0	5·6 4·0	5·6 4·0	5·6 3·9	5·6 3·9	5·6 3·9	58·2
58·5	6·0 4·2	6·0 4·2	6·0 4·2	6·0 4·2	6·0 4·1	5·9 4·1	5·9 4·1	58·5
58·8	6·4 4·4	6·4 4·4	6·4 4·4	6·3 4·4	6·3 4·3	6·3 4·3	6·2 4·2	58·8
59·1	6·8 4·6	6·8 4·6	6·7 4·6	6·7 4·6	6·7 4·5	6·6 4·5	6·6 4·4	59·1
59·4	7·2 4·8	7·1 4·8	7·1 4·8	7·1 4·8	7·0 4·7	7·0 4·7	6·9 4·6	59·4
59·7	7·5 5·1	7·5 5·0	7·5 5·0	7·5 5·0	7·4 4·9	7·3 4·8	7·2 4·7	59·7
60·0	7·9 5·3	7·9 5·3	7·9 5·2	7·8 5·2	7·8 5·1	7·7 5·0	7·6 4·9	60·0
60·3	8·3 5·5	8·3 5·5	8·2 5·4	8·2 5·4	8·1 5·3	8·0 5·2	7·9 5·1	60·3
60·6	8·7 5·7	8·6 5·7	8·6 5·7	8·5 5·6	8·5 5·5	8·4 5·4	8·2 5·3	60·6
60·9	9·1 5·9	9·0 5·9	9·0 5·9	8·9 5·8	8·8 5·7	8·7 5·6	8·6 5·4	60·9
61·2	9·5 6·2	9·4 6·1	9·4 6·1	9·3 6·0	9·2 5·9	9·1 5·8	8·9 5·6	61·2
61·5	9·8 6·4	9·8 6·3	9·7 6·3	9·7 6·2	9·5 6·1	9·4 5·9	9·2 5·8	61·5

DIP

Ht. of Eye	Corrⁿ	Ht. of Eye	Ht. of Eye	Corrⁿ	Ht. of Eye
m		ft.	m		ft.
2·4	−2·8	8·0	9·5	−5·5	31·5
2·6	−2·9	8·6	9·9	−5·6	32·7
2·8	−3·0	9·2	10·3	−5·7	33·9
3·0	−3·1	9·8	10·6	−5·8	35·1
3·2	−3·2	10·5	11·0	−5·9	36·3
3·4	−3·3	11·2	11·4	−6·0	37·6
3·6	−3·4	11·9	11·8	−6·1	38·9
3·8	−3·5	12·6	12·2	−6·2	40·1
4·0	−3·6	13·3	12·6	−6·3	41·5
4·3	−3·7	14·1	13·0	−6·4	42·8
4·5	−3·8	14·9	13·4	−6·5	44·2
4·7	−3·9	15·7	13·8	−6·6	45·5
5·0	−4·0	16·5	14·2	−6·7	46·9
5·2	−4·1	17·4	14·7	−6·8	48·4
5·5	−4·2	18·3	15·1	−6·9	49·8
5·8	−4·3	19·1	15·5	−7·0	51·3
6·1	−4·4	20·1	16·0	−7·1	52·8
6·3	−4·5	21·0	16·5	−7·2	54·3
6·6	−4·6	22·0	16·9	−7·3	55·8
6·9	−4·7	22·9	17·4	−7·4	57·4
7·2	−4·8	23·9	17·9	−7·5	58·9
7·5	−4·9	24·9	18·4	−7·6	60·5
7·9	−5·0	26·0	18·8	−7·7	62·1
8·2	−5·1	27·1	19·3	−7·8	63·8
8·5	−5·2	28·1	19·8	−7·9	65·4
8·8	−5·3	29·2	20·4	−8·0	67·1
9·2	−5·4	30·4	20·9	−8·1	68·8
9·5		31·5	21·4		70·5

MOON CORRECTION TABLE

The correction is in two parts, the first correction is taken from the upper part of the table with argument apparent altitude, and the second from the lower part with argument H.P., in the same column as that from which the first correction was taken. Separate corrections are given in the lower part for lower (L) and upper (U) limbs. All corrections are to be **added** to apparent altitude, *but* 30′ *is to be subtracted from the altitude of the upper limb.*

For corrections for pressure and temperature see page A4.

For bubble sextant observations ignore dip, take the mean of upper and lower limb corrections and subtract 15′ from the altitude.

App. Alt. = Apparent altitude = Sextant altitude corrected for index error and dip.

ALTITUDE CORRECTION TABLES 35°–90°—MOON

App. Alt.	35°–39° Corrⁿ	40°–44° Corrⁿ	45°–49° Corrⁿ	50°–54° Corrⁿ	55°–59° Corrⁿ	60°–64° Corrⁿ	65°–69° Corrⁿ	70°–74° Corrⁿ	75°–79° Corrⁿ	80°–84° Corrⁿ	85°–89° Corrⁿ	App. Alt.
00	35 56·5	40 53·7	45 50·5	50 46·9	55 43·1	60 38·9	65 34·6	70 30·1	75 25·3	80 20·5	85 15·6	00
10	56·4	53·6	50·4	46·8	42·9	38·8	34·4	29·9	25·2	20·4	15·6	10
20	56·3	53·5	50·2	46·7	42·8	38·7	34·3	29·7	25·0	20·2	15·3	20
30	56·2	53·4	50·1	46·5	42·7	38·5	34·1	29·6	24·9	20·0	15·1	30
40	56·2	53·3	50·0	46·4	42·5	38·4	34·0	29·4	24·7	19·9	15·0	40
50	56·1	53·2	49·9	46·3	42·4	38·2	33·8	29·3	24·5	19·7	14·8	50
00	36 56·0	41 53·1	46 49·8	51 46·2	56 42·3	61 38·1	66 33·7	71 29·1	76 24·4	81 19·6	86 14·6	00
10	55·9	53·0	49·7	46·0	42·1	37·9	33·5	29·0	24·2	19·4	14·5	10
20	55·8	52·8	49·5	45·9	42·0	37·8	33·4	28·8	24·1	19·2	14·3	20
30	55·7	52·7	49·4	45·8	41·8	37·7	33·2	28·7	23·9	19·1	14·1	30
40	55·6	52·6	49·3	45·7	41·7	37·5	33·1	28·5	23·8	18·9	14·0	40
50	55·5	52·5	49·2	45·5	41·6	37·4	32·9	28·3	23·6	18·7	13·8	50
00	37 55·4	42 52·4	47 49·1	52 45·4	57 41·4	62 37·2	67 32·8	72 28·2	77 23·4	82 18·6	87 13·7	00
10	55·3	52·3	49·0	45·3	41·3	37·1	32·6	28·0	23·3	18·4	13·5	10
20	55·2	52·2	48·8	45·2	41·2	36·9	32·5	27·9	23·1	18·2	13·3	20
30	55·1	52·1	48·7	45·0	41·0	36·8	32·3	27·7	22·9	18·1	13·2	30
40	55·0	52·0	48·6	44·9	40·9	36·6	32·2	27·6	22·8	17·9	13·0	40
50	55·0	51·9	48·5	44·8	40·8	36·5	32·0	27·4	22·6	17·8	12·8	50
00	38 54·9	43 51·8	48 48·4	53 44·6	58 40·6	63 36·4	68 31·9	73 27·2	78 22·5	83 17·6	88 12·7	00
10	54·8	51·7	48·2	44·5	40·5	36·2	31·7	27·1	22·3	17·4	12·5	10
20	54·7	51·6	48·1	44·4	40·3	36·1	31·6	26·9	22·1	17·3	12·3	20
30	54·6	51·5	48·0	44·2	40·2	35·9	31·4	26·8	22·0	17·1	12·2	30
40	54·5	51·4	47·9	44·1	40·1	35·8	31·3	26·6	21·8	16·9	12·0	40
50	54·4	51·2	47·8	44·0	39·9	35·6	31·1	26·5	21·7	16·8	11·8	50
00	39 54·3	44 51·1	49 47·6	54 43·9	59 39·8	64 35·5	69 31·0	74 26·3	79 21·5	84 16·6	89 11·7	00
10	54·2	51·0	47·5	43·7	39·6	35·3	30·8	26·1	21·3	16·5	11·5	10
20	54·1	50·9	47·4	43·6	39·5	35·2	30·7	26·0	21·2	16·3	11·4	20
30	54·0	50·8	47·3	43·5	39·4	35·0	30·5	25·8	21·0	16·1	11·2	30
40	53·9	50·7	47·2	43·3	39·2	34·9	30·4	25·7	20·9	16·0	11·0	40
50	53·8	50·6	47·0	43·2	39·1	34·7	30·2	25·5	20·7	15·8	10·9	50

H.P.	L U	L U	L U	L U	L U	L U	L U	L U	L U	L U	L U	H.P.
54·0	1·1 1·7	1·3 1·9	1·5 2·1	1·7 2·4	2·0 2·6	2·3 2·9	2·6 3·2	2·9 3·5	3·2 3·8	3·5 4·1	3·8 4·5	54·0
54·3	1·4 1·8	1·6 2·0	1·8 2·2	2·0 2·5	2·3 2·7	2·5 3·0	2·8 3·2	3·0 3·5	3·3 3·8	3·6 4·1	3·9 4·4	54·3
54·6	1·7 2·0	1·9 2·2	2·1 2·4	2·3 2·6	2·5 2·8	2·7 3·0	3·0 3·3	3·3 3·5	3·5 3·8	3·7 4·1	4·0 4·3	54·6
54·9	2·0 2·2	2·2 2·3	2·3 2·5	2·5 2·7	2·7 2·9	2·9 3·1	3·2 3·3	3·4 3·5	3·6 3·8	3·9 4·0	4·1 4·3	54·9
55·2	2·3 2·3	2·5 2·4	2·6 2·6	2·8 2·8	3·0 2·9	3·2 3·1	3·4 3·3	3·6 3·5	3·8 3·7	4·0 4·0	4·2 4·2	55·2
55·5	2·7 2·5	2·8 2·6	2·9 2·7	3·1 2·9	3·2 3·0	3·4 3·2	3·6 3·4	3·7 3·5	3·9 3·7	4·1 3·9	4·3 4·1	55·5
55·8	3·0 2·6	3·1 2·7	3·2 2·8	3·3 3·0	3·5 3·1	3·6 3·3	3·8 3·4	3·9 3·6	4·1 3·7	4·2 3·9	4·4 4·0	55·8
56·1	3·3 2·8	3·4 2·9	3·5 3·0	3·6 3·1	3·7 3·2	3·8 3·3	4·0 3·4	4·1 3·6	4·2 3·7	4·4 3·8	4·5 4·0	56·1
56·4	3·6 2·9	3·7 3·0	3·8 3·1	3·9 3·2	3·9 3·3	4·0 3·4	4·1 3·5	4·3 3·6	4·4 3·7	4·5 3·8	4·6 3·9	56·4
56·7	3·9 3·1	4·0 3·1	4·1 3·2	4·1 3·3	4·2 3·3	4·3 3·4	4·3 3·5	4·4 3·6	4·5 3·7	4·6 3·8	4·7 3·8	56·7
57·0	4·3 3·2	4·3 3·3	4·3 3·3	4·4 3·4	4·4 3·4	4·5 3·5	4·5 3·5	4·6 3·6	4·7 3·6	4·7 3·7	4·8 3·8	57·0
57·3	4·6 3·4	4·6 3·4	4·6 3·4	4·6 3·5	4·7 3·5	4·7 3·5	4·7 3·6	4·8 3·6	4·8 3·6	4·8 3·7	4·9 3·7	57·3
57·6	4·9 3·6	4·9 3·6	4·9 3·6	4·9 3·6	4·9 3·6	4·9 3·6	4·9 3·6	4·9 3·6	5·0 3·6	5·0 3·6	5·0 3·6	57·6
57·9	5·2 3·7	5·2 3·7	5·2 3·7	5·2 3·7	5·2 3·7	5·1 3·6	5·1 3·6	5·1 3·6	5·1 3·6	5·1 3·6	5·1 3·6	57·9
58·2	5·5 3·9	5·5 3·8	5·5 3·8	5·4 3·8	5·4 3·7	5·4 3·7	5·3 3·7	5·3 3·6	5·3 3·6	5·2 3·6	5·2 3·5	58·2
58·5	5·9 4·0	5·8 4·0	5·8 3·9	5·7 3·9	5·6 3·8	5·6 3·8	5·5 3·7	5·5 3·6	5·4 3·6	5·3 3·5	5·3 3·4	58·5
58·8	6·2 4·2	6·1 4·1	6·0 4·1	6·0 4·0	5·9 3·9	5·8 3·8	5·7 3·7	5·6 3·6	5·5 3·5	5·4 3·5	5·3 3·4	58·8
59·1	6·5 4·3	6·4 4·3	6·3 4·2	6·2 4·1	6·1 4·0	6·0 3·9	5·9 3·8	5·8 3·6	5·7 3·5	5·6 3·4	5·4 3·3	59·1
59·4	6·8 4·5	6·7 4·4	6·6 4·3	6·5 4·2	6·4 4·1	6·2 3·9	6·1 3·8	6·0 3·7	5·8 3·5	5·7 3·4	5·5 3·2	59·4
59·7	7·1 4·6	7·0 4·5	6·9 4·4	6·8 4·3	6·6 4·1	6·5 4·0	6·3 3·8	6·2 3·7	6·0 3·5	5·8 3·3	5·6 3·2	59·7
60·0	7·5 4·8	7·3 4·7	7·2 4·5	7·0 4·4	6·9 4·2	6·7 4·0	6·5 3·9	6·3 3·7	6·1 3·5	5·9 3·3	5·7 3·1	60·0
60·3	7·8 5·0	7·6 4·8	7·5 4·7	7·3 4·5	7·1 4·3	6·9 4·1	6·7 3·9	6·5 3·7	6·3 3·5	6·0 3·2	5·8 3·0	60·3
60·6	8·1 5·1	7·9 5·0	7·7 4·8	7·6 4·6	7·3 4·4	7·1 4·2	6·9 3·9	6·7 3·7	6·4 3·4	6·2 3·2	5·9 2·9	60·6
60·9	8·4 5·3	8·2 5·1	8·0 4·9	7·8 4·7	7·6 4·5	7·3 4·2	7·1 4·0	6·8 3·7	6·6 3·4	6·3 3·2	6·0 2·9	60·9
61·2	8·7 5·4	8·5 5·2	8·3 5·0	8·1 4·8	7·8 4·5	7·6 4·3	7·3 4·0	7·0 3·7	6·7 3·4	6·4 3·1	6·1 2·8	61·2
61·5	9·1 5·6	8·8 5·4	8·6 5·1	8·3 4·9	8·1 4·6	7·8 4·3	7·5 4·0	7·2 3·7	6·9 3·4	6·5 3·1	6·2 2·7	61·5

G.M.T.	ARIES G.H.A.	VENUS −4.2 G.H.A.	VENUS Dec.	MARS −0.1 G.H.A.	MARS Dec.	JUPITER −1.6 G.H.A.	JUPITER Dec.	SATURN −0.2 G.H.A.	SATURN Dec.
4 00	103 13.3	149 57.9	S 15 28.5	72 13.5	N13 51.1	145 27.7	S17 01.2	12 53.8	N22 24.5
01	118 15.8	165 00.6	28.0	87 15.1	51.4	160 29.6	01.1	27 56.4	24.5
02	133 18.2	180 03.3	27.4	102 16.6	51.8	175 31.5	00.9	42 59.1	24.5
03	148 20.7	195 06.0	.. 26.9	117 18.2	.. 52.2	190 33.4	.. 00.7	58 01.8	.. 24.5
04	163 23.2	210 08.8	26.3	132 19.8	52.5	205 35.4	00.6	73 04.5	24.5
05	178 25.6	225 11.5	25.8	147 21.3	52.9	220 37.3	00.4	88 07.2	24.6
06	193 28.1	240 14.2	S15 25.2	162 22.9	N13 53.2	235 39.2	S17 00.3	103 09.8	N22 24.6
07	208 30.5	255 17.0	24.7	177 24.4	53.6	250 41.1	17 00.1	118 12.5	24.6
08	223 33.0	270 19.7	24.1	192 26.0	54.0	265 43.0	16 59.9	133 15.2	24.6
F 09	238 35.5	285 22.4	.. 23.6	207 27.6	.. 54.3	280 44.9	.. 59.8	148 17.9	.. 24.6
R 10	253 37.9	300 25.2	23.0	222 29.1	54.7	295 46.8	59.6	163 20.6	24.6
I 11	268 40.4	315 28.0	22.5	237 30.7	55.0	310 48.7	59.4	178 23.2	24.6
D 12	283 42.9	330 30.7	S15 21.9	252 32.2	N13 55.4	325 50.6	S16 59.3	193 25.9	N22 24.6
A 13	298 45.3	345 33.5	21.4	267 33.8	55.8	340 52.6	59.1	208 28.6	24.6
Y 14	313 47.8	0 36.3	20.8	282 35.4	56.1	355 54.5	59.0	223 31.3	24.6
15	328 50.3	15 39.0	.. 20.3	297 36.9	.. 56.5	10 56.4	.. 58.8	238 33.9	.. 24.6
16	343 52.7	30 41.8	19.7	312 38.5	56.9	25 58.3	58.6	253 36.6	24.6
17	358 55.2	45 44.6	19.2	327 40.0	57.2	41 00.2	58.5	268 39.3	24.6
18	13 57.7	60 47.4	S15 18.7	342 41.6	N13 57.6	56 02.1	S16 58.3	283 42.0	N22 24.6
19	29 00.1	75 50.2	18.1	357 43.1	57.9	71 04.0	58.1	298 44.7	24.6
20	44 02.6	90 53.0	17.6	12 44.7	58.3	86 05.9	58.0	313 47.3	24.6
21	59 05.0	105 55.8	.. 17.0	27 46.2	.. 58.7	101 07.8	.. 57.8	328 50.0	.. 24.6
22	74 07.5	120 58.6	16.5	42 47.8	59.0	116 09.8	57.7	343 52.7	24.6
23	89 10.0	136 01.4	16.0	57 49.3	59.4	131 11.7	57.5	358 55.4	24.7
5 00	104 12.4	151 04.2	S15 15.4	72 50.9	N13 59.7	146 13.6	S16 57.3	13 58.0	N22 24.7
01	119 14.9	166 07.0	14.9	87 52.4	14 00.1	161 15.5	57.2	29 00.7	24.7
02	134 17.4	181 09.9	14.4	102 54.0	00.5	176 17.4	57.0	44 03.4	24.7
03	149 19.8	196 12.7	.. 13.8	117 55.5	.. 00.8	191 19.3	.. 56.8	59 06.1	.. 24.7
04	164 22.3	211 15.5	13.3	132 57.1	01.2	206 21.2	56.7	74 08.8	24.7
05	179 24.8	226 18.4	12.8	147 58.6	01.6	221 23.1	56.5	89 11.4	24.7
06	194 27.2	241 21.2	S15 12.2	163 00.2	N14 01.9	236 25.0	S16 56.3	104 14.1	N22 24.7
07	209 29.7	256 24.0	11.7	178 01.7	02.3	251 26.9	56.2	119 16.8	24.7
S 08	224 32.1	271 26.9	11.2	193 03.2	02.6	266 28.9	56.0	134 19.5	24.7
A 09	239 34.6	286 29.8	.. 10.6	208 04.8	.. 03.0	281 30.8	.. 55.9	149 22.1	.. 24.7
T 10	254 37.1	301 32.6	10.1	223 06.3	03.4	296 32.7	55.7	164 24.8	24.7
U 11	269 39.5	316 35.5	09.6	238 07.9	03.7	311 34.6	55.5	179 27.5	24.7
R 12	284 42.0	331 38.3	S15 09.0	253 09.4	N14 04.1	326 36.5	S16 55.4	194 30.2	N22 24.7
D 13	299 44.5	346 41.2	08.5	268 11.0	04.5	341 38.4	55.2	209 32.8	24.7
A 14	314 46.9	1 44.1	08.0	283 12.5	04.8	356 40.3	55.0	224 35.5	24.7
Y 15	329 49.4	16 47.0	.. 07.5	298 14.0	.. 05.2	11 42.2	.. 54.9	239 38.2	.. 24.7
16	344 51.9	31 49.9	06.9	313 15.6	05.6	26 44.1	54.7	254 40.9	24.8
17	359 54.3	46 52.8	06.4	328 17.1	05.9	41 46.0	54.5	269 43.5	24.8
18	14 56.8	61 55.7	S15 05.9	343 18.7	N14 06.3	56 47.9	S16 54.4	284 46.2	N22 24.8
19	29 59.3	76 58.5	05.4	358 20.2	06.6	71 49.8	54.2	299 48.9	24.8
20	45 01.7	92 01.5	04.8	13 21.7	07.0	86 51.8	54.1	314 51.6	24.8
21	60 04.2	107 04.4	.. 04.3	28 23.3	.. 07.4	101 53.7	.. 53.9	329 54.2	.. 24.8
22	75 06.6	122 07.3	03.8	43 24.8	07.7	116 55.6	53.7	344 56.9	24.8
23	90 09.1	137 10.2	03.3	58 26.3	08.1	131 57.5	53.6	359 59.6	24.8
6 00	105 11.6	152 13.1	S15 02.8	73 27.9	N14 08.5	146 59.4	S16 53.4	15 02.3	N22 24.8
01	120 14.0	167 16.0	02.3	88 29.4	08.8	162 01.3	53.2	30 05.0	24.8
02	135 16.5	182 19.0	01.7	103 30.9	09.2	177 03.2	53.1	45 07.6	24.8
03	150 19.0	197 21.9	.. 01.2	118 32.5	.. 09.6	192 05.1	.. 52.9	60 10.3	.. 24.8
04	165 21.4	212 24.9	00.7	133 34.0	09.9	207 07.0	52.7	75 13.0	24.8
05	180 23.9	227 27.8	15 00.3	148 35.5	10.3	222 08.9	52.6	90 15.7	24.8
06	195 26.4	242 30.7	S14 59.7	163 37.1	N14 10.7	237 10.8	S16 52.4	105 18.3	N22 24.8
07	210 28.8	257 33.7	59.2	178 38.6	11.0	252 12.7	52.2	120 21.0	24.8
08	225 31.3	272 36.7	58.7	193 40.1	11.4	267 14.7	52.1	135 23.7	24.8
S 09	240 33.8	287 39.6	.. 58.1	208 41.6	.. 11.8	282 16.6	.. 51.9	150 26.4	.. 24.9
U 10	255 36.2	302 42.6	57.6	223 43.2	12.1	297 18.5	51.7	165 29.0	24.9
N 11	270 38.7	317 45.6	57.1	238 44.7	12.5	312 20.4	51.6	180 31.7	24.9
D 12	285 41.1	332 48.5	S14 56.6	253 46.2	N14 12.8	327 22.3	S16 51.4	195 34.4	N22 24.9
A 13	300 43.6	347 51.5	56.1	268 47.8	13.2	342 24.2	51.3	210 37.1	24.9
Y 14	315 46.1	2 54.5	55.6	283 49.3	13.6	357 26.1	51.1	225 39.7	24.9
15	330 48.5	17 57.5	.. 55.1	298 50.8	.. 13.9	12 28.0	.. 50.9	240 42.4	.. 24.9
16	345 51.0	33 00.5	54.6	313 52.3	14.3	27 29.9	50.8	255 45.1	24.9
17	0 53.5	48 03.5	54.1	328 53.9	14.7	42 31.8	50.6	270 47.8	24.9
18	15 55.9	63 06.5	S14 53.6	343 55.4	N14 15.0	57 33.7	S16 50.4	285 50.4	N22 24.9
19	30 58.4	78 09.5	53.1	358 56.9	15.4	72 35.6	50.3	300 53.1	24.9
20	46 00.9	93 12.5	52.6	13 58.4	15.8	87 37.5	50.1	315 55.8	24.9
21	61 03.3	108 15.5	.. 52.1	28 59.9	.. 16.1	102 39.4	.. 49.9	330 58.4	.. 24.9
22	76 05.8	123 18.5	51.6	44 01.5	16.5	117 41.4	49.8	346 01.1	24.9
23	91 08.3	138 21.6	51.1	59 03.0	16.9	132 43.3	49.6	1 03.8	24.9
Mer. Pass. 17 00.4	v 2.9 d 0.5	v 1.5 d 0.4		v 1.9 d 0.2		v 2.7 d 0.0			

STARS

Name	S.H.A.	Dec.
Acamar	315 40.5	S 40 24.6
Achernar	335 48.5	S 57 22.3
Acrux	173 42.4	S 62 57.1
Adhara	255 35.3	S 28 56.2
Aldebaran	291 23.0	N 16 27.5
Alioth	166 46.4	N 56 05.6
Alkaid	153 22.2	N 49 26.2
Al Na'ir	28 21.0	S 47 05.4
Alnilam	276 16.0	S 1 13.1
Alphard	218 24.8	S 8 32.8
Alphecca	126 36.2	N 26 47.9
Alpheratz	358 14.2	N 28 57.1
Altair	62 37.4	N 8 48.0
Ankaa	353 44.8	S 42 27.0
Antares	113 02.8	S 26 22.5
Arcturus	146 22.8	N 19 18.8
Atria	108 31.7	S 68 58.8
Avior	234 29.5	S 59 25.5
Bellatrix	279 03.4	N 6 19.6
Betelgeuse	271 32.9	N 7 24.2
Canopus	264 08.7	S 52 40.9
Capella	281 17.7	N 45 58.5
Deneb	49 52.1	N 45 11.4
Denebola	183 03.6	N 14 42.8
Diphda	349 25.5	S 18 07.8
Dubhe	194 27.3	N 61 53.1
Elnath	278 49.6	N 28 35.3
Eltanin	91 00.4	N 51 29.4
Enif	34 16.4	N 9 45.4
Fomalhaut	15 56.6	S 29 45.7
Gacrux	172 33.9	S 56 57.9
Gienah	176 22.7	S 17 23.9
Hadar	149 30.2	S 60 14.7
Hamal	328 34.0	N 23 20.6
Kaus Aust.	84 23.4	S 34 23.9
Kochab	137 19.2	N 74 15.3
Markab	14 07.9	N 15 04.1
Menkar	314 45.8	N 3 59.4
Menkent	148 42.6	S 36 14.5
Miaplacidus	221 45.3	S 69 36.5
Mirfak	309 22.4	N 49 46.5
Nunki	76 35.2	S 26 19.8
Peacock	54 06.2	S 56 49.2
Pollux	244 03.4	N 28 05.3
Procyon	245 30.3	N 5 17.5
Rasalhague	96 34.2	N 12 34.6
Regulus	208 14.7	N 12 05.5
Rigel	281 40.1	S 8 13.9
Rigil Kent.	140 32.5	S 60 43.5
Sabik	102 46.7	S 15 41.6
Schedar	350 14.4	N 56 24.1
Shaula	97 02.4	S 37 05.1
Sirius	258 59.4	S 16 40.9
Spica	159 02.5	S 11 01.6
Suhail	223 13.8	S 43 19.6
Vega	80 59.4	N 38 45.5
Zuben'ubi	137 38.3	S 15 56.1

	S.H.A.	Mer. Pass.
Venus	46 51.8	13 53
Mars	328 38.4	19 07
Jupiter	42 01.1	14 13
Saturn	269 45.6	23 00

1974 JANUARY 4, 5, 6 (FRI., SAT., SUN.)

G.M.T.	SUN G.H.A.	Dec.	MOON G.H.A.	v	Dec.	d	H.P.
d h	° ′	° ′	° ′	′	° ′	′	′
4 00	178 49·8	S22 47·0	65 51·3	8·0	N18 51·3	8·9	58·7
01	193 49·5	46·7	80 18·3	7·8	19 00·2	8·8	58·8
02	208 49·3	46·5	94 45·1	7·7	19 09·0	8·7	58·8
03	223 49·0 ··	46·2	109 11·8	7·6	19 17·7	8·5	58·8
04	238 48·7	46·0	123 38·4	7·5	19 26·2	8·5	58·9
05	253 48·4	45·7	138 04·9	7·3	19 34·7	8·4	58·9
06	268 48·1	S22 45·5	152 31·2	7·3	N19 43·1	8·2	59·0
07	283 47·8	45·2	166 57·5	7·1	19 51·3	8·2	59·0
08	298 47·5	45·0	181 23·6	7·0	19 59·5	8·0	59·0
F 09	313 47·3 ··	44·7	195 49·6	7·0	20 07·5	7·9	59·1
R 10	328 47·0	44·4	210 15·6	6·8	20 15·4	7·8	59·1
I 11	343 46·7	44·2	224 41·4	6·6	20 23·2	7·7	59·2
D 12	358 46·4	S22 43·9	239 07·0	6·6	N20 30·9	7·6	59·2
A 13	13 46·1	43·7	253 32·6	6·5	20 38·5	7·4	59·2
Y 14	28 45·8	43·4	267 58·1	6·3	20 45·9	7·4	59·3
15	43 45·6 ··	43·1	282 23·4	6·2	20 53·3	7·2	59·3
16	58 45·3	42·9	296 48·6	6·2	21 00·5	7·1	59·4
17	73 45·0	42·6	311 13·8	6·0	21 07·6	6·9	59·4
18	88 44·7	S22 42·3	325 38·8	5·9	N21 14·5	6·8	59·4
19	103 44·4	42·1	340 03·7	5·8	21 21·3	6·7	59·5
20	118 44·1	41·8	354 28·5	5·6	21 28·0	6·6	59·5
21	133 43·9 ··	41·5	8 53·1	5·6	21 34·6	6·4	59·6
22	148 43·6	41·3	23 17·7	5·5	21 41·0	6·3	59·6
23	163 43·3	41·0	37 42·2	5·3	21 47·3	6·1	59·6
5 00	178 43·0	S22 40·7	52 06·5	5·3	N21 53·4	6·1	59·7
01	193 42·7	40·5	66 30·8	5·2	21 59·5	5·8	59·7
02	208 42·5	40·2	80 55·0	5·0	22 05·3	5·8	59·7
03	223 42·2 ··	39·9	95 19·0	5·0	22 11·1	5·6	59·8
04	238 41·9	39·6	109 43·0	4·8	22 16·7	5·4	59·8
05	253 41·6	39·4	124 06·8	4·7	22 22·1	5·3	59·9
06	268 41·3	S22 39·1	138 30·5	4·7	N22 27·4	5·2	59·9
07	283 41·1	38·8	152 54·2	4·5	22 32·6	5·0	59·9
S 08	298 40·8	38·5	167 17·7	4·5	22 37·6	4·8	60·0
A 09	313 40·5 ··	38·3	181 41·2	4·3	22 42·4	4·7	60·0
T 10	328 40·2	38·0	196 04·5	4·3	22 47·1	4·6	60·0
U 11	343 39·9	37·7	210 27·8	4·2	22 51·7	4·4	60·1
R 12	358 39·7	S22 37·4	224 51·0	4·1	N22 56·1	4·2	60·1
D 13	13 39·4	37·1	239 14·1	4·0	23 00·3	4·1	60·1
A 14	28 39·1	36·9	253 37·1	3·9	23 04·4	3·9	60·2
Y 15	43 38·8 ··	36·6	268 00·0	3·8	23 08·3	3·8	60·2
16	58 38·5	36·3	282 22·8	3·7	23 12·1	3·6	60·2
17	73 38·3	36·0	296 45·5	3·7	23 15·7	3·4	60·3
18	88 38·0	S22 35·7	311 08·2	3·5	N23 19·1	3·3	60·3
19	103 37·7	35·4	325 30·7	3·5	23 22·4	3·1	60·3
20	118 37·4	35·2	339 53·2	3·5	23 25·5	2·9	60·4
21	133 37·2 ··	34·9	354 15·7	3·3	23 28·4	2·8	60·4
22	148 36·9	34·6	8 38·0	3·3	23 31·2	2·6	60·4
23	163 36·6	34·3	23 00·3	3·2	23 33·8	2·4	60·5
6 00	178 36·3	S22 34·0	37 22·5	3·1	N23 36·2	2·3	60·5
01	193 36·1	33·7	51 44·6	3·1	23 38·5	2·1	60·5
02	208 35·8	33·4	66 06·7	3·0	23 40·6	1·9	60·6
03	223 35·5 ··	33·1	80 28·7	2·9	23 42·5	1·8	60·6
04	238 35·2	32·8	94 50·6	2·9	23 44·3	1·6	60·6
05	253 34·9	32·5	109 12·5	2·8	23 45·9	1·3	60·7
06	268 34·7	S22 32·3	123 34·3	2·8	N23 47·2	1·3	60·7
07	283 34·4	32·0	137 56·1	2·7	23 48·5	1·0	60·7
08	298 34·1	31·7	152 17·8	2·7	23 49·5	0·9	60·7
S 09	313 33·8 ··	31·4	166 39·5	2·6	23 50·4	0·7	60·8
U 10	328 33·6	31·1	181 01·1	2·6	23 51·1	0·5	60·8
N 11	343 33·3	30·8	195 22·7	2·5	23 51·6	0·3	60·8
D 12	358 33·0	S22 30·5	209 44·2	2·5	N23 51·9	0·2	60·9
A 13	13 32·8	30·2	224 05·7	2·5	23 52·1	0·1	60·9
Y 14	28 32·5	29·9	238 27·2	2·4	23 52·0	0·1	60·9
15	43 32·2 ··	29·6	252 48·6	2·4	23 51·8	0·4	61·0
16	58 31·9	29·3	267 10·0	2·3	23 51·4	0·5	61·0
17	73 31·7	29·0	281 31·3	2·3	23 50·9	0·8	61·0
18	88 31·4	S22 28·7	295 52·7	2·3	N23 50·1	0·9	61·0
19	103 31·1	28·4	310 14·0	2·2	23 49·2	1·2	61·0
20	118 30·8	28·1	324 35·2	2·3	23 48·0	1·3	61·0
21	133 30·6 ··	27·8	338 56·5	2·2	23 46·7	1·4	61·1
22	148 30·3	27·5	353 17·7	2·3	23 45·3	1·7	61·1
23	163 30·0	27·2	7 39·0	2·2	23 43·6	1·9	61·1
S.D.	16·3 d 0·3		S.D. 16·1		16·4		16·6

Moonrise

Lat.	Twilight Naut.	Civil	Sun-rise	4	5	6	7
°	h m	h m	h m	h m	h m	h m	h m
N 72	08 20	10 31	■	□	□	□	□
N 70	08 02	09 43	■	08 20	□	□	□
68	07 47	09 12	11 32	09 40	□	□	□
66	07 35	08 50	10 20	10 18	10 18	10 37	12 18
64	07 25	08 31	09 45	10 45	11 02	11 44	13 07
62	07 16	08 16	09 19	11 06	11 31	12 19	13 39
60	07 08	08 04	09 00	11 23	11 54	12 45	14 02
N 58	07 01	07 53	08 44	11 37	12 12	13 06	14 21
56	06 55	07 43	08 30	11 50	12 28	13 22	14 36
54	06 49	07 35	08 18	12 01	12 41	13 37	14 50
52	06 44	07 27	08 07	12 11	12 53	13 49	15 02
50	06 39	07 20	07 58	12 19	13 03	14 00	15 12
45	06 28	07 05	07 38	12 38	13 25	14 23	15 34
N 40	06 18	06 52	07 22	12 53	13 42	14 42	15 51
35	06 09	06 41	07 08	13 06	13 57	14 57	16 06
30	06 01	06 30	06 57	13 17	14 10	15 11	16 19
20	05 45	06 12	06 36	13 36	14 32	15 34	16 41
N 10	05 29	05 55	06 18	13 53	14 51	15 54	17 00
0	05 13	05 39	06 02	14 09	15 09	16 13	17 17
S 10	04 55	05 22	05 45	14 25	15 27	16 31	17 35
20	04 33	05 02	05 26	14 42	15 47	16 51	17 54
30	04 05	04 38	05 05	15 02	16 09	17 15	18 16
35	03 47	04 23	04 52	15 14	16 22	17 28	18 28
40	03 25	04 06	04 38	15 27	16 38	17 44	18 43
45	02 56	03 44	04 21	15 43	16 56	18 03	19 00
S 50	02 13	03 16	03 59	16 03	17 18	18 26	19 22
52	01 48	03 01	03 49	16 12	17 29	18 37	19 32
54	01 11	02 45	03 37	16 23	17 42	18 50	19 43
56	////	02 24	03 24	16 35	17 56	19 05	19 56
58	////	01 57	03 08	16 49	18 12	19 22	20 11
S 60	////	01 17	02 49	17 05	18 33	19 43	20 29

Moonset

Lat.	Sun-set	Twilight Civil	Naut.	4	5	6	7
°	h m	h m	h m	h m	h m	h m	h m
N 72	■	13 40	15 51	□	□	□	□
N 70	■	14 27	16 09	07 14	□	□	□
68	12 38	14 58	16 23	05 56	□	□	□
66	13 50	15 21	16 35	05 19	07 21	09 14	09 49
64	14 25	15 39	16 46	04 52	06 37	08 07	08 59
62	14 51	15 54	16 54	04 32	06 08	07 31	08 28
60	15 11	16 06	17 02	04 16	05 46	07 06	08 04
N 58	15 27	16 17	17 09	04 02	05 28	06 45	07 45
56	15 41	16 27	17 15	03 50	05 13	06 28	07 29
54	15 53	16 36	17 21	03 39	05 00	06 14	07 15
52	16 03	16 44	17 27	03 30	04 49	06 02	07 03
50	16 13	16 51	17 32	03 22	04 39	05 51	06 53
45	16 33	17 06	17 43	03 04	04 18	05 28	06 30
N 40	16 49	17 19	17 53	02 50	04 01	05 09	06 12
35	17 02	17 30	18 02	02 38	03 46	04 54	05 57
30	17 14	17 40	18 10	02 28	03 34	04 40	05 44
20	17 34	17 58	18 26	02 10	03 13	04 17	05 21
N 10	17 52	18 15	18 41	01 54	02 54	03 58	05 02
0	18 09	18 32	18 57	01 40	02 37	03 39	04 43
S 10	18 26	18 49	19 16	01 25	02 20	03 20	04 25
20	18 44	19 09	19 38	01 10	02 02	03 01	04 05
30	19 05	19 33	20 05	00 52	01 41	02 38	03 42
35	19 17	19 47	20 23	00 42	01 28	02 24	03 29
40	19 32	20 05	20 46	00 30	01 14	02 09	03 13
45	19 49	20 26	21 14	00 16	00 58	01 50	02 55
S 50	20 11	20 54	21 56	24 27	00 37	01 27	02 32
52	20 21	21 08	22 21	24 16	00 16	01 16	02 20
54	20 32	21 25	22 56	24 04	00 04	01 03	02 08
56	20 46	21 45	////	23 50	24 40	00 49	01 53
58	21 02	22 12	////	23 33	24 32	00 32	01 36
S 60	21 20	22 51	////	23 33	24 12	00 12	01 18

Day	SUN Eqn. of Time 00h	12h	Mer. Pass.	MOON Mer. Pass. Upper	Lower	Age	Phase
	m s	m s	h m	h m	h m	d	
4	04 40	04 54	12 05	20 23	07 54	11	●
5	05 07	05 21	12 05	21 24	08 53	12	
6	05 34	05 47	12 06	22 28	09 56	13	

1974 MARCH 23, 24, 25 (SAT., SUN., MON.)

G.M.T. d h	ARIES G.H.A.	VENUS -4.2 G.H.A.	Dec.	MARS +1.3 G.H.A.	Dec.	JUPITER -1.6 G.H.A.	Dec.	SATURN +0.3 G.H.A.	Dec.	Name	S.H.A.	Dec.
23 00	180 06.1	222 15.1	S 13 28.7	108 22.4	N 23 58.7	204 31.5	S 11 03.0	91 58.0	N 22 37.7	Acamar	315 40.9	S 40 24.6
01	195 08.6	237 15.3	28.3	123 23.3	58.9	219 33.4	02.8	107 00.3	37.7	Achernar	335 49.0	S 57 22.1
02	210 11.0	252 15.5	28.0	138 24.2	59.1	234 35.3	02.6	122 02.7	37.7	Acrux	173 41.7	S 62 57.5
03	225 13.5	267 15.7 ..	27.6	153 25.1 ..	59.2	249 37.3 ..	02.4	137 05.0 ..	37.7	Adhara	255 35.6	S 28 56.5
04	240 16.0	282 15.9	27.3	168 26.0	59.4	264 39.2	02.2	152 07.4	37.7	Aldebaran	291 23.3	N 16 27.5
05	255 18.4	297 16.1	26.9	183 26.9	59.6	279 41.1	02.0	167 09.7	37.7			
06	270 20.9	312 16.3	S 13 26.6	198 27.8	N 23 59.8	294 43.1	S 11 01.8	182 12.1	N 22 37.7	Alioth	166 45.8	N 56 05.7
07	285 23.4	327 16.5	26.2	213 28.7	24 00.0	309 45.0	01.6	197 14.4	37.7	Alkaid	153 21.5	N 49 26.2
S 08	300 25.8	342 16.7	25.8	228 29.6	00.1	324 46.9	01.4	212 16.8	37.7	Al Na'ir	28 20.8	S 47 05.1
A 09	315 28.3	357 16.8 ..	25.5	243 30.5 ..	00.3	339 48.8 ..	01.2	227 19.1 ..	37.7	Alnilam	276 16.2	S 1 13.2
T 10	330 30.8	12 17.0	25.1	258 31.3	00.5	354 50.8	01.0	242 21.5	37.8	Alphard	218 24.7	S 8 33.0
U 11	345 33.2	27 17.2	24.8	273 32.2	00.7	9 52.7	00.8	257 23.8	37.8			
R 12	0 35.7	42 17.4	S 13 24.4	288 33.1	N 24 00.8	24 54.6	S 11 00.6	272 26.2	N 22 37.8	Alphecca	126 35.6	N 26 47.7
D 13	15 38.2	57 17.6	24.0	303 34.0	01.0	39 56.6	00.4	287 28.5	37.8	Alpheratz	358 14.3	N 28 56.9
A 14	30 40.6	72 17.8	23.7	318 34.9	01.2	54 58.5	00.2	302 30.9	37.8	Altair	62 37.0	N 8 47.8
Y 15	45 43.1	87 18.0 ..	23.3	333 35.8 ..	01.4	70 00.4	11 00.0	317 33.2 ..	37.8	Ankaa	353 45.0	S 42 26.8
16	60 45.5	102 18.2	22.9	348 36.7	01.5	85 02.3	10 59.8	332 35.6	37.8	Antares	113 02.2	S 26 22.6
17	75 48.0	117 18.4	22.6	3 37.6	01.7	100 04.3	59.6	347 37.9	37.8			
18	90 50.5	132 18.6	S 13 22.2	18 38.5	N 24 01.9	115 06.2	S 10 59.4	2 40.3	N 22 37.8	Arcturus	146 22.2	N 19 18.7
19	105 52.9	147 18.7	21.8	33 39.4	02.0	130 08.1	59.2	17 42.6	37.8	Atria	108 30.3	S 68 58.8
20	120 55.4	162 18.9	21.5	48 40.3	02.2	145 10.1	59.0	32 44.9	37.8	Avior	234 29.8	S 59 25.9
21	135 57.9	177 19.1 ..	21.1	63 41.2 ..	02.4	160 12.0 ..	58.9	47 47.3 ..	37.9	Bellatrix	279 03.6	N 6 19.6
22	151 00.3	192 19.3	20.7	78 42.1	02.6	175 13.9	58.7	62 49.6	37.9	Betelgeuse	271 33.1	N 7 24.1
23	166 02.8	207 19.5	20.4	93 42.9	02.7	190 15.8	58.5	77 52.0	37.9			
24 00	181 05.3	222 19.7	S 13 20.0	108 43.8	N 24 02.9	205 17.8	S 10 58.3	92 54.3	N 22 37.9	Canopus	264 09.2	S 52 41.2
01	196 07.7	237 19.8	19.6	123 44.7	03.1	220 19.7	58.1	107 56.7	37.9	Capella	281 18.0	N 45 58.6
02	211 10.2	252 20.0	19.2	138 45.6	03.3	235 21.6	57.9	122 59.0	37.9	Deneb	49 51.8	N 45 11.1
03	226 12.7	267 20.2 ..	18.9	153 46.5 ..	03.4	250 23.6 ..	57.7	138 01.4 ..	37.9	Denebola	183 03.2	N 14 42.7
04	241 15.1	282 20.4	18.5	168 47.4	03.6	265 25.5	57.5	153 03.7	37.9	Diphda	349 25.6	S 18 07.7
05	256 17.6	297 20.6	18.1	183 48.3	03.8	280 27.4	57.3	168 06.0	37.9			
06	271 20.0	312 20.7	S 13 17.7	198 49.2	N 24 03.9	295 29.4	S 10 57.1	183 08.4	N 22 37.9	Dubhe	194 26.8	N 61 53.3
07	286 22.5	327 20.9	17.3	213 50.1	04.1	310 31.3	56.9	198 10.7	37.9	Elnath	278 49.8	N 28 35.3
08	301 25.0	342 21.1	17.0	228 51.0	04.3	325 33.2	56.7	213 13.1	37.9	Eltanin	90 59.8	N 51 29.2
S 09	316 27.4	357 21.3 ..	16.6	243 51.8 ..	04.4	340 35.1 ..	56.5	228 15.4 ..	38.0	Enif	34 16.2	N 9 45.3
U 10	331 29.9	12 21.4	16.2	258 52.7	04.6	355 37.1	56.3	243 17.8	38.0	Fomalhaut	15 56.6	S 29 45.5
N 11	346 32.4	27 21.6	15.8	273 53.6	04.8	10 39.0	56.1	258 20.1	38.0			
D 12	1 34.8	42 21.8	S 13 15.5	288 54.5	N 24 05.0	25 40.9	S 10 55.9	273 22.4	N 22 38.0	Gacrux	172 33.2	S 56 58.3
A 13	16 37.3	57 21.9	15.1	303 55.4	05.1	40 42.9	55.7	288 24.8	38.0	Gienah	176 22.2	S 17 24.2
Y 14	31 39.8	72 22.1	14.7	318 56.3	05.3	55 44.8	55.5	303 27.1	38.0	Hadar	149 29.2	S 60 15.0
15	46 42.2	87 22.3 ..	14.3	333 57.2 ..	05.5	70 46.7 ..	55.3	318 29.5 ..	38.0	Hamal	328 34.3	N 23 20.5
16	61 44.7	102 22.5	13.9	348 58.1	05.6	85 48.7	55.1	333 31.8	38.0	Kaus Aust.	84 22.8	S 34 23.8
17	76 47.1	117 22.6	13.5	3 59.0	05.8	100 50.6	54.9	348 34.2	38.0			
18	91 49.6	132 22.8	S 13 13.1	18 59.8	N 24 06.0	115 52.5	S 10 54.7	3 36.5	N 22 38.0	Kochab	137 17.7	N 74 15.3
19	106 52.1	147 23.0	12.8	34 00.7	06.1	130 54.5	54.5	18 38.8	38.0	Markab	14 07.9	N 15 03.9
20	121 54.5	162 23.1	12.4	49 01.6	06.3	145 56.4	54.3	33 41.2	38.1	Menkar	314 46.0	N 3 59.3
21	136 57.0	177 23.3 ..	12.0	64 02.5 ..	06.4	160 58.3 ..	54.1	48 43.5 ..	38.1	Menkent	148 42.0	S 36 14.8
22	151 59.5	192 23.5	11.6	79 03.4	06.6	176 00.2	53.9	63 45.9	38.1	Miaplacidus	221 45.4	S 69 37.0
23	167 01.9	207 23.6	11.2	94 04.3	06.8	191 02.2	53.7	78 48.2	38.1			
25 00	182 04.4	222 23.8	S 13 10.8	109 05.2	N 24 07.0	206 04.1	S 10 53.5	93 50.5	N 22 38.1	Mirfak	309 22.9	N 49 46.4
01	197 06.9	237 23.9	10.4	124 06.1	07.1	221 06.0	53.3	108 52.9	38.1	Nunki	76 34.7	S 26 19.8
02	212 09.3	252 24.1	10.0	139 06.9	07.3	236 08.0	53.1	123 55.2	38.1	Peacock	54 05.6	S 56 48.9
03	227 11.8	267 24.3 ..	09.6	154 07.8 ..	07.5	251 09.9 ..	52.9	138 57.6 ..	38.1	Pollux	244 03.5	N 28 05.3
04	242 14.3	282 24.4	09.2	169 08.7	07.6	266 11.8	52.7	153 59.9	38.1	Procyon	245 30.3	N 5 17.4
05	257 16.7	297 24.6	08.8	184 09.6	07.8	281 13.8	52.5	169 02.2	38.1			
06	272 19.2	312 24.7	S 13 08.4	199 10.5	N 24 08.0	296 15.7	S 10 52.3	184 04.6	N 22 38.1	Rasalhague	96 33.7	N 12 34.5
07	287 21.6	327 24.9	08.0	214 11.4	08.1	311 17.6	52.1	199 06.9	38.2	Regulus	208 14.5	N 12 05.4
08	302 24.1	342 25.0	07.6	229 12.3	08.3	326 19.6	51.9	214 09.3	38.2	Rigel	281 40.4	S 8 14.0
M 09	317 26.6	357 25.2 ..	07.2	244 13.2 ..	08.5	341 21.5 ..	51.7	229 11.6 ..	38.2	Rigil Kent.	140 31.4	S 60 43.7
O 10	332 29.0	12 25.4	06.8	259 14.0	08.6	356 23.4	51.5	244 13.9	38.2	Sabik	102 46.2	S 15 41.7
N 11	347 31.5	27 25.5	06.4	274 14.9	08.8	11 25.4	51.3	259 16.3	38.2			
D 12	2 34.0	42 25.7	S 13 06.0	289 15.8	N 24 09.0	26 27.3	S 10 51.1	274 18.6	N 22 38.2	Schedar	350 14.8	N 56 23.8
A 13	17 36.4	57 25.8	05.6	304 16.7	09.1	41 29.2	50.9	289 21.0	38.2	Shaula	97 01.7	S 37 05.1
Y 14	32 38.9	72 26.0	05.2	319 17.6	09.3	56 31.1	50.7	304 23.3	38.2	Sirius	258 59.6	S 16 41.1
15	47 41.4	87 26.1 ..	04.8	334 18.5 ..	09.4	71 33.1 ..	50.5	319 25.6 ..	38.2	Spica	159 01.9	S 11 01.9
16	62 43.8	102 26.3	04.4	349 19.3	09.6	86 35.0	50.3	334 28.0	38.2	Suhail	223 13.8	S 43 20.0
17	77 46.3	117 26.4	04.0	4 20.2	09.8	101 37.0	50.1	349 30.3	38.2			
18	92 48.7	132 26.6	S 13 03.6	19 21.1	N 24 09.9	116 38.9	S 10 49.9	4 32.6	N 22 38.2	Vega	80 58.9	N 38 45.3
19	107 51.2	147 26.7	03.2	34 22.0	10.1	131 40.8	49.7	19 35.0	38.3	Zuben'ubi	137 37.7	S 15 56.3
20	122 53.7	162 26.8	02.8	49 22.9	10.2	146 42.8	49.5	34 37.3	38.3		S.H.A.	Mer. Pass.
21	137 56.1	177 27.0 ..	02.4	64 23.8 ..	10.4	161 44.7 ..	49.3	49 39.6 ..	38.3	Venus	41 14.4	9 11
22	152 58.6	192 27.1	02.0	79 24.7	10.6	176 46.6	49.2	64 42.0	38.3	Mars	287 38.6	16 44
23	168 01.1	207 27.3	01.6	94 25.5	10.7	191 48.6	49.0	79 44.3	38.3	Jupiter	24 12.5	10 17
Mer. Pass. 11 53.7		v 0.2	d 0.4	v 0.9	d 0.2	v 1.9	d 0.2	v 2.3	d 0.0	Saturn	271 49.1	17 46

1974 MARCH 23, 24, 25 (SAT., SUN., MON.)

SUN and MOON — G.M.T.

G.M.T. d h	SUN G.H.A.	SUN Dec.	MOON G.H.A.	v	MOON Dec.	d	H.P.
23 00	178 17.1	N 0 47.3	189 53.2	14.5	N 1 13.5	12.4	55.7
01	193 17.3	48.3	204 26.7	14.5	1 25.9	12.5	55.7
02	208 17.5	49.3	219 00.2	14.5	1 38.4	12.5	55.7
03	223 17.7	·· 50.3	233 33.7	14.4	1 50.9	12.5	55.8
04	238 17.9	51.2	248 07.1	14.4	2 03.4	12.5	55.8
05	253 18.1	52.2	262 40.5	14.3	2 15.9	12.4	55.8
06	268 18.3	N 0 53.2	277 13.8	14.4	N 2 28.3	12.5	55.8
S 07	283 18.5	54.2	291 47.2	14.3	2 40.8	12.5	55.8
A 08	298 18.6	55.2	306 20.5	14.2	2 53.3	12.5	55.9
A 09	313 18.8	·· 56.2	320 53.7	14.3	3 05.8	12.4	55.9
T 10	328 19.0	57.2	335 27.0	14.2	3 18.2	12.5	55.9
U 11	343 19.2	58.1	350 00.2	14.1	3 30.7	12.5	55.9
R 12	358 19.4	N 0 59.1	4 33.3	14.1	N 3 43.2	12.4	55.9
D 13	13 19.6	1 00.1	19 06.4	14.1	3 55.6	12.5	56.0
A 14	28 19.8	01.1	33 39.5	14.1	4 08.1	12.4	56.0
Y 15	43 20.0	·· 02.1	48 12.6	14.0	4 20.5	12.4	56.0
16	58 20.1	03.1	62 45.6	13.9	4 32.9	12.4	56.0
17	73 20.3	04.1	77 18.5	13.9	4 45.3	12.4	56.1
18	88 20.5	N 1 05.0	91 51.4	13.9	N 4 57.7	12.4	56.1
19	103 20.7	06.0	106 24.3	13.9	5 10.1	12.4	56.1
20	118 20.9	07.0	120 57.2	13.8	5 22.5	12.4	56.1
21	133 21.1	·· 08.0	135 30.0	13.7	5 34.9	12.3	56.1
22	148 21.3	09.0	150 02.7	13.7	5 47.2	12.4	56.2
23	163 21.5	10.0	164 35.4	13.7	5 59.6	12.3	56.2
24 00	178 21.6	N 1 11.0	179 08.1	13.6	N 6 11.9	12.3	56.2
01	193 21.8	11.9	193 40.7	13.5	6 24.2	12.2	56.2
02	208 22.0	12.9	208 13.2	13.6	6 36.4	12.3	56.2
03	223 22.2	·· 13.9	222 45.8	13.4	6 48.7	12.2	56.3
04	238 22.4	14.9	237 18.2	13.5	7 00.9	12.2	56.3
05	253 22.6	15.9	251 50.7	13.3	7 13.1	12.2	56.3
06	268 22.8	N 1 16.9	266 23.0	13.3	N 7 25.3	12.2	56.3
S 07	283 23.0	17.9	280 55.3	13.3	7 37.5	12.1	56.4
U 08	298 23.1	18.8	295 27.6	13.2	7 49.6	12.1	56.4
N 09	313 23.3	·· 19.8	309 59.8	13.2	8 01.7	12.1	56.4
D 10	328 23.5	20.8	324 32.0	13.1	8 13.8	12.0	56.4
A 11	343 23.7	21.8	339 04.1	13.1	8 25.8	12.1	56.4
Y 12	358 23.9	N 1 22.8	353 36.2	13.0	N 8 37.9	11.9	56.5
13	13 24.1	23.8	8 08.2	12.9	8 49.8	12.0	56.5
14	28 24.3	24.7	22 40.1	12.9	9 01.8	11.9	56.5
15	43 24.5	·· 25.7	37 12.0	12.8	9 13.7	11.9	56.5
16	58 24.7	26.7	51 43.8	12.8	9 25.6	11.9	56.6
17	73 24.8	27.7	66 15.6	12.7	9 37.5	11.8	56.6
18	88 25.0	N 1 28.7	80 47.3	12.7	N 9 49.3	11.8	56.6
19	103 25.2	29.7	95 19.0	12.5	10 01.1	11.7	56.6
20	118 25.4	30.7	109 50.5	12.6	10 12.8	11.7	56.6
21	133 25.6	·· 31.6	124 22.1	12.5	10 24.5	11.6	56.7
22	148 25.8	32.6	138 53.6	12.4	10 36.1	11.7	56.7
23	163 26.0	33.6	153 25.0	12.3	10 47.8	11.5	56.7
25 00	178 26.2	N 1 34.6	167 56.3	12.3	N10 59.3	11.5	56.7
01	193 26.3	35.6	182 27.6	12.2	11 10.8	11.5	56.8
02	208 26.5	36.6	196 58.8	12.2	11 22.3	11.5	56.8
03	223 26.7	·· 37.5	211 30.0	12.1	11 33.8	11.3	56.8
04	238 26.9	38.5	226 01.1	12.0	11 45.1	11.4	56.8
05	253 27.1	39.5	240 32.1	11.9	11 56.5	11.2	56.8
06	268 27.3	N 1 40.5	255 03.0	11.9	N12 07.7	11.3	56.9
M 07	283 27.5	41.5	269 33.9	11.9	12 19.0	11.2	56.9
O 08	298 27.7	42.5	284 04.8	11.7	12 30.2	11.1	56.9
N 09	313 27.9	·· 43.4	298 35.5	11.7	12 41.3	11.0	56.9
D 10	328 28.0	44.4	313 06.2	11.6	12 52.3	11.1	56.9
A 11	343 28.2	45.4	327 36.8	11.6	13 03.4	10.9	57.0
Y 12	358 28.4	N 1 46.4	342 07.4	11.5	N13 14.3	10.9	57.0
13	13 28.6	47.4	356 37.9	11.4	13 25.2	10.8	57.0
14	28 28.8	48.4	11 08.3	11.3	13 36.0	10.8	57.0
15	43 29.0	·· 49.3	25 38.6	11.3	13 46.8	10.7	57.0
16	58 29.2	50.3	40 08.9	11.2	13 57.5	10.7	57.1
17	73 29.4	51.3	54 39.1	11.1	14 08.2	10.5	57.1
18	88 29.6	N 1 52.3	69 09.2	11.0	N14 18.7	10.5	57.1
19	103 29.7	53.3	83 39.2	11.0	14 29.2	10.5	57.1
20	118 29.9	54.3	98 09.2	10.9	14 39.7	10.4	57.1
21	133 30.1	·· 55.2	112 39.1	10.9	14 50.1	10.3	57.2
22	148 30.3	56.2	127 09.0	10.7	15 00.4	10.2	57.2
23	163 30.5	57.2	141 38.7	10.7	15 10.6	10.2	57.2
	S.D. 16.1	d 1.0	S.D. 15.2		15.4		15.5

Twilight, Sunrise and Moonrise

Lat.	Twilight Naut.	Twilight Civil	Sun-rise	Moonrise 23	24	25	26
N 72	02 57	04 31	05 41	05 03	04 43	04 18	03 40
N 70	03 20	04 41	05 43	05 06	04 53	04 38	04 18
68	03 37	04 49	05 45	05 08	05 01	04 53	04 44
66	03 51	04 56	05 47	05 10	05 08	05 06	05 05
64	04 02	05 01	05 49	05 12	05 14	05 16	05 21
62	04 11	05 06	05 50	05 13	05 19	05 25	05 35
60	04 19	05 10	05 51	05 15	05 23	05 33	05 47
N 58	04 26	05 13	05 52	05 16	05 27	05 40	05 57
56	04 32	05 16	05 53	05 17	05 30	05 46	06 06
54	04 37	05 18	05 54	05 18	05 34	05 52	06 14
52	04 41	05 21	05 55	05 19	05 37	05 57	06 21
50	04 45	05 23	05 55	05 19	05 39	06 01	06 27
45	04 53	05 27	05 57	05 21	05 45	06 11	06 41
N 40	04 59	05 31	05 58	05 23	05 50	06 19	06 53
35	05 04	05 34	05 59	05 24	05 54	06 26	07 03
30	05 08	05 36	06 00	05 25	05 58	06 33	07 11
20	05 13	05 39	06 01	05 27	06 04	06 44	07 26
N 10	05 17	05 41	06 02	05 29	06 10	06 53	07 40
0	05 19	05 42	06 03	05 31	06 15	07 02	07 52
S 10	05 19	05 43	06 04	05 32	06 21	07 11	08 05
20	05 17	05 43	06 05	05 34	06 27	07 21	08 18
30	05 14	05 42	06 05	05 36	06 34	07 33	08 34
35	05 11	05 41	06 06	05 38	06 37	07 39	08 43
40	05 08	05 39	06 06	05 39	06 42	07 47	08 53
45	05 03	05 38	06 07	05 41	06 47	07 55	09 05
S 50	04 57	05 35	06 07	05 43	06 53	08 06	09 20
52	04 54	05 34	06 08	05 44	06 56	08 11	09 27
54	04 51	05 32	06 08	05 45	07 00	08 17	09 35
56	04 47	05 31	06 08	05 46	07 03	08 23	09 44
58	04 43	05 29	06 08	05 47	07 07	08 29	09 54
S 60	04 38	05 27	06 09	05 48	07 12	08 37	10 05

Sunset, Twilight and Moonset

Lat.	Sun-set	Twilight Civil	Twilight Naut.	Moonset 23	24	25	26
N 72	18 35	19 45	21 22	18 57	20 58	23 19	□
N 70	18 32	19 35	20 58	18 50	20 41	22 42	25 13
68	18 30	19 27	20 40	18 44	20 27	22 17	24 18
66	18 28	19 20	20 25	18 39	20 15	21 58	23 45
64	18 26	19 14	20 14	18 35	20 07	21 42	23 21
62	18 25	19 09	20 04	18 31	19 59	21 29	23 02
60	18 23	19 05	19 56	18 28	19 52	21 18	22 46
N 58	18 22	19 02	19 49	18 25	19 46	21 09	22 33
56	18 21	18 58	19 43	18 23	19 41	21 01	22 22
54	18 20	18 56	19 38	18 20	19 36	20 54	22 12
52	18 19	18 53	19 33	18 18	19 31	20 47	22 03
50	18 18	18 51	19 29	18 16	19 28	20 41	21 55
45	18 17	18 46	19 21	18 12	19 21	20 28	21 39
N 40	18 16	18 43	19 14	18 09	19 13	20 18	21 25
35	18 14	18 40	19 10	18 06	19 07	20 09	21 13
30	18 13	18 37	19 05	18 03	19 02	20 01	21 03
20	18 12	18 34	19 00	17 59	18 53	19 48	20 46
N 10	18 10	18 32	18 56	17 55	18 45	19 37	20 31
0	18 08	18 30	18 54	17 52	18 38	19 26	20 17
S 10	18 07	18 30	18 54	17 48	18 30	19 15	20 03
20	18 05	18 30	18 55	17 44	18 22	19 04	19 48
30	18 03	18 31	19 00	17 40	18 14	18 50	19 31
35	18 02	18 33	19 04	17 38	18 09	18 43	19 21
40	18 01	18 34	19 09	17 35	18 03	18 34	19 10
45	18 00	18 37	19 15	17 32	17 56	18 23	18 57
S 50	17 59	18 41	19 25	17 28	17 49	18 12	18 41
52	17 58	18 42	19 27	17 26	17 45	18 06	18 33
54	17 58	18 44	19 31	17 24	17 41	18 00	18 25
56	17 57	18 45	19 35	17 22	17 36	17 53	18 15
58	17 56	18 47	19 39	17 20	17 31	17 46	18 05
S 60	17 56	18 49	19 44	17 17	17 26	17 37	17 53

SUN and MOON — Phenomena

Day	SUN Eqn. of Time 00h	12h	Mer. Pass.	MOON Mer. Pass. Upper	Lower	Age	Phase
23	06 52	06 43	12 07	11 41	24 07	29	
24	06 34	06 25	12 06	12 26	00 00	01	
25	06 16	06 07	12 06	13 14	00 50	02	

1974 JUNE 24, 25, 26 (MON., TUES., WED.)

G.M.T.	ARIES G.H.A.	VENUS −3.4 G.H.A.	Dec.	MARS +2.0 G.H.A.	Dec.	JUPITER −2.1 G.H.A.	Dec.	SATURN +0.2 G.H.A.	Dec.	STARS Name	S.H.A.	Dec.
24 00	271 46.0	215 57.0 N17	51.7	139 48.2 N19	11.9	282 44.7 S 5	59.2	173 39.5 N22	38.3	Acamar	315 40.7	S 40 24.2
01	286 48.5	230 56.4	52.5	154 49.0	11.4	297 47.1	59.1	188 41.6	38.3	Achernar	335 48.6	S 57 21.6
02	301 51.0	245 55.9	53.2	169 49.9	11.0	312 49.5	59.1	203 43.7	38.3	Acrux	173 42.0	S 62 57.9
03	316 53.4	260 55.4 ··	53.9	184 50.8 ··	10.6	327 51.8 ··	59.1	218 45.8 ··	38.2	Adhara	255 35.8	S 28 56.3
04	331 55.9	275 54.8	54.6	199 51.7	10.2	342 54.2	59.0	233 47.9	38.2	Aldebaran	291 23.2	N 16 27.5
05	346 58.4	290 54.3	55.3	214 52.6	09.7	357 56.5	59.0	248 50.0	38.2			
06	2 00.8	305 53.8 N17	56.1	229 53.5 N19	09.3	12 58.9 S 5	59.0	263 52.1 N22	38.2	Alioth	166 46.1	N 56 06.1
07	17 03.3	320 53.2	56.8	244 54.4	08.9	28 01.3	59.0	278 54.2	38.2	Alkaid	153 21.6	N 49 26.6
08	32 05.7	335 52.7	57.5	259 55.3	08.5	43 03.6	58.9	293 56.4	38.2	Al Na'ir	28 20.0	S 47 04.8
M 09	47 08.2	350 52.1 ··	58.2	274 56.2 ··	08.1	58 06.0 ··	58.9	308 58.5 ··	38.1	Alnilam	276 16.3	S 1 13.0
O 10	62 10.7	5 51.6	58.9	289 57.1	07.6	73 08.3	58.9	324 00.6	38.1	Alphard	218 25.0	S 8 33.0
N 11	77 13.1	20 51.1 17	59.6	304 58.0	07.2	88 10.7	58.8	339 02.7	38.1			
D 12	92 15.6	35 50.5 N18	00.4	319 58.9 N19	06.8	103 13.1 S 5	58.8	354 04.8 N22	38.1	Alphecca	126 35.4	N 26 48.1
A 13	107 18.1	50 50.0	01.1	334 59.8	06.4	118 15.4	58.8	9 06.9	38.1	Alpheratz	358 13.7	N 28 56.9
Y 14	122 20.5	65 49.4	01.8	350 00.7	05.9	133 17.8	58.7	24 09.0	38.1	Altair	62 36.4	N 8 48.1
15	137 23.0	80 48.9 ··	02.5	5 01.6 ··	05.5	148 20.1 ··	58.7	39 11.1 ··	38.1	Ankaa	353 44.4	S 42 26.3
16	152 25.5	95 48.3	03.2	20 02.5	05.1	163 22.5	58.7	54 13.3	38.0	Antares	113 01.8	S 26 22.7
17	167 27.9	110 47.8	03.9	35 03.4	04.7	178 24.9	58.7	69 15.4	38.0			
18	182 30.4	125 47.3 N18	04.6	50 04.3 N19	04.2	193 27.2 S 5	58.6	84 17.5 N22	38.0	Arcturus	146 22.1	N 19 18.9
19	197 32.9	140 46.7	05.3	65 05.2	03.8	208 29.6	58.6	99 19.6	38.0	Atria	108 29.3	S 68 59.1
20	212 35.3	155 46.2	06.0	80 06.1	03.4	223 32.0	58.6	114 21.7	38.0	Avior	234 30.5	S 59 25.9
21	227 37.8	170 45.6 ··	06.8	95 07.0 ··	03.0	238 34.3 ··	58.5	129 23.8 ··	38.0	Bellatrix	279 03.7	N 6 19.6
22	242 40.2	185 45.1	07.5	110 07.9	02.5	253 36.7	58.5	144 25.9	38.0	Betelgeuse	271 33.2	N 7 24.2
23	257 42.7	200 44.5	08.2	125 08.8	02.1	268 39.1	58.5	159 28.0	37.9			
25 00	272 45.2	215 44.0 N18	08.9	140 09.7 N19	01.7	283 41.4 S 5	58.5	174 30.2 N22	37.9	Canopus	264 09.7	S 52 40.9
01	287 47.6	230 43.4	09.6	155 10.6	01.3	298 43.8	58.4	189 32.3	37.9	Capella	281 18.1	N 45 58.4
02	302 50.1	245 42.9	10.3	170 11.5	00.8	313 46.2	58.4	204 34.4	37.9	Deneb	49 51.0	N 45 11.3
03	317 52.6	260 42.3 ··	11.0	185 12.4 ··	00.4	328 48.5 ··	58.4	219 36.5 ··	37.9	Denebola	183 03.4	N 14 42.9
04	332 55.0	275 41.8	11.7	200 13.3 19	00.0	343 50.9	58.3	234 38.6	37.9	Diphda	349 25.2	S 18 07.4
05	347 57.5	290 41.2	12.4	215 14.2 18	59.6	358 53.3	58.3	249 40.7	37.9			
06	3 00.0	305 40.7 N18	13.1	230 15.1 N18	59.1	13 55.6 S 5	58.3	264 42.8 N22	37.8	Dubhe	194 27.5	N 61 53.5
07	18 02.4	320 40.1	13.8	245 16.0	58.7	28 58.0	58.3	279 44.9	37.8	Elnath	278 49.9	N 28 35.2
T 08	33 04.9	335 39.6	14.5	260 16.9	58.3	44 00.4	58.2	294 47.1	37.8	Eltanin	90 59.2	N 51 29.5
U 09	48 07.4	350 39.0 ··	15.2	275 17.8 ··	57.8	59 02.7 ··	58.2	309 49.2 ··	37.8	Enif	34 15.6	N 9 45.5
E 10	63 09.8	5 38.5	15.9	290 18.7	57.4	74 05.1	58.2	324 51.3	37.8	Fomalhaut	15 56.0	S 29 45.2
S 11	78 12.3	20 37.9	16.6	305 19.7	57.0	89 07.5	58.2	339 53.4	37.8			
D 12	93 14.7	35 37.4 N18	17.3	320 20.6 N18	56.6	104 09.8 S 5	58.1	354 55.5 N22	37.7	Gacrux	172 33.5	S 56 58.6
A 13	108 17.2	50 36.8	18.0	335 21.5	56.1	119 12.2	58.1	9 57.6	37.7	Gienah	176 22.4	S 17 24.2
Y 14	123 19.7	65 36.3	18.7	350 22.4	55.7	134 14.6	58.1	24 59.7	37.7	Hadar	149 29.1	S 60 15.4
15	138 22.1	80 35.7 ··	19.4	5 23.3 ··	55.3	149 16.9 ··	58.1	40 01.8 ··	37.7	Hamal	328 33.9	N 23 20.5
16	153 24.6	95 35.2	20.1	20 24.2	54.8	164 19.3	58.0	55 04.0	37.7	Kaus Aust.	84 22.1	S 34 23.8
17	168 27.1	110 34.6	20.8	35 25.1	54.4	179 21.7	58.0	70 06.1	37.7			
18	183 29.5	125 34.0 N18	21.5	50 26.0 N18	54.0	194 24.1 S 5	58.0	85 08.2 N22	37.6	Kochab	137 17.9	N 74 15.8
19	198 32.0	140 33.5	22.1	65 26.9	53.5	209 26.4	57.9	100 10.3	37.6	Markab	14 07.3	N 15 04.1
20	213 34.5	155 32.9	22.8	80 27.8	53.1	224 28.8	57.9	115 12.4	37.6	Menkar	314 45.8	N 3 59.5
21	228 36.9	170 32.4 ··	23.5	95 28.7 ··	52.7	239 31.2 ··	57.9	130 14.5 ··	37.6	Menkent	148 41.9	S 36 15.0
22	243 39.4	185 31.8	24.2	110 29.6	52.3	254 33.5	57.9	145 16.6	37.6	Miaplacidus	221 46.6	S 69 37.0
23	258 41.8	200 31.3	24.9	125 30.5	51.8	269 35.9	57.8	160 18.7	37.6			
26 00	273 44.3	215 30.7 N18	25.6	140 31.4 N18	51.4	284 38.3 S 5	57.8	175 20.9 N22	37.6	Mirfak	309 22.6	N 49 46.2
01	288 46.8	230 30.1	26.3	155 32.3	51.0	299 40.7	57.8	190 23.0	37.6	Nunki	76 34.1	S 26 19.7
02	303 49.2	245 29.6	27.0	170 33.2	50.5	314 43.0	57.8	205 25.1	37.5	Peacock	54 04.5	S 56 48.8
03	318 51.7	260 29.0 ··	27.7	185 34.1 ··	50.1	329 45.4 ··	57.7	220 27.2 ··	37.5	Pollux	244 03.7	N 28 05.3
04	333 54.2	275 28.5	28.3	200 35.0	49.7	344 47.8	57.7	235 29.3	37.5	Procyon	245 30.6	N 5 17.4
05	348 56.6	290 27.9	29.0	215 35.9	49.2	359 50.2	57.7	250 31.4	37.5			
06	3 59.1	305 27.3 N18	29.7	230 36.8 N18	48.8	14 52.5 S 5	57.7	265 33.5 N22	37.5	Rasalhague	96 33.2	N 12 34.7
W 07	19 01.6	320 26.8	30.4	245 37.7	48.4	29 54.9	57.7	280 35.6	37.5	Regulus	208 14.7	N 12 05.5
E 08	34 04.0	335 26.2	31.1	260 38.6	47.9	44 57.3	57.6	295 37.8	37.4	Rigel	281 40.4	S 8 13.8
D 09	49 06.5	350 25.6 ··	31.8	275 39.5 ··	47.5	59 59.7 ··	57.6	310 39.9 ··	37.4	Rigil Kent.	140 31.2	S 60 44.1
N 10	64 09.0	5 25.1	32.4	290 40.4	47.1	75 02.0	57.6	325 42.0	37.4	Sabik	102 45.7	S 15 41.7
E 11	79 11.4	20 24.5	33.1	305 41.3	46.6	90 04.4	57.6	340 44.1	37.4			
S 12	94 13.9	35 24.0 N18	33.8	320 42.2 N18	46.2	105 06.8 S 5	57.5	355 46.2 N22	37.4	Schedar	350 14.0	N 56 23.7
D 13	109 16.3	50 23.4	34.5	335 43.1	45.8	120 09.2	57.5	10 48.3	37.4	Shaula	97 01.1	S 37 05.2
A 14	124 18.8	65 22.8	35.2	350 44.0	45.3	135 11.5	57.5	25 50.4	37.4	Sirius	258 59.8	S 16 40.9
Y 15	139 21.3	80 22.3 ··	35.8	5 44.9 ··	44.9	150 13.9 ··	57.5	40 52.5 ··	37.3	Spica	159 01.9	S 11 01.9
16	154 23.7	95 21.7	36.5	20 45.8	44.5	165 16.3	57.4	55 54.7	37.3	Suhail	223 14.3	S 43 20.0
17	169 26.2	110 21.1	37.2	35 46.7	44.0	180 18.7	57.4	70 56.8	37.3			
18	184 28.7	125 20.6 N18	37.9	50 47.7 N18	43.6	195 21.1 S 5	57.4	85 58.9 N22	37.3	Vega	80 58.3	N 38 45.6
19	199 31.1	140 20.0	38.5	65 48.6	43.2	210 23.4	57.4	101 01.0	37.3	Zuben'ubi	137 37.5	S 15 56.3
20	214 33.6	155 19.4	39.2	80 49.5	42.7	225 25.8	57.4	116 03.1	37.3		S.H.A.	Mer. Pass.
21	229 36.1	170 18.9 ··	39.9	95 50.4 ··	42.3	240 28.2 ··	57.3	131 05.2 ··	37.2		° '	h m
22	244 38.5	185 18.3	40.5	110 51.3	41.9	255 30.6	57.3	146 07.3	37.2	Venus	302 58.8	9 37
23	259 41.0	200 17.7	41.2	125 52.2	41.4	270 32.9	57.3	161 09.4	37.2	Mars	227 24.6	14 38
Mer. Pass.	5 48.0	v −0.6	d 0.7	v 0.9	d 0.4	v 2.4	d 0.0	v 2.1	d 0.0	Jupiter	10 56.3	5 04
										Saturn	261 45.0	12 20

1974 JUNE 24, 25, 26 (MON., TUES., WED.)

G.M.T.	SUN G.H.A.	Dec.	MOON G.H.A.	v	Dec.	d	H.P.	Lat.	Twilight Naut.	Civil	Sun-rise	Moonrise 24	25	26	27
d h	° '	° '	° '	'	° '	'	'	°	h m	h m	h m	h m	h m	h m	h m
								N 72	□	□	□	08 31	10 40	12 45	14 52
24 00	179 27·2	N23 25·5	126 05·2	9·2	N 8 38·8	13·3	60·1	N 70	□	□	□	08 41	10 41	12 37	14 33
01	194 27·0	25·5	140 33·4	9·2	8 25·5	13·4	60·1	68	□	□	□	08 49	10 41	12 31	14 19
02	209 26·9	25·4	155 01·6	9·2	8 12·1	13·4	60·1	66	□	□		08 55	10 42	12 25	14 07
03	224 26·8 ··	25·4	169 29·8	9·4	7 58·7	13·5	60·1	64	////	////	01 32	09 01	10 43	12 21	13 57
04	239 26·6	25·3	183 58·2	9·4	7 45·2	13·5	60·0	62	////	////	02 10	09 06	10 43	12 17	13 49
05	254 26·5	25·3	198 26·6	9·5	7 31·7	13·5	60·0	60	////	00 51	02 37	09 10	10 43	12 14	13 42
06	269 26·4	N23 25·3	212 55·1	9·5	N 7 18·2	13·5	60·0	N 58	////	01 42	02 57	09 14	10 44	12 11	13 36
07	284 26·2	25·2	227 23·6	9·6	7 04·7	13·6	60·0	56	////	02 12	03 14	09 17	10 44	12 08	13 30
08	299 26·1	25·2	241 52·2	9·7	6 51·1	13·6	59·9	54	00 47	02 34	03 28	09 20	10 44	12 06	13 26
M 09	314 26·0 ··	25·1	256 20·9	9·7	6 37·5	13·7	59·9	52	01 34	02 52	03 41	09 23	10 44	12 04	13 21
O 10	329 25·8	25·1	270 49·6	9·8	6 23·8	13·6	59·9	50	02 01	03 07	03 51	09 25	10 45	12 02	13 17
N 11	344 25·7	25·0	285 18·4	9·8	6 10·2	13·7	59·9	45	02 47	03 37	04 14	09 30	10 45	11 58	13 09
D 12	359 25·6	N23 25·0	299 47·2	9·9	N 5 56·5	13·7	59·8	N 40	03 18	03 59	04 32	09 35	10 46	11 54	13 01
A 13	14 25·4	24·9	314 16·1	10·0	5 42·8	13·7	59·8	35	03 41	04 17	04 47	09 38	10 46	11 51	12 55
Y 14	29 25·3	24·9	328 45·1	10·0	5 29·1	13·8	59·8	30	03 59	04 33	05 00	09 42	10 46	11 49	12 50
15	44 25·2 ··	24·8	343 14·1	10·1	5 15·3	13·7	59·7	20	04 28	04 58	05 22	09 48	10 47	11 44	12 41
16	59 25·0	24·8	357 43·2	10·2	5 01·6	13·8	59·7	N 10	04 51	05 18	05 41	09 53	10 47	11 40	12 33
17	74 24·9	24·7	12 12·4	10·1	4 47·8	13·8	59·7	0	05 10	05 36	05 59	09 57	10 48	11 37	12 25
18	89 24·8	N23 24·7	26 41·5	10·3	N 4 34·0	13·8	59·7	S 10	05 27	05 53	06 16	10 02	10 48	11 33	12 18
19	104 24·6	24·6	41 10·8	10·3	4 20·2	13·8	59·6	20	05 43	06 11	06 35	10 07	10 49	11 30	12 10
20	119 24·5	24·6	55 40·1	10·3	4 06·4	13·8	59·6	30	06 00	06 30	06 56	10 13	10 50	11 25	12 01
21	134 24·4 ··	24·5	70 09·4	10·5	3 52·6	13·8	59·6	35	06 08	06 40	07 08	10 16	10 50	11 23	11 56
22	149 24·2	24·5	84 38·9	10·4	3 38·8	13·9	59·6	40	06 18	06 52	07 22	10 20	10 50	11 20	11 50
23	164 24·1	24·4	99 08·3	10·5	3 25·0	13·9	59·5	45	06 28	07 05	07 39	10 24	10 51	11 17	11 44
25 00	179 24·0	N23 24·4	113 37·8	10·6	N 3 11·1	13·8	59·5	S 50	06 40	07 21	08 00	10 29	10 52	11 13	11 36
01	194 23·8	24·3	128 07·4	10·6	2 57·3	13·8	59·5	52	06 45	07 29	08 10	10 31	10 52	11 12	11 32
02	209 23·7	24·3	142 37·0	10·6	2 43·5	13·9	59·4	54	06 51	07 37	08 21	10 34	10 52	11 10	11 28
03	224 23·5 ··	24·2	157 06·6	10·7	2 29·6	13·9	59·4	56	06 57	07 46	08 34	10 37	10 53	11 08	11 24
04	239 23·4	24·1	171 36·3	10·7	2 15·8	13·9	59·4	58	07 04	07 57	08 48	10 40	10 53	11 06	11 19
05	254 23·3	24·1	186 06·0	10·8	2 02·0	13·9	59·3	S 60	07 11	08 08	09 06	10 43	10 53	11 03	11 13

G.M.T.	SUN G.H.A.	Dec.	MOON G.H.A.	v	Dec.	d	H.P.	Lat.	Sun-set	Twilight Civil	Naut.	Moonset 24	25	26	27
06	269 23·1	N23 24·0	200 35·8	10·8	N 1 48·1	13·8	59·3	N 72	□	□	□	23 04	22 44	22 24	21 59
07	284 23·0	24·0	215 05·6	10·9	1 34·3	13·8	59·3	N 70	□	□	□	22 59	22 47	22 34	22 19
T 08	299 22·9	23·9	229 35·5	10·9	1 20·5	13·9	59·3	68	□	□	□	22 56	22 49	22 43	22 35
U 09	314 22·7 ··	23·8	244 05·4	11·0	1 06·7	13·8	59·2	66	□	□	////	22 53	22 51	22 50	22 49
E 10	329 22·6	23·8	258 35·4	10·9	0 52·9	13·9	59·2	64	22 32	////	////	22 50	22 53	22 56	23 00
S 11	344 22·5	23·7	273 05·3	11·1	0 39·1	13·9	59·2	62	21 54	////	////	22 48	22 54	23 01	23 09
D 12	359 22·3	N23 23·6	287 35·4	11·0	N 0 25·3	13·8	59·1	60	21 28	23 13	////	22 46	22 56	23 06	23 17
A 13	14 22·2	23·6	302 05·4	11·1	N 0 11·5	13·7	59·1	N 58	21 07	22 23	////	22 45	22 57	23 10	23 24
Y 14	29 22·1	23·5	316 35·5	11·1	S 0 02·2	13·9	59·1	56	20 51	21 53	////	22 43	22 58	23 14	23 31
15	44 21·9 ··	23·5	331 05·6	11·2	0 16·0	13·8	59·0	54	20 36	21 31	23 17	22 41	22 59	23 17	23 37
16	59 21·8	23·4	345 35·8	11·2	0 29·7	13·7	59·0	52	20 24	21 13	22 31	22 40	23 00	23 20	23 41
17	74 21·7	23·3	0 06·0	11·2	0 43·4	13·7	59·0	50	20 13	20 58	22 03	22 38	23 01	23 23	23 46
18	89 21·5	N23 23·3	14 36·2	11·3	S 0 57·1	13·7	59·0	45	19 51	20 28	21 18	22 36	23 02	23 29	23 56
19	104 21·4	23·2	29 06·5	11·2	1 10·8	13·8	58·9	N 40	19 33	20 06	20 47	22 34	23 03	23 34	24 05
20	119 21·3	23·2	43 36·7	11·3	1 24·4	13·7	58·9	35	19 18	19 47	20 24	22 32	23 05	23 38	24 12
21	134 21·2 ··	23·0	58 07·0	11·4	1 38·1	13·6	58·9	30	19 05	19 32	20 05	22 30	23 06	23 42	24 18
22	149 21·0	23·0	72 37·4	11·4	1 51·7	13·5	58·9	20	18 43	19 07	19 37	22 27	23 08	23 49	24 29
23	164 20·9	22·9	87 07·8	11·3	2 05·2	13·6	58·8	N 10	18 24	18 47	19 14	22 24	23 10	23 54	24 39
26 00	179 20·8	N23 22·8	101 38·1	11·5	S 2 18·8	13·5	58·8	0	18 06	18 29	18 55	22 22	23 11	24 00	00 00
01	194 20·6	22·7	116 08·6	11·4	2 32·3	13·5	58·7	S 10	17 49	18 11	18 38	22 19	23 13	24 05	00 05
02	209 20·5	22·7	130 39·0	11·5	2 45·8	13·5	58·7	20	17 30	17 54	18 22	22 16	23 14	24 11	00 11
03	224 20·4 ··	22·6	145 09·5	11·4	2 59·3	13·4	58·7	30	17 09	17 35	18 05	22 13	23 16	24 18	00 18
04	239 20·2	22·5	159 39·9	11·5	3 12·7	13·4	58·6	35	16 57	17 25	17 57	22 11	23 17	24 22	00 22
05	254 20·1	22·5	174 10·4	11·6	3 26·1	13·4	58·6	40	16 42	17 13	17 47	22 09	23 19	24 27	00 27
06	269 20·0	N23 22·3	188 41·0	11·5	S 3 39·5	13·4	58·6	45	16 26	16 59	17 37	22 06	23 20	24 32	00 32
W 07	284 19·8	22·3	203 11·5	11·6	3 52·9	13·3	58·6	S 50	16 05	16 41	17 25	22 03	23 22	24 38	00 38
E 08	299 19·7	22·2	217 42·1	11·5	4 06·2	13·2	58·5	52	15 55	16 36	17 20	22 02	23 23	24 41	00 41
D 09	314 19·6 ··	22·1	232 12·6	11·6	4 19·4	13·2	58·5	54	15 44	16 28	17 14	22 00	23 23	24 44	00 44
N 10	329 19·4	22·1	246 43·2	11·6	4 32·7	13·1	58·5	56	15 31	16 19	17 08	21 59	23 24	24 47	00 47
E 11	344 19·3	22·0	261 13·8	11·7	4 45·9	13·1	58·4	58	15 17	16 09	17 01	21 57	23 25	24 51	00 51
S 12	359 19·2	N23 21·9	275 44·5	11·6	S 4 59·0	13·2	58·4	S 60	14 59	15 57	16 53	21 54	23 26	24 56	00 56
D 13	14 19·0	21·8	290 15·1	11·6	5 12·2	13·0	58·3								
A 14	29 18·9	21·7	304 45·7	11·7	5 25·2	13·1	58·3								
Y 15	44 18·8 ··	21·7	319 16·4	11·7	5 38·3	13·0	58·3								
16	59 18·6	21·6	333 47·1	11·6	5 51·3	12·9	58·3								
17	74 18·5	21·5	348 17·7	11·7	6 04·2	12·9	58·2								

G.M.T.	SUN G.H.A.	Dec.	MOON G.H.A.	v	Dec.	d	H.P.	Day	SUN Eqn. of Time 00h	12h	Mer. Pass.	MOON Mer. Pass. Upper	Lower	Age	Phase
18	89 18·4	N23 21·3	2 48·4	11·7	S 6 17·1	12·9	58·2		m s	m s	h m	h m	h m		
19	104 18·2	21·3	17 19·1	11·7	6 30·0	12·8	58·2	24	02 11	02 17	12 02	16 09	03 44	04	
20	119 18·1 ··	21·2	31 49·8	11·7	6 42·8	12·8	58·1	25	02 24	02 30	12 03	17 00	04 35	05	
21	134 18·0 ··	21·1	46 20·5	11·7	6 55·6	12·7	58·1	26	02 37	02 43	12 03	17 48	05 24	06	
22	149 17·9	21·1	60 51·2	11·8	7 08·3	12·7	58·1								
23	164 17·7	21·0	75 22·0	11·7	7 21·0	12·6	58·1								
S.D.	15·8	d 0·1	S.D. 16·3		16·1		15·9								

G.M.T. d h	ARIES G.H.A.	VENUS −3.3 G.H.A.	Dec.	MARS +2.0 G.H.A.	Dec.	JUPITER −2.4 G.H.A.	Dec.	SATURN +0.3 G.H.A.	Dec.	STARS Name	S.H.A.	Dec.
30 00	307 15.0	205 45.1	N22 37.7	153 19.5	N11 57.1	318 37.4	S 6 20.6	204 09.5	N22 20.8	Acamar	315 40.4	S 40 24.0
01	322 17.5	220 44.3	37.5	168 20.5	56.5	333 40.0	20.7	219 11.7	20.7	Achernar	335 48.2	S 57 21.5
02	337 20.0	235 43.5	37.4	183 21.5	55.9	348 42.6	20.8	234 13.8	20.7	Acrux	173 42.3	S 62 57.8
03	352 22.4	250 42.7	.. 37.3	198 22.4	.. 55.3	3 45.3	.. 20.8	249 15.9	.. 20.7	Adhara	255 35.7	S 28 56.1
04	7 24.9	265 41.9	37.1	213 23.4	54.8	18 47.9	20.9	264 18.1	20.7	Aldebaran	291 23.0	N 16 27.6
05	22 27.4	280 41.1	37.0	228 24.4	54.2	33 50.5	21.0	279 20.2	20.6			
06	37 29.8	295 40.3	N22 36.9	243 25.4	N11 53.6	48 53.1	S 6 21.1	294 22.3	N22 20.6	Alioth	166 46.3	N 56 06.0
07	52 32.3	310 39.5	36.8	258 26.3	53.0	63 55.8	21.2	309 24.5	20.6	Alkaid	153 21.8	N 49 26.6
T 08	67 34.8	325 38.7	36.6	273 27.3	52.5	78 58.4	21.2	324 26.6	20.6	Al Na'ir	28 19.7	S 47 04.8
U 09	82 37.2	340 37.9	.. 36.5	288 28.3	.. 51.9	94 01.0	.. 21.3	339 28.7	.. 20.5	Alnilam	276 16.1	S 1 13.0
E 10	97 39.7	355 37.1	36.4	303 29.3	51.3	109 03.6	21.4	354 30.9	20.5	Alphard	218 25.0	S 8 32.9
S 11	112 42.1	10 36.2	36.2	318 30.2	50.7	124 06.3	21.5	9 33.0	20.5			
D 12	127 44.6	25 35.4	N22 36.1	333 31.2	N11 50.2	139 08.9	S 6 21.6	24 35.1	N22 20.5	Alphecca	126 35.5	N 26 48.1
A 13	142 47.1	40 34.6	36.0	348 32.2	49.6	154 11.5	21.6	39 37.3	20.4	Alpheratz	358 13.5	N 28 57.1
Y 14	157 49.5	55 33.8	35.8	3 33.2	49.0	169 14.1	21.7	54 39.4	20.4	Altair	62 36.3	N 8 48.2
15	172 52.0	70 33.0	.. 35.7	18 34.1	.. 48.4	184 16.8	.. 21.8	69 41.5	.. 20.4	Ankaa	353 44.1	S 42 26.3
16	187 54.5	85 32.2	35.5	33 35.1	47.9	199 19.4	21.9	84 43.7	20.4	Antares	113 01.8	S 26 22.7
17	202 56.9	100 31.4	35.4	48 36.1	47.3	214 22.0	22.0	99 45.8	20.3			
18	217 59.4	115 30.6	N22 35.2	63 37.1	N11 46.7	229 24.6	S 6 22.0	114 48.0	N22 20.3	Arcturus	146 22.3	N 19 19.0
19	233 01.9	130 29.8	35.1	78 38.0	46.1	244 27.3	22.1	129 50.1	20.3	Atria	108 29.5	S 68 59.2
20	248 04.3	145 29.0	35.0	93 39.0	45.6	259 29.9	22.2	144 52.2	20.3	Avior	234 30.6	S 59 25.7
21	263 06.8	160 28.2	.. 34.8	108 40.0	.. 45.0	274 32.5	.. 22.3	159 54.4	.. 20.2	Bellatrix	279 03.5	N 6 19.7
22	278 09.3	175 27.4	34.7	123 41.0	44.4	289 35.2	22.4	174 56.5	20.2	Betelgeuse	271 33.1	N 7 24.2
23	293 11.7	190 26.6	34.5	138 41.9	43.8	304 37.8	22.4	189 58.6	20.2			
31 00	308 14.2	205 25.8	N22 34.4	153 42.9	N11 43.3	319 40.4	S 6 22.5	205 00.8	N22 20.2	Canopus	264 09.5	S 52 40.7
01	323 16.6	220 25.0	34.2	168 43.9	42.7	334 43.0	22.6	220 02.9	20.1	Capella	281 17.8	N 45 58.3
02	338 19.1	235 24.2	34.1	183 44.9	42.1	349 45.7	22.7	235 05.0	20.1	Deneb	49 50.9	N 45 11.5
03	353 21.6	250 23.4	.. 33.9	198 45.9	.. 41.5	4 48.3	.. 22.8	250 07.2	.. 20.1	Denebola	183 03.5	N 14 42.9
04	8 24.0	265 22.6	33.7	213 46.8	40.9	19 50.9	22.9	265 09.3	20.1	Diphda	349 24.9	S 18 07.3
05	23 26.5	280 21.8	33.6	228 47.8	40.4	34 53.6	22.9	280 11.4	20.0			
06	38 29.0	295 21.0	N22 33.4	243 48.8	N11 39.8	49 56.2	S 6 23.0	295 13.6	N22 20.0	Dubhe	194 27.7	N 61 53.4
W 07	53 31.4	310 20.2	33.3	258 49.8	39.2	64 58.8	23.1	310 15.7	20.0	Elnath	278 49.7	N 28 35.2
E 08	68 33.9	325 19.4	33.1	273 50.7	38.6	80 01.5	23.2	325 17.8	20.0	Eltanin	90 59.2	N 51 29.7
D 09	83 36.4	340 18.6	.. 33.0	288 51.7	.. 38.1	95 04.1	.. 23.3	340 20.0	.. 19.9	Enif	34 15.4	N 9 45.7
N 10	98 38.8	355 17.8	32.8	303 52.7	37.5	110 06.7	23.3	355 22.1	19.9	Fomalhaut	15 55.7	S 29 45.1
E 11	113 41.3	10 17.0	32.6	318 53.7	36.9	125 09.3	23.4	10 24.3	19.9			
S 12	128 43.8	25 16.2	N22 32.5	333 54.6	N11 36.3	140 12.0	S 6 23.5	25 26.4	N22 19.9	Gacrux	172 33.7	S 56 58.6
D 13	143 46.2	40 15.4	32.3	348 55.6	35.7	155 14.6	23.6	40 28.5	19.8	Gienah	176 22.5	S 17 24.2
A 14	158 48.7	55 14.6	32.1	3 56.6	35.2	170 17.2	23.7	55 30.7	19.8	Hadar	149 29.4	S 60 15.4
Y 15	173 51.1	70 13.8	.. 32.0	18 57.6	.. 34.6	185 19.9	.. 23.8	70 32.8	.. 19.8	Hamal	328 33.6	N 23 20.6
16	188 53.6	85 12.9	31.8	33 58.5	34.0	200 22.5	23.8	85 34.9	19.8	Kaus Aust.	84 22.0	S 34 23.9
17	203 56.1	100 12.1	31.6	48 59.5	33.4	215 25.1	23.9	100 37.1	19.7			
18	218 58.5	115 11.3	N22 31.5	64 00.5	N11 32.9	230 27.8	S 6 24.0	115 39.2	N22 19.7	Kochab	137 18.5	N 74 15.8
19	234 01.0	130 10.5	31.3	79 01.5	32.3	245 30.4	24.1	130 41.3	19.7	Markab	14 07.1	N 15 04.2
20	249 03.5	145 09.7	31.1	94 02.5	31.7	260 33.0	24.2	145 43.5	19.7	Menkar	314 45.6	N 3 59.6
21	264 05.9	160 08.9	.. 30.9	109 03.4	.. 31.1	275 35.7	.. 24.3	160 45.6	.. 19.6	Menkent	148 42.0	S 36 14.9
22	279 08.4	175 08.1	30.8	124 04.4	30.5	290 38.3	24.3	175 47.8	19.6	Miaplacidus	221 46.8	S 69 36.9
23	294 10.9	190 07.3	30.6	139 05.4	30.0	305 40.9	24.4	190 49.9	19.6			
1 00	309 13.3	205 06.5	N22 30.4	154 06.4	N11 29.4	320 43.6	S 6 24.5	205 52.0	N22 19.5	Mirfak	309 22.2	N 49 46.2
01	324 15.8	220 05.7	30.2	169 07.3	28.8	335 46.2	24.6	220 54.2	19.5	Nunki	76 34.0	S 26 19.7
02	339 18.3	235 04.9	30.1	184 08.3	28.2	350 48.9	24.7	235 56.3	19.5	Peacock	54 04.3	S 56 48.9
03	354 20.7	250 04.1	.. 29.9	199 09.3	.. 27.6	5 51.5	.. 24.8	250 58.4	.. 19.5	Pollux	244 03.6	N 28 05.3
04	9 23.2	265 03.3	29.7	214 10.3	27.1	20 54.1	24.8	266 00.6	19.4	Procyon	245 30.5	N 5 17.5
05	24 25.6	280 02.5	29.5	229 11.3	26.5	35 56.8	24.9	281 02.7	19.4			
06	39 28.1	295 01.7	N22 29.3	244 12.2	N11 25.9	50 59.4	S 6 25.0	296 04.9	N22 19.4	Rasalhague	96 33.2	N 12 34.8
T 07	54 30.6	310 00.9	29.1	259 13.2	25.3	66 02.0	25.1	311 07.0	19.4	Regulus	208 14.7	N 12 05.5
H 08	69 33.0	325 00.1	29.0	274 14.2	24.7	81 04.7	25.2	326 09.1	19.3	Rigel	281 40.2	S 8 13.7
U 09	84 35.5	339 59.3	.. 28.8	289 15.2	.. 24.2	96 07.3	.. 25.3	341 11.3	.. 19.3	Rigil Kent.	140 31.5	S 60 44.1
R 10	99 38.0	354 58.5	28.6	304 16.1	23.6	111 10.0	25.4	356 13.4	19.3	Sabik	102 45.7	S 15 41.7
11	114 40.4	9 57.7	28.4	319 17.1	23.0	126 12.6	25.4	11 15.5	19.3			
S 12	129 42.9	24 56.9	N22 28.2	334 18.1	N11 22.4	141 15.2	S 6 25.5	26 17.7	N22 19.2	Schedar	350 13.6	N 56 23.8
D 13	144 45.4	39 56.1	28.0	349 19.1	21.8	156 17.9	25.6	41 19.8	19.2	Shaula	96 01.1	S 37 05.7
A 14	159 47.8	54 55.3	27.8	4 20.1	21.2	171 20.5	25.7	56 22.0	19.2	Sirius	258 59.7	S 16 40.8
Y 15	174 50.3	69 54.5	.. 27.6	19 21.0	.. 20.7	186 23.2	.. 25.8	71 24.1	.. 19.2	Spica	159 02.0	S 11 01.8
16	189 52.8	84 53.7	27.4	34 22.0	20.1	201 25.8	25.9	86 26.2	19.1	Suhail	223 14.3	S 43 19.4
17	204 55.2	99 52.9	27.2	49 23.0	19.5	216 28.4	26.0	101 28.4	19.1			
18	219 57.7	114 52.1	N22 27.0	64 24.0	N11 18.9	231 31.1	S 6 26.0	116 30.5	N22 19.1	Vega	80 58.3	N 38 45.8
19	235 00.1	129 51.3	26.8	79 25.0	18.3	246 33.7	26.1	131 32.6	19.1	Zuben'ubi	137 37.6	S 15 56.3
20	250 02.6	144 50.5	26.6	94 26.0	17.8	261 36.3	26.2	146 34.8	19.0		S.H.A.	Mer. Pass.
21	265 05.1	159 49.7	.. 26.4	109 26.9	.. 17.2	276 39.0	.. 26.3	161 36.9	.. 19.0	Venus	257 11.6	10 19
22	280 07.5	174 48.9	26.2	124 27.9	16.6	291 41.6	26.4	176 39.1	19.0	Mars	205 28.7	13 44
23	295 10.0	189 48.1	26.0	139 28.9	16.0	306 44.3	26.5	191 41.2	19.0	Jupiter	11 26.2	2 41
Mer. Pass. 3 26.5		v −0.8 d 0.2		v 1.0 d 0.6		v 2.6 d 0.1		v 2.1 d 0.0		Saturn	256 46.6	10 18

304

SUN and MOON — G.M.T.

G.M.T. d h	SUN G.H.A.	SUN Dec.	MOON G.H.A.	v	MOON Dec.	d	H.P.
30 00	178 23·7	N18 39·5	47 08·4	10·6	S22 55·2	0·7	54·7
01	193 23·7	38·9	61 38·0	10·6	22 54·5	0·8	54·7
02	208 23·8	38·3	76 07·6	10·6	22 53·7	0·9	54·7
03	223 23·8 · ·	37·7	90 37·2	10·7	22 52·8	1·1	54·7
04	238 23·8	37·1	105 06·9	10·7	22 51·7	1·1	54·7
05	253 23·8	36·5	119 36·6	10·7	22 50·6	1·3	54·7
06	268 23·8	N18 35·9	134 06·3	10·7	S22 49·3	1·3	54·6
07	283 23·9	35·3	148 36·0	10·8	22 48·0	1·5	54·6
08	298 23·9	34·7	163 05·8	10·8	22 46·5	1·6	54·6
09	313 23·9 · ·	34·1	177 35·6	10·8	22 44·9	1·7	54·6
10	328 23·9	33·5	192 05·4	10·9	22 43·2	1·8	54·6
11	343 24·0	32·9	206 35·3	10·9	22 41·4	1·9	54·6
12	358 24·0	N18 32·3	221 05·2	10·9	S22 39·5	2·1	54·5
13	13 24·0	31·7	235 35·1	10·9	22 37·4	2·1	54·5
14	28 24·0	31·1	250 05·0	11·0	22 35·3	2·3	54·5
15	43 24·1 · ·	30·5	264 35·0	11·0	22 33·0	2·3	54·5
16	58 24·1	29·9	279 05·0	11·0	22 30·7	2·5	54·5
17	73 24·1	29·3	293 35·0	11·1	22 28·2	2·5	54·5
18	88 24·1	N18 28·7	308 05·1	11·1	S22 25·7	2·7	54·5
19	103 24·2	28·1	322 35·2	11·2	22 23·0	2·8	54·5
20	118 24·2	27·4	337 05·4	11·1	22 20·2	2·9	54·4
21	133 24·2 · ·	26·8	351 35·5	11·2	22 17·3	3·0	54·4
22	148 24·3	26·2	6 05·7	11·3	22 14·3	3·0	54·4
23	163 24·3	25·6	20 36·0	11·3	22 11·3	3·2	54·4
31 00	178 24·3	N18 25·0	35 06·3	11·3	S22 08·1	3·3	54·4
01	193 24·3	24·4	49 36·6	11·4	22 04·8	3·4	54·4
02	208 24·4	23·8	64 07·0	11·3	22 01·4	3·6	54·4
03	223 24·4 · ·	23·2	78 37·3	11·5	21 57·8	3·6	54·4
04	238 24·4	22·6	93 07·8	11·4	21 54·2	3·7	54·3
05	253 24·5	22·0	107 38·2	11·6	21 50·5	3·8	54·3
06	268 24·5	N18 21·4	122 08·8	11·5	S21 46·7	3·9	54·3
07	283 24·5	20·7	136 39·3	11·6	21 42·8	4·0	54·3
08	298 24·5	20·1	151 09·9	11·6	21 38·8	4·1	54·3
09	313 24·6 · ·	19·5	165 40·5	11·7	21 34·7	4·2	54·3
10	328 24·6	18·9	180 11·2	11·7	21 30·5	4·3	54·3
11	343 24·6	18·3	194 41·9	11·8	21 26·2	4·4	54·3
12	358 24·7	N18 17·7	209 12·7	11·8	S21 21·8	4·5	54·3
13	13 24·7	17·1	223 43·5	11·8	21 17·3	4·6	54·3
14	28 24·7	16·4	238 14·3	11·9	21 12·7	4·7	54·2
15	43 24·8 · ·	15·8	252 45·2	11·9	21 08·0	4·8	54·2
16	58 24·8	15·2	267 16·1	11·9	21 03·2	4·9	54·2
17	73 24·8	14·6	281 47·0	12·1	20 58·3	5·0	54·2
18	88 24·9	N18 14·0	296 18·1	12·0	S20 53·3	5·1	54·2
19	103 24·9	13·4	310 49·1	12·1	20 48·2	5·2	54·2
20	118 24·9	12·7	325 20·2	12·1	20 43·0	5·2	54·2
21	133 25·0 · ·	12·1	339 51·3	12·2	20 37·8	5·4	54·2
22	148 25·0	11·5	354 22·5	12·2	20 32·4	5·4	54·2
23	163 25·0	10·9	8 53·7	12·3	20 27·0	5·6	54·2
1 00	178 25·1	N18 10·3	23 25·0	12·3	S20 21·4	5·6	54·2
01	193 25·1	09·6	37 56·3	12·4	20 15·8	5·7	54·1
02	208 25·1	09·0	52 27·7	12·4	20 10·1	5·8	54·1
03	223 25·2 · ·	08·4	66 59·1	12·4	20 04·3	5·9	54·1
04	238 25·2	07·8	81 30·5	12·5	19 58·4	6·0	54·1
05	253 25·2	07·1	96 02·0	12·6	19 52·4	6·1	54·1
06	268 25·3	N18 06·5	110 33·6	12·6	S19 46·3	6·1	54·1
07	283 25·3	05·9	125 05·2	12·6	19 40·2	6·3	54·1
08	298 25·3	05·3	139 36·8	12·7	19 33·9	6·3	54·1
09	313 25·4 · ·	04·6	154 08·5	12·7	19 27·6	6·4	54·1
10	328 25·4	04·0	168 40·2	12·8	19 21·2	6·5	54·1
11	343 25·5	03·4	183 12·0	12·8	19 14·7	6·6	54·1
12	358 25·5	N18 02·8	197 43·8	12·8	S19 08·1	6·7	54·1
13	13 25·5	02·1	212 15·6	12·9	19 01·4	6·7	54·1
14	28 25·6	01·5	226 47·5	13·0	18 54·7	6·9	54·1
15	43 25·6 · ·	00·9	241 19·5	13·0	18 47·8	6·9	54·1
16	58 25·6	18 00·2	255 51·5	13·0	18 40·9	7·0	54·0
17	73 25·7	17 59·6	270 23·5	13·1	18 33·9	7·1	54·0
18	88 25·7	N17 59·0	284 56·6	13·2	S18 26·8	7·1	54·0
19	103 25·8	58·4	299 27·8	13·2	18 19·7	7·2	54·0
20	118 25·8	57·7	314 00·0	13·2	18 12·5	7·3	54·0
21	133 25·8 · ·	57·1	328 32·2	13·3	18 05·2	7·4	54·0
22	148 25·9	56·5	343 04·5	13·3	17 57·8	7·5	54·0
23	163 25·9	55·8	357 36·8	13·4	17 50·3	7·5	54·0

S.D. 15·8 d 0·6 | S.D. 14·9 14·8 14·7

Twilight / Sunrise / Moonrise

Lat.	Twilight Naut.	Twilight Civil	Sun-rise	Moonrise 30	31	1	2
N 72	□	□	□	■	■	22 51	21 28
N 70	////	////	01 11	■	■	21 23	20 57
68	////	////	02 07	■	20 58	20 43	20 34
66	////	////	02 39	20 04	20 13	20 16	20 16
64	////	01 30	03 03	19 22	19 43	19 55	20 01
62	////	02 09	03 22	18 54	19 21	19 38	19 49
60	////	02 35	03 37	18 32	19 02	19 23	19 38
N 58	01 22	02 55	03 50	18 14	18 47	19 11	19 29
56	01 57	03 12	04 01	17 59	18 34	19 01	19 21
54	02 22	03 26	04 11	17 47	18 23	18 51	19 14
52	02 41	03 37	04 19	17 35	18 13	18 43	19 07
50	02 56	03 48	04 27	17 25	18 04	18 35	19 01
45	03 26	04 09	04 43	17 04	17 45	18 19	18 49
N 40	03 49	04 26	04 57	16 47	17 29	18 06	18 38
35	04 06	04 40	05 08	16 33	17 16	17 55	18 29
30	04 21	04 52	05 18	16 20	17 05	17 45	18 21
20	04 43	05 11	05 35	15 59	16 45	17 28	18 07
N 10	05 01	05 27	05 49	15 40	16 28	17 13	17 55
0	05 16	05 41	06 03	15 23	16 12	16 59	17 44
S 10	05 29	05 54	06 16	15 05	15 56	16 45	17 33
20	05 41	06 07	06 30	14 47	15 38	16 30	17 20
30	05 52	06 21	06 46	14 25	15 19	16 12	17 06
35	05 58	06 29	06 56	14 13	15 07	16 02	16 58
40	06 05	06 37	07 06	13 58	14 54	15 51	16 49
45	06 11	06 47	07 19	13 41	14 38	15 37	16 38
S 50	06 19	06 58	07 34	13 20	14 18	15 20	16 25
52	06 22	07 03	07 41	13 10	14 09	15 13	16 19
54	06 26	07 09	07 48	12 58	13 59	15 04	16 12
56	06 29	07 15	07 57	12 45	13 47	14 54	16 04
58	06 34	07 22	08 07	12 30	13 33	14 43	15 55
S 60	06 38	07 29	08 18	12 12	13 17	14 30	15 45

Sunset / Twilight / Moonset

Lat.	Sun-set	Twilight Civil	Twilight Naut.	Moonset 30	31	1	2
N 72	22 52	////	////	■	■	23 43	26 38
N 70	22 01	////	////	■	■	■	01 10
68	21 30	////	////	■	23 57	25 48	01 48
66	21 07	22 37	////	23 51	24 41	00 41	02 15
64	20 49	22 01	////	23 50	25 11	01 11	02 35
62	20 34	21 35	////	24 20	00 20	01 33	02 52
60	20 21	21 15	22 46	00 00	00 59	02 06	03 17
N 58	20 20	21 15	22 12	00 16	01 13	02 29	03 27
56	20 10	20 59	22 14	00 29	01 26	02 29	03 36
54	20 01	20 46	21 49	00 42	01 38	02 38	03 44
52	19 52	20 34	21 30	00 51	01 47	02 45	03 51
50	19 44	20 24	21 15	01 00	01 56	02 52	03 57
45	19 29	20 02	20 45	01 19	02 13	03 05	04 06
N 40	19 15	19 46	20 23	01 31	02 25	03 21	04 19
35	19 04	19 32	20 06	01 46	02 39	03 34	04 29
30	18 54	19 20	19 52	01 58	02 51	03 45	04 39
20	18 38	19 01	19 29	02 20	03 12	04 03	04 54
N 10	18 23	18 45	19 11	02 39	03 30	04 20	05 08
0	18 10	18 32	18 57	02 57	03 47	04 35	05 21
S 10	17 56	18 19	18 44	03 15	04 03	04 50	05 34
20	17 43	18 06	18 32	03 34	04 21	05 06	05 47
30	17 28	17 52	18 21	03 55	04 42	05 24	06 03
35	17 17	17 44	18 15	04 08	04 54	05 35	06 11
40	17 07	17 36	18 08	04 23	05 08	05 47	06 22
45	16 55	17 26	18 02	04 40	05 24	06 01	06 33
S 50	16 41	17 15	17 54	05 01	05 44	06 19	06 48
52	16 35	17 10	17 51	05 12	05 54	06 27	06 54
54	16 28	17 04	17 48	05 23	06 04	06 36	07 02
56	16 20	16 58	17 44	05 36	06 16	06 47	07 10
58	16 11	16 52	17 40	05 52	06 30	06 58	07 19
S 60	15 55	16 44	17 36	06 10	06 46	07 12	07 30

SUN and MOON summary

Day	SUN Eqn. of Time 00h	12h	SUN Mer. Pass.	MOON Mer. Pass. Upper	Lower	Age	Phase
30	06 25	06 24	12 06	21 35	09 10	11	○
31	06 23	06 21	12 06	22 23	09 59	12	
1	06 20	06 18	12 06	23 10	10 47	13	

1974 OCTOBER 19, 20, 21 (SAT., SUN., MON.)

G.M.T.	ARIES G.H.A.	VENUS −3.5 G.H.A.	Dec.	MARS +1.8 G.H.A.	Dec.	JUPITER −2.3 G.H.A.	Dec.	SATURN +0.3 G.H.A.	Dec.
19 00	27 05·3	187 40·9	S 6 49·6	184 53·6	S 8 45·2	46 31·5	S 9 43·6	276 50·7	N21 38·9
01	42 07·7	202 40·5	50·8	199 54·5	45·8	61 34·0	43·7	291 53·1	38·9
02	57 10·2	217 40·0	52·1	214 55·5	46·4	76 36·6	43·7	306 55·5	38·9
03	72 12·6	232 39·6	·· 53·3	229 56·4	·· 47·1	91 39·2	·· 43·8	321 57·9	·· 38·9
04	87 15·1	247 39·1	54·5	244 57·3	47·7	106 41·8	43·8	337 00·3	38·9
05	102 17·6	262 38·7	55·7	259 58·2	48·3	121 44·4	43·8	352 02·7	38·9
06	117 20·0	277 38·3	S 6 56·9	274 59·1	S 8 49·0	136 47·0	S 9 43·9	7 05·1	N21 38·9
07	132 22·5	292 37·8	58·2	290 00·0	49·6	151 49·6	43·9	22 07·5	38·9
S 08	147 25·0	307 37·4	6 59·4	305 00·9	50·2	166 52·2	44·0	37 09·9	38·9
A 09	162 27·4	322 36·9	7 00·6	320 01·8	·· 50·9	181 54·7	·· 44·0	52 12·3	·· 38·9
T 10	177 29·9	337 36·5	01·8	335 02·7	51·5	196 57·3	44·0	67 14·7	38·9
U 11	192 32·4	352 36·1	03·0	350 03·6	52·1	211 59·9	44·1	82 17·1	38·9
R 12	207 34·8	7 35·6	S 7 04·2	5 04·5	S 8 52·8	227 02·5	S 9 44·1	97 19·5	N21 38·9
D 13	222 37·3	22 35·2	05·4	20 05·4	53·4	242 05·1	44·2	112 21·9	38·9
A 14	237 39·7	37 34·7	06·7	35 06·3	54·0	257 07·7	44·2	127 24·3	38·8
Y 15	252 42·2	52 34·3	·· 07·9	50 07·2	·· 54·7	272 10·3	·· 44·2	142 26·7	·· 38·8
16	267 44·7	67 33·8	09·1	65 08·1	55·3	287 12·8	44·3	157 29·2	38·8
17	282 47·1	82 33·4	10·3	80 09·0	55·9	302 15·4	44·3	172 31·6	38·8
18	297 49·6	97 33·0	S 7 11·5	95 09·9	S 8 56·6	317 18·0	S 9 44·4	187 34·0	N21 38·8
19	312 52·1	112 32·5	12·7	110 10·8	57·2	332 20·6	44·4	202 36·4	38·8
20	327 54·5	127 32·1	13·9	125 11·7	57·8	347 23·2	44·4	217 38·8	38·8
21	342 57·0	142 31·6	·· 15·2	140 12·6	·· 58·5	2 25·8	·· 44·5	232 41·2	·· 38·8
22	357 59·5	157 31·2	16·4	155 13·5	59·1	17 28·3	44·5	247 43·6	38·8
23	13 01·9	172 30·7	17·6	170 14·4	8 59·7	32 30·9	44·6	262 46·0	38·8
20 00	28 04·4	187 30·3	S 7 18·8	185 15·3	S 9 00·4	47 33·5	S 9 44·6	277 48·4	N21 38·8
01	43 06·9	202 29·8	20·0	200 16·2	01·0	62 36·1	44·6	292 50·8	38·8
02	58 09·3	217 29·4	21·2	215 17·1	01·6	77 38·7	44·7	307 53·2	38·8
03	73 11·8	232 29·0	·· 22·4	230 18·0	·· 02·3	92 41·2	·· 44·7	322 55·6	·· 38·8
04	88 14·2	247 28·5	23·6	245 18·9	02·9	107 43·8	44·8	337 58·0	38·8
05	103 16·7	262 28·1	24·8	260 19·8	03·5	122 46·4	44·8	353 00·4	38·8
06	118 19·2	277 27·6	S 7 26·1	275 20·7	S 9 04·2	137 49·0	S 9 44·8	8 02·8	N21 38·8
07	133 21·6	292 27·2	27·3	290 21·6	04·8	152 51·6	44·9	23 05·2	38·7
S 08	148 24·1	307 26·7	28·5	305 22·4	05·4	167 54·1	44·9	38 07·7	38·7
U 09	163 26·6	322 26·3	·· 29·7	320 23·3	·· 06·0	182 56·7	·· 44·9	53 10·1	·· 38·7
N 10	178 29·0	337 25·8	30·9	335 24·2	06·7	197 59·3	45·0	68 12·5	38·7
11	193 31·5	352 25·4	32·1	350 25·1	07·3	213 01·9	45·0	83 14·9	38·7
D 12	208 34·0	7 24·9	S 7 33·3	5 26·0	S 9 07·9	228 04·5	S 9 45·1	98 17·3	N21 38·7
A 13	223 36·4	22 24·5	34·5	20 26·9	08·6	243 07·0	45·1	113 19·7	38·7
Y 14	238 38·9	37 24·0	35·7	35 27·8	09·2	258 09·6	45·1	128 22·1	38·7
15	253 41·4	52 23·6	·· 36·9	50 28·7	·· 09·8	273 12·2	·· 45·2	143 24·5	38·7
16	268 43·8	67 23·1	38·1	65 29·6	10·5	288 14·8	45·2	158 26·9	38·7
17	283 46·3	82 22·7	39·4	80 30·5	11·1	303 17·3	45·2	173 29·3	38·7
18	298 48·7	97 22·2	S 7 40·6	95 31·4	S 9 11·7	318 19·9	S 9 45·3	188 31·7	N21 38·7
19	313 51·2	112 21·8	41·8	110 32·3	12·4	333 22·5	45·3	203 34·2	38·7
20	328 53·7	127 21·3	43·0	125 33·2	13·0	348 25·1	45·3	218 36·6	38·7
21	343 56·1	142 20·9	·· 44·2	140 34·1	·· 13·6	3 27·6	·· 45·4	233 39·0	·· 38·7
22	358 58·6	157 20·4	45·4	155 35·0	14·2	18 30·2	45·4	248 41·4	38·7
23	14 01·1	172 20·0	46·6	170 35·9	14·9	33 32·8	45·5	263 43·8	38·7
21 00	29 03·5	187 19·5	S 7 47·8	185 36·8	S 9 15·5	48 35·4	S 9 45·5	278 46·2	N21 38·7
01	44 06·0	202 19·1	49·0	200 37·7	16·1	63 37·9	45·5	293 48·6	38·7
02	59 08·5	217 18·6	50·2	215 38·6	16·8	78 40·5	45·6	308 51·0	38·7
03	74 10·9	232 18·2	·· 51·4	230 39·5	·· 17·4	93 43·1	·· 45·6	323 53·4	·· 38·7
04	89 13·4	247 17·7	52·6	245 40·4	18·0	108 45·7	45·6	338 55·9	38·6
05	104 15·9	262 17·3	53·8	260 41·3	18·6	123 48·2	45·7	353 58·3	38·6
06	119 18·3	277 16·8	S 7 55·0	275 42·2	S 9 19·3	138 50·8	S 9 45·7	9 00·7	N21 38·6
07	134 20·8	292 16·4	56·2	290 43·1	19·9	153 53·4	45·7	24 03·1	38·6
M 08	149 23·2	307 15·9	57·4	305 44·0	20·5	168 55·9	45·8	39 05·5	38·6
O 09	164 25·7	322 15·4	·· 58·6	320 44·8	·· 21·2	183 58·5	·· 45·8	54 07·9	·· 38·6
N 10	179 28·2	337 15·0	7 59·8	335 45·7	21·8	199 01·1	45·8	69 10·3	38·6
11	194 30·6	352 14·5	8 01·0	350 46·6	22·4	214 03·7	45·9	84 12·7	38·6
D 12	209 33·1	7 14·1	S 8 02·2	5 47·5	S 9 23·1	229 06·2	S 9 45·9	99 15·2	N21 38·6
A 13	224 35·6	22 13·6	03·4	20 48·4	23·7	244 08·8	45·9	114 17·6	38·6
Y 14	239 38·0	37 13·2	04·6	35 49·3	24·3	259 11·4	46·0	129 20·0	38·6
15	254 40·5	52 12·7	·· 05·8	50 50·2	·· 24·9	274 13·9	·· 46·0	144 22·4	38·6
16	269 43·0	67 12·3	07·0	65 51·1	25·6	289 16·5	46·0	159 24·8	38·6
17	284 45·4	82 11·8	08·2	80 52·0	26·2	304 19·1	46·1	174 27·2	38·6
18	299 47·9	97 11·3	S 8 09·4	95 52·9	S 9 26·8	319 21·6	S 9 46·1	189 29·6	N21 38·6
19	314 50·3	112 10·9	10·6	110 53·8	27·4	334 24·2	46·1	204 32·1	38·6
20	329 52·8	127 10·4	11·8	125 54·7	28·1	349 26·8	46·2	219 34·5	38·6
21	344 55·3	142 10·0	·· 13·0	140 55·6	·· 28·7	4 29·3	·· 46·2	234 36·9	·· 38·6
22	359 57·7	157 09·5	14·2	155 56·4	29·3	19 31·9	46·2	249 39·3	38·6
23	15 00·2	172 09·0	15·4	170 57·3	30·0	34 34·5	46·3	264 41·7	38·6
Mer. Pass. 22 04·1		v −0·4	d 1·2	v 0·9	d 0·6	v 2·6	d 0·0	v 2·4	d 0·0

STARS

Name	S.H.A.	Dec.
Acamar	315 39·9	S 40 24·1
Achernar	335 47·6	S 57 21·7
Acrux	173 42·5	S 62 57·5
Adhara	255 35·2	S 28 56·0
Aldebaran	291 22·4	N 16 27·6
Alioth	166 46·5	N 56 05·7
Alkaid	153 22·1	N 49 26·3
Al Na'ir	28 19·7	S 47 05·0
Alnilam	276 15·6	S 1 12·9
Alphard	218 24·7	S 8 32·9
Alphecca	126 35·9	N 26 48·1
Alpheratz	358 13·2	N 28 57·4
Altair	62 36·5	N 8 48·3
Ankaa	353 43·8	S 42 26·5
Antares	113 02·1	S 26 22·6
Arcturus	146 22·5	N 19 18·8
Atria	108 30·4	S 68 59·2
Avior	234 30·0	S 59 25·4
Bellatrix	279 02·9	N 6 19·8
Betelgeuse	271 32·5	N 7 24·3
Canopus	264 08·8	S 52 40·6
Capella	281 17·0	N 45 58·3
Deneb	49 51·2	N 45 11·8
Denebola	183 03·4	N 14 42·7
Diphda	349 24·6	S 18 07·3
Dubhe	194 27·5	N 61 53·0
Elnath	278 49·0	N 28 35·2
Eltanin	90 59·9	N 51 29·8
Enif	34 15·4	N 9 45·8
Fomalhaut	15 55·6	S 29 45·3
Gacrux	172 33·9	S 56 58·3
Gienah	176 22·4	S 17 24·1
Hadar	149 29·8	S 60 15·1
Hamal	328 33·2	N 23 20·8
Kaus Aust.	84 22·4	S 34 23·9
Kochab	137 19·8	N 74 15·6
Markab	14 07·0	N 15 04·4
Menkar	314 45·1	N 3 59·7
Menkent	148 42·2	S 36 14·8
Miaplacidus	221 46·2	S 69 36·6
Mirfak	309 21·5	N 49 46·4
Nunki	76 34·3	S 26 19·7
Peacock	54 04·7	S 56 49·1
Pollux	244 03·1	N 28 05·2
Procyon	245 30·0	N 5 17·5
Rasalhague	96 33·5	N 12 34·8
Regulus	208 14·5	N 12 05·4
Rigel	281 39·7	S 8 13·6
Rigil Kent.	140 32·0	S 60 43·9
Sabik	102 46·0	S 15 41·6
Schedar	350 13·1	N 56 24·2
Shaula	97 01·5	S 37 05·2
Sirius	258 59·2	S 16 40·7
Spica	159 02·1	S 11 01·8
Suhail	223 13·9	S 43 19·6
Vega	80 58·7	N 38 45·9
Zuben'ubi	137 37·9	S 15 56·2

	S.H.A.	Mer. Pass.
Venus	159 25·9	11 30
Mars	157 10·9	11 38
Jupiter	19 29·1	20 46
Saturn	249 44·0	5 28

1974 OCTOBER 19, 20, 21 (SAT., SUN., MON.)

SUN and MOON

G.M.T. d h	SUN G.H.A.	SUN Dec.	MOON G.H.A.	v	MOON Dec.	d	H.P.
19 00	183 42·8	S 9 45·7	139 42·1	8·6	S21 59·6	2·0	56·6
01	198 42·9	46·6	154 09·7	8·6	22 01·6	1·9	56·6
02	213 43·0	47·5	168 37·3	8·6	22 03·5	1·7	56·6
03	228 43·1	·· 48·4	183 04·9	8·7	22 05·2	1·7	56·5
04	243 43·2	49·3	197 32·6	8·7	22 06·9	1·5	56·5
05	258 43·3	50·2	212 00·3	8·8	22 08·4	1·3	56·5
06	273 43·5	S 9 51·1	226 28·1	8·7	S22 09·7	1·3	56·4
07	288 43·6	52·0	240 55·8	8·8	22 11·0	1·1	56·4
08	303 43·7	52·9	255 23·6	8·9	22 12·1	1·0	56·4
09	318 43·8	·· 53·8	269 51·5	8·8	22 13·1	0·9	56·3
10	333 43·9	54·7	284 19·3	9·0	22 14·0	0·7	56·3
11	348 44·0	55·6	298 47·3	8·9	22 14·7	0·7	56·3
12	3 44·2	S 9 56·6	313 15·2	9·0	S22 15·4	0·5	56·2
13	18 44·3	57·5	327 43·2	9·0	22 15·9	0·4	56·2
14	33 44·4	58·4	342 11·2	9·0	22 16·3	0·2	56·2
15	48 44·5	9 59·3	356 39·2	9·1	22 16·5	0·2	56·2
16	63 44·6	10 00·2	11 07·3	9·1	22 16·7	0·0	56·1
17	78 44·7	01·1	25 35·4	9·2	22 16·7	0·1	56·1
18	93 44·8	S10 02·0	40 03·6	9·2	S22 16·6	0·2	56·1
19	108 44·9	02·9	54 31·8	9·3	22 16·4	0·3	56·0
20	123 45·1	03·8	69 00·1	9·3	22 16·1	0·5	56·0
21	138 45·2	·· 04·7	83 28·4	9·3	22 15·6	0·6	56·0
22	153 45·3	05·6	97 56·7	9·4	22 15·0	0·6	55·9
23	168 45·4	06·5	112 25·1	9·4	22 14·4	0·8	55·9
20 00	183 45·5	S10 07·4	126 53·5	9·5	S22 13·6	1·0	55·9
01	198 45·6	08·3	141 22·0	9·5	22 12·6	1·0	55·9
02	213 45·7	09·2	155 50·5	9·5	22 11·6	1·2	55·8
03	228 45·8	·· 10·1	170 19·0	9·6	22 10·4	1·2	55·8
04	243 46·0	11·0	184 47·6	9·7	22 09·2	1·4	55·8
05	258 46·1	11·9	199 16·3	9·7	22 07·8	1·5	55·7
06	273 46·2	S10 12·8	213 45·0	9·7	S22 06·3	1·6	55·7
07	288 46·3	13·7	228 13·7	9·8	22 04·7	1·8	55·7
08	303 46·4	14·6	242 42·5	9·9	22 02·9	1·8	55·7
09	318 46·5	·· 15·5	257 11·4	9·9	22 01·1	2·0	55·6
10	333 46·6	16·4	271 40·3	10·0	21 59·1	2·0	55·6
11	348 46·7	17·3	286 09·3	10·0	21 57·1	2·2	55·6
12	3 46·8	S10 18·2	300 38·3	10·0	S21 54·9	2·3	55·6
13	18 46·9	19·1	315 07·3	10·1	21 52·6	2·4	55·5
14	33 47·0	20·0	329 36·4	10·2	21 50·2	2·5	55·5
15	48 47·1	·· 20·9	344 05·6	10·2	21 47·7	2·6	55·5
16	63 47·3	21·8	358 34·8	10·3	21 45·1	2·7	55·4
17	78 47·4	22·7	13 04·1	10·3	21 42·4	2·9	55·4
18	93 47·5	S10 23·6	27 33·4	10·4	S21 39·5	2·9	55·4
19	108 47·6	24·5	42 02·8	10·4	21 36·6	3·1	55·4
20	123 47·7	25·3	56 32·2	10·5	21 33·5	3·1	55·3
21	138 47·8	·· 26·2	71 01·7	10·5	21 30·4	3·3	55·3
22	153 47·9	27·1	85 31·2	10·6	21 27·1	3·3	55·3
23	168 48·0	28·0	100 00·8	10·7	21 23·8	3·5	55·3
21 00	183 48·1	S10 28·9	114 30·5	10·7	S21 20·3	3·5	55·2
01	198 48·2	29·8	129 00·2	10·8	21 16·8	3·7	55·2
02	213 48·3	30·7	143 30·0	10·8	21 13·1	3·8	55·2
03	228 48·4	·· 31·6	157 59·8	10·9	21 09·3	3·8	55·2
04	243 48·5	32·5	172 29·7	10·9	21 05·5	4·0	55·2
05	258 48·6	33·4	186 59·6	11·0	21 01·5	4·1	55·1
06	273 48·7	S10 34·3	201 29·6	11·1	S20 57·4	4·1	55·1
07	288 48·8	35·2	215 59·7	11·1	20 53·3	4·3	55·1
08	303 48·9	36·1	230 29·8	11·2	20 49·0	4·4	55·0
09	318 49·0	·· 37·0	245 00·0	11·2	20 44·6	4·4	55·0
10	333 49·1	37·9	259 30·2	11·3	20 40·2	4·6	55·0
11	348 49·2	38·7	274 00·5	11·4	20 35·6	4·6	55·0
12	3 49·3	S10 39·6	288 30·9	11·4	S20 31·0	4·8	55·0
13	18 49·4	40·5	303 01·3	11·5	20 26·2	4·8	54·9
14	33 49·5	41·4	317 31·8	11·5	20 21·4	4·9	54·9
15	48 49·6	·· 42·3	332 02·3	11·6	20 16·5	5·1	54·9
16	63 49·7	43·2	346 32·9	11·6	20 11·4	5·1	54·9
17	78 49·8	44·1	1 03·5	11·7	20 06·3	5·2	54·9
18	93 49·9	S10 45·0	15 34·2	11·8	S20 01·1	5·3	54·9
19	108 50·0	45·9	30 05·0	11·8	19 55·8	5·4	54·8
20	123 50·1	46·8	44 35·8	11·9	19 50·4	5·4	54·8
21	138 50·2	·· 47·6	59 06·7	12·0	19 45·0	5·6	54·8
22	153 50·3	48·5	73 37·7	12·0	19 39·4	5·7	54·8
23	168 50·4	49·4	88 08·7	12·0	19 33·7	5·7	54·8
S.D.	16·1	d 0·9	S.D. 15·3		15·1		15·0

Twilight, Sunrise and Moonrise

Lat.	Naut.	Civil	Sun-rise	Moonrise 19	20	21	22
N 72	05 15	06 34	07 47	■	■	■	17 00
N 70	05 16	06 27	07 33	■	■	■	15 49
68	05 18	06 22	07 21	■	15 39	15 19	15 11
66	05 18	06 18	07 11	13 41	14 21	14 38	14 45
64	05 19	06 14	07 03	13 00	13 44	14 10	14 24
62	05 19	06 11	06 57	12 31	13 18	13 48	14 08
60	05 20	06 08	06 50	12 09	12 57	13 30	13 54
N 58	05 20	06 05	06 45	11 52	12 40	13 16	13 42
56	05 20	06 03	06 41	11 37	12 26	13 03	13 31
54	05 19	06 00	06 36	11 24	12 13	12 52	13 22
52	05 19	05 58	06 33	11 13	12 02	12 42	13 14
50	05 19	05 56	06 29	11 03	11 53	12 33	13 07
45	05 18	05 52	06 22	10 42	11 32	12 15	12 51
N 40	05 16	05 48	06 15	10 25	11 16	12 00	12 38
35	05 15	05 44	06 10	10 10	11 02	11 47	12 27
30	05 13	05 41	06 05	09 58	10 49	11 36	12 17
20	05 08	05 34	05 56	09 37	10 29	11 16	12 00
N 10	05 03	05 28	05 49	09 18	10 10	11 00	11 45
0	04 56	05 21	05 42	09 01	09 54	10 44	11 32
S 10	04 48	05 13	05 34	08 44	09 37	10 28	11 18
20	04 38	05 04	05 26	08 26	09 19	10 11	11 03
30	04 24	04 53	05 17	08 05	08 58	09 52	10 46
35	04 15	04 46	05 12	07 52	08 46	09 41	10 36
40	04 04	04 38	05 06	07 38	08 31	09 28	10 25
45	03 51	04 28	04 59	07 22	08 15	09 12	10 12
S 50	03 34	04 16	04 50	07 01	07 54	08 53	09 55
52	03 25	04 10	04 46	06 51	07 45	08 44	09 48
54	03 16	04 04	04 42	06 40	07 34	08 34	09 39
56	03 05	03 57	04 37	06 28	07 21	08 23	09 29
58	02 52	03 48	04 32	06 13	07 07	08 10	09 18
S 60	02 37	03 39	04 25	05 56	06 49	07 54	09 06

Sunset, Twilight and Moonset

Lat.	Sun-set	Civil	Naut.	Moonset 19	20	21	22
N 72	15 41	16 55	18 13	■	■	■	18 39
N 70	15 56	17 01	18 12	■	■	■	19 49
68	16 08	17 06	18 11	■	16 37	18 40	20 26
66	16 17	17 11	18 10	16 46	17 55	19 21	20 52
64	16 25	17 15	18 10	17 28	18 31	19 49	21 12
62	16 32	17 18	18 09	17 56	18 58	20 10	21 28
60	16 38	17 21	18 09	18 18	19 18	20 27	21 41
N 58	16 44	17 24	18 09	18 36	19 36	20 41	21 52
56	16 49	17 26	18 09	18 51	19 49	20 54	22 02
54	16 53	17 29	18 10	19 04	20 01	21 04	22 11
52	16 56	17 31	18 10	19 15	20 12	21 14	22 19
50	17 00	17 33	18 10	19 25	20 22	21 22	22 26
45	17 08	17 37	18 11	19 46	20 42	21 40	22 41
N 40	17 14	17 42	18 13	20 03	20 58	21 55	22 53
35	17 20	17 45	18 15	20 17	21 12	22 07	23 03
30	17 25	17 49	18 17	20 30	21 24	22 18	23 12
20	17 33	17 55	18 21	20 51	21 44	22 36	23 28
N 10	17 41	18 02	18 27	21 09	22 02	22 52	23 41
0	17 48	18 09	18 34	21 27	22 18	23 07	23 54
S 10	17 56	18 17	18 42	21 44	22 34	23 23	24 06
20	18 04	18 26	18 53	22 02	22 52	23 38	24 20
30	18 13	18 38	19 07	22 23	23 12	23 56	24 35
35	18 19	18 45	19 16	22 35	23 24	24 06	00 06
40	18 25	18 53	19 27	22 50	23 37	24 18	00 18
45	18 32	19 03	19 40	23 06	23 53	24 32	00 32
S 50	18 41	19 15	19 58	23 27	24 13	00 13	00 49
52	18 45	19 21	20 07	23 37	24 22	00 22	00 57
54	18 49	19 27	20 16	23 48	24 31	00 31	01 06
56	18 54	19 35	20 27	24 01	00 01	00 44	01 16
58	19 00	19 43	20 40	24 15	00 15	00 57	01 28
S 60	19 06	19 53	20 56	24 32	00 32	01 13	01 41

SUN and MOON

Day	SUN Eqn. of Time 00h	12h	Mer. Pass.	MOON Mer. Pass. Upper	Lower	Age	Phase
19	14 51	14 56	11 45	15 14	02 47	04	
20	15 02	15 07	11 45	16 06	03 40	05	
21	15 12	15 17	11 45	16 56	04 31	06	

1974 OCT. 31, NOV. 1, 2 (THURS., FRI., SAT.)

G.M.T.	ARIES G.H.A.	VENUS −3.5 G.H.A.	Dec.	MARS +1.8 G.H.A.	Dec.	JUPITER −2.2 G.H.A.	Dec.	SATURN +0.2 G.H.A.	Dec.	Name	S.H.A.	Dec.
31 00	38 54.9	185 21.3	S12 26.5	189 06.9	S11 43.6	58 43.7	S 9 50.2	288 30.8	N21 38.2	Acamar	315 39.8	S 40 24.2
01	53 57.4	200 20.7	27.6	204 07.8	44.2	73 46.2	50.2	303 33.3	38.2	Achernar	335 47.6	S 57 21.8
02	68 59.8	215 20.2	28.7	219 08.7	44.8	88 48.7	50.2	318 35.7	38.2	Acrux	173 42.4	S 62 57.5
03	84 02.3	230 19.7	.. 29.8	234 09.5	.. 45.4	103 51.2	.. 50.2	333 38.2	.. 38.2	Adhara	255 35.1	S 28 56.1
04	99 04.8	245 19.1	30.9	249 10.4	46.0	118 53.7	50.2	348 40.7	38.2	Aldebaran	291 22.3	N 16 27.6
05	114 07.2	260 18.6	32.0	264 11.2	46.6	133 56.2	50.2	3 43.1	38.2			
06	129 09.7	275 18.0	S12 33.1	279 12.1	S11 47.2	148 58.7	S 9 50.2	18 45.6	N21 38.3	Alioth	166 46.5	N 56 05.6
T 07	144 12.2	290 17.5	34.2	294 12.9	47.8	164 01.2	50.2	33 48.1	38.3	Alkaid	153 22.1	N 49 26.2
H 08	159 14.6	305 17.0	35.3	309 13.8	48.4	179 03.7	50.2	48 50.5	38.3	Al Na'ir	28 19.8	S 47 05.1
U 09	174 17.1	320 16.4	.. 36.4	324 14.6	.. 49.0	194 06.2	.. 50.2	63 53.0	.. 38.3	Alnilam	276 15.5	S 1 12.9
R 10	189 19.6	335 15.9	37.5	339 15.5	49.6	209 08.7	50.2	78 55.4	38.3	Alphard	218 24.6	S 8 32.9
S 11	204 22.0	350 15.3	38.6	354 16.3	50.2	224 11.1	50.2	93 57.9	38.3			
D 12	219 24.5	5 14.8	S12 39.7	9 17.2	S11 50.8	239 13.6	S 9 50.2	109 00.4	N21 38.3	Alphecca	126 35.9	N 26 48.0
A 13	234 26.9	20 14.2	40.8	24 18.0	51.4	254 16.1	50.2	124 02.8	38.3	Alpheratz	358 13.2	N 28 57.4
Y 14	249 29.4	35 13.7	41.9	39 18.9	52.0	269 18.6	50.2	139 05.3	38.3	Altair	62 36.5	N 8 48.3
15	264 31.9	50 13.1	.. 43.0	54 19.7	.. 52.6	284 21.1	.. 50.2	154 07.8	.. 38.3	Ankaa	353 43.8	S 42 26.5
16	279 34.3	65 12.6	44.1	69 20.6	53.2	299 23.6	50.2	169 10.2	38.3	Antares	113 02.1	S 26 22.6
17	294 36.8	80 12.1	45.2	84 21.5	53.8	314 26.1	50.2	184 12.7	38.3			
18	309 39.3	95 11.5	S12 46.3	99 22.3	S11 54.4	329 28.6	S 9 50.2	199 15.2	N21 38.3	Arcturus	146 22.5	N 19 18.8
19	324 41.7	110 11.0	47.4	114 23.2	55.0	344 31.1	50.2	214 17.6	38.3	Atria	108 30.5	S 68 59.1
20	339 44.2	125 10.4	48.5	129 24.0	55.6	359 33.6	50.2	229 20.1	38.3	Avior	234 29.8	S 59 25.4
21	354 46.7	140 09.9	.. 49.6	144 24.9	.. 56.2	14 36.1	.. 50.2	244 22.5	.. 38.3	Bellatrix	279 02.8	N 6 19.7
22	9 49.1	155 09.3	50.7	159 25.7	56.8	29 38.5	50.2	259 25.0	38.3	Betelgeuse	271 32.4	N 7 24.2
23	24 51.6	170 08.8	51.8	174 26.6	57.4	44 41.0	50.2	274 27.5	38.3			
1 00	39 54.0	185 08.2	S12 52.9	189 27.4	S11 58.0	59 43.5	S 9 50.2	289 29.9	N21 38.3	Canopus	264 08.7	S 52 40.7
01	54 56.5	200 07.7	54.0	204 28.3	58.6	74 46.0	50.2	304 32.4	38.3	Capella	281 16.9	N 45 58.4
02	69 59.0	215 07.1	55.1	219 29.1	59.2	89 48.5	50.2	319 34.9	38.3	Deneb	49 51.2	N 45 11.8
03	85 01.4	230 06.6	.. 56.2	234 30.0	11 59.8	104 51.0	.. 50.2	334 37.3	.. 38.3	Denebola	183 03.4	N 14 42.7
04	100 03.9	245 06.0	57.3	249 30.8	12 00.4	119 53.5	50.2	349 39.8	38.3	Diphda	349 24.6	S 18 07.3
05	115 06.4	260 05.5	58.4	264 31.7	01.0	134 55.9	50.2	4 42.3	38.3			
06	130 08.8	275 04.9	S12 59.4	279 32.5	S12 01.6	149 58.4	S 9 50.2	19 44.7	N21 38.3	Dubhe	194 27.4	N 61 52.9
07	145 11.3	290 04.4	13 00.5	294 33.4	02.2	165 00.9	50.2	34 47.2	38.3	Elnath	278 48.9	N 28 35.2
F 08	160 13.8	305 03.8	01.6	309 34.2	02.8	180 03.4	50.2	49 49.7	38.3	Eltanin	91 00.0	N 51 29.8
R 09	175 16.2	320 03.3	.. 02.7	324 35.1	.. 03.4	195 05.9	.. 50.2	64 52.1	.. 38.3	Enif	34 15.5	N 9 45.8
I 10	190 18.7	335 02.7	03.8	339 35.9	04.0	210 08.4	50.2	79 54.6	38.3	Fomalhaut	15 55.6	S 29 45.3
D 11	205 21.2	350 02.1	04.9	354 36.8	04.6	225 10.9	50.2	94 57.1	38.3			
A 12	220 23.6	5 01.6	S13 06.0	9 37.6	S12 05.2	240 13.3	S 9 50.2	109 59.5	N21 38.3	Gacrux	172 33.8	S 56 58.2
Y 13	235 26.1	20 01.0	07.1	24 38.4	05.8	255 15.8	50.2	125 02.0	38.3	Gienah	176 22.4	S 17 24.1
14	250 28.5	35 00.5	08.2	39 39.3	06.4	270 18.3	50.2	140 04.5	38.3	Hadar	149 29.8	S 60 15.1
15	265 31.0	49 59.9	.. 09.3	54 40.1	.. 07.0	285 20.8	.. 50.2	155 07.0	.. 38.3	Hamal	328 33.1	N 23 20.8
16	280 33.5	64 59.4	10.3	69 41.0	07.6	300 23.3	50.2	170 09.4	38.3	Kaus Aust.	84 22.4	S 34 23.9
17	295 35.9	79 58.8	11.4	84 41.8	08.2	315 25.8	50.2	185 11.9	38.3			
18	310 38.4	94 58.2	S13 12.5	99 42.7	S12 08.8	330 28.2	S 9 50.2	200 14.4	N21 38.3	Kochab	137 19.9	N 74 15.5
19	325 40.9	109 57.7	13.6	114 43.5	09.4	345 30.7	50.2	215 16.8	38.3	Markab	14 07.0	N 15 04.5
20	340 43.3	124 57.1	14.7	129 44.4	10.0	0 33.2	50.2	230 19.3	38.3	Menkar	314 45.0	N 3 59.7
21	355 45.8	139 56.6	.. 15.8	144 45.2	.. 10.6	15 35.7	.. 50.2	245 21.8	.. 38.3	Menkent	148 42.2	S 36 14.8
22	10 48.3	154 56.0	16.8	159 46.1	11.2	30 38.2	50.2	260 24.2	38.3	Miaplacidus	221 46.0	S 69 36.6
23	25 50.7	169 55.5	17.9	174 46.9	11.8	45 40.6	50.2	275 26.7	38.3			
2 00	40 53.2	184 54.9	S13 19.0	189 47.8	S12 12.4	60 43.1	S 9 50.2	290 29.2	N21 38.3	Mirfak	309 21.4	N 49 46.4
01	55 55.7	199 54.3	20.1	204 48.6	12.9	75 45.6	50.2	305 31.6	38.3	Nunki	76 34.3	S 26 19.7
02	70 58.1	214 53.8	21.2	219 49.5	13.5	90 48.1	50.2	320 34.1	38.4	Peacock	54 04.8	S 56 49.1
03	86 00.6	229 53.2	.. 22.3	234 50.3	.. 14.1	105 50.6	.. 50.2	335 36.6	.. 38.4	Pollux	244 03.0	N 28 05.2
04	101 03.0	244 52.6	23.3	249 51.1	14.7	120 53.0	50.2	350 39.1	38.4	Procyon	245 29.9	N 5 17.4
05	116 05.5	259 52.1	24.4	264 52.0	15.3	135 55.5	50.2	5 41.5	38.4			
06	131 08.0	274 51.5	S13 25.5	279 52.8	S12 15.9	150 58.0	S 9 50.2	20 44.0	N21 38.4	Rasalhague	96 33.6	N 12 34.8
07	146 10.4	289 51.0	26.6	294 53.7	16.5	166 00.5	50.2	35 46.5	38.4	Regulus	208 14.4	N 12 05.4
S 08	161 12.9	304 50.4	27.6	309 54.5	17.1	181 02.9	50.2	50 49.0	38.4	Rigel	281 39.6	S 8 13.6
A 09	176 15.4	319 49.8	.. 28.7	324 55.4	.. 17.7	196 05.4	.. 50.2	65 51.4	.. 38.4	Rigil Kent.	140 32.0	S 60 43.9
T 10	191 17.8	334 49.3	29.8	339 56.2	18.3	211 07.9	50.2	80 53.9	38.4	Sabik	102 46.0	S 15 41.6
U 11	206 20.3	349 48.7	30.9	354 57.1	18.9	226 10.4	50.2	95 56.4	38.4			
R 12	221 22.8	4 48.1	S13 32.0	9 57.9	S12 19.5	241 12.8	S 9 50.1	110 58.8	N21 38.4	Schedar	350 13.2	N 56 24.3
D 13	236 25.2	19 47.6	33.0	24 58.7	20.1	256 15.3	50.1	126 01.3	38.4	Shaula	97 01.5	S 37 05.2
A 14	251 27.7	34 47.0	34.1	39 59.6	20.7	271 17.8	50.1	141 03.8	38.4	Sirius	258 59.1	S 16 40.7
Y 15	266 30.1	49 46.4	.. 35.2	55 00.4	.. 21.3	286 20.3	.. 50.1	156 06.3	.. 38.4	Spica	159 02.1	S 11 01.8
16	281 32.6	64 45.9	36.2	70 01.3	21.9	301 22.7	50.1	171 08.7	38.4	Suhail	223 13.8	S 43 19.6
17	296 35.1	79 45.3	37.3	85 02.1	22.5	316 25.2	50.1	186 11.2	38.4			
18	311 37.5	94 44.7	S13 38.4	100 03.0	S12 23.1	331 27.7	S 9 50.1	201 13.7	N21 38.4	Vega	80 58.8	N 38 45.9
19	326 40.0	109 44.2	39.5	115 03.8	23.7	346 30.2	50.1	216 16.2	38.4	Zuben'ubi	137 37.8	S 15 56.2
20	341 42.5	124 43.6	40.5	130 04.6	24.3	1 32.6	50.1	231 18.6	38.4		S.H.A.	Mer. Pass.
21	356 44.9	139 43.0	.. 41.6	145 05.5	.. 24.9	16 35.1	.. 50.1	246 21.1	.. 38.4		° '	h m
22	11 47.4	154 42.4	42.7	160 06.3	25.4	31 37.6	50.1	261 23.6	38.4	Venus	145 14.2	11 40
23	26 49.9	169 41.9	43.7	175 07.2	26.0	46 40.1	50.1	276 26.1	38.4	Mars	149 33.4	11 22
Mer. Pass. 21 16.9		v −0.6	d 1.1	v 0.8	d 0.6	v 2.5	d 0.0	v 2.5	d 0.0	Jupiter	19 49.5	19 58
										Saturn	249 35.9	4 41

G.M.T.	SUN		MOON					Lat.	Twilight		Sun-rise	Moonrise			
									Naut.	Civil		31	1	2	3
	G.H.A.	Dec.	G.H.A.	v	Dec.	d	H.P.	°	h m	h m	h m	h m	h m	h m	h m
d h	° '	° '	° '	'	° '	'	'	N 72	06 04	07 27	08 54	12 17	□	□	□
31 00	184 04·7	S13 54·7	5 43·3	10·4	N16 26·4	8·5	56·8	N 70	06 00	07 14	08 28	13 49	□	□	□
01	199 04·7	55·5	20 12·7	10·4	16 34·9	8·5	56·8	68	05 57	07 04	08 09	14 29	14 24	14 14	15 18
02	214 04·8	56·3	34 42·1	10·3	16 43·4	8·4	56·9	66	05 54	06 55	07 53	14 56	15 08	15 37	16 38
03	229 04·8	·· 57·1	49 11·4	10·2	16 51·8	8·3	56·9	64	05 51	06 48	07 41	15 18	15 38	16 14	17 15
04	244 04·8	58·0	63 40·6	10·1	17 00·1	8·2	56·9	62	05 49	06 41	07 30	15 35	16 01	16 41	17 42
05	259 04·9	58·8	78 09·7	10·0	17 08·3	8·1	56·9	60	05 46	06 36	07 21	15 49	16 19	17 02	18 02
06	274 04·9	S13 59·6	92 38·7	10·0	N17 16·4	8·1	56·9	N 58	05 44	06 31	07 13	16 02	16 34	17 19	18 19
07	289 04·9	14 00·4	107 07·7	9·9	17 24·5	7·9	57·0	56	05 42	06 26	07 06	16 12	16 47	17 33	18 34
T 08	304 04·9	01·2	121 36·6	9·8	17 32·4	7·9	57·0	54	05 40	06 22	07 00	16 22	16 58	17 46	18 46
H 09	319 05·0	·· 02·0	136 05·4	9·8	17 40·3	7·8	57·0	52	05 38	06 18	06 54	16 30	17 08	17 57	18 57
U 10	334 05·0	02·8	150 34·2	9·6	17 48·1	7·6	57·0	50	05 37	06 15	06 49	16 38	17 17	18 07	19 06
R 11	349 05·0	03·7	165 02·8	9·6	17 55·7	7·6	57·1	45	05 33	06 07	06 38	16 54	17 37	18 27	19 27
S 12	4 05·1	S14 04·5	179 31·4	9·5	N18 03·3	7·5	57·1	N 40	05 28	06 00	06 28	17 08	17 52	18 44	19 43
D 13	19 05·1	05·3	193 59·9	9·5	18 10·8	7·4	57·1	35	05 24	05 54	06 21	17 19	18 05	18 58	19 57
A 14	34 05·1	06·1	208 28·4	9·3	18 18·2	7·4	57·1	30	05 21	05 49	06 13	17 29	18 17	19 10	20 09
Y 15	49 05·1	·· 06·9	222 56·7	9·3	18 25·6	7·2	57·2	20	05 12	05 39	06 01	17 46	18 37	19 32	20 30
16	64 05·2	07·7	237 25·0	9·2	18 32·8	7·1	57·2	N 10	05 04	05 29	05 50	18 01	18 54	19 50	20 48
17	79 05·2	08·5	251 53·2	9·2	18 39·9	7·0	57·2	0	04 54	05 19	05 40	18 16	19 10	20 07	21 05
18	94 05·2	S14 09·3	266 21·4	9·1	N18 46·9	6·9	57·2	S 10	04 43	05 08	05 30	18 30	19 26	20 24	21 22
19	109 05·2	10·1	280 49·5	8·9	18 53·8	6·9	57·2	20	04 29	04 56	05 19	18 45	19 44	20 43	21 40
20	124 05·3	10·9	295 17·4	9·0	19 00·7	6·7	57·3	30	04 11	04 41	05 06	19 03	20 04	21 04	22 00
21	139 05·3	·· 11·8	309 45·4	8·8	19 07·4	6·6	57·3	35	03 59	04 31	04 58	19 13	20 16	21 16	22 12
22	154 05·3	12·6	324 13·2	8·8	19 14·0	6·5	57·3	40	03 45	04 21	04 50	19 25	20 29	21 30	22 26
23	169 05·3	13·4	338 41·0	8·7	19 20·5	6·4	57·3	45	03 28	04 08	04 40	19 39	20 45	21 47	22 43
1 00	184 05·4	S14 14·2	353 08·7	8·6	N19 26·9	6·3	57·4	S 50	03 06	03 51	04 27	19 57	21 05	22 08	23 03
01	199 05·4	15·0	7 36·3	8·6	19 33·2	6·2	57·4	52	02 54	03 44	04 22	20 05	21 15	22 19	23 13
02	214 05·4	15·8	22 03·9	8·5	19 39·4	6·1	57·4	54	02 41	03 35	04 15	20 14	21 25	22 30	23 23
03	229 05·4	·· 16·6	36 31·4	8·4	19 45·5	6·0	57·4	56	02 26	03 25	04 08	20 24	21 38	22 43	23 36
04	244 05·4	17·4	50 58·8	8·4	19 51·5	5·8	57·4	58	02 07	03 13	04 00	20 36	21 52	22 58	23 50
05	259 05·5	18·2	65 26·2	8·3	19 57·3	5·8	57·5	S 60	01 43	03 00	03 51	20 49	22 08	23 15	24 07
06	274 05·5	S14 19·0	79 53·5	8·2	N20 03·1	5·6	57·5		Sun-	Twilight		Moonset			
07	289 05·5	19·8	94 20·7	8·2	20 08·7	5·5	57·5	Lat.	set	Civil	Naut.	31	1	2	3
08	304 05·5	20·6	108 47·9	8·0	20 14·2	5·5	57·5								
F 09	319 05·5	·· 21·4	123 14·9	8·1	20 19·7	5·3	57·5	°	h m	h m	h m	h m	h m	h m	h m
R 10	334 05·6	22·2	137 42·0	7·9	20 25·0	5·1	57·6	N 72	14 32	15 59	17 21	11 33	□	□	□
I 11	349 05·6	23·0	152 08·9	7·9	20 30·1	5·1	57·6	N 70	14 58	16 12	17 25	10 02	□	□	□
D 12	4 05·6	S14 23·8	166 35·8	7·9	N20 35·2	5·0	57·6	68	15 17	16 22	17 29	09 23	11 20	13 28	14 24
A 13	19 05·6	24·6	181 02·7	7·7	20 40·2	4·8	57·6	66	15 33	16 31	17 32	08 56	10 36	12 05	13 04
Y 14	34 05·6	25·4	195 29·4	7·7	20 45·0	4·7	57·7	64	15 45	16 38	17 35	08 36	10 07	11 27	12 27
15	49 05·7	·· 26·2	209 56·1	7·7	20 49·7	4·6	57·7	62	15 56	16 45	17 38	08 19	09 44	11 01	12 00
16	64 05·7	27·0	224 22·8	7·6	20 54·3	4·4	57·7	60	16 06	16 50	17 40	08 05	09 27	10 40	11 39
17	79 05·7	27·8	238 49·4	7·5	20 58·7	4·4	57·7								
18	94 05·7	S14 28·6	253 15·9	7·5	N21 03·1	4·2	57·7	N 58	16 13	16 56	17 42	07 54	09 12	10 23	11 22
19	109 05·7	29·4	267 42·4	7·4	21 07·3	4·1	57·8	56	16 21	17 00	17 44	07 43	08 59	10 09	11 08
20	124 05·7	30·2	282 08·8	7·3	21 11·4	4·0	57·8	54	16 27	17 04	17 46	07 34	08 48	09 56	10 55
21	139 05·8	·· 31·0	296 35·1	7·4	21 15·4	3·8	57·8	52	16 33	17 08	17 48	07 26	08 38	09 45	10 44
22	154 05·8	31·8	311 01·5	7·2	21 19·2	3·7	57·8	50	16 38	17 12	17 50	07 19	08 29	09 36	10 35
23	169 05·8	32·6	325 27·7	7·2	21 22·9	3·6	57·8	45	16 49	17 20	17 54	07 04	08 11	09 15	10 14
2 00	184 05·8	S14 33·4	339 53·9	7·2	N21 26·5	3·5	57·9	N 40	16 58	17 27	17 58	06 51	07 56	08 59	09 57
01	199 05·8	34·2	354 20·1	7·1	21 30·0	3·3	57·9	35	17 06	17 33	18 02	06 41	07 43	08 45	09 43
02	214 05·8	35·0	8 46·2	7·0	21 33·3	3·2	57·9	30	17 14	17 38	18 06	06 31	07 32	08 33	09 31
03	229 05·8	·· 35·8	23 12·2	7·0	21 36·5	3·1	57·9	20	17 26	17 49	18 15	06 15	07 13	08 12	09 10
04	244 05·9	36·6	37 38·2	7·0	21 39·6	2·9	57·9	N 10	17 37	17 59	18 23	06 02	06 57	07 54	08 52
05	259 05·9	37·4	52 04·2	6·9	21 42·5	2·8	57·9	0	17 47	18 09	18 33	05 49	06 41	07 37	08 35
06	274 05·9	S14 38·2	66 30·1	6·8	N21 45·3	2·7	58·0	S 10	17 58	18 20	18 45	05 36	06 26	07 20	08 17
S 07	289 05·9	39·0	80 55·9	6·9	21 48·0	2·5	58·0	20	18 09	18 32	18 59	05 22	06 10	07 02	07 59
A 08	304 05·9	39·8	95 21·8	6·7	21 50·5	2·4	58·0	30	18 22	18 47	19 17	05 06	05 51	06 42	07 38
T 09	319 05·9	·· 40·6	109 47·5	6·8	21 52·9	2·3	58·0	35	18 30	18 57	19 29	04 57	05 40	06 29	07 25
U 10	334 05·9	41·4	124 13·3	6·7	21 55·2	2·1	58·0	40	18 39	19 07	19 43	04 46	05 27	06 15	07 11
R 11	349 05·9	42·2	138 39·0	6·6	21 57·3	2·0	58·1	45	18 48	19 21	20 00	04 34	05 13	05 59	06 54
R 12	4 06·0	S14 43·0	153 04·6	6·6	N21 59·3	1·9	58·1	S 50	19 01	19 37	20 23	04 19	04 55	05 39	06 33
D 13	19 06·0	43·7	167 30·3	6·6	22 01·2	1·7	58·1	52	19 07	19 45	20 35	04 12	04 46	05 29	06 23
A 14	34 06·0	44·5	181 55·9	6·5	22 02·9	1·6	58·1	54	19 13	19 54	20 48	04 05	04 37	05 18	06 12
Y 15	49 06·0	·· 45·3	196 21·4	6·5	22 04·5	1·5	58·1	56	19 20	20 04	21 04	03 56	04 26	05 06	05 59
16	64 06·0	46·1	210 46·9	6·5	22 06·0	1·3	58·1	58	19 28	20 16	21 24	03 47	04 14	04 52	05 44
17	79 06·0	46·9	225 12·4	6·5	22 07·3	1·2	58·1	S 60	19 38	20 30	21 49	03 36	04 00	04 35	05 26
18	94 06·0	S14 47·7	239 37·9	6·4	N22 08·5	1·0	58·2		SUN			MOON			
19	109 06·0	48·5	254 03·3	6·4	22 09·5	0·9	58·2	Day	Eqn. of Time		Mer.	Mer. Pass.		Age	Phase
20	124 06·0	49·3	268 28·7	6·3	22 10·4	0·8	58·2		00ʰ	12ʰ	Pass.	Upper	Lower		
21	139 06·0	·· 50·1	282 54·1	6·4	22 11·2	0·6	58·2		m s	m s	h m	h m	h m	d	
22	154 06·0	50·8	297 19·5	6·3	22 11·8	0·5	58·2	31	16 19	16 20	11 44	24 28	12 02	16	●
23	169 06·0	51·6	311 44·8	6·3	22 12·3	0·3	58·3	1	16 21	16 22	11 44	00 28	12 56	17	
	S.D. 16·1	d 0·8	S.D. 15·6		15·7		15·8	2	16 23	16 24	11 44	01 14	13 52	18	

309

8 s	SUN PLANETS	ARIES	MOON	v or d	Corrⁿ	v or d	Corrⁿ	v or d	Corrⁿ
00	2 00·0	2 00·3	1 54·5	0·0	0·0	6·0	0·9	12·0	1·7
01	2 00·3	2 00·6	1 54·8	0·1	0·0	6·1	0·9	12·1	1·7
02	2 00·5	2 00·8	1 55·0	0·2	0·0	6·2	0·9	12·2	1·7
03	2 00·8	2 01·1	1 55·2	0·3	0·0	6·3	0·9	12·3	1·7
04	2 01·0	2 01·3	1 55·5	0·4	0·1	6·4	0·9	12·4	1·8
05	2 01·3	2 01·6	1 55·7	0·5	0·1	6·5	0·9	12·5	1·8
06	2 01·5	2 01·8	1 56·0	0·6	0·1	6·6	0·9	12·6	1·8
07	2 01·8	2 02·1	1 56·2	0·7	0·1	6·7	0·9	12·7	1·8
08	2 02·0	2 02·3	1 56·4	0·8	0·1	6·8	1·0	12·8	1·8
09	2 02·3	2 02·6	1 56·7	0·9	0·1	6·9	1·0	12·9	1·8
10	2 02·5	2 02·8	1 56·9	1·0	0·1	7·0	1·0	13·0	1·8
11	2 02·8	2 03·1	1 57·2	1·1	0·2	7·1	1·0	13·1	1·9
12	2 03·0	2 03·3	1 57·4	1·2	0·2	7·2	1·0	13·2	1·9
13	2 03·3	2 03·6	1 57·6	1·3	0·2	7·3	1·0	13·3	1·9
14	2 03·5	2 03·8	1 57·9	1·4	0·2	7·4	1·0	13·4	1·9
15	2 03·8	2 04·1	1 58·1	1·5	0·2	7·5	1·1	13·5	1·9
16	2 04·0	2 04·3	1 58·4	1·6	0·2	7·6	1·1	13·6	1·9
17	2 04·3	2 04·6	1 58·6	1·7	0·2	7·7	1·1	13·7	1·9
18	2 04·5	2 04·8	1 58·8	1·8	0·3	7·8	1·1	13·8	2·0
19	2 04·8	2 05·1	1 59·1	1·9	0·3	7·9	1·1	13·9	2·0
20	2 05·0	2 05·3	1 59·3	2·0	0·3	8·0	1·1	14·0	2·0
21	2 05·3	2 05·6	1 59·5	2·1	0·3	8·1	1·1	14·1	2·0
22	2 05·5	2 05·8	1 59·8	2·2	0·3	8·2	1·2	14·2	2·0
23	2 05·8	2 06·1	2 00·0	2·3	0·3	8·3	1·2	14·3	2·0
24	2 06·0	2 06·3	2 00·3	2·4	0·3	8·4	1·2	14·4	2·0
25	2 06·3	2 06·6	2 00·5	2·5	0·4	8·5	1·2	14·5	2·1
26	2 06·5	2 06·8	2 00·7	2·6	0·4	8·6	1·2	14·6	2·1
27	2 06·8	2 07·1	2 01·0	2·7	0·4	8·7	1·2	14·7	2·1
28	2 07·0	2 07·3	2 01·2	2·8	0·4	8·8	1·2	14·8	2·1
29	2 07·3	2 07·6	2 01·5	2·9	0·4	8·9	1·3	14·9	2·1
30	2 07·5	2 07·8	2 01·7	3·0	0·4	9·0	1·3	15·0	2·1
31	2 07·8	2 08·1	2 01·9	3·1	0·4	9·1	1·3	15·1	2·1
32	2 08·0	2 08·4	2 02·2	3·2	0·5	9·2	1·3	15·2	2·2
33	2 08·3	2 08·6	2 02·4	3·3	0·5	9·3	1·3	15·3	2·2
34	2 08·5	2 08·9	2 02·6	3·4	0·5	9·4	1·3	15·4	2·2
35	2 08·8	2 09·1	2 02·9	3·5	0·5	9·5	1·3	15·5	2·2
36	2 09·0	2 09·4	2 03·1	3·6	0·5	9·6	1·4	15·6	2·2
37	2 09·3	2 09·6	2 03·4	3·7	0·5	9·7	1·4	15·7	2·2
38	2 09·5	2 09·9	2 03·6	3·8	0·5	9·8	1·4	15·8	2·2
39	2 09·8	2 10·1	2 03·8	3·9	0·6	9·9	1·4	15·9	2·3
40	2 10·0	2 10·4	2 04·1	4·0	0·6	10·0	1·4	16·0	2·3
41	2 10·3	2 10·6	2 04·3	4·1	0·6	10·1	1·4	16·1	2·3
42	2 10·5	2 10·9	2 04·6	4·2	0·6	10·2	1·4	16·2	2·3
43	2 10·8	2 11·1	2 04·8	4·3	0·6	10·3	1·5	16·3	2·3
44	2 11·0	2 11·4	2 05·0	4·4	0·6	10·4	1·5	16·4	2·3
45	2 11·3	2 11·6	2 05·3	4·5	0·6	10·5	1·5	16·5	2·3
46	2 11·5	2 11·9	2 05·5	4·6	0·7	10·6	1·5	16·6	2·4
47	2 11·8	2 12·1	2 05·7	4·7	0·7	10·7	1·5	16·7	2·4
48	2 12·0	2 12·4	2 06·0	4·8	0·7	10·8	1·5	16·8	2·4
49	2 12·3	2 12·6	2 06·2	4·9	0·7	10·9	1·5	16·9	2·4
50	2 12·5	2 12·9	2 06·5	5·0	0·7	11·0	1·6	17·0	2·4
51	2 12·8	2 13·1	2 06·7	5·1	0·7	11·1	1·6	17·1	2·4
52	2 13·0	2 13·4	2 06·9	5·2	0·7	11·2	1·6	17·2	2·4
53	2 13·3	2 13·6	2 07·2	5·3	0·8	11·3	1·6	17·3	2·5
54	2 13·5	2 13·9	2 07·4	5·4	0·8	11·4	1·6	17·4	2·5
55	2 13·8	2 14·1	2 07·7	5·5	0·8	11·5	1·6	17·5	2·5
56	2 14·0	2 14·4	2 07·9	5·6	0·8	11·6	1·6	17·6	2·5
57	2 14·3	2 14·6	2 08·1	5·7	0·8	11·7	1·7	17·7	2·5
58	2 14·5	2 14·9	2 08·4	5·8	0·8	11·8	1·7	17·8	2·5
59	2 14·8	2 15·1	2 08·6	5·9	0·8	11·9	1·7	17·9	2·5
60	2 15·0	2 15·4	2 08·9	6·0	0·9	12·0	1·7	18·0	2·6

9 s	SUN PLANETS	ARIES	MOON	v or d	Corrⁿ	v or d	Corrⁿ	v or d	Corrⁿ
00	2 15·0	2 15·4	2 08·9	0·0	0·0	6·0	1·0	12·0	1·9
01	2 15·3	2 15·6	2 09·1	0·1	0·0	6·1	1·0	12·1	1·9
02	2 15·5	2 15·9	2 09·3	0·2	0·0	6·2	1·0	12·2	1·9
03	2 15·8	2 16·1	2 09·6	0·3	0·0	6·3	1·0	12·3	1·9
04	2 16·0	2 16·4	2 09·8	0·4	0·1	6·4	1·0	12·4	2·0
05	2 16·3	2 16·6	2 10·0	0·5	0·1	6·5	1·0	12·5	2·0
06	2 16·5	2 16·9	2 10·3	0·6	0·1	6·6	1·0	12·6	2·0
07	2 16·8	2 17·1	2 10·5	0·7	0·1	6·7	1·1	12·7	2·0
08	2 17·0	2 17·4	2 10·8	0·8	0·1	6·8	1·1	12·8	2·0
09	2 17·3	2 17·6	2 11·0	0·9	0·1	6·9	1·1	12·9	2·0
10	2 17·5	2 17·9	2 11·2	1·0	0·2	7·0	1·1	13·0	2·1
11	2 17·8	2 18·1	2 11·5	1·1	0·2	7·1	1·1	13·1	2·1
12	2 18·0	2 18·4	2 11·7	1·2	0·2	7·2	1·1	13·2	2·1
13	2 18·3	2 18·6	2 12·0	1·3	0·2	7·3	1·2	13·3	2·1
14	2 18·5	2 18·9	2 12·2	1·4	0·2	7·4	1·2	13·4	2·1
15	2 18·8	2 19·1	2 12·4	1·5	0·2	7·5	1·2	13·5	2·1
16	2 19·0	2 19·4	2 12·7	1·6	0·3	7·6	1·2	13·6	2·2
17	2 19·3	2 19·6	2 12·9	1·7	0·3	7·7	1·2	13·7	2·2
18	2 19·5	2 19·9	2 13·1	1·8	0·3	7·8	1·2	13·8	2·2
19	2 19·8	2 20·1	2 13·4	1·9	0·3	7·9	1·3	13·9	2·2
20	2 20·0	2 20·4	2 13·6	2·0	0·3	8·0	1·3	14·0	2·2
21	2 20·3	2 20·6	2 13·9	2·1	0·3	8·1	1·3	14·1	2·2
22	2 20·5	2 20·9	2 14·1	2·2	0·3	8·2	1·3	14·2	2·2
23	2 20·8	2 21·1	2 14·3	2·3	0·4	8·3	1·3	14·3	2·3
24	2 21·0	2 21·4	2 14·6	2·4	0·4	8·4	1·3	14·4	2·3
25	2 21·3	2 21·6	2 14·8	2·5	0·4	8·5	1·3	14·5	2·3
26	2 21·5	2 21·9	2 15·1	2·6	0·4	8·6	1·4	14·6	2·3
27	2 21·8	2 22·1	2 15·3	2·7	0·4	8·7	1·4	14·7	2·3
28	2 22·0	2 22·4	2 15·5	2·8	0·4	8·8	1·4	14·8	2·3
29	2 22·3	2 22·6	2 15·8	2·9	0·5	8·9	1·4	14·9	2·4
30	2 22·5	2 22·9	2 16·0	3·0	0·5	9·0	1·4	15·0	2·4
31	2 22·8	2 23·1	2 16·2	3·1	0·5	9·1	1·4	15·1	2·4
32	2 23·0	2 23·4	2 16·5	3·2	0·5	9·2	1·5	15·2	2·4
33	2 23·3	2 23·6	2 16·7	3·3	0·5	9·3	1·5	15·3	2·4
34	2 23·5	2 23·9	2 17·0	3·4	0·5	9·4	1·5	15·4	2·4
35	2 23·8	2 24·1	2 17·2	3·5	0·6	9·5	1·5	15·5	2·5
36	2 24·0	2 24·4	2 17·4	3·6	0·6	9·6	1·5	15·6	2·5
37	2 24·3	2 24·6	2 17·7	3·7	0·6	9·7	1·5	15·7	2·5
38	2 24·5	2 24·9	2 17·9	3·8	0·6	9·8	1·6	15·8	2·5
39	2 24·8	2 25·1	2 18·2	3·9	0·6	9·9	1·6	15·9	2·5
40	2 25·0	2 25·4	2 18·4	4·0	0·6	10·0	1·6	16·0	2·5
41	2 25·3	2 25·6	2 18·6	4·1	0·6	10·1	1·6	16·1	2·5
42	2 25·5	2 25·9	2 18·9	4·2	0·7	10·2	1·6	16·2	2·6
43	2 25·8	2 26·1	2 19·1	4·3	0·7	10·3	1·6	16·3	2·6
44	2 26·0	2 26·4	2 19·3	4·4	0·7	10·4	1·6	16·4	2·6
45	2 26·3	2 26·7	2 19·6	4·5	0·7	10·5	1·7	16·5	2·6
46	2 26·5	2 26·9	2 19·8	4·6	0·7	10·6	1·7	16·6	2·6
47	2 26·8	2 27·2	2 20·1	4·7	0·7	10·7	1·7	16·7	2·6
48	2 27·0	2 27·4	2 20·3	4·8	0·8	10·8	1·7	16·8	2·7
49	2 27·3	2 27·7	2 20·5	4·9	0·8	10·9	1·7	16·9	2·7
50	2 27·5	2 27·9	2 20·8	5·0	0·8	11·0	1·7	17·0	2·7
51	2 27·8	2 28·2	2 21·0	5·1	0·8	11·1	1·8	17·1	2·7
52	2 28·0	2 28·4	2 21·3	5·2	0·8	11·2	1·8	17·2	2·7
53	2 28·3	2 28·7	2 21·5	5·3	0·8	11·3	1·8	17·3	2·7
54	2 28·5	2 28·9	2 21·7	5·4	0·9	11·4	1·8	17·4	2·8
55	2 28·8	2 29·2	2 22·0	5·5	0·9	11·5	1·8	17·5	2·8
56	2 29·0	2 29·4	2 22·2	5·6	0·9	11·6	1·8	17·6	2·8
57	2 29·3	2 29·7	2 22·5	5·7	0·9	11·7	1·9	17·7	2·8
58	2 29·5	2 29·9	2 22·7	5·8	0·9	11·8	1·9	17·8	2·8
59	2 29·8	2 30·2	2 22·9	5·9	0·9	11·9	1·9	17·9	2·8
60	2 30·0	2 30·4	2 23·2	6·0	1·0	12·0	1·9	18·0	2·9

14ᵐ

s	SUN PLANETS	ARIES	MOON	v or Corrⁿ d	v or Corrⁿ d	v or Corrⁿ d
	° ′	° ′	° ′	′ ′	′ ′	′ ′
00	3 30·0	3 30·6	3 20·4	0·0 0·0	6·0 1·5	12·0 2·9
01	3 30·3	3 30·8	3 20·7	0·1 0·0	6·1 1·5	12·1 2·9
02	3 30·5	3 31·1	3 20·9	0·2 0·0	6·2 1·5	12·2 2·9
03	3 30·8	3 31·3	3 21·1	0·3 0·1	6·3 1·5	12·3 3·0
04	3 31·0	3 31·6	3 21·4	0·4 0·1	6·4 1·5	12·4 3·0
05	3 31·3	3 31·8	3 21·6	0·5 0·1	6·5 1·6	12·5 3·0
06	3 31·5	3 32·1	3 21·9	0·6 0·1	6·6 1·6	12·6 3·0
07	3 31·8	3 32·3	3 22·1	0·7 0·2	6·7 1·6	12·7 3·1
08	3 32·0	3 32·6	3 22·3	0·8 0·2	6·8 1·6	12·8 3·1
09	3 32·3	3 32·8	3 22·6	0·9 0·2	6·9 1·7	12·9 3·1
10	3 32·5	3 33·1	3 22·8	1·0 0·2	7·0 1·7	13·0 3·1
11	3 32·8	3 33·3	3 23·1	1·1 0·3	7·1 1·7	13·1 3·2
12	3 33·0	3 33·6	3 23·3	1·2 0·3	7·2 1·7	13·2 3·2
13	3 33·3	3 33·8	3 23·5	1·3 0·3	7·3 1·8	13·3 3·2
14	3 33·5	3 34·1	3 23·8	1·4 0·3	7·4 1·8	13·4 3·2
15	3 33·8	3 34·3	3 24·0	1·5 0·4	7·5 1·8	13·5 3·3
16	3 34·0	3 34·6	3 24·3	1·6 0·4	7·6 1·8	13·6 3·3
17	3 34·3	3 34·8	3 24·5	1·7 0·4	7·7 1·9	13·7 3·3
18	3 34·5	3 35·1	3 24·7	1·8 0·4	7·8 1·9	13·8 3·3
19	3 34·8	3 35·3	3 25·0	1·9 0·5	7·9 1·9	13·9 3·4
20	3 35·0	3 35·6	3 25·2	2·0 0·5	8·0 1·9	14·0 3·4
21	3 35·3	3 35·8	3 25·4	2·1 0·5	8·1 2·0	14·1 3·4
22	3 35·5	3 36·1	3 25·7	2·2 0·5	8·2 2·0	14·2 3·4
23	3 35·8	3 36·3	3 25·9	2·3 0·6	8·3 2·0	14·3 3·5
24	3 36·0	3 36·6	3 26·2	2·4 0·6	8·4 2·0	14·4 3·5
25	3 36·3	3 36·8	3 26·4	2·5 0·6	8·5 2·1	14·5 3·5
26	3 36·5	3 37·1	3 26·6	2·6 0·6	8·6 2·1	14·6 3·5
27	3 36·8	3 37·3	3 26·9	2·7 0·7	8·7 2·1	14·7 3·6
28	3 37·0	3 37·6	3 27·1	2·8 0·7	8·8 2·1	14·8 3·6
29	3 37·3	3 37·8	3 27·4	2·9 0·7	8·9 2·2	14·9 3·6
30	3 37·5	3 38·1	3 27·6	3·0 0·7	9·0 2·2	15·0 3·6
31	3 37·8	3 38·3	3 27·8	3·1 0·7	9·1 2·2	15·1 3·6
32	3 38·0	3 38·6	3 28·1	3·2 0·8	9·2 2·2	15·2 3·7
33	3 38·3	3 38·8	3 28·3	3·3 0·8	9·3 2·2	15·3 3·7
34	3 38·5	3 39·1	3 28·5	3·4 0·8	9·4 2·3	15·4 3·7
35	3 38·8	3 39·3	3 28·8	3·5 0·8	9·5 2·3	15·5 3·7
36	3 39·0	3 39·6	3 29·0	3·6 0·9	9·6 2·3	15·6 3·8
37	3 39·3	3 39·8	3 29·3	3·7 0·9	9·7 2·3	15·7 3·8
38	3 39·5	3 40·1	3 29·5	3·8 0·9	9·8 2·4	15·8 3·8
39	3 39·8	3 40·4	3 29·7	3·9 0·9	9·9 2·4	15·9 3·8
40	3 40·0	3 40·6	3 30·0	4·0 1·0	10·0 2·4	16·0 3·9
41	3 40·3	3 40·9	3 30·2	4·1 1·0	10·1 2·4	16·1 3·9
42	3 40·5	3 41·1	3 30·5	4·2 1·0	10·2 2·5	16·2 3·9
43	3 40·8	3 41·4	3 30·7	4·3 1·0	10·3 2·5	16·3 3·9
44	3 41·0	3 41·6	3 30·9	4·4 1·1	10·4 2·5	16·4 4·0
45	3 41·3	3 41·9	3 31·2	4·5 1·1	10·5 2·5	16·5 4·0
46	3 41·5	3 42·1	3 31·4	4·6 1·1	10·6 2·6	16·6 4·0
47	3 41·8	3 42·4	3 31·6	4·7 1·1	10·7 2·6	16·7 4·0
48	3 42·0	3 42·6	3 31·9	4·8 1·2	10·8 2·6	16·8 4·1
49	3 42·3	3 42·9	3 32·1	4·9 1·2	10·9 2·6	16·9 4·1
50	3 42·5	3 43·1	3 32·4	5·0 1·2	11·0 2·7	17·0 4·1
51	3 42·8	3 43·4	3 32·6	5·1 1·2	11·1 2·7	17·1 4·1
52	3 43·0	3 43·6	3 32·9	5·2 1·3	11·2 2·7	17·2 4·2
53	3 43·3	3 43·9	3 33·1	5·3 1·3	11·3 2·7	17·3 4·2
54	3 43·5	3 44·1	3 33·3	5·4 1·3	11·4 2·9	17·4 4·2
55	3 43·8	3 44·4	3 33·6	5·5 1·3	11·5 2·8	17·5 4·2
56	3 44·0	3 44·6	3 33·8	5·6 1·4	11·6 2·8	17·6 4·3
57	3 44·3	3 44·9	3 34·0	5·7 1·4	11·7 2·8	17·7 4·3
58	3 44·5	3 45·1	3 34·3	5·8 1·4	11·8 2·9	17·8 4·3
59	3 44·8	3 45·4	3 34·5	5·9 1·4	11·9 2·9	17·9 4·3
60	3 45·0	3 45·6	3 34·8	6·0 1·5	12·0 2·9	18·0 4·4

15ᵐ

s	SUN PLANETS	ARIES	MOON	v or Corrⁿ d	v or Corrⁿ d	v or Corrⁿ d
	° ′	° ′	° ′	′ ′	′ ′	′ ′
00	3 45·0	3 45·6	3 34·8	0·0 0·0	6·0 1·6	12·0 3·1
01	3 45·3	3 45·9	3 35·0	0·1 0·0	6·1 1·6	12·1 3·1
02	3 45·5	3 46·1	3 35·2	0·2 0·1	6·2 1·6	12·2 3·2
03	3 45·8	3 46·4	3 35·5	0·3 0·1	6·3 1·6	12·3 3·2
04	3 46·0	3 46·6	3 35·7	0·4 0·1	6·4 1·7	12·4 3·2
05	3 46·3	3 46·9	3 35·9	0·5 0·1	6·5 1·7	12·5 3·2
06	3 46·5	3 47·1	3 36·2	0·6 0·2	6·6 1·7	12·6 3·3
07	3 46·8	3 47·4	3 36·4	0·7 0·2	6·7 1·7	12·7 3·3
08	3 47·0	3 47·6	3 36·7	0·8 0·2	6·8 1·8	12·8 3·3
09	3 47·3	3 47·9	3 36·9	0·9 0·2	6·9 1·8	12·9 3·3
10	3 47·5	3 48·1	3 37·1	1·0 0·3	7·0 1·8	13·0 3·4
11	3 47·8	3 48·4	3 37·4	1·1 0·3	7·1 1·8	13·1 3·4
12	3 48·0	3 48·6	3 37·6	1·2 0·3	7·2 1·9	13·2 3·4
13	3 48·3	3 48·9	3 37·9	1·3 0·3	7·3 1·9	13·3 3·4
14	3 48·5	3 49·1	3 38·1	1·4 0·4	7·4 1·9	13·4 3·5
15	3 48·8	3 49·4	3 38·3	1·5 0·4	7·5 1·9	13·5 3·5
16	3 49·0	3 49·6	3 38·6	1·6 0·4	7·6 2·0	13·6 3·5
17	3 49·3	3 49·9	3 38·8	1·7 0·4	7·7 2·0	13·7 3·5
18	3 49·5	3 50·1	3 39·0	1·8 0·5	7·8 2·0	13·8 3·6
19	3 49·8	3 50·4	3 39·3	1·9 0·5	7·9 2·0	13·9 3·6
20	3 50·0	3 50·6	3 39·5	2·0 0·5	8·0 2·1	14·0 3·6
21	3 50·3	3 50·9	3 39·8	2·1 0·5	8·1 2·1	14·1 3·6
22	3 50·5	3 51·1	3 40·0	2·2 0·6	8·2 2·1	14·2 3·7
23	3 50·8	3 51·4	3 40·2	2·3 0·6	8·3 2·1	14·3 3·7
24	3 51·0	3 51·6	3 40·5	2·4 0·6	8·4 2·2	14·4 3·7
25	3 51·3	3 51·9	3 40·7	2·5 0·6	8·5 2·2	14·5 3·7
26	3 51·5	3 52·1	3 41·0	2·6 0·7	8·6 2·2	14·6 3·8
27	3 51·8	3 52·4	3 41·2	2·7 0·7	8·7 2·2	14·7 3·8
28	3 52·0	3 52·6	3 41·4	2·8 0·7	8·8 2·3	14·8 3·8
29	3 52·3	3 52·9	3 41·7	2·9 0·7	8·9 2·3	14·9 3·8
30	3 52·5	3 53·1	3 41·9	3·0 0·8	9·0 2·3	15·0 3·9
31	3 52·8	3 53·4	3 42·1	3·1 0·8	9·1 2·4	15·1 3·9
32	3 53·0	3 53·6	3 42·4	3·2 0·8	9·2 2·4	15·2 3·9
33	3 53·3	3 53·9	3 42·6	3·3 0·9	9·3 2·4	15·3 3·9
34	3 53·5	3 54·1	3 42·9	3·4 0·9	9·4 2·4	15·4 4·0
35	3 53·8	3 54·4	3 43·1	3·5 0·9	9·5 2·5	15·5 4·0
36	3 54·0	3 54·6	3 43·3	3·6 0·9	9·6 2·5	15·6 4·0
37	3 54·3	3 54·9	3 43·6	3·7 1·0	9·7 2·5	15·7 4·1
38	3 54·5	3 55·1	3 43·8	3·8 1·0	9·8 2·5	15·8 4·1
39	3 54·8	3 55·4	3 44·1	3·9 1·0	9·9 2·6	15·9 4·1
40	3 55·0	3 55·6	3 44·3	4·0 1·0	10·0 2·6	16·0 4·1
41	3 55·3	3 55·9	3 44·5	4·1 1·1	10·1 2·6	16·1 4·2
42	3 55·5	3 56·1	3 44·8	4·2 1·1	10·2 2·6	16·2 4·2
43	3 55·8	3 56·4	3 45·0	4·3 1·1	10·3 2·7	16·3 4·2
44	3 56·0	3 56·6	3 45·2	4·4 1·1	10·4 2·7	16·4 4·2
45	3 56·3	3 56·9	3 45·5	4·5 1·2	10·5 2·7	16·5 4·3
46	3 56·5	3 57·1	3 45·7	4·6 1·2	10·6 2·7	16·6 4·3
47	3 56·8	3 57·4	3 46·0	4·7 1·2	10·7 2·8	16·7 4·3
48	3 57·0	3 57·6	3 46·2	4·8 1·2	10·8 2·8	16·8 4·3
49	3 57·3	3 57·9	3 46·4	4·9 1·3	10·9 2·8	16·9 4·4
50	3 57·5	3 58·2	3 46·7	5·0 1·3	11·0 2·8	17·0 4·4
51	3 57·8	3 58·4	3 46·9	5·1 1·3	11·1 2·9	17·1 4·4
52	3 58·0	3 58·7	3 47·2	5·2 1·3	11·2 2·9	17·2 4·4
53	3 58·3	3 58·9	3 47·4	5·3 1·4	11·3 2·9	17·3 4·5
54	3 58·5	3 59·2	3 47·6	5·4 1·4	11·4 2·9	17·4 4·5
55	3 58·8	3 59·4	3 47·9	5·5 1·4	11·5 3·0	17·5 4·5
56	3 59·0	3 59·7	3 48·1	5·6 1·4	11·6 3·0	17·6 4·5
57	3 59·3	3 59·9	3 48·4	5·7 1·5	11·7 3·0	17·7 4·6
58	3 59·5	4 00·2	3 48·6	5·8 1·5	11·8 3·0	17·8 4·6
59	3 59·8	4 00·4	3 48·8	5·9 1·5	11·9 3·1	17·9 4·6
60	4 00·0	4 00·7	3 49·1	6·0 1·6	12·0 3·1	18·0 4·7

20	SUN PLANETS	ARIES	MOON	v or d Corrⁿ	v or d Corrⁿ	v or d Corrⁿ
s	° ′	° ′	° ′	′ ′	′ ′	′ ′
00	5 00·0	5 00·8	4 46·3	0·0 0·0	6·0 2·1	12·0 4·1
01	5 00·3	5 01·1	4 46·6	0·1 0·0	6·1 2·1	12·1 4·1
02	5 00·5	5 01·3	4 46·8	0·2 0·1	6·2 2·1	12·2 4·2
03	5 00·8	5 01·6	4 47·0	0·3 0·1	6·3 2·2	12·3 4·2
04	5 01·0	5 01·8	4 47·3	0·4 0·1	6·4 2·2	12·4 4·2
05	5 01·3	5 02·1	4 47·5	0·5 0·2	6·5 2·2	12·5 4·3
06	5 01·5	5 02·3	4 47·8	0·6 0·2	6·6 2·3	12·6 4·3
07	5 01·8	5 02·6	4 48·0	0·7 0·2	6·7 2·3	12·7 4·3
08	5 02·0	5 02·8	4 48·2	0·8 0·3	6·8 2·3	12·8 4·4
09	5 02·3	5 03·1	4 48·5	0·9 0·3	6·9 2·4	12·9 4·4
10	5 02·5	5 03·3	4 48·7	1·0 0·3	7·0 2·4	13·0 4·4
11	5 02·8	5 03·6	4 49·0	1·1 0·4	7·1 2·4	13·1 4·5
12	5 03·0	5 03·8	4 49·2	1·2 0·4	7·2 2·5	13·2 4·5
13	5 03·3	5 04·1	4 49·4	1·3 0·4	7·3 2·5	13·3 4·5
14	5 03·5	5 04·3	4 49·7	1·4 0·5	7·4 2·5	13·4 4·6
15	5 03·8	5 04·6	4 49·9	1·5 0·5	7·5 2·6	13·5 4·6
16	5 04·0	5 04·8	4 50·2	1·6 0·5	7·6 2·6	13·6 4·6
17	5 04·3	5 05·1	4 50·4	1·7 0·6	7·7 2·6	13·7 4·7
18	5 04·5	5 05·3	4 50·6	1·8 0·6	7·8 2·7	13·8 4·7
19	5 04·8	5 05·6	4 50·9	1·9 0·6	7·9 2·7	13·9 4·7
20	5 05·0	5 05·8	4 51·1	2·0 0·7	8·0 2·7	14·0 4·8
21	5 05·3	5 06·1	4 51·3	2·1 0·7	8·1 2·8	14·1 4·8
22	5 05·5	5 06·3	4 51·6	2·2 0·8	8·2 2·8	14·2 4·9
23	5 05·8	5 06·6	4 51·8	2·3 0·8	8·3 2·8	14·3 4·9
24	5 06·0	5 06·8	4 52·1	2·4 0·8	8·4 2·9	14·4 4·9
25	5 06·3	5 07·1	4 52·3	2·5 0·9	8·5 2·9	14·5 5·0
26	5 06·5	5 07·3	4 52·5	2·6 0·9	8·6 2·9	14·6 5·0
27	5 06·8	5 07·6	4 52·8	2·7 0·9	8·7 3·0	14·7 5·0
28	5 07·0	5 07·8	4 53·0	2·8 1·0	8·8 3·0	14·8 5·1
29	5 07·3	5 08·1	4 53·3	2·9 1·0	8·9 3·0	14·9 5·1
30	5 07·5	5 08·3	4 53·5	3·0 1·0	9·0 3·1	15·0 5·1
31	5 07·8	5 08·6	4 53·7	3·1 1·1	9·1 3·1	15·1 5·2
32	5 08·0	5 08·8	4 54·0	3·2 1·1	9·2 3·1	15·2 5·2
33	5 08·3	5 09·1	4 54·2	3·3 1·1	9·3 3·2	15·3 5·2
34	5 08·5	5 09·3	4 54·4	3·4 1·2	9·4 3·2	15·4 5·3
35	5 08·8	5 09·6	4 54·7	3·5 1·2	9·5 3·2	15·5 5·3
36	5 09·0	5 09·8	4 54·9	3·6 1·2	9·6 3·3	15·6 5·3
37	5 09·3	5 10·1	4 55·2	3·7 1·3	9·7 3·3	15·7 5·4
38	5 09·5	5 10·3	4 55·4	3·8 1·3	9·8 3·3	15·8 5·4
39	5 09·8	5 10·6	4 55·6	3·9 1·3	9·9 3·4	15·9 5·4
40	5 10·0	5 10·8	4 55·9	4·0 1·4	10·0 3·4	16·0 5·5
41	5 10·3	5 11·1	4 56·1	4·1 1·4	10·1 3·5	16·1 5·5
42	5 10·5	5 11·4	4 56·4	4·2 1·4	10·2 3·5	16·2 5·5
43	5 10·8	5 11·6	4 56·6	4·3 1·5	10·3 3·5	16·3 5·6
44	5 11·0	5 11·9	4 56·8	4·4 1·5	10·4 3·6	16·4 5·6
45	5 11·3	5 12·1	4 57·1	4·5 1·5	10·5 3·6	16·5 5·6
46	5 11·5	5 12·4	4 57·3	4·6 1·6	10·6 3·6	16·6 5·7
47	5 11·8	5 12·6	4 57·5	4·7 1·6	10·7 3·7	16·7 5·7
48	5 12·0	5 12·9	4 57·8	4·8 1·6	10·8 3·7	16·8 5·7
49	5 12·3	5 13·1	4 58·0	4·9 1·7	10·9 3·7	16·9 5·8
50	5 12·5	5 13·4	4 58·3	5·0 1·7	11·0 3·8	17·0 5·8
51	5 12·8	5 13·6	4 58·5	5·1 1·7	11·1 3·8	17·1 5·8
52	5 13·0	5 13·9	4 58·7	5·2 1·8	11·2 3·8	17·2 5·9
53	5 13·3	5 14·1	4 59·0	5·3 1·8	11·3 3·9	17·3 5·9
54	5 13·5	5 14·4	4 59·2	5·4 1·8	11·4 3·9	17·4 5·9
55	5 13·8	5 14·6	4 59·5	5·5 1·9	11·5 3·9	17·5 6·0
56	5 14·0	5 14·9	4 59·7	5·6 1·9	11·6 4·0	17·6 6·0
57	5 14·3	5 15·1	5 00·0	5·7 1·9	11·7 4·0	17·7 6·0
58	5 14·5	5 15·4	5 00·2	5·8 2·0	11·8 4·0	17·8 6·1
59	5 14·8	5 15·6	5 00·4	5·9 2·0	11·9 4·1	17·9 6·1
60	5 15·0	5 15·9	5 00·7	6·0 2·1	12·0 4·1	18·0 6·2

21	SUN PLANETS	ARIES	MOON	v or d Corrⁿ	v or d Corrⁿ	v or d Corrⁿ
s	° ′	° ′	° ′	′ ′	′ ′	′ ′
00	5 15·0	5 15·9	5 00·7	0·0 0·0	6·0 2·2	12·0 4·3
01	5 15·3	5 16·1	5 00·9	0·1 0·0	6·1 2·2	12·1 4·3
02	5 15·5	5 16·4	5 01·1	0·2 0·1	6·2 2·2	12·2 4·4
03	5 15·8	5 16·6	5 01·4	0·3 0·1	6·3 2·3	12·3 4·4
04	5 16·0	5 16·9	5 01·6	0·4 0·1	6·4 2·3	12·4 4·4
05	5 16·3	5 17·1	5 01·8	0·5 0·2	6·5 2·3	12·5 4·5
06	5 16·5	5 17·4	5 02·1	0·6 0·2	6·6 2·4	12·6 4·5
07	5 16·8	5 17·6	5 02·3	0·7 0·3	6·7 2·4	12·7 4·6
08	5 17·0	5 17·9	5 02·6	0·8 0·3	6·8 2·4	12·8 4·6
09	5 17·3	5 18·1	5 02·8	0·9 0·3	6·9 2·5	12·9 4·6
10	5 17·5	5 18·4	5 03·0	1·0 0·4	7·0 2·5	13·0 4·7
11	5 17·8	5 18·6	5 03·3	1·1 0·4	7·1 2·5	13·1 4·7
12	5 18·0	5 18·9	5 03·5	1·2 0·4	7·2 2·6	13·2 4·7
13	5 18·3	5 19·1	5 03·8	1·3 0·5	7·3 2·6	13·3 4·8
14	5 18·5	5 19·4	5 04·0	1·4 0·5	7·4 2·7	13·4 4·8
15	5 18·8	5 19·6	5 04·2	1·5 0·5	7·5 2·7	13·5 4·8
16	5 19·0	5 19·9	5 04·5	1·6 0·6	7·6 2·7	13·6 4·9
17	5 19·3	5 20·1	5 04·7	1·7 0·6	7·7 2·8	13·7 4·9
18	5 19·5	5 20·4	5 04·9	1·8 0·6	7·8 2·8	13·8 4·9
19	5 19·8	5 20·6	5 05·2	1·9 0·7	7·9 2·8	13·9 5·0
20	5 20·0	5 20·9	5 05·4	2·0 0·7	8·0 2·9	14·0 5·0
21	5 20·3	5 21·1	5 05·7	2·1 0·7	8·1 2·9	14·1 5·1
22	5 20·5	5 21·4	5 05·9	2·2 0·8	8·2 2·9	14·2 5·1
23	5 20·8	5 21·6	5 06·1	2·3 0·8	8·3 3·0	14·3 5·1
24	5 21·0	5 21·9	5 06·4	2·4 0·9	8·4 3·0	14·4 5·2
25	5 21·3	5 22·1	5 06·6	2·5 0·9	8·5 3·0	14·5 5·2
26	5 21·5	5 22·4	5 06·9	2·6 0·9	8·6 3·1	14·6 5·2
27	5 21·8	5 22·6	5 07·1	2·7 1·0	8·7 3·1	14·7 5·3
28	5 22·0	5 22·9	5 07·3	2·8 1·0	8·8 3·2	14·8 5·3
29	5 22·3	5 23·1	5 07·6	2·9 1·0	8·9 3·2	14·9 5·3
30	5 22·5	5 23·4	5 07·8	3·0 1·1	9·0 3·2	15·0 5·4
31	5 22·8	5 23·6	5 08·0	3·1 1·1	9·1 3·3	15·1 5·4
32	5 23·0	5 23·9	5 08·3	3·2 1·1	9·2 3·3	15·2 5·4
33	5 23·3	5 24·1	5 08·5	3·3 1·2	9·3 3·3	15·3 5·5
34	5 23·5	5 24·4	5 08·8	3·4 1·2	9·4 3·4	15·4 5·5
35	5 23·8	5 24·6	5 09·0	3·5 1·3	9·5 3·4	15·5 5·6
36	5 24·0	5 24·9	5 09·2	3·6 1·3	9·6 3·4	15·6 5·6
37	5 24·3	5 25·1	5 09·5	3·7 1·3	9·7 3·5	15·7 5·6
38	5 24·5	5 25·4	5 09·7	3·8 1·4	9·8 3·5	15·8 5·7
39	5 24·8	5 25·6	5 10·0	3·9 1·4	9·9 3·5	15·9 5·7
40	5 25·0	5 25·9	5 10·2	4·0 1·4	10·0 3·6	16·0 5·7
41	5 25·3	5 26·1	5 10·4	4·1 1·5	10·1 3·6	16·1 5·8
42	5 25·5	5 26·4	5 10·7	4·2 1·5	10·2 3·7	16·2 5·8
43	5 25·8	5 26·6	5 10·9	4·3 1·5	10·3 3·7	16·3 5·8
44	5 26·0	5 26·9	5 11·1	4·4 1·6	10·4 3·7	16·4 5·9
45	5 26·3	5 27·1	5 11·4	4·5 1·6	10·5 3·8	16·5 5·9
46	5 26·5	5 27·4	5 11·6	4·6 1·6	10·6 3·8	16·6 5·9
47	5 26·8	5 27·6	5 11·9	4·7 1·7	10·7 3·8	16·7 6·0
48	5 27·0	5 27·9	5 12·1	4·8 1·7	10·8 3·9	16·8 6·0
49	5 27·3	5 28·1	5 12·3	4·9 1·8	10·9 3·9	16·9 6·1
50	5 27·5	5 28·4	5 12·6	5·0 1·8	11·0 3·9	17·0 6·1
51	5 27·8	5 28·6	5 12·8	5·1 1·8	11·1 4·0	17·1 6·1
52	5 28·0	5 28·9	5 13·1	5·2 1·9	11·2 4·0	17·2 6·2
53	5 28·3	5 29·1	5 13·3	5·3 1·9	11·3 4·0	17·3 6·2
54	5 28·5	5 29·4	5 13·5	5·4 1·9	11·4 4·1	17·4 6·2
55	5 28·8	5 29·7	5 13·8	5·5 2·0	11·5 4·1	17·5 6·3
56	5 29·0	5 29·9	5 14·0	5·6 2·0	11·6 4·2	17·6 6·3
57	5 29·3	5 30·2	5 14·3	5·7 2·0	11·7 4·2	17·7 6·3
58	5 29·5	5 30·4	5 14·5	5·8 2·1	11·8 4·2	17·8 6·4
59	5 29·8	5 30·7	5 14·7	5·9 2·1	11·9 4·3	17·9 6·4
60	5 30·0	5 30·9	5 15·0	6·0 2·2	12·0 4·3	18·0 6·5

34	SUN PLANETS	ARIES	MOON	v or Corrn d	v or Corrn d	v or Corrn d
s	° ′	° ′	° ′	′ ′	′ ′	′ ′
00	8 30·0	8 31·4	8 06·8	0·0 0·0	6·0 3·5	12·0 6·9
01	8 30·3	8 31·6	8 07·0	0·1 0·1	6·1 3·5	12·1 7·0
02	8 30·5	8 31·9	8 07·2	0·2 0·1	6·2 3·6	12·2 7·0
03	8 30·8	8 32·1	8 07·5	0·3 0·2	6·3 3·6	12·3 7·1
04	8 31·0	8 32·4	8 07·7	0·4 0·2	6·4 3·7	12·4 7·1
05	8 31·3	8 32·6	8 08·0	0·5 0·3	6·5 3·7	12·5 7·2
06	8 31·5	8 32·9	8 08·2	0·6 0·3	6·6 3·8	12·6 7·2
07	8 31·8	8 33·2	8 08·4	0·7 0·4	6·7 3·9	12·7 7·3
08	8 32·0	8 33·4	8 08·7	0·8 0·5	6·8 3·9	12·8 7·4
09	8 32·3	8 33·7	8 08·9	0·9 0·5	6·9 4·0	12·9 7·4
10	8 32·5	8 33·9	8 09·2	1·0 0·6	7·0 4·0	13·0 7·5
11	8 32·8	8 34·2	8 09·4	1·1 0·6	7·1 4·1	13·1 7·5
12	8 33·0	8 34·4	8 09·6	1·2 0·7	7·2 4·1	13·2 7·6
13	8 33·3	8 34·7	8 09·9	1·3 0·7	7·3 4·2	13·3 7·6
14	8 33·5	8 34·9	8 10·1	1·4 0·8	7·4 4·3	13·4 7·7
15	8 33·8	8 35·2	8 10·3	1·5 0·9	7·5 4·3	13·5 7·8
16	8 34·0	8 35·4	8 10·6	1·6 0·9	7·6 4·4	13·6 7·8
17	8 34·3	8 35·7	8 10·8	1·7 1·0	7·7 4·4	13·7 7·9
18	8 34·5	8 35·9	8 11·1	1·8 1·0	7·8 4·5	13·8 7·9
19	8 34·8	8 36·2	8 11·3	1·9 1·1	7·9 4·5	13·9 8·0
20	8 35·0	8 36·4	8 11·5	2·0 1·2	8·0 4·6	14·0 8·1
21	8 35·3	8 36·7	8 11·8	2·1 1·2	8·1 4·7	14·1 8·1
22	8 35·5	8 36·9	8 12·0	2·2 1·3	8·2 4·7	14·2 8·2
23	8 35·8	8 37·2	8 12·3	2·3 1·3	8·3 4·8	14·3 8·2
24	8 36·0	8 37·4	8 12·5	2·4 1·4	8·4 4·8	14·4 8·3
25	8 36·3	8 37·7	8 12·7	2·5 1·4	8·5 4·9	14·5 8·3
26	8 36·5	8 37·9	8 13·0	2·6 1·5	8·6 4·9	14·6 8·4
27	8 36·8	8 38·2	8 13·2	2·7 1·6	8·7 5·0	14·7 8·5
28	8 37·0	8 38·4	8 13·4	2·8 1·6	8·8 5·1	14·8 8·5
29	8 37·3	8 38·7	8 13·7	2·9 1·7	8·9 5·1	14·9 8·6
30	8 37·5	8 38·9	8 13·9	3·0 1·7	9·0 5·2	15·0 8·6
31	8 37·8	8 39·2	8 14·2	3·1 1·8	9·1 5·2	15·1 8·7
32	8 38·0	8 39·4	8 14·4	3·2 1·8	9·2 5·3	15·2 8·7
33	8 38·3	8 39·7	8 14·6	3·3 1·9	9·3 5·3	15·3 8·8
34	8 38·5	8 39·9	8 14·9	3·4 2·0	9·4 5·4	15·4 8·9
35	8 38·8	8 40·2	8 15·1	3·5 2·0	9·5 5·5	15·5 8·9
36	8 39·0	8 40·4	8 15·4	3·6 2·1	9·6 5·5	15·6 9·0
37	8 39·3	8 40·7	8 15·6	3·7 2·1	9·7 5·6	15·7 9·0
38	8 39·5	8 40·9	8 15·8	3·8 2·2	9·8 5·6	15·8 9·1
39	8 39·8	8 41·2	8 16·1	3·9 2·2	9·9 5·7	15·9 9·1
40	8 40·0	8 41·4	8 16·3	4·0 2·3	10·0 5·8	16·0 9·2
41	8 40·3	8 41·7	8 16·5	4·1 2·4	10·1 5·8	16·1 9·3
42	8 40·5	8 41·9	8 16·8	4·2 2·4	10·2 5·9	16·2 9·3
43	8 40·8	8 42·2	8 17·0	4·3 2·5	10·3 5·9	16·3 9·4
44	8 41·0	8 42·4	8 17·3	4·4 2·5	10·4 6·0	16·4 9·4
45	8 41·3	8 42·7	8 17·5	4·5 2·6	10·5 6·0	16·5 9·5
46	8 41·5	8 42·9	8 17·7	4·6 2·6	10·6 6·1	16·6 9·5
47	8 41·8	8 43·2	8 18·0	4·7 2·7	10·7 6·2	16·7 9·6
48	8 42·0	8 43·4	8 18·2	4·8 2·8	10·8 6·2	16·8 9·7
49	8 42·3	8 43·7	8 18·5	4·9 2·8	10·9 6·3	16·9 9·7
50	8 42·5	8 43·9	8 18·7	5·0 2·9	11·0 6·3	17·0 9·8
51	8 42·8	8 44·2	8 18·9	5·1 2·9	11·1 6·4	17·1 9·8
52	8 43·0	8 44·4	8 19·2	5·2 3·0	11·2 6·4	17·2 9·9
53	8 43·3	8 44·7	8 19·4	5·3 3·0	11·3 6·5	17·3 9·9
54	8 43·5	8 44·9	8 19·7	5·4 3·1	11·4 6·6	17·4 10·0
55	8 43·8	8 45·2	8 19·9	5·5 3·2	11·5 6·6	17·5 10·1
56	8 44·0	8 45·4	8 20·1	5·6 3·2	11·6 6·7	17·6 10·1
57	8 44·3	8 45·7	8 20·4	5·7 3·3	11·7 6·7	17·7 10·2
58	8 44·5	8 45·9	8 20·6	5·8 3·3	11·8 6·8	17·8 10·2
59	8 44·8	8 46·2	8 20·8	5·9 3·4	11·9 6·8	17·9 10·3
60	8 45·0	8 46·4	8 21·1	6·0 3·5	12·0 6·9	18·0 10·4

35	SUN PLANETS	ARIES	MOON	v or Corrn d	v or Corrn d	v or Corrn d
s	° ′	° ′	° ′	′ ′	′ ′	′ ′
00	8 45·0	8 46·4	8 21·1	0·0 0·0	6·0 3·6	12·0 7·1
01	8 45·3	8 46·7	8 21·3	0·1 0·1	6·1 3·6	12·1 7·2
02	8 45·5	8 46·9	8 21·6	0·2 0·1	6·2 3·7	12·2 7·2
03	8 45·8	8 47·2	8 21·8	0·3 0·2	6·3 3·7	12·3 7·3
04	8 46·0	8 47·4	8 22·0	0·4 0·2	6·4 3·8	12·4 7·3
05	8 46·3	8 47·7	8 22·3	0·5 0·3	6·5 3·8	12·5 7·4
06	8 46·5	8 47·9	8 22·5	0·6 0·4	6·6 3·9	12·6 7·5
07	8 46·8	8 48·2	8 22·8	0·7 0·4	6·7 4·0	12·7 7·5
08	8 47·0	8 48·4	8 23·0	0·8 0·5	6·8 4·0	12·8 7·6
09	8 47·3	8 48·7	8 23·2	0·9 0·5	6·9 4·1	12·9 7·6
10	8 47·5	8 48·9	8 23·5	1·0 0·6	7·0 4·1	13·0 7·7
11	8 47·8	8 49·2	8 23·7	1·1 0·7	7·1 4·2	13·1 7·8
12	8 48·0	8 49·4	8 23·9	1·2 0·7	7·2 4·3	13·2 7·8
13	8 48·3	8 49·7	8 24·2	1·3 0·8	7·3 4·3	13·3 7·9
14	8 48·5	8 49·9	8 24·4	1·4 0·8	7·4 4·4	13·4 7·9
15	8 48·8	8 50·2	8 24·7	1·5 0·9	7·5 4·4	13·5 8·0
16	8 49·0	8 50·4	8 24·9	1·6 0·9	7·6 4·5	13·6 8·0
17	8 49·3	8 50·7	8 25·1	1·7 1·0	7·7 4·6	13·7 8·1
18	8 49·5	8 50·9	8 25·4	1·8 1·1	7·8 4·6	13·8 8·2
19	8 49·8	8 51·2	8 25·6	1·9 1·1	7·9 4·7	13·9 8·2
20	8 50·0	8 51·5	8 25·9	2·0 1·2	8·0 4·7	14·0 8·3
21	8 50·3	8 51·7	8 26·1	2·1 1·2	8·1 4·8	14·1 8·3
22	8 50·5	8 52·0	8 26·3	2·2 1·3	8·2 4·9	14·2 8·4
23	8 50·8	8 52·2	8 26·6	2·3 1·4	8·3 4·9	14·3 8·5
24	8 51·0	8 52·5	8 26·8	2·4 1·4	8·4 5·0	14·4 8·5
25	8 51·3	8 52·7	8 27·0	2·5 1·5	8·5 5·0	14·5 8·6
26	8 51·5	8 53·0	8 27·3	2·6 1·5	8·6 5·1	14·6 8·6
27	8 51·8	8 53·2	8 27·5	2·7 1·6	8·7 5·1	14·7 8·7
28	8 52·0	8 53·5	8 27·8	2·8 1·7	8·8 5·2	14·8 8·8
29	8 52·3	8 53·7	8 28·0	2·9 1·7	8·9 5·3	14·9 8·8
30	8 52·5	8 54·0	8 28·2	3·0 1·8	9·0 5·3	15·0 8·9
31	8 52·8	8 54·2	8 28·5	3·1 1·8	9·1 5·4	15·1 8·9
32	8 53·0	8 54·5	8 28·7	3·2 1·9	9·2 5·4	15·2 9·0
33	8 53·3	8 54·7	8 29·0	3·3 2·0	9·3 5·5	15·3 9·1
34	8 53·5	8 55·0	8 29·2	3·4 2·0	9·4 5·6	15·4 9·1
35	8 53·8	8 55·2	8 29·4	3·5 2·1	9·5 5·6	15·5 9·2
36	8 54·0	8 55·5	8 29·7	3·6 2·1	9·6 5·7	15·6 9·2
37	8 54·3	8 55·7	8 29·9	3·7 2·2	9·7 5·7	15·7 9·3
38	8 54·5	8 56·0	8 30·2	3·8 2·2	9·8 5·8	15·8 9·3
39	8 54·8	8 56·2	8 30·4	3·9 2·3	9·9 5·9	15·9 9·4
40	8 55·0	8 56·5	8 30·6	4·0 2·4	10·0 5·9	16·0 9·5
41	8 55·3	8 56·7	8 30·9	4·1 2·4	10·1 6·0	16·1 9·5
42	8 55·5	8 57·0	8 31·1	4·2 2·5	10·2 6·0	16·2 9·6
43	8 55·8	8 57·2	8 31·3	4·3 2·5	10·3 6·1	16·3 9·6
44	8 56·0	8 57·5	8 31·6	4·4 2·6	10·4 6·2	16·4 9·7
45	8 56·3	8 57·7	8 31·8	4·5 2·7	10·5 6·2	16·5 9·8
46	8 56·5	8 58·0	8 32·1	4·6 2·7	10·6 6·3	16·6 9·8
47	8 56·8	8 58·2	8 32·3	4·7 2·8	10·7 6·3	16·7 9·9
48	8 57·0	8 58·5	8 32·5	4·8 2·8	10·8 6·4	16·8 9·9
49	8 57·3	8 58·7	8 32·8	4·9 2·9	10·9 6·4	16·9 10·0
50	8 57·5	8 59·0	8 33·0	5·0 3·0	11·0 6·5	17·0 10·1
51	8 57·8	8 59·2	8 33·3	5·1 3·0	11·1 6·6	17·1 10·1
52	8 58·0	8 59·5	8 33·5	5·2 3·1	11·2 6·6	17·2 10·2
53	8 58·3	8 59·7	8 33·7	5·3 3·1	11·3 6·7	17·3 10·2
54	8 58·5	9 00·0	8 34·0	5·4 3·2	11·4 6·7	17·4 10·3
55	8 58·8	9 00·2	8 34·2	5·5 3·3	11·5 6·8	17·5 10·4
56	8 59·0	9 00·5	8 34·4	5·6 3·3	11·6 6·9	17·6 10·4
57	8 59·3	9 00·7	8 34·7	5·7 3·4	11·7 6·9	17·7 10·5
58	8 59·5	9 01·0	8 34·9	5·8 3·4	11·8 7·0	17·8 10·5
59	8 59·8	9 01·2	8 35·2	5·9 3·5	11·9 7·0	17·9 10·6
60	9 00·0	9 01·5	8 35·4	6·0 3·6	12·0 7·1	18·0 10·7

50	SUN PLANETS	ARIES	MOON	v or Corrⁿ d		v or Corrⁿ d		v or Corrⁿ d	
s	° ′	° ′	° ′	′	′	′	′	′	′
00	12 30·0	12 32·1	11 55·8	0·0	0·0	6·0	5·1	12·0	10·1
01	12 30·3	12 32·3	11 56·1	0·1	0·1	6·1	5·1	12·1	10·2
02	12 30·5	12 32·6	11 56·3	0·2	0·2	6·2	5·2	12·2	10·3
03	12 30·8	12 32·8	11 56·5	0·3	0·3	6·3	5·3	12·3	10·4
04	12 31·0	12 33·1	11 56·8	0·4	0·3	6·4	5·4	12·4	10·4
05	12 31·3	12 33·3	11 57·0	0·5	0·4	6·5	5·5	12·5	10·5
06	12 31·5	12 33·6	11 57·3	0·6	0·5	6·6	5·6	12·6	10·6
07	12 31·8	12 33·8	11 57·5	0·7	0·6	6·7	5·6	12·7	10·7
08	12 32·0	12 34·1	11 57·7	0·8	0·7	6·8	5·7	12·8	10·8
09	12 32·3	12 34·3	11 58·0	0·9	0·8	6·9	5·8	12·9	10·9
10	12 32·5	12 34·6	11 58·2	1·0	0·8	7·0	5·9	13·0	10·9
11	12 32·8	12 34·8	11 58·5	1·1	0·9	7·1	6·0	13·1	11·0
12	12 33·0	12 35·1	11 58·7	1·2	1·0	7·2	6·1	13·2	11·1
13	12 33·3	12 35·3	11 58·9	1·3	1·1	7·3	6·1	13·3	11·2
14	12 33·5	12 35·6	11 59·2	1·4	1·2	7·4	6·2	13·4	11·3
15	12 33·8	12 35·8	11 59·4	1·5	1·3	7·5	6·3	13·5	11·4
16	12 34·0	12 36·1	11 59·7	1·6	1·3	7·6	6·4	13·6	11·4
17	12 34·3	12 36·3	11 59·9	1·7	1·4	7·7	6·5	13·7	11·5
18	12 34·5	12 36·6	12 00·1	1·8	1·5	7·8	6·6	13·8	11·6
19	12 34·8	12 36·8	12 00·4	1·9	1·6	7·9	6·6	13·9	11·7
20	12 35·0	12 37·1	12 00·6	2·0	1·7	8·0	6·7	14·0	11·8
21	12 35·3	12 37·3	12 00·8	2·1	1·8	8·1	6·8	14·1	11·9
22	12 35·5	12 37·6	12 01·1	2·2	1·9	8·2	6·9	14·2	12·0
23	12 35·8	12 37·8	12 01·3	2·3	1·9	8·3	7·0	14·3	12·0
24	12 36·0	12 38·1	12 01·6	2·4	2·0	8·4	7·1	14·4	12·1
25	12 36·3	12 38·3	12 01·8	2·5	2·1	8·5	7·2	14·5	12·2
26	12 36·5	12 38·6	12 02·0	2·6	2·2	8·6	7·2	14·6	12·3
27	12 36·8	12 38·8	12 02·3	2·7	2·3	8·7	7·3	14·7	12·4
28	12 37·0	12 39·1	12 02·5	2·8	2·4	8·8	7·4	14·8	12·5
29	12 37·3	12 39·3	12 02·8	2·9	2·4	8·9	7·5	14·9	12·5
30	12 37·5	12 39·6	12 03·0	3·0	2·5	9·0	7·6	15·0	12·6
31	12 37·8	12 39·8	12 03·2	3·1	2·6	9·1	7·7	15·1	12·7
32	12 38·0	12 40·1	12 03·5	3·2	2·7	9·2	7·7	15·2	12·8
33	12 38·3	12 40·3	12 03·7	3·3	2·8	9·3	7·8	15·3	12·9
34	12 38·5	12 40·6	12 03·9	3·4	2·9	9·4	7·9	15·4	13·0
35	12 38·8	12 40·8	12 04·2	3·5	2·9	9·5	8·0	15·5	13·0
36	12 39·0	12 41·1	12 04·4	3·6	3·0	9·6	8·1	15·6	13·1
37	12 39·3	12 41·3	12 04·7	3·7	3·1	9·7	8·2	15·7	13·2
38	12 39·5	12 41·6	12 04·9	3·8	3·2	9·8	8·2	15·8	13·3
39	12 39·8	12 41·8	12 05·1	3·9	3·3	9·9	8·3	15·9	13·4
40	12 40·0	12 42·1	12 05·4	4·0	3·4	10·0	8·4	16·0	13·5
41	12 40·3	12 42·3	12 05·6	4·1	3·5	10·1	8·5	16·1	13·6
42	12 40·5	12 42·6	12 05·9	4·2	3·5	10·2	8·6	16·2	13·6
43	12 40·8	12 42·8	12 06·1	4·3	3·6	10·3	8·7	16·3	13·7
44	12 41·0	12 43·1	12 06·3	4·4	3·7	10·4	8·8	16·4	13·8
45	12 41·3	12 43·3	12 06·6	4·5	3·8	10·5	8·8	16·5	13·9
46	12 41·5	12 43·6	12 06·8	4·6	3·9	10·6	8·9	16·6	14·0
47	12 41·8	12 43·8	12 07·0	4·7	4·0	10·7	9·0	16·7	14·1
48	12 42·0	12 44·1	12 07·3	4·8	4·0	10·8	9·1	16·8	14·1
49	12 42·3	12 44·3	12 07·5	4·9	4·1	10·9	9·2	16·9	14·2
50	12 42·5	12 44·6	12 07·8	5·0	4·2	11·0	9·3	17·0	14·3
51	12 42·8	12 44·8	12 08·0	5·1	4·3	11·1	9·3	17·1	14·4
52	12 43·0	12 45·1	12 08·2	5·2	4·4	11·2	9·4	17·2	14·5
53	12 43·3	12 45·3	12 08·5	5·3	4·5	11·3	9·5	17·3	14·6
54	12 43·5	12 45·6	12 08·7	5·4	4·5	11·4	9·6	17·4	14·6
55	12 43·8	12 45·8	12 09·0	5·5	4·6	11·5	9·7	17·5	14·7
56	12 44·0	12 46·1	12 09·2	5·6	4·7	11·6	9·8	17·6	14·8
57	12 44·3	12 46·3	12 09·4	5·7	4·8	11·7	9·8	17·7	14·9
58	12 44·5	12 46·6	12 09·7	5·8	4·9	11·8	9·9	17·8	15·0
59	12 44·8	12 46·8	12 09·9	5·9	5·0	11·9	10·0	17·9	15·1
60	12 45·0	12 47·1	12 10·2	6·0	5·1	12·0	10·1	18·0	15·2

51	SUN PLANETS	ARIES	MOON	v or Corrⁿ d		v or Corrⁿ d		v or Corrⁿ d	
s	° ′	° ′	° ′	′	′	′	′	′	′
00	12 45·0	12 47·1	12 10·2	0·0	0·0	6·0	5·2	12·0	10·3
01	12 45·3	12 47·3	12 10·4	0·1	0·1	6·1	5·2	12·1	10·4
02	12 45·5	12 47·6	12 10·6	0·2	0·2	6·2	5·3	12·2	10·5
03	12 45·8	12 47·8	12 10·9	0·3	0·3	6·3	5·4	12·3	10·6
04	12 46·0	12 48·1	12 11·1	0·4	0·3	6·4	5·5	12·4	10·6
05	12 46·3	12 48·3	12 11·3	0·5	0·4	6·5	5·6	12·5	10·7
06	12 46·5	12 48·6	12 11·6	0·6	0·5	6·6	5·7	12·6	10·8
07	12 46·8	12 48·8	12 11·8	0·7	0·6	6·7	5·8	12·7	10·9
08	12 47·0	12 49·1	12 12·1	0·8	0·7	6·8	5·8	12·8	11·0
09	12 47·3	12 49·4	12 12·3	0·9	0·8	6·9	5·9	12·9	11·1
10	12 47·5	12 49·6	12 12·5	1·0	0·9	7·0	6·0	13·0	11·2
11	12 47·8	12 49·9	12 12·8	1·1	0·9	7·1	6·1	13·1	11·2
12	12 48·0	12 50·1	12 13·0	1·2	1·0	7·2	6·2	13·2	11·3
13	12 48·3	12 50·4	12 13·3	1·3	1·1	7·3	6·3	13·3	11·4
14	12 48·5	12 50·6	12 13·5	1·4	1·2	7·4	6·4	13·4	11·5
15	12 48·8	12 50·9	12 13·7	1·5	1·3	7·5	6·4	13·5	11·6
16	12 49·0	12 51·1	12 14·0	1·6	1·4	7·6	6·5	13·6	11·7
17	12 49·3	12 51·4	12 14·2	1·7	1·5	7·7	6·6	13·7	11·8
18	12 49·5	12 51·6	12 14·4	1·8	1·5	7·8	6·7	13·8	11·8
19	12 49·8	12 51·9	12 14·7	1·9	1·6	7·9	6·8	13·9	11·9
20	12 50·0	12 52·1	12 14·9	2·0	1·7	8·0	6·9	14·0	12·0
21	12 50·3	12 52·4	12 15·2	2·1	1·8	8·1	7·0	14·1	12·1
22	12 50·5	12 52·6	12 15·4	2·2	1·9	8·2	7·1	14·2	12·2
23	12 50·8	12 52·9	12 15·6	2·3	2·0	8·3	7·1	14·3	12·3
24	12 51·0	12 53·1	12 15·9	2·4	2·1	8·4	7·2	14·4	12·4
25	12 51·3	12 53·4	12 16·1	2·5	2·1	8·5	7·3	14·5	12·4
26	12 51·5	12 53·6	12 16·4	2·6	2·2	8·6	7·4	14·6	12·5
27	12 51·8	12 53·9	12 16·6	2·7	2·3	8·7	7·5	14·7	12·6
28	12 52·0	12 54·1	12 16·8	2·8	2·4	8·8	7·6	14·8	12·7
29	12 52·3	12 54·4	12 17·1	2·9	2·5	8·9	7·6	14·9	12·8
30	12 52·5	12 54·6	12 17·3	3·0	2·6	9·0	7·7	15·0	12·9
31	12 52·8	12 54·9	12 17·5	3·1	2·7	9·1	7·8	15·1	13·0
32	12 53·0	12 55·1	12 17·8	3·2	2·7	9·2	7·9	15·2	13·0
33	12 53·3	12 55·4	12 18·0	3·3	2·8	9·3	8·0	15·3	13·1
34	12 53·5	12 55·6	12 18·3	3·4	2·9	9·4	8·1	15·4	13·2
35	12 53·8	12 55·9	12 18·5	3·5	3·0	9·5	8·2	15·5	13·3
36	12 54·0	12 56·1	12 18·7	3·6	3·1	9·6	8·2	15·6	13·4
37	12 54·3	12 56·4	12 19·0	3·7	3·2	9·7	8·3	15·7	13·5
38	12 54·5	12 56·6	12 19·2	3·8	3·3	9·8	8·4	15·8	13·6
39	12 54·8	12 56·9	12 19·5	3·9	3·3	9·9	8·5	15·9	13·6
40	12 55·0	12 57·1	12 19·7	4·0	3·4	10·0	8·6	16·0	13·7
41	12 55·3	12 57·4	12 19·9	4·1	3·5	10·1	8·7	16·1	13·8
42	12 55·5	12 57·6	12 20·2	4·2	3·6	10·2	8·8	16·2	13·9
43	12 55·8	12 57·9	12 20·4	4·3	3·7	10·3	8·8	16·3	14·0
44	12 56·0	12 58·1	12 20·6	4·4	3·8	10·4	8·9	16·4	14·1
45	12 56·3	12 58·4	12 20·9	4·5	3·9	10·5	9·0	16·5	14·2
46	12 56·5	12 58·6	12 21·1	4·6	3·9	10·6	9·1	16·6	14·3
47	12 56·8	12 58·9	12 21·4	4·7	4·0	10·7	9·2	16·7	14·3
48	12 57·0	12 59·1	12 21·6	4·8	4·1	10·8	9·3	16·8	14·4
49	12 57·3	12 59·4	12 21·8	4·9	4·2	10·9	9·4	16·9	14·5
50	12 57·5	12 59·6	12 22·1	5·0	4·3	11·0	9·4	17·0	14·6
51	12 57·8	12 59·9	12 22·3	5·1	4·4	11·1	9·5	17·1	14·7
52	12 58·0	13 00·1	12 22·6	5·2	4·5	11·2	9·6	17·2	14·8
53	12 58·3	13 00·4	12 22·8	5·3	4·5	11·3	9·7	17·3	14·8
54	12 58·5	13 00·6	12 23·0	5·4	4·6	11·4	9·8	17·4	14·9
55	12 58·8	13 00·9	12 23·3	5·5	4·7	11·5	9·9	17·5	15·0
56	12 59·0	13 01·1	12 23·5	5·6	4·8	11·6	10·0	17·6	15·1
57	12 59·3	13 01·4	12 23·8	5·7	4·9	11·7	10·0	17·7	15·2
58	12 59·5	13 01·6	12 24·0	5·8	5·0	11·8	10·1	17·8	15·3
59	12 59·8	13 01·9	12 24·2	5·9	5·1	11·9	10·2	17·9	15·4
60	13 00·0	13 02·1	12 24·5	6·0	5·2	12·0	10·3	18·0	15·5

58ᵐ

58	SUN PLANETS	ARIES	MOON	v or Corrⁿ d	v or Corrⁿ d	v or Corrⁿ d
00	14 30·0	14 32·4	13 50·4	0·0 0·0	6·0 5·9	12·0 11·7
01	14 30·3	14 32·6	13 50·6	0·1 0·1	6·1 5·9	12·1 11·8
02	14 30·5	14 32·9	13 50·8	0·2 0·2	6·2 6·0	12·2 11·9
03	14 30·8	14 33·1	13 51·1	0·3 0·3	6·3 6·1	12·3 12·0
04	14 31·0	14 33·4	13 51·3	0·4 0·4	6·4 6·2	12·4 12·1
05	14 31·3	14 33·6	13 51·6	0·5 0·5	6·5 6·3	12·5 12·2
06	14 31·5	14 33·9	13 51·8	0·6 0·6	6·6 6·4	12·6 12·3
07	14 31·8	14 34·1	13 52·0	0·7 0·7	6·7 6·5	12·7 12·4
08	14 32·0	14 34·4	13 52·3	0·8 0·8	6·8 6·6	12·8 12·5
09	14 32·3	14 34·6	13 52·5	0·9 0·9	6·9 6·7	12·9 12·6
10	14 32·5	14 34·9	13 52·8	1·0 1·0	7·0 6·8	13·0 12·7
11	14 32·8	14 35·1	13 53·0	1·1 1·1	7·1 6·9	13·1 12·8
12	14 33·0	14 35·4	13 53·2	1·2 1·2	7·2 7·0	13·2 12·9
13	14 33·3	14 35·6	13 53·5	1·3 1·3	7·3 7·1	13·3 13·0
14	14 33·5	14 35·9	13 53·7	1·4 1·4	7·4 7·2	13·4 13·1
15	14 33·8	14 36·1	13 53·9	1·5 1·5	7·5 7·3	13·5 13·2
16	14 34·0	14 36·4	13 54·2	1·6 1·6	7·6 7·4	13·6 13·3
17	14 34·3	14 36·6	13 54·4	1·7 1·7	7·7 7·5	13·7 13·4
18	14 34·5	14 36·9	13 54·7	1·8 1·8	7·8 7·6	13·8 13·5
19	14 34·8	14 37·1	13 54·9	1·9 1·9	7·9 7·7	13·9 13·6
20	14 35·0	14 37·4	13 55·1	2·0 2·0	8·0 7·8	14·0 13·7
21	14 35·3	14 37·6	13 55·4	2·1 2·0	8·1 7·9	14·1 13·8
22	14 35·5	14 37·9	13 55·6	2·2 2·1	8·2 8·0	14·2 13·8
23	14 35·8	14 38·1	13 55·9	2·3 2·2	8·3 8·1	14·3 13·9
24	14 36·0	14 38·4	13 56·1	2·4 2·3	8·4 8·2	14·4 14·0
25	14 36·3	14 38·6	13 56·3	2·5 2·4	8·5 8·3	14·5 14·1
26	14 36·5	14 38·9	13 56·6	2·6 2·5	8·6 8·4	14·6 14·2
27	14 36·8	14 39·2	13 56·8	2·7 2·6	8·7 8·5	14·7 14·3
28	14 37·0	14 39·4	13 57·0	2·8 2·7	8·8 8·6	14·8 14·4
29	14 37·3	14 39·7	13 57·3	2·9 2·8	8·9 8·7	14·9 14·5
30	14 37·5	14 39·9	13 57·5	3·0 2·9	9·0 8·8	15·0 14·6
31	14 37·8	14 40·2	13 57·8	3·1 3·0	9·1 8·9	15·1 14·7
32	14 38·0	14 40·4	13 58·0	3·2 3·1	9·2 9·0	15·2 14·8
33	14 38·3	14 40·7	13 58·2	3·3 3·2	9·3 9·1	15·3 14·9
34	14 38·5	14 40·9	13 58·5	3·4 3·3	9·4 9·2	15·4 15·0
35	14 38·8	14 41·2	13 58·7	3·5 3·4	9·5 9·3	15·5 15·1
36	14 39·0	14 41·4	13 59·0	3·6 3·5	9·6 9·4	15·6 15·2
37	14 39·3	14 41·7	13 59·2	3·7 3·6	9·7 9·5	15·7 15·3
38	14 39·5	14 41·9	13 59·4	3·8 3·7	9·8 9·6	15·8 15·4
39	14 39·8	14 42·2	13 59·7	3·9 3·8	9·9 9·7	15·9 15·5
40	14 40·0	14 42·4	13 59·9	4·0	10·0 9·8	16·0 15·6
41	14 40·3	14 42·7	14 00·1	4·1 4·0	10·1 9·8	16·1 15·7
42	14 40·5	14 42·9	14 00·4	4·2 4·1	10·2 9·9	16·2 15·8
43	14 40·8	14 43·2	14 00·6	4·3 4·2	10·3 10·0	16·3 15·9
44	14 41·0	14 43·4	14 00·9	4·4 4·3	10·4 10·1	16·4 16·0
45	14 41·3	14 43·7	14 01·1	4·5 4·4	10·5 10·2	16·5 16·1
46	14 41·5	14 43·9	14 01·3	4·6 4·5	10·6 10·3	16·6 16·2
47	14 41·8	14 44·2	14 01·6	4·7 4·6	10·7 10·4	16·7 16·3
48	14 42·0	14 44·4	14 01·8	4·8 4·7	10·8 10·5	16·8 16·4
49	14 42·3	14 44·7	14 02·1	4·9 4·8	10·9 10·6	16·9 16·5
50	14 42·5	14 44·9	14 02·3	5·0 4·9	11·0 10·7	17·0 16·6
51	14 42·8	14 45·2	14 02·5	5·1 5·0	11·1 10·8	17·1 16·7
52	14 43·0	14 45·4	14 02·8	5·2 5·1	11·2 10·9	17·2 16·8
53	14 43·3	14 45·7	14 03·0	5·3 5·2	11·3 11·0	17·3 16·9
54	14 43·5	14 45·9	14 03·3	5·4 5·3	11·4 11·1	17·4 17·0
55	14 43·8	14 46·2	14 03·5	5·5 5·4	11·5 11·2	17·5 17·1
56	14 44·0	14 46·4	14 03·7	5·6 5·5	11·6 11·3	17·6 17·2
57	14 44·3	14 46·7	14 04·0	5·7 5·6	11·7 11·4	17·7 17·3
58	14 44·5	14 46·9	14 04·2	5·8 5·7	11·8 11·5	17·8 17·4
59	14 44·8	14 47·2	14 04·4	5·9 5·8	11·9 11·6	17·9 17·5
60	14 45·0	14 47·4	14 04·7	6·0 5·9	12·0 11·7	18·0 17·6

59ᵐ

59	SUN PLANETS	ARIES	MOON	v or Corrⁿ d	v or Corrⁿ d	v or Corrⁿ d
00	14 45·0	14 47·4	14 04·7	0·0 0·0	6·0 6·0	12·0 11·9
01	14 45·3	14 47·7	14 04·9	0·1 0·1	6·1 6·0	12·1 12·0
02	14 45·5	14 47·9	14 05·2	0·2 0·2	6·2 6·1	12·2 12·1
03	14 45·8	14 48·2	14 05·4	0·3 0·3	6·3 6·2	12·3 12·2
04	14 46·0	14 48·4	14 05·6	0·4 0·4	6·4 6·3	12·4 12·3
05	14 46·3	14 48·7	14 05·9	0·5 0·5	6·5 6·4	12·5 12·4
06	14 46·5	14 48·9	14 06·1	0·6 0·6	6·6 6·5	12·6 12·5
07	14 46·8	14 49·2	14 06·4	0·7 0·7	6·7 6·6	12·7 12·6
08	14 47·0	14 49·4	14 06·6	0·8 0·8	6·8 6·7	12·8 12·7
09	14 47·3	14 49·7	14 06·8	0·9 0·9	6·9 6·8	12·9 12·8
10	14 47·5	14 49·9	14 07·1	1·0 1·0	7·0 6·9	13·0 12·9
11	14 47·8	14 50·2	14 07·3	1·1 1·1	7·1 7·0	13·1 13·0
12	14 48·0	14 50·4	14 07·5	1·2 1·2	7·2 7·1	13·2 13·1
13	14 48·3	14 50·7	14 07·8	1·3 1·3	7·3 7·2	13·3 13·2
14	14 48·5	14 50·9	14 08·0	1·4 1·4	7·4 7·3	13·4 13·3
15	14 48·8	14 51·2	14 08·3	1·5 1·5	7·5 7·4	13·5 13·4
16	14 49·0	14 51·4	14 08·5	1·6 1·6	7·6 7·5	13·6 13·5
17	14 49·3	14 51·7	14 08·7	1·7 1·7	7·7 7·6	13·7 13·6
18	14 49·5	14 51·9	14 09·0	1·8 1·8	7·8 7·7	13·8 13·7
19	14 49·8	14 52·2	14 09·2	1·9 1·9	7·9 7·8	13·9 13·8
20	14 50·0	14 52·4	14 09·5	2·0 2·0	8·0 7·9	14·0 13·9
21	14 50·3	14 52·7	14 09·7	2·1 2·1	8·1 8·0	14·1 14·0
22	14 50·5	14 52·9	14 09·9	2·2 2·2	8·2 8·1	14·2 14·1
23	14 50·8	14 53·2	14 10·2	2·3 2·3	8·3 8·2	14·3 14·2
24	14 51·0	14 53·4	14 10·4	2·4 2·4	8·4 8·3	14·4 14·3
25	14 51·3	14 53·7	14 10·6	2·5 2·5	8·5 8·4	14·5 14·4
26	14 51·5	14 53·9	14 10·9	2·6 2·6	8·6 8·5	14·6 14·5
27	14 51·8	14 54·2	14 11·1	2·7 2·7	8·7 8·6	14·7 14·6
28	14 52·0	14 54·4	14 11·4	2·8 2·8	8·8 8·7	14·8 14·7
29	14 52·3	14 54·7	14 11·6	2·9 2·9	8·9 8·8	14·9 14·8
30	14 52·5	14 54·9	14 11·8	3·0 3·0	9·0 8·9	15·0 14·9
31	14 52·8	14 55·2	14 12·1	3·1 3·1	9·1 9·0	15·1 15·0
32	14 53·0	14 55·4	14 12·3	3·2 3·2	9·2 9·1	15·2 15·1
33	14 53·3	14 55·7	14 12·6	3·3 3·3	9·3 9·2	15·3 15·2
34	14 53·5	14 55·9	14 12·8	3·4 3·4	9·4 9·3	15·4 15·3
35	14 53·8	14 56·2	14 13·0	3·5 3·5	9·5 9·4	15·5 15·4
36	14 54·0	14 56·4	14 13·3	3·6 3·6	9·6 9·5	15·6 15·5
37	14 54·3	14 56·7	14 13·5	3·7 3·7	9·7 9·6	15·7 15·6
38	14 54·5	14 56·9	14 13·8	3·8 3·8	9·8 9·7	15·8 15·7
39	14 54·8	14 57·2	14 14·0	3·9 3·9	9·9 9·8	15·9 15·8
40	14 55·0	14 57·5	14 14·2	4·0 4·0	10·0 9·9	16·0 15·9
41	14 55·3	14 57·7	14 14·5	4·1 4·1	10·1 10·0	16·1 16·0
42	14 55·5	14 58·0	14 14·7	4·2 4·2	10·2 10·1	16·2 16·1
43	14 55·8	14 58·2	14 14·9	4·3 4·3	10·3 10·2	16·3 16·2
44	14 56·0	14 58·5	14 15·2	4·4 4·4	10·4 10·3	16·4 16·3
45	14 56·3	14 58·7	14 15·4	4·5 4·5	10·5 10·4	16·5 16·4
46	14 56·5	14 59·0	14 15·7	4·6 4·6	10·6 10·5	16·6 16·5
47	14 56·8	14 59·2	14 15·9	4·7 4·7	10·7 10·6	16·7 16·6
48	14 57·0	14 59·5	14 16·1	4·8 4·8	10·8 10·7	16·8 16·7
49	14 57·3	14 59·7	14 16·4	4·9 4·9	10·9 10·8	16·9 16·8
50	14 57·5	15 00·0	14 16·6	5·0 5·0	11·0 10·9	17·0 16·9
51	14 57·8	15 00·2	14 16·9	5·1 5·1	11·1 11·0	17·1 17·0
52	14 58·0	15 00·5	14 17·1	5·2 5·2	11·2 11·1	17·2 17·1
53	14 58·3	15 00·7	14 17·3	5·3 5·3	11·3 11·2	17·3 17·2
54	14 58·5	15 01·0	14 17·6	5·4 5·4	11·4 11·3	17·4 17·3
55	14 58·8	15 01·2	14 17·8	5·5 5·5	11·5 11·4	17·5 17·4
56	14 59·0	15 01·5	14 18·0	5·6 5·6	11·6 11·5	17·6 17·5
57	14 59·3	15 01·7	14 18·3	5·7 5·7	11·7 11·6	17·7 17·6
58	14 59·5	15 02·0	14 18·5	5·8 5·8	11·8 11·7	17·8 17·7
59	14 59·8	15 02·2	14 18·8	5·9 5·9	11·9 11·8	17·9 17·8
60	15 00·0	15 02·5	14 19·0	6·0 6·0	12·0 11·9	18·0 17·9

TABLES FOR INTERPOLATING SUNRISE, MOONRISE, ETC.

TABLE I—FOR LATITUDE

Tabular Interval			Difference between the times for consecutive latitudes																
10°	5°	2°	5m	10m	15m	20m	25m	30m	35m	40m	45m	50m	55m	60m	1h 05m	1h 10m	1h 15m	1h 20m
o ′	o ′	o ′	m	m	m	m	m	m	m	m	m	m	m	m	h m	h m	h m	h m
0 30	0 15	0 06	0	0	1	1	1	1	1	2	2	2	2	2	0 02	0 02	0 02	0 02
1 00	0 30	0 12	0	1	1	2	2	3	3	3	4	4	4	5	05	05	05	05
1 30	0 45	0 18	1	1	2	3	3	4	4	5	5	6	7	7	07	07	07	07
2 00	1 00	0 24	1	2	3	4	5	5	6	7	7	8	9	10	10	10	10	10
2 30	1 15	0 30	1	2	4	5	6	7	8	9	9	10	11	12	12	13	13	13
3 00	1 30	0 36	1	3	4	6	7	8	9	10	11	12	13	14	0 15	0 15	0 16	0 16
3 30	1 45	0 42	2	3	5	7	8	10	11	12	13	14	16	17	18	18	19	19
4 00	2 00	0 48	2	4	6	8	9	11	13	14	15	16	18	19	20	21	22	22
4 30	2 15	0 54	2	4	7	9	11	13	15	16	18	19	21	22	23	24	25	26
5 00	2 30	1 00	2	5	7	10	12	14	16	18	20	22	23	25	26	27	28	29
5 30	2 45	1 06	3	5	8	11	13	16	18	20	22	24	26	28	0 29	0 30	0 31	0 32
6 00	3 00	1 12	3	6	9	12	14	17	20	22	24	26	29	31	32	33	34	36
6 30	3 15	1 18	3	6	10	13	16	19	22	24	26	29	31	34	36	37	38	40
7 00	3 30	1 24	3	7	10	14	17	20	23	26	29	31	34	37	39	41	42	44
7 30	3 45	1 30	4	7	11	15	18	22	25	28	31	34	37	40	43	44	46	48
8 00	4 00	1 36	4	8	12	16	20	23	27	30	34	37	41	44	0 47	0 48	0 51	0 53
8 30	4 15	1 42	4	8	13	17	21	25	29	33	36	40	44	48	0 51	0 53	0 56	0 58
9 00	4 30	1 48	4	9	13	18	22	27	31	35	39	43	47	52	0 55	0 58	1 01	1 04
9 30	4 45	1 54	5	9	14	19	24	28	33	38	42	47	51	56	1 00	1 04	1 08	1 12
10 00	5 00	2 00	5	10	15	20	25	30	35	40	45	50	55	60	1 05	1 10	1 15	1 20

Table I is for interpolating the L.M.T. of sunrise, twilight, moonrise, etc., for latitude. It is to be entered, in the appropriate column on the left, with the difference between true latitude and the nearest tabular latitude which is *less* than the true latitude; and with the argument at the top which is the nearest value of the difference between the times for the tabular latitude and the next higher one; the correction so obtained is applied to the time for the tabular latitude; the sign of the correction can be seen by inspection. It is to be noted that the interpolation is not linear, so that when using this table it is essential to take out the tabular phenomenon for the latitudè *less* than the true latitude.

TABLE II—FOR LONGITUDE

Long. East or West	Difference between the times for given date and preceding date (for east longitude) or for given date and following date (for west longitude)																		
	10m	20m	30m	40m	50m	60m	1h + 10m	20m	30m	1h + 40m	50m	60m	2h 10m	2h 20m	2h 30m	2h 40m	2h 50m	3h 00m
o	m	m	m	m	m	m	m	m	m	m	m	m	h m	h m	h m	h m	h m	h m
0	0	0	0	0	0	0	0	0	0	0	0	0	0 00	0 00	0 00	0 00	0 00	0 00
10	0	1	1	1	1	2	2	2	2	3	3	3	04	04	04	04	05	05
20	1	1	2	2	3	3	4	4	5	6	6	7	07	08	08	09	09	10
30	1	2	2	3	4	5	6	7	7	8	9	10	11	12	12	13	14	15
40	1	2	3	4	6	7	8	9	10	11	12	13	14	16	17	18	19	20
50	1	3	4	6	7	8	10	11	12	14	15	17	0 18	0 19	0 21	0 22	0 24	0 25
60	2	3	5	7	8	10	12	13	15	17	18	20	22	23	25	27	28	30
70	2	4	6	8	10	12	14	16	17	19	21	23	25	27	29	31	33	35
80	2	4	7	9	11	13	16	18	20	22	24	27	29	31	33	36	38	40
90	2	5	7	10	12	15	17	20	22	25	27	30	32	35	37	40	42	45
100	3	6	8	11	14	17	19	22	25	28	31	33	0 36	0 39	0 42	0 44	0 47	0 50
110	3	6	9	12	15	18	21	24	27	31	34	37	40	43	46	49	0 52	0 55
120	3	7	10	13	17	20	23	27	30	33	37	40	43	47	50	53	0 57	1 00
130	4	7	11	14	18	22	25	29	32	36	40	43	47	51	54	0 58	1 01	1 05
140	4	8	12	16	19	23	27	31	35	39	43	47	51	54	0 58	1 02	1 06	1 10
150	4	8	13	17	21	25	29	33	38	42	46	50	0 54	0 58	1 03	1 07	1 11	1 15
160	4	9	13	18	22	27	31	36	40	44	49	53	0 58	1 02	1 07	1 11	1 16	1 20
170	5	9	14	19	24	28	33	38	42	47	52	57	1 01	1 06	1 11	1 16	1 20	1 25
180	5	10	15	20	25	30	35	40	45	50	55	60	1 05	1 10	1 15	1 20	1 25	1 30

Table II is for interpolating the L.M.T. of moonrise, moonset and the Moon's meridian passage for longitude. It is entered with longitude and with the difference between the times for the given date and for the preceding date (in east longitudes) or following date (in west longitudes). The correction is normally *added* for west longitudes and *subtracted* for east longitudes, but if, as occasionally happens, the times become earlier each day instead of later, the signs of the corrections must be reversed.

316

POLARIS (POLE STAR) TABLES, 1974
FOR DETERMINING LATITUDE FROM SEXTANT ALTITUDE AND FOR AZIMUTH

L.H.A. ARIES	0°– 9°	10°– 19°	20°– 29°	30°– 39°	40°– 49°	50°– 59°	60°– 69°	70°– 79°	80°– 89°	90°– 99°	100°– 109°	110°– 119°
	a_0	a_0	a_0	a_0	a_0	a_0	a_0	a_0	a_0	a_0	a_0	a_0
0	0 15·6	0 11·5	0 08·9	0 07·8	0 08·3	0 10·4	0 13·9	0 18·9	0 25·0	0 32·2	0 40·2	0 48·7
1	15·1	11·2	08·7	07·8	08·5	10·7	14·4	19·4	25·7	33·0	41·0	49·6
2	14·7	10·9	08·6	07·8	08·6	11·0	14·8	20·0	26·4	33·7	41·9	50·5
3	14·2	10·6	08·4	07·8	08·8	11·3	15·3	20·6	27·1	34·5	42·7	51·4
4	13·8	10·3	08·3	07·8	09·0	11·6	15·7	21·2	27·8	35·3	43·6	52·3
5	0 13·4	0 10·0	0 08·2	0 07·9	0 09·2	0 12·0	0 16·2	0 21·8	0 28·5	0 36·1	0 44·4	0 53·1
6	13·0	09·8	08·1	07·9	09·4	12·3	16·7	22·4	29·2	36·9	45·3	54·0
7	12·6	09·5	08·0	08·0	09·6	12·7	17·2	23·0	29·9	37·7	46·1	54·9
8	12·2	09·3	07·9	08·1	09·8	13·1	17·8	23·7	30·7	38·5	47·0	55·8
9	11·9	09·1	07·9	08·2	10·1	13·5	18·3	24·3	31·4	39·4	47·9	56·7
10	0 11·5	0 08·9	0 07·8	0 08·3	0 10·4	0 13·9	0 18·9	0 25·0	0 32·2	0 40·2	0 48·7	0 57·6

Lat.	a_1	a_1	a_1	a_1	a_1	a_1	a_1	a_1	a_1	a_1	a_1	a_1
0	0·5	0·6	0·6	0·6	0·6	0·5	0·5	0·4	0·3	0·2	0·2	0·2
10	·5	·6	·6	·6	·6	·5	·5	·4	·4	·3	·2	·2
20	·5	·6	·6	·6	·6	·6	·5	·5	·4	·4	·3	·3
30	·6	·6	·6	·6	·6	·6	·5	·5	·5	·4	·4	·4
40	0·6	0·6	0·6	0·6	0·6	0·6	0·6	0·5	0·5	0·5	0·5	0·5
45	·6	·6	·6	·6	·6	·6	·6	·6	·5	·5	·5	·5
50	·6	·6	·6	·6	·6	·6	·6	·6	·6	·6	·6	·6
55	·6	·6	·6	·6	·6	·6	·6	·6	·7	·7	·7	·7
60	·6	·6	·6	·6	·6	·6	·7	·7	·7	·8	·8	·8
62	0·7	0·6	0·6	0·6	0·6	0·6	0·7	0·7	0·8	0·8	0·8	0·9
64	·7	·6	·6	·6	·6	·7	·7	·8	·8	·9	0·9	0·9
66	·7	·6	·6	·6	·6	·7	·7	·8	·9	0·9	1·0	1·0
68	0·7	0·6	0·6	0·6	0·6	0·7	0·7	0·8	0·9	1·0	1·0	1·1

Month	a_2	a_2	a_2	a_2	a_2	a_2	a_2	a_2	a_2	a_2	a_2	a_2
Jan.	0·7	0·7	0·7	0·7	0·8	0·8	0·8	0·8	0·7	0·7	0·7	0·7
Feb.	·6	·7	·7	·7	·8	·8	·8	·8	·9	·9	·8	·8
Mar.	·5	·5	·6	·7	·7	·8	·8	·9	·9	·9	·9	0·9
Apr.	0·3	0·4	0·5	0·5	0·6	0·7	0·7	0·8	0·8	0·9	0·9	1·0
May	·2	·3	·3	·4	·4	·5	·6	·6	·7	·8	·8	0·9
June	·2	·2	·2	·3	·3	·4	·4	·5	·6	·6	·7	·8
July	0·2	0·2	0·2	0·2	0·2	0·3	0·3	0·4	0·4	0·5	0·5	0·6
Aug.	·4	·3	·3	·3	·3	·3	·3	·3	·3	·3	·4	·4
Sept.	·5	·5	·4	·4	·3	·3	·3	·3	·3	·3	·3	·3
Oct.	0·7	0·7	0·6	0·6	0·5	0·4	0·4	0·3	0·3	0·3	0·3	0·2
Nov.	0·9	0·9	·8	·7	·7	·6	·5	·5	·4	·3	·3	·3
Dec.	1·0	1·0	0·9	0·9	0·8	0·8	0·7	0·6	0·5	0·5	0·4	0·3

Lat.	AZIMUTH											
0	0·4	0·2	0·1	0·0	359·8	359·7	359·5	359·4	359·3	359·2	359·2	359·2
20	0·4	0·3	0·1	0·0	359·8	359·6	359·5	359·5	359·3	359·2	359·1	359·1
40	0·5	0·3	0·1	359·9	359·7	359·6	359·4	359·2	359·1	359·0	358·9	
50	0·6	0·4	0·2	359·9	359·7	359·5	359·3	359·1	358·9	358·8	358·7	358·7
55	0·7	0·4	0·2	359·9	359·7	359·4	359·2	359·0	358·8	358·7	358·6	358·5
60	0·8	0·5	0·2	359·9	359·6	359·3	359·1	358·8	358·6	358·5	358·4	358·3
65	0·9	0·6	0·2	359·9	359·5	359·2	358·9	358·6	358·4	358·2	358·1	358·0

Latitude = Apparent altitude (corrected for refraction) $- 1° + a_0 + a_1 + a_2$

The table is entered with L.H.A. Aries to determine the column to be used; each column refers to a range of 10°. a_0 is taken, with mental interpolation, from the upper table with the units of L.H.A. Aries in degrees as argument; a_1, a_2 are taken, without interpolation, from the second and third tables with arguments latitude and month respectively. a_0, a_1, a_2 are always positive. The final table gives the azimuth of *Polaris*.

POLARIS (POLE STAR) TABLES, 1974
FOR DETERMINING LATITUDE FROM SEXTANT ALTITUDE AND FOR AZIMUTH

L.H.A. ARIES	120°–129°	130°–139°	140°–149°	150°–159°	160°–169°	170°–179°	180°–189°	190°–199°	200°–209°	210°–219°	220°–229°	230°–239°
	a_0	a_0	a_0	a_0	a_0	a_0	a_0	a_0	a_0	a_0	a_0	a_0
0	0 57·6	1 06·5	1 15·1	1 23·2	1 30·6	1 37·0	1 42·2	1 46·2	1 48·7	1 49·8	1 49·3	1 47·3
1	58·5	07·3	15·9	24·0	31·3	37·6	42·7	46·5	48·9	49·8	49·2	47·0
2	0 59·4	08·2	16·8	24·7	31·9	38·1	43·1	46·8	49·1	49·8	49·0	46·7
3	1 00·3	09·1	17·6	25·5	32·6	38·7	43·6	47·1	49·2	49·8	48·9	46·4
4	01·1	10·0	18·4	26·2	33·3	39·2	44·0	47·4	49·3	49·8	48·7	46·1
5	1 02·0	1 10·8	1 19·2	1 27·0	1 33·9	1 39·8	1 44·4	1 47·6	1 49·4	1 49·7	1 48·5	1 45·8
6	02·9	11·7	20·0	27·7	34·5	40·3	44·8	47·9	49·5	49·7	48·3	45·4
7	03·8	12·5	20·8	28·5	35·2	40·8	45·2	48·1	49·6	49·6	48·1	45·1
8	04·7	13·4	21·6	29·2	35·8	41·3	45·5	48·3	49·7	49·5	47·8	44·7
9	05·6	14·2	22·4	29·9	36·4	41·8	45·9	48·5	49·7	49·4	47·6	44·3
10	1 06·5	1 15·1	1 23·2	1 30·6	1 37·0	1 42·2	1 46·2	1 48·7	1 49·8	1 49·3	1 47·3	1 43·9

Lat.	a_1	a_1	a_1	a_1	a_1	a_1	a_1	a_1	a_1	a_1	a_1	a_1
0	0·2	0·2	0·2	0·3	0·4	0·4	0·5	0·6	0·6	0·6	0·6	0·5
10	·2	·2	·3	·3	·4	·5	·5	·6	·6	·6	·6	·5
20	·3	·3	·3	·4	·4	·5	·5	·6	·6	·6	·6	·6
30	·4	·4	·4	·4	·5	·5	·6	·6	·6	·6	·6	·6
40	0·5	0·5	0·5	0·5	0·5	0·6	0·6	0·6	0·6	0·6	0·6	0·6
45	·5	·5	·5	·5	·6	·6	·6	·6	·6	·6	·6	·6
50	·6	·6	·6	·6	·6	·6	·6	·6	·6	·6	·6	·6
55	·7	·7	·7	·7	·6	·6	·6	·6	·6	·6	·6	·6
60	·8	·8	·8	·7	·7	·7	·6	·6	·6	·6	·6	·6
62	0·9	0·8	0·8	0·8	0·7	0·7	0·7	0·6	0·6	0·6	0·6	0·6
64	0·9	0·9	·9	·8	·8	·7	·7	·6	·6	·6	·6	·7
66	1·0	1·0	0·9	0·9	·8	·7	·7	·6	·6	·6	·6	·7
68	1·1	1·1	1·0	0·9	0·9	0·8	0·7	0·6	0·6	0·6	0·6	0·7

Month	a_2	a_2	a_2	a_2	a_2	a_2	a_2	a_2	a_2	a_2	a_2	a_2
Jan.	0·7	0·6	0·6	0·6	0·6	0·5	0·5	0·5	0·5	0·5	0·4	0·4
Feb.	·8	·8	·7	·7	·7	·6	·6	·5	·5	·5	·4	·4
Mar.	0·9	0·9	0·9	0·9	·8	·8	·7	·7	·6	·5	·5	·4
Apr.	1·0	1·0	1·0	1·0	0·9	0·9	0·9	0·8	0·7	0·7	0·6	0·5
May	0·9	1·0	1·0	1·0	1·0	1·0	1·0	0·9	0·9	·8	·8	·7
June	·8	0·9	0·9	1·0	1·0	1·0	1·0	1·0	1·0	0·9	0·9	·8
July	0·7	0·7	0·8	0·8	0·9	0·9	1·0	1·0	1·0	1·0	1·0	0·9
Aug.	·5	·6	·6	·7	·7	·8	0·8	0·9	0·9	0·9	0·9	·9
Sept.	·3	·4	·4	·5	·5	·6	·7	·7	·8	·8	·9	·9
Oct.	0·3	0·3	0·3	0·3	0·4	0·4	0·5	0·5	0·6	0·6	0·7	0·8
Nov.	·2	·2	·2	·2	·2	·3	·3	·3	·4	·5	·5	·6
Dec.	0·3	0·2	0·2	0·2	0·2	0·2	0·2	0·2	0·3	0·3	0·4	0·4

Lat.						AZIMUTH						
0	359·2	359·2	359·2	359·3	359·4	359·5	359·6	359·8	359·9	0·0	0·2	0·3
20	359·1	359·1	359·2	359·2	359·3	359·5	359·6	359·7	359·9	0·0	0·2	0·4
40	358·9	358·9	359·0	359·1	359·2	359·3	359·5	359·7	359·9	0·1	0·2	0·4
50	358·7	358·7	358·8	358·9	359·0	359·2	359·4	359·6	359·8	0·1	0·3	0·5
55	358·5	358·6	358·6	358·8	358·9	359·1	359·3	359·6	359·8	0·1	0·3	0·6
60	358·3	358·4	358·5	358·6	358·8	359·0	359·2	359·5	359·8	0·1	0·4	0·7
65	358·0	358·1	358·2	358·3	358·6	358·8	359·1	359·4	359·8	0·1	0·4	0·8

ILLUSTRATION

On 1974 January 22 at G.M.T. 23ʰ 13ᵐ 48ˢ in longitude W. 37° 14′ the corrected sextant altitude of *Polaris* was 49° 31′·6.

From the daily pages:		
	°	′
G.H.A. Aries (23ʰ)	106	54·5
Increment (13ᵐ 48ˢ)	3	27·6
Longitude (west)	−37	14
L.H.A. Aries	73	08

Corr. Sext. Alt.	49 31·6
a_0 (argument 73° 08′)	0 20·7
a_1 (lat. 50° approx.)	0·6
a_2 (January)	0·8
Sum −1° = Lat. =	48 53·7

318

POLARIS (POLE STAR) TABLES, 1974
FOR DETERMINING LATITUDE FROM SEXTANT ALTITUDE AND FOR AZIMUTH

L.H.A. ARIES	240°–249°	250°–259°	260°–269°	270°–279°	280°–289°	290°–299°	300°–309°	310°–319°	320°–329°	330°–339°	340°–349°	350°–359°
	a_0	a_0	a_0	a_0	a_0	a_0	a_0	a_0	a_0	a_0	a_0	$\cdot a_0$
°	° ′	° ′	° ′	° ′	° ′	° ′	° ′	° ′	° ′	° ′	° ′	° ′
0	1 43·9	1 39·1	1 33·1	1 26·1	1 18·2	1 09·7	1 00·9	0 52·0	0 43·3	0 35·1	0 27·6	0 21·0
1	43·5	38·5	32·4	25·3	17·4	08·8	1 00·0	51·1	42·5	34·3	26·9	20·4
2	43·0	38·0	31·8	24·5	16·5	08·0	0 59·1	50·3	41·6	33·5	26·2	19·8
3	42·6	37·4	31·1	23·8	15·7	07·1	58·2	49·4	40·8	32·8	25·5	19·3
4	42·1	36·8	30·4	23·0	14·9	06·2	57·4	48·5	40·0	32·0	24·8	18·7
5	1 41·6	1 36·2	1 29·7	1 22·2	1 14·0	1 05·3	0 56·5	0 47·6	0 39·1	0 31·2	0 24·2	0 18·2
6	41·2	35·6	29·0	21·4	13·2	04·5	55·6	46·8	38·3	30·5	23·5	17·6
7	40·7	35·0	28·3	20·6	12·3	03·6	54·7	45·9	37·5	29·8	22·9	17·1
8	40·1	34·4	27·5	19·8	11·4	02·7	53·8	45·0	36·7	29·0	22·2	16·6
9	39·6	33·7	26·8	19·0	10·6	01·8	52·9	44·2	35·9	28·3	21·6	16·1
10	1 39·1	1 33·1	1 26·1	1 18·2	1 09·7	1 00·9	0 52·0	0 43·3	0 35·1	0 27·6	0 21·0	0 15·6

Lat.	a_1	a_1	a_1	a_1	a_1	a_1	a_1	a_1	a_1	a_1	a_1	a_1
°	′	′	′	′	′	′	′	′	′	′	′	′
0	0·5	0·4	0·3	0·2	0·2	0·2	0·2	0·2	0·2	0·3	0·4	0·4
10	·5	·4	·4	·3	·2	·2	·2	·2	·3	·3	·4	·5
20	·5	·5	·4	·4	·3	·3	·3	·3	·3	·4	·4	·5
30	·5	·5	·5	·4	·4	·4	·4	·4	·4	·4	·5	·5
40	0·6	0·5	0·5	0·5	0·5	0·5	0·5	0·5	0·5	0·5	0·5	0·6
45	·6	·6	·6	·5	·5	·5	·5	·5	·5	·5	·6	·6
50	·6	·6	·6	·6	·6	·6	·6	·6	·6	·6	·6	·6
55	·6	·6	·7	·7	·7	·7	·7	·7	·7	·7	·6	·6
60	·7	·7	·7	·8	·8	·8	·8	·8	·8	·7	·7	·7
62	0·7	0·7	0·8	0·8	0·8	0·9	0·9	0·8	0·8	0·8	0·7	0·7
64	·7	·8	·8	·9	·9	·9	·9	·9	·9	·9	·8	·7
66	·7	·8	·9	0·9	1·0	1·0	1·0	1·0	0·9	·9	·8	·7
68	0·7	0·8	0·9	1·0	1·0	1·1	1·1	1·1	1·0	0·9	0·9	0·8

Month	a_2	a_2	a_2	a_2	a_2	a_2	a_2	a_2	a_2	a_2	a_2	a_2
	′	′	′	′	′	′	′	′	′	′	′	′
Jan.	0·4	0·4	0·5	0·5	0·5	0·5	0·5	0·6	0·6	0·6	0·6	0·7
Feb.	·4	·4	·3	·3	·4	·4	·4	·4	·5	·5	·5	·6
Mar.	·4	·3	·3	·3	·3	·3	·3	·3	·3	·3	·4	·4
Apr.	0·5	0·4	0·4	0·3	0·3	0·2	0·2	0·2	0·2	0·2	0·3	0·3
May	·6	·6	·5	·4	·4	·3	·3	·2	·2	·2	·2	·2
June	·8	·7	·6	·6	·5	·4	·4	·3	·3	·2	·2	·2
July	0·9	0·8	0·8	0·7	0·7	0·6	0·5	0·5	0·4	0·4	0·3	0·3
Aug.	·9	·9	·9	·9	·8	·8	·7	·6	·6	·5	·5	·4
Sept.	·9	·9	·9	·9	·9	0·9	·9	·8	·8	·7	·7	·6
Oct.	0·8	0·9	0·9	0·9	0·9	1·0	0·9	0·9	0·9	0·9	0·8	0·8
Nov.	·7	·7	·8	·9	·9	0·9	1·0	1·0	1·0	1·0	1·0	0·9
Dec.	0·5	0·6	0·7	0·7	0·8	0·9	1·0	1·0	1·0	1·0	1·0	1·0

Lat.	AZIMUTH											
°	°	°	°	°	°	°	°	°	°	°	°	°
0	0·5	0·6	0·7	0·8	0·8	0·8	0·8	0·8	0·8	0·7	0·6	0·5
20	0·5	0·6	0·7	0·8	0·9	0·9	0·9	0·9	0·8	0·8	0·7	0·5
40	0·6	0·8	0·9	1·0	1·1	1·1	1·1	1·1	1·0	0·9	0·8	0·7
50	0·7	0·9	1·0	1·2	1·3	1·3	1·3	1·3	1·2	1·1	1·0	0·8
55	0·8	1·0	1·2	1·3	1·4	1·5	1·5	1·5	1·4	1·3	1·1	0·9
60	0·9	1·1	1·3	1·5	1·6	1·7	1·7	1·7	1·6	1·4	1·3	1·0
65	1·1	1·3	1·6	1·8	1·9	2·0	2·0	2·0	1·9	1·7	1·5	1·2

Latitude = Apparent altitude (corrected for refraction) − 1° + a_0 + a_1 + a_2

The table is entered with L.H.A. Aries to determine the column to be used; each column refers to a range of 10°. a_0 is taken, with mental interpolation, from the upper table with the units of L.H.A. Aries in degrees as argument; a_1, a_2 are taken, without interpolation, from the second and third tables with arguments latitude and month respectively. a_0, a_1, a_2 are always positive. The final table gives the azimuth of *Polaris*.